PLAYING THE HERO:
READING THE IRISH SAGA *TÁIN BÓ CÚAILNGE*

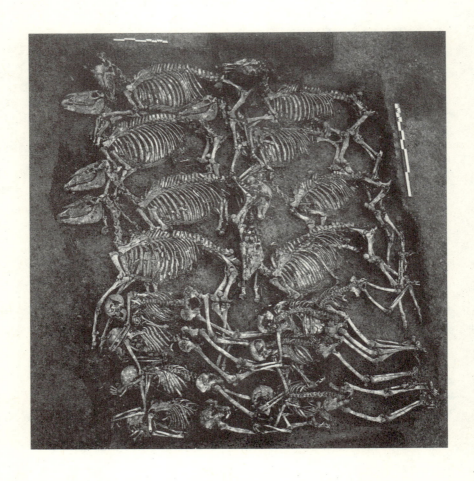

'The Ghost Cavalry of Gondole' from an ongoing excavation in the precincts of the Gaulish oppidum of Gondole, near Clermont-Ferront. Photograph: U. Cabezuelo/Inrap. Used by permission.

ANN DOOLEY

Playing the Hero:
Reading the Irish Saga
Táin Bó Cúailnge

UNIVERSITY OF TORONTO PRESS
Toronto Buffalo London

© University of Toronto Press Incorporated 2006
Toronto Buffalo London
Printed in Canada

ISBN-13: 978-0-8020-3832-6
ISBN-10: 0-8020-3832-8

Printed on acid-free paper

Library and Archives Canada Cataloguing in Publication

Dooley, Ann, 1943–
   Playing the hero : reading the Irish saga Táin bó Cúailnge / Ann Dooley.

   Includes bibliographical references and index.
   ISBN-13: 978-0-8020-3832-6
   ISBN-10: 0-8020-3832-8

   1. Táin bó Cúailnge.   I. Title.

   PB1397.T33D66 2006   891.6'231   C2006-900898-1

University of Toronto Press acknowledges the financial assistance to its
publishing program of the Canadian Council for the Arts and the
Ontario Arts Council.

This book has been published with the help of a grant from the Humanities
and Social Sciences Federation of Canada, using funds provided by the
Social Sciences and Humanities Research Council of Canada.

University of Toronto Press acknowledges the financial support for its
publishing activities of the Government of Canada through the Book
Publishing Industry Development Program (BPIDP).

For Alain Stoclet and for Michael Dooley (†2006)

Contents

Acknowledgments

This work is the result of many years of teaching and studying the *Táin* with a succession of wonderful undergraduate and graduate students. For their input, their enthusiasm, and their insights I am profoundly grateful. Some of these students are at the beginning of their academic careers, some are now in the world of academic teaching themselves; they know who they are and I am immensely proud of them. They have been the energizing force behind the flowering of Celtic Studies at the University of Toronto. My thanks to SSHRC for two summer grants-in-aid which enabled me to study the great medieval Irish codexes first-hand. Suzanne Rancourt of the University of Toronto Press, for her efficacious persistence and patience, has richly earned my thanks, as have the two anonymous readers for the Press for their most helpful comments. I thank Barbara Porter at the University of Toronto Press, and also my friend Carolyn Wood, formerly of University of Toronto Press. Especially I thank Ruth Pincoe for her enormously helpful work on licking a very ungainly manuscript into shape.

My colleagues and friends have also contributed hugely, through discussion, forbearance, and general encouragement, even when it was not always obvious to them or to myself where my work was headed. I thank my great colleagues Máirín, David, and Jean at the Celtic Studies Program, to whom I owe the privilege of working in an environment that is the envy of the University for its warmth and good fellowship. My friends Harry Roe and his wife Medora have given generously of support and hospitality over the years. I thank Harry for his careful reading of the manuscript and for his many helpful suggestions. I thank my Toronto friend of longest standing, Jacqueline Brunning, for the many ways she helped me, making sure I got home safely on many a late night of work for us both. My good friends Jeremy Harman, James Carley, Anne Hutchison, Jocelyn Hillgarth, Fred Unwalla, and my many friends in Ireland – foremost among them my cousin Máirín Ní Dhonnchadha – have always been unstinting in their encouragement and support. A special thanks to Joep Leerssen and Ann Rigney for all the rich and stimulating discussion of ideas that always flows in their company, and for the steadfast warmth of their friendship. My friend Simon Waegemaekers read the Introduction at an early stage and helped reduce some of my turgid prose to manageable chunks of meaning. My own family in Ireland is, as always, my key to sanity; to my beloved parents, brothers, and sisters I owe more than I can ever express. Finally, this book would never have come into being without my dearest husband, Alain Stoclet. His steadfast and loving support through thick and thin, his belief in my ability to complete this project, and his passionate interest in it have never faltered; as well as this, the constant example he himself has provided in the arena of medieval studies, of scrupulous, research-based scholarship at its very best, has been my intellectual beacon and ideal for many years. To him and to my beloved brother Michael this book is dedicated.

PLAYING THE HERO:
READING THE IRISH SAGA *TÁIN BÓ CÚAILNGE*

Introduction: Reading This Saga

'Ithaka'

As you set out for Ithaka
hope your road is a long one,
full of adventure, full of discovery.
Laistrygonians, Cyclops,
angry Poseidon – don't be afraid of them:
you'll never find things like that on your way
as long as you keep your thoughts raised high,
as long as a rare excitement
stirs your spirit and your body,
Laistrygonians, Cyclops,
wild Poseidon – you won't encounter them
unless you bring them along inside your soul,
unless your soul sets them up in front of you.

Hope your road is a long one.
May there be many summer mornings when,
with what pleasure, what joy,
you enter harbours you are seeing for the first time;

...

Keep Ithaka always in your mind.
Arriving there is what you're destined for.
But don't hurry the journey at all.
Better if it lasts for years,

so you're old by the time you reach the island,
wealthy with all you've gained on the way,
not expecting Ithaka to make you rich.
Ithaka gave you the marvelous journey.
Without her you would not have set out.
She has nothing left to give you now.

And if you find her poor, Ithaka won't have fooled you.
Wise as you will become, so full of experience,
you'll have understood by then what these Ithakas mean.

C.P. Cavafy, *Collected Poems*, trans. Edmund Keeley

Setting Out

This study comprises a series of thematic essays grouped around the main saga representation of the Irish martial hero Cú Chulainn. It thus takes as its focus the early development of the *Táin Bó Cúailnge* textual tradition. At some point, probably in the ninth century, a text was put together that presumes to describe certain events in Ireland which the Irish annalistic tradition claims took place around the time of Christ. The armies of the rulers of the western province, Connacht, combined with representative groups from all other provinces, attempt to steal a prize bull, the Brown Bull of Cooley, from the province of Ulster. The Ulstermen are suffering under a strange debility, leaving the province undefended but for a young adolescent, Cú Chulainn, who single-handedly guards the borders of the province until the king of Ulster and his men have recovered sufficiently to mount a counteroffensive. The allied armies are repelled but succeed in taking the bull with them. The saga ends with a fight to the death between the Ulster beast and his Connacht rival, finishing when the Brown Bull of Cooley finally returns to the North to die in his native place. Complicating the whole narrative is the fact that the deposed king of Ulster, Fergus mac Roich, and his men are in the service of Medb, the queen of Connacht; this creates a grave problem of loyalty with which this flawed figure Fergus, who is also sleeping with queen Medb, must grapple at every turn of the action. Attached to this tale from an early period are a number of small 'foretales' that set the scene and provide additional motivation and clarification.

The bulk of the text is in a version of Irish which has been dated to the ninth century, but there are also passages that evoke an earlier poetic language. Surviving textual versions of the saga begin with an incomplete copy in the great Clonmacnoise manuscript, Lebor na hUidre (LU), itself a work of long-drawn-out composition with scribal input from the eleventh and twelfth centuries. Other copies in later fifteenth-century manuscripts enable scholars to complete the text. This text, which is designated Recension I, shows many internal marks of reworking and later additions, so that scholars hesitate to describe it as a literary product with any high degree of finish.[1] Towards the middle of the twelfth century an unknown author took this version and reworked it into a much more coherent narrative, providing a new beginning, eliminating reduplication of episodes, and toning down some of the rougher aspects of the old story. This is the version that, shortly after its composition, was copied into that other great medieval codex, the Book of Leinster (LL), kept at the monastery of Oughaval in the south midlands.[2] This version is known as Recension II, and it is with the relation between these two versions that I am most concerned in this study.[3]

The *Táin Bó Cúailnge* is the work that best represents various stages of the 'epicisation' of Irish saga writing so that, from a generic point of view, it is at certain moments legitimate to invoke for it the major structural model of epic, a model that will come up for consideration at a number of points of this study, and principally in chapter 5. I have not ordered the chapters of this study, however, according to any overarching structural, theoretical, or critical rubric: I choose to present microstudies of sample text sequences that yield results on a local level of textual understanding rather than corral the whole into the service of a larger literary concept to which I would then attempt to fit the text. Neither have I attempted a straightforward commentary-type approach, which would provide a linear closely observed account of the whole text: this is not a study that can be used as a convenient *vade mecum* for potential readers. For these reasons there may be disappointment for the general reader or student who would hope for a complete account of the entire saga under clearly pre-announced unified themes. I adopt a circumspect approach because I do not wish to foreclose too soon on issues of *what* texts mean: the nature of the work would not be served best by reductionist treatments that would ignore its very complex and altogether fascinating textual history. Rather, in this study I am more interested in all the complex and varied aspects of *how* texts – and this text in particular – reveal themselves, of how it is they *come to mean*. I have adopted this stance even though most scholars and readers of the text would agree that there is an underlying dynamic and high-relief profile to the narrative of the *Táin*: it presents a textual vehicle for the display of an exemplary master hero, one who is amply and sharply enough delineated that he can bear comparison with other heroic figures from the early literary traditions of the Indo-European language world. It is tempting to continue a scholarly tradition that sees Cú Chulainn as such: the youth from the Ulster borderlands indeed bestrides his saga like a colossus; however, to borrow phrasing from the saga itself, some trees, indeed whole forests, may have to be first cut down in order to have a clearer line of sight to him.

'Keep at a Tangent'[4]

Thus my title signals something other than a general straight 'heroic' reading of the text. As the participle 'playing' implies, I am concerned to tease out, with the help of a number of textualizing tactics, what goes into the construction of words and actions in the Irish heroic narrative. In viewing and in following the hero in the work, it is necessary to underline the position that, whatever the interpretative process adopted, the hero's only reality is textual; he is a part of the texture of the text and cannot be separated from it. It might be said that my concern is more with the text in the hero than with the hero in the text. Thus, it is inevitable that at times some limited use of reading tactics falling under the general rubrics of post-structuralist and deconstructionist approaches may be deployed. Consequently, among other things, the reader is alerted to expect some of the clearing of the ground that such approaches require: in identifying, for example, the complementary roles of sender(s) and receiver(s) in the negotiation of narrative splicing in the text, especially in the internal storytelling scenes of the Boyhood Deeds narration (chapter 4); in clarifying the roles of the actors of enunciation when it becomes important to view the text as a medium of communication, and the corresponding roles of encoders and decoders of that text when the discussion turns to readers and their implied ways of receiving the work.[5] Characters such as Cú Chulainn do not indeed exist for present purposes outside their fictional frames of the words graphed on a page; they are rather actors of represented enunciation. Each occupies a discursive space that is distinctive but also contingent with the discursive sites of others, and all compete with the author himself for control of their medium.[6]

I am less interested in the larger textual structurings and more in the communicative process involved in textual production. Nevertheless, awareness of the relations between the text and its situation of communication, that is between the text and its functional poles of sender and receiver (aka author and reader), means that one must take into full account the conditions of communication: the text is not just generated by but also acts upon its author: s/he produces and in that production also changes it. The process may itself profoundly influence other works of the author who, even while he/they are acting in relative anonymity, can be seen as creative towards the received text and creative because of the text;[7] this is even more so the case as here where the 'author' represents all those who have had a hand in the transmission of the work. The reader too acts on the text; he completes it, catalyzes it, and, even as I now do, rewrites it, or allows it to come into the contemporary conditions of its existence.[8]

The role of the reader will preoccupy us much for the simple reason that it has proved notoriously problematical to dig up the hidden users of these ancient texts. Different theoreticians suggest different tactics to deal with scoping the range of freedoms which the decoder/reader has at his disposal. For Eco – to take an obvious example – a text has to be actualized in its implicit content by the reader, but,

> In order to make sense of a text, that is, to understand it, the reader has to 'fill' the text with a number of textual inferences, connected to a large set of presuppositions defined by a given context (knowledge basis, background assumptions, construction of schemata, links between schemata and text, system of values, construction of point of view, and so on).[9]

Or, to take Rastier's definition of context, which is less pre-occupied with schemata and more friendly to literary issues: communication happens when the reader/decoder has competence in the sociolectal system structures posed by the sender/author, structures identified in a literary work as genres and discourses.[10]

The question as posed by semioticians concerning the limits on the authority of the decoder is one that directly concerns my treatment of the *Táin* and I will return to it later in this Introduction when I speak of the tension between historical and mythic traditions of discourse. It will become clear to readers that in thinking about the *Táin* my bias is towards the idea of the 'open text' and of 'reading things into texts.'

Jonathan Culler's remarks defending readerly play are still worth consideration:

> an excessive propensity to treat as significant elements which might be considered fortuitous may actually be the best source of the insights into language and literature that we seek, a quality to be cultivated rather than shunned ... It would be sad indeed, if fear of 'over-interpretation' should lead us to avoid or repress the state of wonder at the play of texts.[11]

Tipping and Tapping[12]

Play – registering a reader's response to the pleasures of reading – is a feature of treating a work as an open text and is, as my title signals, a major aspect of my enquiry. In taking up a ludic approach to the *Táin* I am helped by the critical spirit of the work itself and the Irish discursive tradition to which it belongs.[13] But shifting and subverting the text's dialectic on behalf of the author(s) should not elide very real issues around the enforcing of cultural hegemony. The hero may be a only a vellum tiger, a graphed verbal entity, but precisely as such he and his text are the serious playthings of social construction, and are never so obscured by verbal ironies as not to be communicable and malleable in the public domain of a shared interpretative community. A constituency of Irish readers has been served over the *longue durée* by successive play with elaborations of Irish heroic idealism in which the figure of Cú Chulainn has played a significant part. This imagined reception community, the Irish nation, has always been marked by fissure, following its relative cultural unity in the first centuries of Irish Christian-derived literacy, and the enjoyment of heroes has not been restricted to the domain of a culturally privileged elite of Gaelic lords and the medieval scholars who served them. Native Irish heroes continued to be as popular in the high towers of antiquarian literary culture as in the open field of storytelling; indeed the co-option of the native hero by the nineteenth-century Protestant ascendancy in order to serve their hegemonic purpose is one of the great enriching ironies of Irish literary history.[14] His variously manifested textual presence, however displaced and transformed from one receiving group to another and from reader to reader, marks a long, if discontinuous, tradition of the desiring gaze of a culture that began with the evocation of the spectator frenzy of the women in the *Táin* and reached its apogee with the erection of the statue of Cú Chulainn in the General Post

Office, Dublin, commissioned by the new Free State to commemorate the 1916 Easter Rising.[15] Given a national history where the cult of the hero has been thus fetishized, critical tools that convey irony, tension, distance, and irreverence are useful when taking a fresh look at a text which is so central to this process in the earlier literary culture that one might speak of its various incarnations as an all-enclosing and repeating discursive loop.

Much of the work of this study will involve a textual analysis of the *Táin* of the type described thus by Barthes: 'Textual analysis does not try to find out what determines the text but rather how the text explodes and disperses.'[16] The chapters of this book are exercises in fissured reading, in taking chances with the text, in moving the structurating goal posts, in changing the name of the game. It is intended as a study that joins with all other readers, ancient, modern, and contemporary, who enjoy playing with and in text. What I have found fascinating is that this ludic end of the spectrum of possible readings has already been considered, albeit with a more disenchanted and snobbish eye, by one of the earliest commentators on the *Táin* work. At the end of the Recension II copy in the Book of Leinster comes the famous scribal colophon which analyses the tale along a traditional rhetorical critique of usefulness or pleasure:

> But I who have written this story, or rather this fable, give no credence to the various incidents related in it. For some things in it are the deceptions of demons, others poetic figments; some are probable, others improbable; while others still are intended for the delectation of the foolish.[17]

The descriptive list is highly content-critical and its terms are cast in a pejorative mode; but each reader is thus also presented at the end of the text with a means for self-classification into readerly categories, depending on how she has responded to the experience of the text in this form. In so far as my main aim in this study is to engage in a pleasurable reading of the texts, I like to think there is honour and huge delight in sitting down with those who have experienced the *Táin* as a site for *delectatio stultorum*.[18]

Play has many systemic levels. Not alone is the hero expressed in a textual matrix; internal to this there are cultural posturings, specific behavioural norms peculiar to his position, and coded reactions between him and his social milieu – in short a complex set of discursive, preprogramed expectations that go into his creation. In this sense

it is important to keep the role of the reader and the constituent enunciative levels of the text clear, to speak of the hero as constrained to act
out his script rather than simply to act. Frequently, in the chapters that
follow, I will point out a number of these verbal plays and performative modes of the hero and the cast of heroic actors. The textual inven-
tions of Recension II provide a good example of what we are looking
for here. As I discuss in chapter 2, I see the famous 'Pillow Talk'
sequence as one such brilliant invention designed with specifically
performative, comedic values in mind.

On another level also I believe it is appropriate to speak of 'playing
the hero.' Cú Chulainn is presented in the work as the youthful hero
par excellence. This key position in the spectrum of the heroic is clearly
marked by the way other characters can themselves be typed as contrastive. Other heroes act as points of reference on an age spectrum,
whether as equally young but foolish (Etarcomal), younger but also
brave (the boy troop), old and wise but impotent (Fergus, Ailill),
downright amoral and misgendered as a competent woman fighter
(Medb), or old and risible but with good intentions (Illiach). For Cú
Chulainn himself, an important sequence in the narrative concerns his
first introduction to the profession of the hero at the age of seven; the
present action of the saga takes place when he has not yet fully
emerged from his adolescent warrior apprenticeship. In both cases he
may be said to have acquired his heroic role by unorthodox means,
first by stealing it and then by being the unmarked outsider in a deadly
game of gods and men which has condemned the Ulster warriors to
impotent indignity. The writing consciously plays with this behavioural ambiguity and this liminal space between childhood and adult-
hood: the hero is mocked – or mocks his audience – as less than the
orthodox fighting male; he hides, disguises himself, fights with unorthodox weapons, allows himself to be seen in undignified situations
(picking lice from his clothing, chasing birds, fooling around on the job
with women, playing hide-and-seek around a hill) and generally slips
in and out of heroic responsibility at will. This creates a doubled sense
of play in the text: on the one hand, an enactment of rule/role fidelity
in acting out the part of a hero, on the other, a mechanism to trip these
rules and create of the hero an anarchic site of social mayhem and narrative suspense. In addition, by factoring in the enunciators' narrator
roles, and their extra-textual commentary one may also view the verbal
deconstruction of the enunciated matter of the work into word games.
The whole becomes an artful performance of a particularly complex

work of storytelling where codes of orality, of inscribing, of writing, of glossing, and finally of secondary production, interweave themselves with a high degree of self-conscious artifice.

The fictional hero himself contains the elements of his own decon-struction, and the play of the text encourages a reader to take an active pleasure in this kind of reading praxis, as I show in chapters 3 and 4. Here, the emphasis is on unpacking the issue of myth in early Irish saga and in exploring the epic links created between the hero and the gods. One other element of the saga world of the *Táin* also encodes a major subversion of the work of the hero. The world of women in the text is richly multifaceted from the point of view of the feminine collec-tivity, and is also marked uniquely by one of the major literary achieve-ments of the *Táin*: the creation of Medb. Chapter 6 takes up the question of how women play the heroic game from their particular gendered social codes. Techniques of feminist reading help to uncover the degree to which male heroic asseveration may be said to be sub-verted by women. Here the challenge lies in finding ways to get around the dominant male master narrators' and authors' mapping of women in order to uncover women's voices behind and in dissonance with the dominant discourse. The final result, however, is not intended to be a straightforward happy feminist reading of the saga as a 'women on top' discovery; to find that women might actually win in this fic-tional world would be to skew the actual structuration of the heroic poetics dominant in the heroic saga genre. Yet, as we shall see in the final chapter, the domain of the feminine strongly influences the sense of the saga's ending.

If women, in the person of Medb, fail here in their drive to power, it is not a serious cause for feminist despair, much less masculinist alarm, as they were never meant to be in serious contention anyway. But the fact that a challenge is mounted means that a culture question is actu-ally posed by the texts, and this may reflect a more than residual uneasiness on the part of authors at the (increasing?) ability of women in medieval Irish society to figure strongly in the male social preserve of waging war. For my intentions in examining the literary text, how-ever, the women of the *Táin* act on a linguistically signifying level as a mark of difference whereby variance and contradiction can trigger a deconstruction of the sign of the hero on a socially gendered level. Thus the chapter on women is intended to present yet another serious form of socially calibrated gaming as a kind of hazarding or raiding from below the boards on which normal male action struts; women are one effective grouping whose very presence leads in to a more widely cast interrogation of the Irish heroic world view.

Whose Hand Is Dealing the Hand Dealt?

One chapter of this study concerns itself with the material aspects of the transmission of the *Táin* by examining the input of one scribe into the actual postmanufacture and maintenance aspects of one textual version: the form we know as Recension I. My concern here has been to ground the idea of the text with as much material realism as possible. To quote Roger Chartier: 'In contrast to the representation of the ideal abstract text – which is stable because it is detached from all material-ity, a representation elaborated by literature itself – it is essential to remember that no text exists outside of the support that enables it to be read.'[19] By paying careful attention to the material aspects of a scribe's work (scribe H) in situ, a number of useful insights can be adduced about the medieval Irish reception of a prestigious text. The conclu-sions on the life of a medieval work such as the *Táin* can be paradoxi-cal: along with the acceptance of considerable fluidity and of glaring sites of deficiency in transmission goes a desire that drives for corre-sponding innovation and, ultimately, an ambition to complete and per-fect a work based on a shifting model of what the text of the *Táin* should include. Caught in transit so to speak, the antiquarian in scribe H can be seen to respect the text's diachronic integrity while taking care to direct the reading of it by explicating it according to the decod-ing tools at his disposal, the gloss and the etymology. At the same time, the writer in him finds the gaps in the text's synchronic facade irresist-ible to his desire to generate more or fuller text. Writer as performer also emerges here: a scribal player entering into the text on another level and '*playing* the hero' in the sense of the puppet-master allowing himself to be seen pulling the strings.[20] Whether this finally generates a valuable activity, a 'better' text, or conversely produces a text that is slipping into a form of entropy, into a repetition of rhetorical gestures with decreasing literary energy can be a risky call to make, and any attempt at judgment must bear in mind the self-imposed restraints of open reading, as I outline above.

The central chapters of the book pick up ideas of performance on the level of myth, once in the Boyhood Deeds sequence and again in the scene of the healing of the hero. Myth has frequently been invoked for Irish heroic literature as a justification for a work of reconstructing fundamental mentalities and structures of 'Celtic mythology' – in other words, a basic systemic code. Although my interests and conclusions on the subject of myth and meaning are rather different from most Celticists, at some point in this Introduction it is necessary to comment on the insights of other Celtic scholars who have contributed mightily to clarifying major issues concerning the *Táin* texts. This seems the proper moment to do so, as these kinds of studies of the work, from the point of view of elucidating *mentalités*, have inevitably also raised basic questions on literary structure.

Pages Like This Our Field[21]

From the great range of previous scholarship on *Táin Bó Cúailnge* I begin with a perceptive literary comment from Will Sayers that may be read as exemplary of his important critical contribution to Irish saga studies: 'The *Táin* as we have it is an episodic work, and the importance of many episodes is in their relevance to central themes rather than in any contribution to the delineation of character or the progress of the narrative.'[22] With this judgment Sayers prefaces an analysis of some of the incidents from the final phases of the *Táin* narrative. To him these incidents are deeply significant for the manner in which they reveal a continuing interest in and an ability to construct cosmogonic statements on the part of medieval Irish *literati*. Herein lies their interest to most Celtic scholars, and it is telling that the exploration of 'literary' critiques, even on a conventional level, moves to the background in this not untypical view of the significance of Irish saga. Character and structure are largely irrelevant because they are too 'literary.' Incidentally grounded but yet crucial, those aspects of an early Irish world-view model which Sayers identifies as the scholar's desiderata in the *Táin* have been further augmented by other items from Irish saga tradition. Such evidence as they provide encourages a modern reader to explore further the status of these narratives as mythic constructs in order to attempt to describe as fully as possible all the constituent elements of that totalizing world view.[23] In this enterprise, by far the most productive and influential body of work has proved to be that of George Dumézil on Indo-European tripartite ideology and social organization.[24] His various explorations of Indo-European traditions, including work on Irish saga, have built up, layer by layer, a description of the major structures and tenets of a common Indo-European ideology in which Irish material seemed to find an easy home. The

Celtic rooms in the Dumézilian version of the Indo-European mythic mansion are consequently described in some detail – first by the Rees brothers, with considerable input from a British pagan Celtic tradition,[25] and then with increasing confidence by the late Proinsias Mac Cana[26] in a way that seems to suggest satisfying correspondences between Celtic traditions and a common Indo-European heritage. This work has an added advantage in that it brings into sharper focus elements of internal congruence between the cultural record of continental or common Celtic and the literary remains of the two major branches of the insular Celtic world, Ireland and Britain.

The Field of Myth

Ideas on myths and their relation to the literary genres of any society have always been with us. Since the heroic age of the great anthropologists in the first half of the last century, we have become accustomed to accept as a given of myth criticism that the cosmogonic and mythic constructs of preliterate peoples are not independent of their social context but provide a basis for the meaningful ordering of human actions on the level of cultural praxis.[27] Seen in this way, the body of early Irish literary tradition could be scrutinized for the light it throws on the socio-cultural history of early Ireland. But in addition to the potential usefulness to cultural historians of literary texts approached from the standpoint of mythology in charting and describing early Irish realities, a structuralist analysis of mythic narratives also claims that such accounts in non-literate and traditional societies are not necessarily passive and static reflectors of social meaning.[28] The structuralist model for myth is of a dynamic process, a play of relations and functions, a mode of exploration and projection, a way of performing meaning rather than a medium of mere reflexive description.[29]

The often posited relation between myth and ritual may also be assumed in the structuralist model through the idea of game and transactional performance, as proposed by Van Gennep, and more recently by Turner and Geertz.[30] Structuralist analysis of the traditional tales of preliterate peoples assumes that the work they do, while deemed to be evident in all narratives in the repertoire, is not bounded by any one narrative field but is necessarily concerned with the contextualist status of all coded and marked discourse in the total repertoire of their respective societies.[31] In this model 'myth' is itself a language and a systemic code; through the classic linguistic operations of metonomy and metaphor, of paradigm and syntax, of opposition and substitution, key aspects of a text's contribution to meaning in relation to the cultural totality may be elucidated.[32] This expansion out from a text-bounded repertoire could constitute a problem for someone who wishes to use a structuralist method to approach a unique but complex work such as the *Táin Bó Cúailnge*. The challenge here is to see if some variant of the structuralist agenda can usefully speak also to the unique significance of an individual text, if careful note is taken of the terms that serve either to link or to differentiate it from the rest of the tradition's repertoire.

The analysis of Sayers, with whose comment I began this discussion, takes its place alongside that of other recent contributors in the field of Celtic scholarship, such as Tomás Ó Cathasaigh, Elizabeth Gray, Joseph F. Nagy, and Kim McCone. All of these represent, as it were, a second generation of scholarship based on and reacting to twentieth-century myth analyses – in particular, the Indo-Europeanist methodologies of the Dumézilian school and the structural insights of Claude Lévi-Strauss.[33] The perceptions of these Celtic scholars and of others working in a similar vein have advanced significantly our understanding of the body of early and medieval Irish tradition. Each of these scholars has taken on board a wide variety of approaches under the general rubric of modern myth criticism. For example, by concentrating on ideas of the archetypal heroic biography and of exemplary myth, Ó Cathasaigh has clarified considerably our understanding of the function of some central texts in the tradition.[34] McCone has argued strenuously against the idea that the survival and deployment of Indo-European features in Irish saga literature is due to an institutional continuity from the distant, common Indo-European past of a native Irish sacral and poetic class, such as was postulated by Mac Cana.[35] But he has equally vigorously presented the case for a survival of some common Indo-European features in the domain of warrior-class institutions, and consequently, in the textual products that express them.[36]

Making an Irish Text Mean

Valuable as their insights are, there still remains the critical problem posed by the implied ranking of possible meanings in Sayers's observation and the consequent apparent downgrading of what one might still consider to be a major aspect of the work of the literary scholar: it is the latter's task to locate and respond to the specific sites of pleasure in exposing the particularly literary operations of the texts in question. The critic of early Irish literature – if one may so posit such a person in the discipline of Irish Studies as currently practised – may reasonably ask what accepting the validity of such an approach signifies for the more specific compositional concerns of textual and narrative under- standing. The question one might then ask of these saga texts is not whether recoverable overarching meanings and constructs may be embodied in the texts, but rather, how does the early Irish culture world enable each narrative tale to write itself? We have generally been inclined to trust a myth approach to yield significant insights as to the deep, almost passive reservoir of meaning in texts, but how does one invert this relation and discover what the operations of 'myth' on the surface are? Does it also enable the rhetorical resources of Irish sagas to present such meanings, and what enhanced sense of structuring major narrative units does predicating the presence of myth supply? Can one actually catch these texts in the process of constructing meaning on mythic lines, and what is the level of self-consciousness or even artifi- ciality attendant on that process?

These are some of the questions I set out to answer in my chapters on myth. I have devoted two chapters to the issue because the more I examine the process of myth encoding in Irish texts, the more I am struck by the difficulty in speaking of possible underlying myths as 'natural' significant discourse.[37] Two issues come into play here: one is the objection, as presented by Bruce Lincoln, that myth is never merely taxonomic, but rather is 'ideology in narrative form.'[38] The second is to expand the primitivist imagining of the site of myth in tales away from orality and its modulations to include myth disseminated in the writ- ten word. To use the favourite structuralist phrase: even in the *Táin* we find that myth is 'always already written' – with the emphasis on 'written.'

The critical parameters of the role of literary commentator on the *Táin*, and on early Irish texts in general, remain fraught with problems for many other reasons. The arbitrariness of the cultural division between Latin and Irish works which has obtained up to recent years is now rightly criticized.[39] The very legitimacy of Irish sagas as literary texts has been questioned in a number of ways:[40] their sole function, it has been asserted, is one of political propaganda, and they serve no aesthetic purpose beyond this delimitation; the first recension of the *Táin* itself has been described by its modern editor as 'nothing more than a mass of workshop materials, not yet assimilated or amalgamated.'[41] In order to relate my study to work that has been influential in the field of Irish saga scholarship, it may be useful for me restate the discussion of the uses and deployment of these texts with an interpretative model of the greatest simplicity.

The Giants and the Giant-Killers

One may posit a basic opposition in significant discourse between the two extremes of narratological form: on the one hand, anecdotal history, an event as lived within time and recounted as linear structure with unproblematic assumptions about the manner in which such discourse fulfils the function of modeling lived and experienced reality; on the other, those story lines standing outside of temporal accounting in a special site called 'tradition,' where readers are invited to consider perdurable and essential culture shapes beneath the narrative skin. These are tales that are driven and constituted by a communal memory that can be just as masterful and interventionist as a modern individual creativity in dictating how a narrative is to be validated. One moves here towards more marked patterning of experience, and towards designs which are deemed capable of embodying transcendental and cosmological modes of significance. The operations of narrative, then, can be seen as existing in the pull of these two tendencies: the fact that there is always a tension between them means that in a traditional narrative such as the *Táin*, which has been patently manipulated by a series of handlers over a *longue durée*, the sheer number of re-tellings and redactions will provide a shifting and unstable play of narrative interest around a presumed 'original' story core.

But this idea of a fixed point of narrative origin carries special problems on a textual level, and not just because, in a postmodernist critical world, we live with the idea that language is a system of differences / *différances* with no fixed positive terms.[42] Thus the appearance of structure may be deceiving; it may itself be an accident, an effect resulting from a number of narrative splices and nodes of interest made by succeeding text handlers. This further implies that the idea of an 'originary' story core may have been imperfectly resolved even in the time period when the story still remained more or less in touch with the circumstances of its genesis.[43] The 'unnatural' pull of a second generic form imposed on material first enunciated in another mode – here in the *Táin Bó Cúailnge*, saga being pulled in the direction of epic and consequently geared to a new centralizing amplitude – may also distort *what* is to expressed in the changed *manner* of its expression. This may be even more the case here, where the work, whether considered as historic commemoration and/or ritual performance, or even cultural fetish, is long distanced from its actual point of cultural origin. For the *Táin*, identification of what might have persisted as the 'significant' narrative core becomes more problematical.[44]

Recent treatments of the question of epic formation in an Indo-European context, to which texts such as the *Táin* may be presumed to have a relation, bear out this sense of duality, of story poised between history and myth. They also reflect some of the ensuing confusion as to the matter of identifying central meaning. Viewed in the light of Bruce Lincoln's work on Indo-European epic tradition, for example, the *Táin* would represent a basic Indo-European cattle-raiding myth, or rather, myth complex, which he illustrates mainly through the Indra/Trita Indo-Iranian version, in which the underlying core seems to be a compact of warrior and god against a serpentine enemy.[45] This paradigm may be more familiar to us in its Graeco-Roman, Herculean version. The key point of departure for Lincoln from the prevailing Dumézilian orthodoxy of the 1960s was that he interprets all this realistically: first, as a model of prime importance in the historical events of Indo-European conquest, and only secondarily and subsequently, as event integrated into a culturally relevant ritual scenario.

In Walter Burkert's master narrative of Indo-European epic action, consideration of the Herculean model of an Indo-European cattle-stealing myth also takes into account a pre-Indo-European model; he posits a pre-urban originary ground, a pastoral cultural setting, so that the model has as a deep structure the mentality of shamanism and foregrounds a ritualized quest of the hero to the other world, the source of both success and hostility.[46] Burkert would see the dual nature of the other-world forces – the sun god is both helper and adversary in different story motifs – as essential to the Indo-European branch of this myth, and would emphasize the hunting and herding tasks of the Herculean-type hero as essential to general societal abilities to decode and become master of the environment. Burkert's underlining of the significance of the Herculean story type of the hero's burden emphasizes two things: the hero as servant of the public weal, and the hero as standing in a certain relationship to the natural world as its guardian and representative.[47]

For Dumézil – and for those Celtic scholars, such as Nagy, Gray, and McCone, who have begun from his premises and gone on to develop and fashion their own perspectives on early Irish narratives – the predominant approach to the *Táin* 'myth' or master code is one of heroic initiation, an approach which provides a brilliant explanation for the Boyhood Deeds narrative sequence, and which locates Cú Chulainn's frenzy, his early actions, and his adopted name firmly in the Indo-European repertoire of warrior biography and male behavioural modes. The anthropological insights offered by Van Gennep's initiation model, and the further development of that model by Turner picked up by Ó Riain, Nagy, and McCone[48] – insights paralleled by the analyses of classicists such as Pierre Vidal-Naquet on Greek warrior initiatory material[49] – have only strengthened the original attraction of Dumézil's claim.[50]

The other side of the paradigm to the mythic and heavily patterned narrative, the *Táin* narrative as reflective of its circumstantial historical context has received fairly continuous attention from Irish scholars. No one model of actual events or clear allegorical relation to actual events, however, seems to account in a conclusive way for the fictive world of the *Táin*. John Kelleher has seen the events of the saga as a metaphor for an ecclesiastical policy that pitted Armagh against its rivals in the early ninth century, and Pádraig Ó Riain has considerably refined this view by suggesting an actual *causa scribendi*.[51] James Carney and Joan Radner have sought clues for the action principally in the political events which pitted various elements of the Uí Néill dynasty against their enemies at various times from the sixth to the ninth centuries; the saga in this light reflects the transposition and utilization of pre-existing materials by Uí Néill propagandists.[52] The lack of a clear historical context, however, may actually constitute its generic real status and impact as a literary text: where its connectedness to *historia* is conspicuous for its absence, one is encouraged to explore the more specifically imaginative modes whereby it was once called into literary existence.

Recent examinations of the *Táin* have added considerable colour and subtlety to the understanding of the narrative on these more literary terms. Hildegard Tristram's collaborative research project on Ulster sagas has played a major role in the recent stages of scholarship on the *Táin*, and her own contributions have been of high significance.[53] Among the more useful aspects of her research is her pursuance of some of the literary ideas of the late James Carney: he had already analysed the early evidence for the evolution of the *Táin* narrative and, in addition to pursuing the theory of an early sixth-century context for the genesis of the work, he also suggested that in the literary milieu of the monastic scriptorium a conscious attempt would have been made to imitate and recreate in the *Táin* certain features of classical epic.[54] Patricia Kelly, in her discussion of the literary value of Recension I, has much that is new and useful to say on the question of the conceptualization of women characters in the *Táin*; she finally opts for a nuanced Dumézilian mythic overview in her conclusion: 'Ultimately concerned with the theme of kingship, the tale deals with the three fundamental areas of mental, martial and material qualities and functions and comments on their relative importance.'[55] Ruairi Ó hUiginn's view of the saga is cautiously inclusive, and phrased in such a way as to allow the text a measure of 'original' mythic features. He also endorses more recent scholarship – his own included – that has emphasized the literary and the Christian Latin, and hence non-traditional, nature of much early Irish saga writing. His summary is useful, if selective, in its emphases:[56]

> we can accept the *Táin* as a literary creation which grew over a period of centuries. A debt to preceding oral traditions must certainly be reckoned with, but the extent of this debt is difficult if not impossible to quantify with any accuracy. It is probable that the force of the tale was originally cosmogonic, and dealt with certain aspects of the creation of the Irish world ... In the course of time these traditions were added to and developed, and there is evidence to suggest that certain aspects of the tale were developed under the influence of classical and biblical material. Christian learning and a desire to establish a place for the Irish in the scheme of world history was certainly responsible for the tales of the Ulster cycle being set at the time of Christ. This in turn led to the *literati* attempting to create a pagan atmosphere for the tales, and the means used for doing so most probably comprised a judicious use of inherited features and traditions coupled with deliberate archaizing features.[57]

From all of the above discussion it is obvious that much of the groundwork for identifying likely underlying codes – whether ideological or cosmogonic – of the *Táin* has already been laid. What I wish to do in this study, and particularly in the two chapters devoted to myth, is nothing so ambitious as to re-designate any new totalizing meaning to the *Táin* as we have it in its early written forms. I wish simply to raise this question of how we might conceive of the interpretative process in the work generally, and as a point of stratagem, to defer further attempts to determine the significant structural design of the whole work. More specifically, given all this good groundwork scholarship already in place, I wish to give myself the freedom to speculate more on the interpretative mechanisms contained within the text itself, to try to understand how the work, being structured in a certain way by its textual custodians, may be said to understand itself. At some level then, it is necessary to posit a degree of knowingness internal to the text, if we are to have a degree of confidence that the text is indeed truly 'about' something and that this something – mythic, or historical, or at least present as a formal heightened ideological or ritual fact – depends on specific discursive operations for its projection. A major aspect of this knowingness is the act of writing itself, whether understood in all its material manifestations (see chapters 1 and 3), or in the wider Derridean sense of 'the multiplicity of meanings embedded within the uniqueness of textual inscription.'[58] Consequently, it is here that I begin in chapter 1.

Ithaka

My citation of Cavafy's poem at the beginning of the Introduction serves a double function. It points to the kind of epic context within which I wish to treat the *Táin* texts: a gestural lifting up of the Irish saga is intended, an implication that an early Irish *magnum opus* can stand shoulder to shoulder with its Greek neighbour. More specifically, however, as the great Edward Said reminds us, 'Ithaka is not itself a goal or *telos* for the homeward-bound hero but an instigation for his journey.'[59] Cavafy's great poem recapitulates and celebrates the *Odyssey*, the literary text, and not the historical place, Ithaka, behind the epic; 'these Ithakas' float free and can only be re-found as types of literary experience, as ways of re-reading. The term is also subject to the rather slyer reaches of Cavafy's understanding of the pleasure of exploration far from home. Away from Ithaka men can be boys; without the constraints of home, men can act out with full intensity their homosocial dreams. Peril there may be, and that peril will tend towards the fear of the feminine and the non-human, but it is all part of a male exploration of a masculinely defined world. Most women in the Irish saga are either trying to do men's work or are seen as queering a male pitch in unwelcome ways. Both Cavafy's queered Ithaka and the two 'homes' of the *Táin*, Cruachain and Emain Macha, are in their own ways places and concepts emptied of domestic satisfaction.

I would, however, want to return a more purely textual valency to the idea of 'Ithaka.' Just as the term Ithaka stands in for the *Odyssey*, so, for me, the wisdom in simplicity of Cavafy's poem symbolizes the great pleasure which the scholarly traversal, conducted with the help of many eager crews of students, over the textual seas and the ports of call of the *Táin*, has afforded me over my years as a teacher. If this particular *Ithaka*, in all its meandering ruminations, will help anyone else to see the Irish saga as a more alluring and more pleasant place, then the journey around Ithaka will have been its own reward.

1 Before Writing: Heroic Inscribing

[GOETHE:] Man does not know how to be mortal. And when he dies, he doesn't even know how to be dead.

[ERNEST HEMINGWAY:] And do you know how to be dead, Johann? ... Do you really believe that the best way to be dead is to waste time chatting with me?

[GOETHE:] Don't make a fool of yourself, Ernest ... You know perfectly well that at this moment we are but the frivolous fantasy of a novelist who lets us say things we would probably never say on our own.

Milan Kundera, 'Homo sentimentalis,' *L'immortalité*

Making a Mark

It has always been perceived that Irish saga tradition in general, and the *Táin* especially so, stands at a particularly complex point of medieval Irish literary history. It shows the marks, or has been seen to bear the signs, of a stretch across a crucial divide in Irish cultural history – namely, the twinned paradigms of the pagan/Christian and oral/written transition. Irish sagas are, so to speak, permanently marked by the fictive trauma of their beginnings in the theatre of conversion and by the apparently radical shift in their modes of communication which this supposes. There are, of course, plenty of textual sites that seem to show a discursive fidelity to a prior oral mode. The *Táin* itself has a major section – 'another version,' according to the scribe – where all the competing characters speak in an elevated vatic mode, the poetic alliterative *rosc* metre of some apparent native antiquity.[1] The Irish transference from oral to written is itself a matter of some myth-making. Medieval Irish learned tradition revisits the site of transition constantly through the creation of numerous parables which belabour the point that a way had to be found by which a hypothesized, pre-existing oral concept of privileged and empowering word might be accommodated within the Christian wisdom repository system of the monastic scriptoria.[2] The challenge that faced Irish writers of the first phase of conversion was that they were in a virtually unique situation from the fact that their adopted religion of the book – and all texts brought in its wake – were rendered in a language, Latin, that would not in any way have been in common use in Ireland.[3] Their consequent extraordinary innovations in the field of language acquisition and pedagogy, and in grammatical studies, writing, and book creation are well known.[4]

This self-consciousness about the nature of language also extended from Christian Latin texts to the writing of vernacular compositions. Both the act of writing – those who wrote – and what was written could and did become objects of veneration in themselves. At the head of vernacular literary tradition stands the figure of St Colum Cille, the subject of the earliest surviving eulogies in Irish, presented by Adomnán in his biography of the saint as a master scribe, one whose life is marked by books and writing – now receiving heavenly glass books from an angel, now closing a glorious saintly life with last acts of sacred writing that offer a final written guarantee of the blessing of God upon the community and his scribe successor.[5] The nature of early, secular Irish society was such that its elites did not greatly utilize the possibilities provided by monastic centres of writing to create a complex bureaucratic record. The relation of writing to power is located on a different plane, one of power display rather than power functionality. Irish secular society had little in the way of developed mercantile exchanges, or little scope available to kings to redirect land-ownership through the enabling legitimation provided by charters or other royal documents.[6] Where writing, as enactment and as object, is put to secular use and accepted into the native system, the relative novelty of the phenomenon ensures that it will not be so naturalized as a social act as to be merely a value-neutral, secular device of record; rather its freshness makes of it an acknowledged pledge, which, when visibly present and/or orally activated in social practice, can carry a considerable charge of power.[7] Thus genealogical lists and king lists could be produced and manipulated, for example, in such a way as to lend material validation to current or emerging power élites at their occasions of assembly display) Praise poems could be composed and then written down to act as a kind of charter to express formal social relations of interdependence between a dominant group and their lesser allies; and these written poems provide a document of abiding legal validity well beyond the immediate impact of their public recital at regional assemblies.⁸ Power relationships in society could also be compacted by written texts composed under the aegis of the Church, as in the case of the transmission of early Irish law, in order to supply its dual enforcers, kings and ecclesiastics, with an effective form of civic controlling order.⁹

Older forms and sites of writing – as public inscription and status display in the lapidary form of boundary, property, or ancestor markers from the repertoire of ogam and other early Christian inscriptions – provide evidence for and continued to play a part under the law in delineating family land bases and the parameters of regional or local hegemonies.[10] Texts could also be engendered and disseminated on a more popular or bastard level as simple displays of the power to command, protect, prohibit, or coerce in the form of charms and religious talismans – that is, as a naive materialization in a written object of the magically controlling power inherent in words themselves.[11] One such model in a legal context involves the proper preliminary procedures for invoking a formal satire or formal distraint against a person:

Benair aibghitir oghaim. blf. 7 aibgitir ua .i. tiasca ai i nainm de; 7 is e a greim-so .i. cros, 7 a cur isin .c. drumaind ar son apaid; doberar ainm cinadh isin drumain eile, 7 ainm cintaigh isin tres drumainn, 7 moladh isin cethramad drumaind; 7 in flesc do sadhudh i forba .x. maide don fhilidh trefhocail, no conadh a forba .x. maide apaid.

[The ogham alphabet is cut, *blf*, and the alphabet of poetry i.e. 'I begin poetry in the name of God,' and this is how it takes effect, i.e. a cross, and it is put on the first arm as a notice, and the name of the offence on the second arm, and the name of the guilty party on the third arm, and praise on the fourth arm, and the rod is to be set in the ground by the poet at the end of the ten-day period of *trefhocal*, or rather at the end of the ten-day period of notice.][12]

Here both the Christian cross and the native ogam script function as tridimensional markers – equally spatial and immanent – of the magical enforcing quality which the ritual and verbal message embodies. Such models also appear and function in texts as a metawriting residuum.[13] There are parallels here: the fiction of the prior oral status of significant discourse is assumed as a basic metaphor of the relation of secular and Christian in the Irish literati's presentation of the model of the transition to literacy as shown by the famous story of Cenn Faeled's impaired memory and his need to turn to writing; in much the same way, (writing is deemed to have its primitive stage as ogam inscription in the presentation of the idea of the heroic past as this is romanticized in the genre of epic saga writing.[14])

In a Field by the River

These two simpler levels of writing are used in the *Táin* and help to establish distance between the represented enunciation of the world of the epic hero (ogam, roughly dressed wood, stone markers, etc.) and the more sophisticated writing model of the text's enunciation. Such monumental markers serve to label the saga world as separate and past, divided from the world of the present by the overt gesture to past historicity and past literacy. Such division is offered on another level by the layering of naming – place-name layers of heroic time that displace an earlier neutral level, and that may or may not have again suffered displacement between the time of saga and the present auctorial time. Successive games of naming, whereby one settlement tradition and its narratives are both inscribed and superseded in the place names of a landscape, is, of course, one of the most important of all taxonomic activities in early Ireland – if its traces in the literary record are an accurate reflection. It is also to be expected that the bulk of place-name lore in the *dindshenchas* tradition, as in the *Táin*, is strongly marked by literary heroic tradition, even when it may actually have come into being by other historical processes, such as legal boundary marking or identifying relations between dominant and client regions.[15] The play the authors make between heroic space and their present historical geography is a major preoccupation in the *Táin*.

In the Irish saga, heroes who die in combat are regularly memorialized according to a set formula. One of the early casualties on the Connacht side is one Úalu.[16]

> *Luid láech amra ara bárach, Úalu a ainm. Gabais liic móir fria ais do thecht darsan n-usce. Do chorostár in glaiss for cúlu oss é cona licc fora thairr. Atá a lecht 7 a lía forsin tsligi ocon glaiss .i. Lía Úaland a ainm.*

[The next day a famous hero, Úalu by name, went forth. He took a large stone on his back in order to make a river crossing. The river turned him upside down so that he had his stone on his belly. His stone and his grave-slab are here by the road at the river – Úalu's Stone is its name.] (ll: 1002–7)

This seems, at first sight, to be a straightforward case of heroic memorialization with a particularly interesting vertical connection to the present world of the scribe: the hero drowns trying to create a stepping-stone passage across the flooding river; he dies and the stone somehow becomes his permanent land monument that has lasted till the present time of writing, forever marked in a generalized world of memory as Úalu's stone. Even so, one notes the crafted verbal symmetries in the tale that work to short-circuit the straight heroic reading: the stone carried on his back becomes the stone on his belly, becomes already his grave slab (note the symmetry of *fri ais* and *for cúlu*, and the pun linking *dar* and *tairr*).[17] The river is stronger than the hero and lays him low in the unheroic pose of belly up.[18] The linguistic congruence between the hero's last act, his death, and his memorialization, makes all flow together as a totally 'natural' fit, a melding of the name of the hero into a landscape of river, road, and ford that is sanctioned by the familiarity implied in the substantive present of the narrator, *atá*; current witness in customary local rhythms of coming and going bring the fate of the hero into the permanent currency of a familiar present 'little' world of ordinary comings and goings thereafter.

The Irish text itself gives further clues: there is a series of words in sequence that play off the lead word *láech* and then off each other semantically and alliteratively: *liac* [flagstone], *lía* [gravestone, landmark], *lía* [flood, spate], and finally *lecht* [grave]. The stone intended as a stepping stone has become a monument in narrated fact, and heroic fate is generated thus by linguistic convergence. In addition there is chiastic play between the *Úalu* of the opening and the *Lia Úaland* place name of the end, between the *luid laech amra* (*l, l, a*) opening of the first sentence and the *Ualu* (*ó, l, a*) of its end. One might say here that language is the sole begetter of action, and nothing that happens has any status outside of a language so manipulated by the enunciator of the text. Even the hero's name is a linguistic issue. There is no common noun, *úalu*, for the textual narrator to play with, but there are suggestive similarities: *úala* (f. n-stem) is a variant of *gúala* [shoulder], and there are numerous references in the annals to place names with this word as a component (for example, *Túaim Dá (G)úalainn, Telach Úalann,* etc.); *úalach* (o-stem) [burden] is also appropriate to the present scenario.[19] So it seems that some linguistic thought went into the creation of this narrative moment; what initially reads like innocent diegesis marked by a suitable heroically styled beginning, *luid láech amra,* [a famous warrior went] is diverted from the simple business of narrated action by the lure of an alliterative string and is transformed into the site for an almost purely linguistic game.

Damning with Faint Praise

An even more striking case is presented by the death of Etarcomal (ll. 1287–1387).[20] Here there is a multiple memorialization which is monumental, inscriptional, and oral: *Cladar a fhert íarom. Sátir a lia. Scríbthar a ainm n-ogaim. Agair a gubae* [Afterwards his gravemound is dug, his stone is raised, his name is written in ogam, the lament for him is raised] (ll. 1835–6). In this formulation, the use of ogam provides the fictional sign of the archaic past for the scene and makes the site heroically marked and lisible in these terms to a future audience. However, despite its efficacy as a sign of permanence, the written aspect of the memorialization ritual is here somewhat redundant, a supplement bracketed between the labour of making the physical monument and the immediacy of the oral lament. Separated from issues of merit a heroic task is done. All phases together compose the heroic scene as the intradiscursive work of memorialization. Nevertheless, some idea of a permanent written trace is left: ogam here provides a convenient code for the marking of the epic landscape intratextually, configuring it for the reading future as the sign of the past – always assuming, in hindsight, that the special class of readers of ogam will be present in that historic future.

A simple sign of a heroic pastness, however, is here trumped by the whole context of the scene. A further consideration here is offered by Carney, who would give Etarcomal an extraordinary importance:[21] his fate – the grisly detail of his mutilated, split body hauled back to the camp by Fergus – would be a mirror of Hector's death scene in the *Iliad,* on the assumption that the Irish were consciously taking their received native saga more and more in the direction of classical epic. Even if this were so, however, the praise/blame dynamic which lies at the heart of these formal memorializations in Irish heroic literature means that heroism has to be adjudicated by poets, and is thus often mediated through a complex enunciation of blame as ambiguous praise. Other levels of considered enunciation also come into play. Thus the scene is left open to a second reading of the site which would override an uncomplicated heroic impress of permanent scribed monument.

Etarcomal is marked as a not untypical young warrior, heedless of counsel and stupidly brave in a situation where he is clearly out of his depth. His name, Etarcomal, if taken as a compound of *eter* and *comal*, could mean 'the mutual agreement' – and clearly his actions are the very negation of this[22] – or, more likely, 'between agreement,' as he is the residue that remains behind after Fergus and Cú Chulainn work out their mutual pact.[23] But it is much more likely that the name derives from the manner of his post-mortem humiliation, 'the spancel': *Atnaig Fergus íarom id n-ercomail tria a dí pherid* [Fergus then put a spancel band through his two heels] (l. 1378). The recomposed name thus mirrors the conditions of his death and his inscriptional memorial is an abiding counter-heroic notice of his miserable end. It is Medb who objects to his humiliation after death and her side that erects the monument. But it is Fergus who, in effect, delivers the reading, the proper – in this instance, unofficial – judgment on him as material for memorability; he disposes of any residual emotions of pity in the scene with an animal-language putdown that is unanswerable in its contrastive alignment with the paragon of heroism: '*Ní tocrád dam dano in t-at[h]echmatud,*' ol Fergus, '*do glieid frisin coin móir nád n-argarad*' [I have no pity for the mongrel,' said Fergus, 'and he fighting with the great hound (Cú Chulainn) for which he is no match'] (ll. 1383–4).

It may also be that there is further diminishing word play in the memorialization formula: the writing part seems to have been pulled out of sequence by the stylistic need to observe the alliterative possibilities between the present middle two formulae: *Sátir a lia. Scríbhtair a ainm n-ogaim*. Over and above this, the verbal constructs that make up the fourfold formula replay mercilessly the first element of his name, Etar: *Cladar, Sátir, Scríbhtair, Agair* represent the kind of patterned cacophony that characterizes satiric utterances in Irish.

The reality content of these heroes as fictional characters is thus wafer thin. No sooner is their earthly heroic career established for the audience than the mind of the Irish encoder is busy on their verbal deconstruction. Indeed, in these cases one might say there is no fixed convention of prioritizing one code or another, naming or acting; those who transmit saga tradition are themselves (re)composing it out of their training in linguistic exegesis. It is testimony to the way in which the *Táin* is already far from a presumed 'simple' and oral point of origin.

Much Ado about a Withe

My next example, the 'myth' of writing-as-talisman in the text, is somewhat more complex. In the early stages of the *Táin*, Cú Chulainn, in an iterative narrative series of actions, throws down a withe inscribed with ogam writing; this action is a proscription which, magically prevents the armies from going any further (ll. 225–6). One may say that here that 'the idea of writing' functions within the text as magically effective, setting up script or the written object itself as potent sign of the main and sole literate hero. The inscribed withe is not effective just as display graffito, a graphic spoor, so to speak, attesting to the intrusive presence of the hero and of his powers to intimidate; more importantly, it attests to his unique power to make a magic composition: the cutting marks found on the wood speak of a unique hand, but it is Cú Chulainn's writing that makes it a magical device. Following the discovery of the withe comes an elaborate verbal ritual in the prose and verse exchanges between Medb, Fergus, the druid, and Ailill in order to decipher the code and process the information. This dialogue appears to follow and to illustrate its own hierarchical decorum of degrees of privileged access to, and legitimated propagation of, heroic information. The withe is deconstructed, so to speak, into its component message parts by Fergus and the druid from different poles of 'knowing':

> 'Anmai,' or Fergus, 'frisin n-id n-ucut. Atá ogam inna menuc, 7 iss ed fil and: 'Ná tíagar secha co n-étar fer ro láa id samlaid cona óenláim, 7 óenshlat día tá, 7 friscuriur mo phopa Fergus.' Fír,' ol Fergus, 'Cú Chulaind rod lá, 7 it é a eich geltatar in mag so.'
>   Ocus dambeir i lláim in druad, 7 cachain Fergus in laíd so sís:
>
> 'Id inso, ced sloindnes dún?
> Ind id cia fo tá a rún?
> Cía lín ro lá insé,
> inn úat[h]ed nó in sochaide?
>
> 'In déne erchóit don [t]shlúag
> má docóiset ude n-úad?

Finnaid, a druíde, ní ar sin
cod frisi farcbad in t-id.'

In druí dixit:

'Crephnas churad caur rod lá
lánaingces for erreda,
astúd rurech ferg i ndá
óenfer co n-óenláim ro lá.

'In nách diá réir slúag ind ríg
inge má ro choilled fír
conid ro lá úaib nammá
óenfer amal fer ro lá.
Nocon fhetur acht insin
ni frisi corthe in t-id.'

id inso .c. s.

Asbert Fergus íarom friu:
'Má sáraighte in n-id se,' ol sé. *'nó má thíasta secha, cia beith i lláim duni nó i*
taig fó glas, ricfe i ndead ind fhir ro scríb in n-ogum n-ind, 7 génaid-side guin
dune díb ría mmatain mani láa nech úaib id samlaid.'
'Ní háil dúinne ém guin dune dín fó chétóir,' ol Ailill. *'Regmai for muincind*
ind fheda móir ucut frind andes, 7 ní ragam tairiseom eter.'

[We are waiting,' said Fergus, 'because of that withe. There is ogam writing on the peg and here is what it is: "Let no one go past until there can be
found a man to throw a withe made of one branch as this is, in the same
way and with one hand. But I except my friend Fergus." In truth,' said
Fergus, 'it is Cú Chulainn who has cast it and it is his horses which have
grazed this plain.' And he put the withe in the druid's hand and chanted
this song:
'Here is a withe. What is its message for us, its secret meaning? How
many put it there? Was it few or many?
Will it bring ruin on the army if they go past it? Find out, O ye druids,
why the withe was left there.'
A druid answered:
'A hero cast it there, the swift stroke of a champion, a source of perplex-
ity to warriors, a hemming in of chiefs with their followers. One man cast
it there with one hand.

Does not the king's army obey him unless they have broken faith? I know no reason why the withe was cast there save that one of you should cast a withe even as one man did.'

Then Fergus said to them: 'If ye flout this withe or if you go past it, though it be in a man's possession or in a locked house, it will go after the man who wrote the ogam inscription, and he will kill one of you before morning unless one of you cast a withe in like manner.' 'It is not our wish that any one of us should be killed at this time,' said Ailill. 'Let us go by the narrow and forested stretch to the south of us. We will not go beyond it at all.] (ll. 268–97)

At first reading the above exchanges are frustrating: the expected sequence of challenge, elucidation, and taking up of challenge does not take place; the druid has no special insight to offer beyond that of Fergus, nor does Ailill have any intention of committing himself to any heroic enterprise, despite the druid's conventional and unfocused exhortations about good warriors keeping faith with their royal leaders and following where they lead. Fergus supplies the practical information on the identity and nature of the charm before and after the druidic performance, while the druids, in response to Fergus'(s) verse questions, put an elegant verse formulation on the general nature of the withe and the proper response to it. For all his proper deference to the experts in verse, Fergus is revealed as the only fully competent exegete with specific and extended 'folkloric' information on the nature of the withe as magical sign. Only he can be said to be literate in Ulster customs and in 'Ulster writing,' the letters of heroes. The true magic of the sign resides, however, not in what is written on it, but rather in its function as a messenger: it has an inherent magical ability to return to its original sender bringing with it the identity of the man foolhardy enough to take up its challenge. Writing in this sense is included as part of the magic package but its presence is then curiously over-ridden by the orality-grounded concept of the magical speaking object.

The difficulty arises on the level of textual transmission. Though the withe signifies after a fashion as I have described, my translation conceals some real problems with the text and raises the question of whether the textual transmitters properly understood their material. The 'folkloric' aspect of the withe is reduced if the text of Recension I is emended to read appositionally, *ricfe indead, in fer ro scrib in n-ogum* [the man who wrote that ogam, he will follow after], thereby making Cú Chulainn, and not the withe, the agent of revenge.[24] But if the precise functioning of the sign is confused, the actual challenge is clear. In their separate response to the withe, Ailill and the armies present a compromise, and this throws up yet another move in the register of the folkloric response by invoking the principle of answering like with like. By not provoking the withe directly but proceeding on a tangential path around it to the nearby wood, they revert to a magical game's most basic functional component: when in doubt about entering into a series of moves involving a piece of carved wood, try the avoidance antidote and solve the dilemma by cutting another kind of wood. Thus Ailill's response also deflects the malign withe in another way: by saying aloud that he will not go beyond it and leaving open the question of what the 'it' refers to (wood or withe), he hopes to find a devious way forward. Thus an intention may be concealed by cloaking it behind another when wooden object and wood are brought into narrative contiguity. Ailill is engaged in a piece of intradiscursive trickery with words, of a kind similar to the verbal sleight of hand of the transmitters themselves.[25]

Track Marks

Writing and reading, then, are present in the saga world of the *Táin* but they occupy an ambiguous zone. They are far from fully functional as modes of textual signification and communication; to readers of the saga, writing 'inside the saga' remains an unstable code reflecting a shadowy image of textual forms from the other side of the oral/written divide. As one sees in the case of the withe above, either the message tends to outrun the medium, or the medium itself is made mystifying. But these games with pieces of writing that I have been describing above, ranging from monumental citation to graffiti, constitute only one item in a still older order of models of inscription and decipherment recessed in the *Táin*. In a pastoral/heroic world the first proficiency of the hero/stalker is an ability to inscribe his mark, erase, manipulate and read the 'book' of nature itself as the great originary residiuum of natural signs. Thus the early Fenian materials which delineate the other paramount Irish hero, Finn, as a shamanistic hunter/tracker/poet are replete with evidence of the priority of this mode of decipherment and knowledge.[26] The primary importance of this aspect of the heroic model has considerable bearing on the rhetorical stratagems that govern the ordering of narrative in the early part of the *Táin*; in the withe incident above, the written object and the evidence of savage grazing were put together by Fergus as two items in a register of readable signs that serve to present Cú Chulainn. I shall revisit this part of the text presently, but an important subset of the intratextual stratagems for the organization and presentation of meaning must first be considered.

Written on the Body

In any staging of the making of meaning in the heroic world, the body of the hero itself takes pride of place. For example, in the popular tale of Finn's accidental burning of his thumb and tasting of the salmon of wisdom, this, his first access to other worldly knowledge, is gained through a wounding and scarification of his own body.[27] The variants of this scene, the thumb bruised in the doorway to the other world, enacts the same process. Subsequently, Finn's other-worldly knowledge can only be accessed by him through a restaging of the wound to the thumb, a gesture which becomes a staple of later Fenian romance narrative.

The body of the warrior hero is also itself a field of signs, always liable to self-manipulation, reconstruction, and disguise in a non-realistic and iconographic mode, as the various descriptions throughout the narrative of Cú Chulainn at peace and at war demonstrate.[28] The body of Cú Chulainn as it is presented in the Fedelm prophecy poem is the most rubricated of all the heroic bodies in the text, the hero's description being built here around the idea of redness. By the end of the saga the hero's body is held together by a totally artificial grid of splints, hoops, and grasses, and even – in a kind of *Third Policeman* transference – the elements of his own chariot. When these are taken off, and the hero is again is allowed to feel the pain of his wounds, he is reinvigorated. His body thus becomes a kind of self-consuming artifact, capable of regenerating itself through the circular play of wounding.

His convalescence and re-entry into fighting form (ll. 3143–50, 3984–96) frames an incident where some of the implications of reading wounds is made most explicit. This incident of heroic reading in the *Táin*, possibly written somewhat later than its saga context presents the most striking virtuoso display of varieties of learned reading and heroic illiteracy.[29] After the Ulster hero, Cethern, is wounded coming to Cú Chulainn's aid, his wounds are 'read' by the diagnosing physicians (ll. 3161–327). Cethern reacts with the instinctive savagery of an illiterate when the first doctors read off the brief scientific prognosis of 'death' from his wounds and he kills them all; but he is marvelously pleased by the joint diagnostic discourse of Cú Chulainn and the Ulster physician Fíngin, who between them reconstitute the narrative of his warrior exploits by decoding the bodily traces of all his fatal encounters. Some of these offer quite startling novel perspectives on figures that are otherwise so familiar and ubiquitous. Consider this, for example:

> Téit Fíngin cuici. Danéici di chéin.
>   'Cotumaici-si,' ol Cethern. Is tend lim in forgom sa cetadomránic.'
>   'Bangal báethúallach insin,' or Fíngin.
>   'Is dóig bid fír, ol Cethern. 'Dománic ben máethainech bánainech lecanfhata chaínmar. Mong find fuirri, 7 dá én óir fora gúalaind, 7 brat tlacht-gorm corcar- rda hi cennfhait impe. Cóicdornn fuillechta di ór ara druim. Craísech foráith fáe- brach étrom ina léim. Claideb benndornach iarna imdae osé amulcach. Is mór a delb. Is é rombí 7 cetadomthánic,'
>   'Aill amae!' or Cú Chulaind. 'Meadb Crúuachan sin.'

[Fíngin came to Cethern. He scrutinized him from a distance. 'Examine me,' said Cethern. 'This first stab I got is painful.' 'This is a wanton and arrogant woman's feat of arms,' replied Fíngin. 'I'd say that's true,' said Cethern. 'A tall beautiful woman, pale-faced and long-visaged came to me. She had thick fair hair and she wore two golden birds on her shoul- der. She had a dark purple hooded cloak around her. On her back she car- ried a five-span shield overlaid in gold. In her hand was a light javelin, keen and sharp-edged. A sword with knobbed hilt ... [?] was across her shoulders. Great was her appearance. She was the first to approach me and wound me. 'Glory be!' said Cú Chulainn, 'that is Medb of Crúachu!']
(ll. 3201–10)

Medb is not described anywhere else in the text, and this unexpected description, though conventional in form, gives a customized image of the virago, armed, hugely impressive, but beautiful and seductive in her own Junoesque way.

Cethern supplies his audience with the raw descriptive data which only he has experienced, and as long as he can spin out the narrative with the counting of his wounds, he can defer the moment of morbid prognosis. In this instance he wishes to be a glorious text – which para- doxically he himself cannot read – and also to control its interpretation. He forces the text of the body to be read in the register of heroic discourse advertisement and not as medical exemplar; but in so doing he cannot delay a final reading of a body about to be rendered meaningless in the physical anonymity of death. That heroic text, however, becomes itself a prize-winning effort, the staging point from which a further chapter can be enacted. Rewarded for his heroic sufferings, Cethern is allowed to exit the scene of the narrative in glory, according to the standard formula of the best heroic choice:

> Is andsin íarom erpais in léig togu dó, im bad buith fora huthar co cend mbliadna 7 beathu dó íarom fa nert trí lá 7 trí n-aidchi fo chétóir do imbirt fora náimdib. Is ed ón íarom do thog-sam.

> [Then the physician offered Cethern a choice: either to be an invalid for a year and then survive, or right then and there to have sufficient strength for three days and three nights in order to attack his enemies. This latter is what Cethern chose.] (ll. 3296–8)

The wounds are the graphs of Cethern's heroic deeds and it would be unthinkable to allow them to fade away: the first text ends with the wounds inscribed on him by Ailill and the Maines; appropriately, the postscript picks up with the reinvigorated hero's assault on Ailill, and with the death of one of the Maines, some of his honour is restored. Beyond this and over the long read, the work of the saga goes on. The movement is from body-marking to reading to final textualization, and beyond text to the free zones of communication of the written literary work. Cethern's glory is preserved for all time through the saga's narrative-within-the-narrative; it could be called 'The reading of Cethern's wound-signs.'[30]

Doing the Math

As is fitting, Cú Chulainn is an excellent reader and writer of the heroic world; there are several examples of his bravura performances in both sign making and sign reading, of which the story of Cethern is one.[31] Cú Chulainn assumes the role of best decoder from the beginning of the action. He asks his charioteer to make a count of the enemy, but he cannot, whereupon Cú Chulainn boasts that he can. Láeg then tells him to get out of the chariot – he is still in the last unbuttoned moments of the previous episode, the love tryst with a maidservant, and so Láeg's rejoinders may be quite sharply pointed:

Tic Cú Culaind isin carpat 7 focheird airdmius forsin lorg iar céin móir.
'Cid tussu,' or Láeg, 'ni réid fort.'
'Is assu ém dam-sa,' ol Cú chulaind, 'oldás dait-siu, air itát trí buada form-sa
.i. búaid roisc 7 intliuchta 7 airdmessa. Ro láosa didiu trá,' ol sé, 'fomus forsaní
sin. Ocht [t]ríc[h]ait chét déac inso,' ol sé, 'ara rím, acht forodlad in t-ochtmad
chét fón slóg n-ule conid mesc fria rím .i. trícha chét na nGalión.'

[Cú Chulainn got out of the chariot and for a long time he estimated the
number of the host. 'Even you,' said Láeg, 'do not find it easy.' 'It is easier
for me, however, than for you. For I have three gifts, namely, the gift of
sight, the gift of understanding, the gift of reckoning. I have reckoned
up the numbers here. There are here eighteen divisions in number, but
the eighteenth division, that is, the division of the Gailióin, has been
distributed among the whole host so that it is confusing to count them.']
ll. 322–9).

What is shown here is a little drama of numeracy fuelled in the standard heroic challenge fashion. The charioteer challenges the hero in a
normal heroic discursive mode to which is added a contextual flavour
of reproach, and the hero responds, somewhat out of code, in a surprisingly formal way by invoking innate intellectual gifts. It is most fascinating, however, to note that the textual transmission of this display
fires scribe Máel Muire (M) of the Lebor na hUidre text to add a marginal codification of his own – on the three greatest 'readings' ever
made in Ireland. What he means by 'made in Ireland' is, of course,
made in the literary Ireland of the sagas' circulation. There is, one
might say, a challenge thrown out by the scribe: if Cú Chulainn can
read and decode superbly, the scribe in his turn can go one better, as it
is he who controls the entire writing and reading agenda. The reader
finds herself caught up in a generating of reading processes that
spreads like a web over enunciated and enunciation alike.

Getting Down to the Text

I cite all these examples of the uses of writing internal to the narrative in
order to emphasize the considerable possibilities for a complex reading
afforded by this self-conscious sense of the hermeneutics of the purely
textual and the paratextual in the *Táin*. This is a self-consciousness
which, paradoxically, may have a great deal to do with the state of
Recension I, the earliest text, itself a product keenly aware of the gaps in

the story and constantly making a virtue of necessity by drawing attention to its own textual pre-history.[32] The scribes establish their own
realm of authority through their constant reference to the written tradition that preceded them.[33] These constant references to other books and
other authors constitutes, as it were, the reality of a legitimating charter
to their profession. Unlike the writers of *Dindshenchas* or *Pseudo-historical* material, however, they feel no compulsion to call on the Christian
God to guarantee the truth claims implied in their activities that record
res gestae. Their formal awareness of the idea of saga tradition, and the
textual nature and components of that narrative tradition, is also the
source of their literary independence. The scribes are never very far
from the awareness of other saga texts, which afford points of *comparanda* with the *Táin* text.[34] Through their literary training they possess
the ability to manipulate and vary the presentation of action so that the
action becomes malleable to the hermeneutical purpose. This works on
the level of punning and etymological play, but it is also evident in narrative construction. Awareness of this is present in the ordering of the
beginning of the story: there is an apparent reluctance by the narrative
controllers to set the narrative free, to release it from the interpretative
and illustrative modes of discourse of which the logical culmination is
the Boyhood Deeds narrative sequence. This sequence is framed as the
answer to Ailill's question, 'who is this hero?' and it serves a double
function. It is, as I will describe in chapter 2, yet another variant in the
difficult process of beginning; but in its strategic placement *in medias res*
it offers a way to foreground a rich thematic contrast of groups and
actors. Against the foreground setting of the Connacht camp, the site of
worthless and inappropriate leaders, exiles, malcontents, mercenaries,
and all the heterogeneous elements which compose the Connacht army,
there is contrasted the distant court at Emain Macha. Here, in the Boyhood Deeds narrative unit, a site is presented for our consideration
where vignettes of hierarchical order and careful pedagogy ensure that
heroic initiative is carefully nurtured and controlled. It is the ideal
social setting for the revealing of the hero. It is simply one more irony
that, at the time the narrative begins, this site is suffering under the general Ulster malaise. Thus, even as the exiles, the tellers of the Boyhood
Deeds tales are trying to impress and terrify the Connacht camp with
the glorious happenings in their old home, they are also whistling in
the dark. They have been driven into exile by a corrupt king, and the
tall tales they spin are now the only defence the province can muster
against the curse which has fallen on it.

But aside from hermeneutic issues concerning the meaning of the narrative arrangement, and based on this preliminary discussion of the internal reading/writing textual self-awareness of the *Táin* saga in general, I propose a first necessary qualification to the idea that the text can offer a transparent access to a heroic world. It is through its very textuality that the work touches in significant ways on the problematics of the hero and his host society. The agenda of heroic myth-making can only be presented through the mindset and the cultural tools of the monastic men of letters. The work as we have it constantly reminds its readers of the difficult and self-conscious task of the literary scholars as they attempt to weave a text out of all the paratextual elements that their received tradition has invested in making up that ideology of the hero. They are, indeed, faithful to the idea of preserving in its fullest possible form the textual evidence they have received; to this end they convey their own managing presence in the text with numerous discourse markers – 'metatextual diegetics' – frequently in Latin but equally richly in the vernacular.[35] Their control is everywhere, whether it be the stiff referencing to textual sources or their much looser references to their own handling of the narrative, with phrases such as *amal ro innisimar remoind* [as we narrated before] (l. 304), *amal atrubrumar remoind* [as we already said] (l. 1232), *amal asrubartmar* [as we said] (l. 1263).[36] Luckily for a modern reader, this conscientiousness about doing narrative properly does not at all conflict with their intention to have as much fun with words as possible, while they serve the interests of their cultural community in writing out a good *Táin*.

2 Opening the *Táin Bó Cúailnge*

'Gablánach in rét an scéluighecht!' [Storytelling is a branching business!]
Acallam na Senórach, saying attributed to St Patrick

Once Upon a Time ...

There is plenty of evidence that the medieval scholars responsible for the forms of the *Táin* as we have them intended to keep a careful control of their narrative and sought out specific effects in their presentation of the saga. What follows here is an attempt to understand better how these effects of presentation function at the outset of the narrative, in order to arrive at a sense of how succeeding generations of literary men envisioned and set about the total literary enterprise of this, the greatest of Irish sagas. I begin with Recension II, then develop some of the themes of the organization of Recension I by way of contrast, and finally circle back to some of the fundamental questions which the nature of the various openings invites.

The contrast between the opening sections of Recension I and Recension II of *Táin Bó Cúailnge* (*TBC*) could not be greater. The reader who begins with Recension II is immediately aware of having come on a particularly brilliant example of the storyteller's art. In narrative tone and tempo the opening devised by the unknown craftsman 'Bearbeiter C' is masterly.[1] From the easy expansiveness of the time-honoured formula *Fecht n-óen* [once upon a time], with which the saga begins, the reader/audience is drawn into an illusion of making, with the textual narrator, an effortless and collusive compact to follow a tale type which promises rich reward and few complications.[2] That the scene is introduced as *com-*

rád chind chercaille [pillow talk, l. 2] further contributes to a sense of having entered a privileged and intimate narrative space. The royal bedroom of Ailill and Medb is like a stage set, replete with promises of access to the 'real deal,' the unguarded confidences and motivations of the principal protagonists. The narrator attends to the show much like a photographer for a modern *Hello!* magazine; he will not be seen to collude or condemn, but neither will he shield his actors from any of their own tawdriness. The tale thus begins far from the field of the heroic; rather, it has its origins in a site of domestic simplicity and private words where one will be led to expect candour and a laying aside of heroic assertion and public display speech. It is set up, apparently casually, as an idle conversation between two intimates. But in their snobbish and unshakeably complacent self-regard it is clear that, even in their most private space, this pair will always be in the process of putting on a show. That Ailill begins the exchange with an assumption of mastery indicates he is in that peculiarly vulnerable male position of post-coital self-complacency – hence the condescending dominance. If so, then the knowing audience can read the comedic signals, and can anticipate that his happy self-regard will not be long in the enjoyment!

Beginning from the potential ambiguity of Ailill's term for Medb, *maith* [well-off, good], locked as it is into a male-dependent position – *is maith ben ben dagfhir* [well for the wife, or, good is the woman, who is the wife of a fine man] – the tone of the dramatic narrative voice segues from indulgent teasing to a kind of mutual social one-upmanship poised on the edge of outrageous and narcissistic self-regard.[3] Medb feels the need to present herself still as the *femme fatale* with a string of suitors, all, of course, unworthy of her until Ailill, whose famed generosity is now expectantly cited. Ailill still plays on the note of the necessary male, the knight bridegroom of romance who rescued a foolish heiress incapable on her own of defending her lands: *do bith-siu ar bantincur mnáa 7 bidba na crích ba nessom duit oc breith do shlait 7 do chrech i fúatach úait* [you were a woman of property and claimants from adjoining lands were openly carrying off spoils and booty from you].[4] With such jaded bedroom games they wind up their considerable energies for the public face-off that follows, and the narrative shifts into the open domain to describe a grand public display of material self-worth, with shades of a rerun of old affiancing, gift-exchange concerns, or of a vulgar, inverted potlach serving no laudable social purpose. Wealth is here displayed not to signal socially sanctioned contracts or royal largesse in goods distribution but rather as an attestation to a lifetime of private greed. This scene too is beautifully played out, just this side of farce; by using the rhetorical mode of the survey list, the audience/ reader takes in successive waves of bathetic cacophony, of wooden vessels thumping, iron pots banging, ornaments jangling, confused herds milling and lowing, etc. Then – irony of ironies! – Medb is finally struck by the galling sexual betrayal of her own bull calf who abandons her herd because he cannot bear to be counted as a woman's chattel: *ba samalta re Meidb ná beth penning a selba lé* [for Medb it was as if her worth was less than a penny] (ll. 74–5). Game, set, and match to Ailill![5]

By now we have lurched into a personal crisis that is rapidly turning into a public concern. The narrative, still with brilliantly controlled tone, and still playing on the farcical, makes the transition to Ulster in search of a bull for Medb. The bull's owner, Dáire mac Fhiachnai, also becomes enmeshed in the escalating cycle of flattery and avidity; he too has his memorable greed-spasm in the comfort of his bed on hearing Medb's sexual invitation: *ra mbertaig co raímdetar úammand a cholchtech faí* [he shook himself so that he burst the seams in the quilts under him] (ll. 98–9). But like Dáire's quilts, the whole bubble of bull-diplomacy presently bursts, the easy loan option on the prize animal turns out to be a sham and is lost in the loose, careless talk of the bit players. By allowing just such a line of bombast – with sudden misdirections that prove impossible for the actants themselves to control – to play out as the rhetorical lead-up to the stage of the saga quest proper, much delicious incidental play is also made of such high-status themes as royal succession and the gendering of the sovereignty symbolic system itself.[6] But the line between (pseudo)-heroic vows and action is finally crossed with the gathering of sufficient critical mass of a military and heroic dimension, such as might properly begin a great saga. War is declared[7] and the narrative connects easily to the traditional and received path of the story from this point on (l. 147). The fact that it is, at base, a beginning that utilizes the traditional 'trivial cause' topos such as Mac Cana has recently described, and that the motif provides a very recognizable narrative ploy for an action of great dimensions, facilitates an audience's acceptance of the lead-in coding.[8] Yet, the fact that it begins from such a morally flawed siting also creates disturbing resonances that flow from this frame narrative to the saga proper.[9] As Mac Cana concludes apropos of the tales which he studies: 'The narrative force of the motif of triviality lies in the gross, even ludicrous, disparity of scale between the immediate "accidental" cause of the conflict and the larger contextual ones.'

Such then, as I see it, is the controlling genius of Thurneysen's 'Bear-beiter C,' and nothing else in Recension II's very capable treatment of the story reaches quite such heights of comedic or dramatic mastery again. What is not clear, however, is the degree to which the introduction itself is *tout court* the entire invention of our genius, or whether he is responsible merely for the dominant tone of sardonic humour. In addition, the formal literary status that such an opening might have for medieval Irish literary classifications remains to be explored below.

But Where's the Bull?

By stark contrast, the opening moves of Recension I have puzzled scholars and frustrated would-be literary analysts of the saga by their austere brevity. There seems no good reason for deeming it an acceptable beginning for such a major literary monument. A bald announcement is made of the mustering of the four provinces under Ailill and Medb at Crúachain. The rhetorical expenditure involved is small: bare gestures thrice repeated towards the literary convention of group identification. The prophecy of Fedelm follows, so at least a way is found to foreground the hero Cú Chulainn and to confer a certain dignity of portent.[10] But no account is given of the bull, the whole cause of contention between Connacht and Ulster. The first casual mention of Dond Cúailnge occurs at ll. 131–2, following on a list of place names. Why the apparent literary failure of a non-opening in U and the re-invention of a beginning in LL? Does some sort of oral/written problematic account for the difference? For a narrative that exists in a performative storytelling tradition, the lack of a clear textual opening would not be troubling because it would be assumed that the existence of a supporting oral performance culture with a similarly acculturated audience takes care of such entry matters in its own way; each listener sets about siting the performance, co-remembering, co-recalling and co-recreating on each occasion of each individual presentation. In this scenario the text exists as adjunct to an oral tradition, and its power is almost wholly subordinated to the performative.

However, this rather simple explanation leaves a large question hovering about how to understand the real conditions governing the term 'audience' for medieval Irish saga. For the reasons advanced at the end of this chapter, my view is that we are more likely to be dealing with an audience being read to from a written version. But are the texts available to readers and/or scribes only, or do they circulate to a mixed literacy collectivity, a mixed reception group where the recounting can easily be reabsorbed back imaginatively into a living tradition of saga-telling with an audience that can appreciate the scholarly conscientiousness of scribal redactors but can also easily supply missing bits?[11] For now it is best to preserve absolute impartiality and deal only with what survives: a physical reality, a text. This Recension I opening, at any rate, yields evidence of a fragmented and imperfect textual transmission history, where the simple, performative entertainment issue of telling a clear story that commands attention from the beginning is of no apparent consequence because there is no attempt to do so. From the evidence of Recension I we cannot be sure that there was such a general audience, but merely books and bookmen and those learning to write.[12] I raise these questions here at the outset, but a way through them can only come after a more detailed discussion of the elements constituting the *Táin*'s ideas of a literary beginning.

A Tale of Two Openings

Immediately after the place-name itinerary list and the mention of the bull in the *LU* version comes the text-manager's first overt intervention to provide a division heading in the narrative. Scribally, it occurs on page 57 of the manuscript, as part of the boxed-in area of the journey list itself; the double lines around the list that serve to differentiate it from the writing of prose narrative are also drawn to enclose this piece of commentary and entitulation:[13] *A Findabair Chúalngi is ass fodáilte in tslóig Hérend fón cóiced do c[h]uingid in tairb. Ár ropo thairsiu sin dochótar céin co ráncatar Findabair. Finit a titulrad. Incipit in scél iar n-urd.* [At Findabair Cuailnge, it is from here that the army of the men of Ireland split up around the province to look for the bull. Because they passed through these places before they got to Findabair.][14] The heading ends. The story begins arranged in order (ll. 131–4). The comment on Findabair Cuailnge as the end of the line is M's alone. Thus a pre-existing gloss on the splitting of the armies also indirectly marks two prior versions of the story and elicits a further gloss from M specific to the list itself. Beginning a new column the scribe repeats, as title to the next segment, *In scél iar n-urd inso sís* [the story arranged in order here below] and provides a large capital O.[15] The two entitulation items conveniently arrange the story around what has happened and what comes next. It is the glossing addition to the list that indicates something that clearly bothers scribe M and that might prove interesting for us to uncover.[16]

Getting from Here to There

The list of some thirty place names presumes to give a complete itinerary of the Connacht armies in the course of their journey to Ulster. As the first taste of what is in store for its audience on this narrative quest, the string of place names is of considerable interest, both for its rhetorical placement and for the information it conveys about the course of the saga itself. The list is offered as a mnemonic tool for an audience – more significantly so, of course, for a reader who sees the mark-up of the page with the places set off in a barred double column which must be read vertically rather than from side to side; it is a verbal map, a means of orientation through a geography which is not necessarily the audience's own, from which the audience can be presumed to get pleasure. How much of it is geographically real and what status it has – a retracing of a public continuous way, a one-off spot diagram on the part of a later scribe, or an actual memory of saga events preserved by tradition – is hard to say, but from the rivers and fords that figure largely and the north and south directions, a regularly used itinerary is probable.[17]

The import of the list is that it can animate a contemporary audience's involvement: to dream of travel is fundamental, to think an army passed on a well-known route renders the saga material more immediate. But the composition of the list is problematical precisely because of failed connections between armies travelling and armies subsequently doing. M's gloss signals the limits of the list as literary prefiguring: the sequence hardly covers the matter of the entire saga in the ensuing narrative. There are only ten places with which an incident is later implicated; of these, two, Methe Togmaill and Methe nEóin (ll. 920–7), are new fictional places keyed only to incidents concerning Medb in the *Táin* itself.[18] The rivers Deind, Delt, and Dubglais are associated with the river Cronn in the list, the river whose rising against the armies – also around the Findabair stage of the journey – will constitute a 'real' part of the narrative (ll. 1158–64).[19] But they do not occur diegetically until almost the end of the saga, as the last items in a list of the rivers of Conaille Muirtheimne (ll. 3145–9), waters to which the wounded native son Cú Chulainn is taken to bathe as a cure for his wounds – a passage, incidentally, that has no equivalent in Recension II.[20] One place also poses a special problem in terms of M's explanatory gloss above. Fid Mór is glossed .i. *Trúailli* by M, and here we have the only place name, Fid Mórtruailli, associated with the *rosc*-styled 'other version' which plays the tale of Fergus and Medb's adultery (ll. 1030–1146, at l. 1063).[21] M's identification of the 'Great Wood' in Cúailnge as the place where Medb commits adultery with Fergus may well be correct. That this is the only one from that segment is still significant: with it the anxiety of the gloss to assert that in the narrative the army passed through all these places before coming to Findabair (Cúailnge) is perhaps explained. M wishes the list to be as congruent as possible with the composite nature of his future text, and hence moves it further away from realistic geographical itinerary.[22]

Except for these three literary places above, all connected with Medb, the whole status of the second half of the list beyond the Findabair in the centre is of little value as a narrative guide.[23] The places themselves may well be real for all that, but in literary terms they are blanks, and there is no further glossing help from the scribes of U to give them any significance.[24] The list becomes mere rhetorical string with no real narrative knots, answerable to nothing more than its own alliterative and rhythmic euphony – other than the need to tether the other end clearly in Conaille Muirtheimne by connecting with other lists localized there.[25] Indeed one might compare the sort of free-floating invention that generated the pet-killing scenes and a rather forced place naming at this point in the narrative with the inventive effort that gave rise to the more fanciful second part of the list itself.

Over and above this, the fact that the place-name box is included by M as part of a process of *titulrad* (naming), different graphically from the surrounding narrative layout, heightens the sense of self-consciousness attendant on the compositional concerns of the narrative controller at this point. Scribe M obviously felt he had to acknowledge, present, and clarify a name from the alternative *rosc* version and to acknowledge the fact of alternative versions. In so doing he may have remained faithful to his narrative, but he also undermined any trust a contemporary reader might have in his reliability as witness to historical and geographical reality. Lists in this respect have an important rhetorical life of their own; they can be generated, much as narrative is, by internal phonological triggers such as alliteration (Sailig, Slaibre, Slechtai, Deind, Deilt, Dubhglaiss) and processes of doubling and looping (Scúaip, Imscúaip). They can be aesthetically pleasurable to an audience/reader beyond their utilitarian function as mirrors and prefigurations of events.

Place-name lists can also provide a way of revealing a local control and bias on the part of individual handlers of the text. In chapter 3, for example, I discuss the place-name glosses of H in LU generally and what they reveal about him. It is clear that the makers of Recension I and its prototype have a sense of how the journey list should go through the north midlands and as far as the vicinity of Kells.[26] Making the small final bridge to Conaille Muirtheimne is, however, much more difficult, and here M's glosses to the body of the narrative are valuable. Once in Muirtheimne, the hero's native place, the border land over which the Ulaid wielded and then lost control, the narrative as a whole recovers confidence and relies on a sharp delineation of location. Beside the core elements of the saga that relate to this area, however, there is a general tendency in the total sweep of the narrative to bring the scene of conflict back into the midlands as much as possible. The final mustering of the Ulstermen, for example, takes place at Slemain Mide, and a number of miscellaneous incidents preceding the great battle take place in the vicinity of the royal assembly site of Tailtiu.[27] M's glosses, moreover, indicate a conscious will to present Christian time as well, as his place names – Gránard (l. 214c), Crossa Caíl (l. 219d, l. 256a), Cennannas (l. 309a), and Scrín Cholaim Cille (LU, l. 4378) – indicate. But such sharpness with respect to glossing and connecting with the geographical reality in the main narrative whenever it suits him to do so is manifestly not carried back into the composition of the lists and their names as a whole. Indeed matters do not improve in Recension II, where the list as such seems to have invited rather careless handling. Lists, then, insofar as they have a creative life of their own, tend to have great difficulty in forming a stable preview of ensuing narrative.

Something on the Trail Up Ahead

I have gone into this very unpromising matter of lists because, in the grand scheme of the onomastics of the *Táin*, other naming processes have received much more attention since they can be seen as sharing features with a recognizable native genre, the *Dinnshenchas* tradition.[28] I wish, rather, to see what a list looks like from a story receiver's point of view and how strong a contribution it makes to the matter of beginning a story. It clearly gives a decided narrative push to the tale's forward impetus at the start; but, as I have pointed out, M's gloss on his list reveals a somewhat worried foreknowledge of difficulties in the eventual progression of his story. The gesture in the list towards doubled construction is, however, a key element in M's handling of his received material. It signals his perception that narrative linearity is not sustained up ahead in the tale and his response shows that the textual scholar in him feels the need to monitor his other role as tale master. Findabair Cúailnge is obviously marked as an important stage in the conflicted textual staging of the tale from M's point of view because he takes the trouble of glossing it, including the note with his major rubric on *titulrad* and *sgél*. Indeed the gloss can be seen to represent an important boundary line where *titulrad* and *sgél* blend.

When the Connacht armies eventually arrive here, at the point of one of the most important bifurcations in the text, a fissure opens which knocks askew the whole idea of the narrative project as a fiction of straight linear and performative-type exposition. For the first arrival in Findabair (ll. 978–1026), the account proceeds smoothly enough and the only hint that something might be wrong is the flurry of minor rewriting of details evident in the spread of manuscript witnesses. There is an apparent need to signal rival versions of finding the bull in the Y version, and M does not provide a 'bull' reference in the heading, such as Y incorporates very early in his text.[29] The fact of the variant version is noted thus by M at l. 1027: *It é sin trá a n-imthechta ó Chúalngi co Machairi iarsin tslicht sa. Dogníat immorro augtair 7 libair aile córugad aile fora n-imthechtaib a Findabair co Conaille .i.* [These then are their journeyings from Cuailgne to Machaire according to this version. But other authors and books give a different version of their movements from Findabair to Conaille as follows]. M, in his original note to the list, has succeeded in warning the reader that something unusual is presented up ahead. It is as if by inserting a break-up gloss on his list, but keeping it graphically separate, he can still afford the fiction of linearity in his places string; this is, after all what a real journey might be like. Thus he maintains his scholarly honesty and at the same time he helps an audience/reader to get over the rupture in the narrative at Findabair, where we have, in fact, not two but three alternative versions of a 'find the bull' action. In the same way, the closing of the list with the river Cronn could also be seen as an attempt to suggest a 'reasonable' narrative in the face of bifurcation; this motif of the magical flooding of the river is also repeated twice, to the potential confusion of the audience/reader (ll. 1000–1, 1158–64).[30]

What we are seeing here is an important clue to our understanding of the mentality of scholarly figures, such as M, who have, with great deliberation, preserved a form of the *Táin* for future generations. The scholar and the creative respondent to the received written tradition of the saga are one and the same person. The scholar's pleasure in the text is an analytic one but he can also read synchronically. Something up ahead in the narrative is left as it is with multiple witnesses to its essence as written artifact – hence authoritative and 'genuine' in a writerly way; it will not be discarded by the person who delights in the lore of the old tales.[31] The creative instincts of the tale-shapers can then be most evident in such humble and unpromising places as a place-name list. Here we are lured in to enjoy such a simple pleasure as a sequence of places, all part of the grand pageant of massed warriors on the march, for which the correct Latin phrase would be *in ordine* (in marching order = *iar n-ord*).[32] This display is part of the epic lure and romance of the tale and must remain. The scholar in M, however, peeps from the margin of the page and taps in a masterly corrective. The creative pleasure of the list will be kept, but M will, with one phrase, indicate the critical function his arrangement is made to bear with respect to the upcoming problems by first framing the whole with a marginal gloss, the mark of a scholarly mode of telling.

Naming First Things First: Recension I

Obviously the term *titulrad* covers the boxed list with which it is packaged. But is it a term that can cover the whole matter of the beginning action up to this time? The word *titul* derives from the Latin *titulus*; *DIL* distributes the meaning of the Irish word between 'title as heading' or 'title as epithet,' and a legal meaning, 'title as legal right.' Of these we need only consider the first, as the others are later developments. The basic meaning here is substantiated by citations from the Würzburg and Milan Glosses: *is titul indi ar chiunn* [what is at the head is a *titul*] (Wb 28a 11); with respect to the 'Titles' of the Psalms: *ni feil titlu remib* [there is no title before them], glossing *non sunt suprascripti* (Ml 2b 4), and connecting with a crucial term *tucaid*: *titulus de fursundvd na tucaite ... frisa rochet in psalmb* [a title to it, revealing the reason why the psalm was sung].[33] This usage of *titul* is also found in the preface and commentary on the *Altus prosator* hymn.[34] *Titulrad* itself is given as 'preface' in *DIL* on the strength of the citation in Recension I. O'Clery's *Glossary* yields another reference: *a titulrad .i. scél .i. a tiumsugud no a cruinniugad* [its entitulation, i.e., story, i.e., its assembly or collection].[35] The O'Clery reading – which may, however, be dependent on the *Táin* citation – gives equivalents that can refer most proximately to a literary process of collecting and arranging variants of a tradition and, at a stretch, to a military action, a mustering. Thus we are left with a paradox, a term which in its strictly literary origins indicates an entitulation, or at most a very brief introduction, that is little more than notational but can also describe the work of *compilatio* and of *ordinatio* proper to the composition of the entire tale.

Moreover, if one accepts the O'Clery entry as having genuine insight, it also can refer to a standard rhetorical *topos*, the mustering and census of armies with which sagas often begin, the possessive pronoun *a* here referring forward to *scél*. So the phrase can also refer to the story's opening action of mustering the army. The term *titulrad* is indeed rich in that it has a strong connection with scriptural and hymnal traditions of learned Irish monastic culture; it is also ambiguous in that the stretching of the term's range by M, its probable inventor, has strained it almost to excess. Though the corroborating evidence for its secondary literary extension is not as secure as one would wish, it would allow us to better see M as a professional discourse arranger. One would hardly have time for a bull at all when the business of marking up a received text is such an intriguing challenge to a professional writer, such as M, that it triggers inventiveness about scholarly words.

Naming Things: Recension II

Recension II, by contrast, presents a whole series of opener-type terms, the most significant of which is contained in an early colophon (ll. 276–8): *Tairngiri 7 remfhástine 7 cendphairt in sceóil 7 fotha a fagbála 7 a dénma, 7 comrád chind chercaille dorigni Ailill 7 Medb i Crúachain connice sain* [The Prophecy, Prediction and Prelude of the Tale/Events, the Background to its Invention and Composition/Reasons for Motivation and Action, and the pillow conversation which Ailill and Medb had in Cruachain, (all these) up to this point].[36] The next section begins: *Sligi na Tána in so 7 tossach in tslúagid 7 anmand na sliged dochúatar cethri ollchóiced Hérend i crích Ulad* [The way of the *Táin* here, the beginning of the hosting and the names of the roads which the four great provinces of Ireland took into the territory of Ulster] (ll. 279–80).

The obvious challenge here is to judge the extent to which these notices function as simple narrative summaries, or as more technical rhetorical *topoi* derived from a tradition of handling the opening of large narratives and from the challenge of treating this one in particular. The first thing to note is the dissimilarity of the technical terms to those employed by M. Thus, the first notice, for all its doubling of descriptive titles, falls into three sections: (a) *tairngire 7 remfháistine* and *cendphairt*, (b) *fotha a fagbála 7 a dénma*, and (c) *comrád chind chercaille*. The first two of these seem to be part of a technical repertoire, though (b) has ambiguities relating to the dual meaning of *scél*, which I noted above. Only (c) refers in a non-technical, summary way to what seems to be an original contribution to the convention of a *Táin* opening. Of these terms it is the middle group (b) that is the most difficult to assess; I shall deal with these terms in detail presently. One may also note that this group of headings counts the narrative elements backwards, beginning with the last incident in the narrative sequence. The second cluster of headings anticipates the action ahead and also counts backward, if one accepts that *Sligi na Tána* refers to the itinerary itself and not to the list.

Thus the LL version separates the place name list from the prefatory material as set up by U. Somewhat later, however, there is a further recapitulative notice from LL, this time in four parts: *Conid innisin do macgnímaib Con Culaind sin for Táin Bó Cúalnge ocus remthús in sceóil 7 na sliged 7 imthechta in tslúaig a Crúachain connici sin. In scél fodessin is ní and fodechtsa* [Thus far then is some account of the youthful deeds of Cú Chulainn on *The Cattle-raid of Cúailnge*, together with the prologue to the tale and (an account of) the route and the host's departure from Crúachain. The story proper is what comes now] (ll. 1214–17).[37] Here there is a slight breakdown of LL's retrospective heading arrangement: *remthús*, (what comes before the beginning) would seem to be the equivalent of U's *titulrad* but, as we have seen, the latter term cannot be accepted as describing anything but the briefest of headings.[38] That LL should, on three occasions, chop what passes for an introduction into three segments – a kind of triple preface[39] – indicates either a certain lack of certitude about what is entailed in beginning this narrative, or more likely, a great personal satisfaction with the way he has mastered the problem of a received lame opening. The shifting dividing line between a preface and the work shows the difficulty of making a clear distinction between those extra-narrative, literary classification issues properly dealt with summarily in a preface, and the constant spillover into it of material proper to the narrative itself. U opts for the austere *titulrad*, LL grapples with the concept in a much more florid manner.[40]

Certain aspects of LL's defining terms can take us further into the question of how these masters of the text saw it, and saw their own work in relation to it. Thus *cendphairt* and *remthús* are reasonable ver-

sions of a term to signify 'preface' and are closest to U's *titulrad*. The Latin borrowing, *pars> pairt*, seems to establish early on a special literary usage, 'tome,' as in *Fel. Ep.*, 136. (*DIL* 494, 173). *Cendphairt* then is easily understood as introductory or heading material, as in the metonymic <u>corp</u> *in sceóil sunna. Finit don* <u>ceannphort</u>.[41] It also glosses Latin *capitulum, epistilia, supermissa columnarum*, but the latter is obviously scribally irrelevant here unless one considers the role of the Eusebian Canons' layout in Irish illuminated manuscripts.[42] The LL phrase, *Conid innisin do macgnímaib Con Chulaind sin for Táin Bó Cúalnge* contains some difficulties for the translator. It is not entirely clear how O'Rahilly takes *innisin*: if she takes it as *in + ní + sin* – definite article, noun (*ní*, thing), and demonstrative pronoun, in parallel with the phrasing of the end of the heading, *in scél fodessin is* <u>n</u> *ann fodechtsa* – then the syntax of the phrase is quite confused. I rather take *innisin* (vbn. of *in-fét*) as a technical *narratio* term here, for example: 'This is a telling of 'The Boyhood Deeds of Cú Chulainn' in/on the *Táin Bó Cúailnge.*'[43] It is not possible to know if the LL scribe here intends to convey that this is <u>his</u> particular selection of 'The Boyhood Deeds,' and hence his own take on a tradition, or whether he claims that this should now be the canonical version of the sequence that is also present but more fully in Recension I. It may be that his comment is not simply extratextual but rather is simply focused on the task in hand. He wishes to signal that there has been a break in the primary narrative flow in order to allow for a staged 'telling' by Fergus and his Ulster companions, thus a narrative that functions on an intradiegetic level.[44] But one may also note here that this notation is very different from the corresponding closing phrase in the Boyhood Deeds section in the YWC versions of Recension I, a phrase which clearly is the product of a scholar concerned with manuscript textual entitulation: *It e Maccerda Con Culaind andso annuas for Táin Bó Cúailnge.*[45]

The phrase *fotha a fagbála 7 a dénma* is translated fairly neutrally by O'Rahilly on literary lines as, 'the basis of its invention and composition.' The terms *fotha, dénam, fagbál,* along with *tucait* are fairly frequent in saga texts: a good example would be the title *Fotha Catha Cnucha* [The Reasons for the Battle of Knock], a Fenian text found in LU, p. 41.[46] With this group we arrive at an exegetical model, *accessus ad auctores*, much favoured in early Ireland for analysing sacred texts. On this model the LL scribe's achievement has been to come up with an actual *causa scribendi* for the saga, something that is missing from Recension I in LU, whether by accident or design.

The *Accessus ad auctores* in Irish Tradition

In order to understand what a medieval Irish scholar might have made of the convention of the *accessus* we can turn to two examples: one is available close at hand in LU itself; the other is the versions of the tale of the recovery of the *Táin*.[47] The preface to the *Amrae Choluim Chille* provides a very good example of how a form of exegesis on sacred texts came to be applied also to texts considered canonical in native Irish tradition. The usage here will serve as a control to the further exploration of the method as applied to saga texts and the *Táin* in particular.

> <u>Loc</u> dond remoculsa (leg. *remfhoculsa*) chetus Druimm Ceta ar is ann do ronad in mórdáil Dromma Ceta. In alio loco i͡m do ronad corp ind immuin o sein immach ut post apparet.
> <u>In-aimsir</u> Aedae meic Anmerech do rigned.
> Perso Dallán Forgaill do Masraigibh Maige Slecht (.i. i mBreifne Connacht [M].
> <u>Tucait</u>. ar rochtain richid dó fein 7 aliis per se. Trí <u>tucaite</u> uero ara tanic Coluim Cille a hAlbain ... (*LU*, 5)

[The <u>place</u> of this <u>preface</u> first, Drom Cet; because it was there that the Assembly of Drom Cet took place. In another place, however, the <u>body</u> of the eulogy was afterwards composed as will be apparent later.

   In the <u>time</u> of Aed mac Ainmerach it was made.

The <u>person</u> was Dallán Forgaill from the Mascraide of Mag Slecht (.i. from Breifne Connacht, [M]).[48]

The <u>cause</u>. To gain the kingdom of heaven for himself and for others through him. Actually there were three <u>reasons</u> for which Colmcille came from Scotland ...].

Here the thrust of the categorization with respect to the work served by the preface is strictly literary. It is only when the coordinates of composition have been established along these lines that the *Tucait* of the Preface begins to dip into the historical context (the three *tucaide*) of the Convention of Drom Cet; in other words, to expand in the direction of extracategorical, narrative content.[49]

My second example, the tale of how the *Táin* was found again, bears directly on transmission of the *Táin*. Although the story of the saga's recovery can only be dealt with briefly here, I will return to it with other concerns in mind at the conclusion of this chapter. There are a number of variants of the tale, the best known being the version in LL, 245b.[50] In one variant, BL Egerton 1782, 87b, obviously related to the longer tale *Tromdám Guaire*, the traditional introduction occurs as follows:

> [C]ethardo connadur da gach eladuin is cuinncesta don eladuin si na Táno.
> Loc di cetamus lige Fergusa maic Roich aitt in rohadnucht ar Mag nAi.
> Tempus autem Díarmato maic Ceruaill in regno Hiberniae.
> Perso di Fergus mac Róich, ar is hé rothirchan dona hexib archena.
> A tucaid sgribhinn dono dia ndechaid Senchán Torpéist cona trí cóica rigecius mnaib maccuib sceo ingenuib leo do shaigid Guaire ri[g] Connacht. Fuidis didiu Guaire essomuin friu 7 rusnothrastar mis for bliadain fo gleri gach maithiusa. Forellsid[51] in ecis autem for mianuib decmuici ardaig enich Guaire do brith 7 rof-restuil in Cuimdiu onechgresa in rig tar a chent, gu mbut oga a n-ocobair.[52]

> [Four enquiries of every work of art are brought to this work, the *Táin*:
> Place firstly: the grave of Fergus mac Roich where he was buried in Mag nAí.
> Time then: when Díarmait mac Cerbaill was king of Ireland.
> Person: Fergus mac Roich, because it was he who chanted it to the scholars.
> Cause of writing it: when Senchán Torpéist came with his one hundred and fifty poets, and their wives, sons and daughters, to visit Guaire, the king of Connacht. Guaire gave them a welcome and he supported them for a year and a month with every good thing. They demanded impossible gifts such as would deprive Guaire of his honour and the Lord adverted the attacks on the king's honour in spite of them so that their desire did not prevail.]

Here one notices again the difficulty of keeping the *causa scribendi* exposition from becoming part of the main tale itself, and from leaping from purely literary aspects of the work to the matter contained therein. In this case, however, the Egerton 1782 text presents a neat summary of a longer version of the quest, probably similar to *Tromdám Guaire*, a text to which it is obviously related.[53]

What conclusions can be drawn from a comparison of these more formal usages of an *accessus ad auctores* type of beginning and the organization of the opening of both *Táin* recensions? To begin with, there is an ultimate common ancestry for the explicatory type of opening narrative organization for both versions that goes back to exegetical models. In the LL version of the saga the author, having plunged straight into a narrative mode with a 'free' narrative marker – *Fecht n-óen* – must then, having offered the Pillow-talk as a very loose form of *causa scribendi*, bring his inventiveness into line by means of a plethora of authoritative entitulations and formal categorizations.[54] In U the only approximation of *accessus* lies in the schematic style with which the saga begins, and in the use of the term *titulrad*. In further comparison with the *Amrae* Preface, one finds additional parallels: there is the equivalent of *tochim* (l. 9) in the deliberative *mordáil* of the *Amrae*, and in the passive and impersonal preterites, *tarcomlad, doecmalta, hetha, fóite*, etc., there is the same deliberate holding back of the syntax from full narrative release. Locations themselves are firmly established: at Crúachain (cited four times before the armies set out) and also by the list of place names which itself promises a preview of the future action. As to *personae*, the leading figures are all mentioned. U also provides a clear time point at which the action begins, *in Lúan iar Samuin* (l. 114). It is LL, however, which provides a clear Irish regnal time marker – the reign of Eochu Feidlech – in the genealogical boasting of Medb. One might say that LL, by using a term such as *fotha*, provides a rich *causa scribendi* of the spillover kind. Mention of reward for the whole work of transcribing and reading the *Táin* comes in the Irish final colophon (ll. 4919–20). This too is a development from the *Amrae* Preface; there the *causa* is the desire for a heavenly reward, and the switch from creating context to displaying literary work involves a belief in the real moral consequences of the compositional task. U works in complete contrast, and only finds time to insert a *causa* – the bull – as an undeveloped afterthought in a note at the very end of the *titulrad* section.

Ancestral Voices Prophesying War

What is common to both versions of the opening is the element of prophecy, even if U does not grant Fedelm and her performance titular status in his prefatory material.[55] LL is particularly fond of the form, as is evident from the way in which he adds to its verse content and takes care to signpost it.[56] From the evidence of U's and W's placement of the scene – even if not so titled – they also considered prophecy as an essential part of the prefatory material of the saga. Furthermore, the prophecy of Fedelm is the first element in the narrative to introduce the high epic themes of bloodshed and heroic singularity. In Lambert's important article on the conceptual basis of insular narrative historical texts there is the assumption that elements such as prophecy are present in insular tradition because of the bedrock of the literary heritage from the late Roman, and/or early Christian west.[57] Thus in British narrative histories two kinds of prophetic strain are evident: one is an idea of 'necessary destiny' (376) as a kind of trace element of a Roman model of historical vision; the other is a reading of historical process as *excidium*, or of destruction of nations and cities as a kind of Old Testament model of divine retribution for communal human folly (379). Hence, according to Lambert, structures of self-fulfilling prophecy are part of a deeply embedded tradition introduced early in insular learned culture.

This deep code of meaning is not so immediately evident as far as Irish saga tradition is concerned and Lambert does not press the point. What is undeniable, however, is that sacred scripture was capable of providing Irish *literati* with their own kind of providential model, more optimistic and less attuned to Old Testament calamity models. By combining the idea of their own pre-Christian history with the Old Testament under the rubric *recht nadúir*, Irish cultural history could be seen as forming one element in a binary typological contrast. As the Old Testament prefigured the New, so too native secular discourse could be structured in a deeply analogical and prophetic way.[58] Whether their sources be in universal World Chronicle or Biblical history, models existed to endow Irish secular sagas with their own appropriate epic weight of destiny, much of it carried by the category of prophecy.[59]

Fixing the Táin

From this detailed look at the conventions of beginning a saga, one may surmise that there is a basic underlying instability in the presentation frame of the *Táin* in both versions. The freshness of the brilliant opening of Recension II may well derive from the fact that it is a new invention, its composer allows himself an entirely free hand; Recension I strictly patrols what is there available to it. The larger question looming here is, what, if anything, was there to work with? I have already used the textual tradition on the finding of the *Táin* in order to focus on the convention of *causa scribendi*. A further look at the attitudes expressed towards the transmission of the great saga in this complex of tales may prove useful at this stage, in that its ostensible purpose is to provide just such a literary history.[60] .

The materials centre around the figure of the poet Senchán Torpéist. A major element in the poetic biography of Senchán is his relationship to King Guaire of Connacht and the account charts out a specific problem in Irish social custom, the often fraught *modus vivendi* between royal patrons and powerful poets with retinues.[61] For both sides the king's demand that he wants to hear a recital of the *Táin* – *Romgab imtholta im erscéluib Tano do faisneis dam* (A), *Táin Bo Cuailnge do faisneis* (D) [I am taken with a great desire to have the famous stories of the *Táin* told me/ to have *Táin Bó Cúailnge* told] – implicates issues of competitive honour to which Senchán must respond.[62] What remains of the *Táin*, however, are mere fragments – *ar nir'-mair don Thain acht blogha di nama roboi ac cach co coitceann* [because there survived of the *Táin* only fragments that were in common currency (D)] – and imperfect memories of Medb, Ailill, the Ulstermen, and Conchobar (D). The poem of invocation to the ghost of Fergus is spoken either by Senchán at St Ciaran's bidding or by Muirgen, his son and emissary:[63]

> *Manib do liic*
> *luaichthech[64] mal-gel*
> *mac Roich, ro fessin*
> *fechtaib co n-éicsib[65]*
> *immán immanachta,[66]*
> *laithiu[67] bruidin*
> *ba Cuailnge[68]*
> *in cech follus*
> *a Ferguis*

> [If this be your stone
> bright one, shining hero,
> I would know, son of Roech,
> in deeds and in disasters
> the fierce driving that was driven,
> in the day of the *Battle*
> *of the Cattle of Cooley,*
> in all clarity, O Fergus]. (ll 32878–909)

Clothed in the language of performative orality, it is still clear that the tale in D conceptualizes a prior written, authoritative *text* of the saga, one which could have been exchanged and sent overseas for the Latin text of Isidore of Seville's *Etymologiae*, known in Ireland as the *Culmen*.[69] Thus the very basis of the myth of saga production posits a written text at the head of the tradition. Orality is now the debris of a prior written tradition, and though the reconstructed myth of the authentic witness from the past in the person of Fergus will mean a return to oral delivery, the Derridean sense of writing as the necessary supplement and the originary form of discourse is valid here in the literal sense. There is also, one notes, a hesitation about the form of the tale they are seeking. It is sometimes referred to as singular, other times as plural, a work of heterogeneous form, comprising prose narrative types, *fecht*, *écht*, and perhaps learned verse, *éicse*. There is also an anxiety about its dispersal and decomposition; it requires a master hand to reclaim and reformat it into a noble tale worthy of a high audience – and also to bring it back to a suitable western aristocratic audience. It also requires a reliable witness, Fergus, one who can tell the tale *ó thús co deiread* (D), because he was there and because, as Ó Coileáin points out, he was already a teller of tales in the *Táin*.[70] It also requires a further morphing of the figure of Fergus himself, from the ghastly wounded warrior of his burial to a more benign form of the great man wearing clothing for an *óenach*, itself an occasion of tale telling. As Ciarán instructs: *Ar roboi Fergus fein isin gliaid sin 7 atat a scela do (leg. go) leir aigi 7 abradh fris co na tardad gráin na hirfuath leis ina dochum, acht amail nothisad do dhail no aenach* [Because Fergus himself was there in that conflict and he knows all the stories, ask him not to bring any ugly or fearsome form with him but to be just as if he were going to an assembly or a fair (D)]. The end product is an official form of the saga, triply guaranteed by the declamation from a witness, by the transforming hand of the master *ollam*, and by the overarching power of the church – with an additional and final stage, the writing down of the whole in *Lebor na hUidre* itself: *rochuir [Senchan] i cairtlibur*, (E); *7 is e do scribh uadha hi .i. Ciaran Cluana, 7 is e loc in roscribh hi, for seichid na huidhre*, (TD). The emphasis given to Ciarán of Clonmacnoise and to western saints, such as Caillín of Fenagh, Finnian of Clonard, Finnian of Moville, and Brendán mac Findloga, makes it clear that this evolving *Táin* tradition is linked to the work of scholars at Clonmacnoise and to the desire to have the definitive written version of the epic in the zone of influence of this monastery.[71]

Other scholars have drawn their own valid conclusions from a study of these fascinating texts. Here I emphasize two aspects that are significant to my purposes. First are some basic ideas about the literary tradition of the saga: the recognition that the *Táin* has a double aspect, that it was felt to possess a unitary integrity but to be made up of registers with variety and episodic difference, and that it had a designated key primary narrator, Fergus, itself a crucial gesture in the setting up of forms of literary shaping, selection, and judgment. Second, the line of memory once bridged, its performative enactment, the official fiction of its re-composition, is transferred immediately into the custodianship of the men of writing. Its written form thus sublimated to talismanic preciousness as a founding saint's relic (it is written on the skin of St Ciarán's best-loved cow), it is now the only form capable of maintaining the saga in its compositional integrity. The tradition of the *Táin's* recovery is almost certainly geared to a textual reconstitutive occasion that seems to be related somewhat closely to a writing event exclusively associated with Clonmacnoise and its traditions .

This fiction of stability, however, can only protect the text in a limited way; it cannot protect it from codicological accidents, such as the loss of folios, a loss most frequently suffered at the beginning or end of a manuscript gathering or gatherings that are geared to accommodate the text of a work. From this perspective a scenario for the saga's provenance that is something other than a knowing embedding in oral tradition might be envisaged. A case might be made that the '*Táin*' textual exemplar from which U scribes worked had already lost its beginning. For the same reason as the early folio loss in his prototype, the author of the LL version of the saga felt free to invent a beginning. In other words, the fact of the great variance between the two surviving recensions, judged from their manuscript witness, might mean that there probably never was a beginning to the *Táin* as either of them knew it.

Back to the Bull

Indeed, a perfectly good candidate for an alternative opening is preserved in the textual tradition of the tale, *Echtra Nerai*.[72] Here the bull Finnbennach is challenged in Cruachain by the calf sired by the Donn Cuailnge (in a cross reference to the *Táin Bó Regamna*); the victory of the Finnbennach causes the calf to bellow; this is then interpreted by the bystanders as asserting that its father would be a match for the Connacht bull. Fergus attempts to stifle the boasting by wounding Bricriu with the gaming pieces but Medb asserts:

'Tonga na dea thungus mo thuath, na tairinnith 7 na coitelfat for cluim na col-
ccuid 7 ni bom blatchcha 7 ni cainfuirim mo taeib 7 ni cainairbiur dergflatha na
finn 7 nicon-airbiur biuth, conamrabat na da tharb sin ar mo uhelaib a comracc.'

['I swear by the gods my people swear by that I shall not rest nor sleep on
down or soft quilts, nor shall I drink buttermilk nor adorn my body, nor
drink red ale nor wine, neither shall I eat anything until these two bulls
appear in combat before me!'][73]

The reference to Bricriu in M's version of the Boyhood Deeds indicates
that he knew this story. Similarly, it is clear that the LL saga tradition,
which knows *Echtra Nerai* as a preliminary story to the *Táin* and which
uses with YBL's version this material of the blow to Bricriu in the ending, would also have been familiar with this suggestion for an opening
motivation. Why its author should then go on to create an entirely new
scene can be best understood as I describe it at the beginning of this
chapter. The only answer must be that the LL 'author' was trying his
hand at new literary invention of a kind that would draw the figure of
Medb into even higher relief.

But it would not do to entirely dismiss all the evidence for oral circulation of the *Táin*. The 'Finding the *Táin*' tradition seems to have kept a
sense of that circulation in popular form of some elements of the work:
... *blogha di ... roboi ac cach co coitceann* ... (D). Recent work done on the
continental *jongleurs*, their performative tradition, and their relationship to written *chansons de geste*, has emphasized the fragmentary or
episodic nature of this oral performative tradition, and has set firmly
apart from it, as an élite cultural item, the written texts of long heroic
works such as the *Chanson de Roland*.[74] Taylor, reviewing Zumthor's
idea of *mouvance* and the revising statements of Lord and Foley on the
oral formula in a discussion of the famous Oxford manuscript of the
Chanson de Roland, states: 'What I wish to stress is that the extended
versions of the chansons de geste, the ones that come down to us, were
essentially clerical creations, that they were not just copied, but com-
piled and delivered by clerics, since only if it took the form of a written
text would a poem have the prestige or authority to command a listener's attention for four thousand lines.'[75] This is also a likely scenario
for the *Táin*. On the one hand, there is a popular knowledge, a tradition
of the cattle raid, which may be either oral or textual fragments stored
in memory, as the reported *blogha* in common circulation attest; on the
other hand, there is the larger creation, the *Táin texts* as we know them,

which also arise out of these badly memorized and fragmented past textual traditions. As the poem on the study methods of a law student attests, medieval Irish scholars pored over texts and took care to memorize a written text:[76]

> *Ogham nach coimhghléighearr colg,*
> *agus an t-oirléigheann ard–*
> *eochracha oslaigthe ghlas*
> *breitheamhan mbras agus mbard.*

> *Meabhraigh seinbhriathra na suadh*
> *agus deighriarfa gach dál,*
> *ní fhuighbhe meabhal ná méal,*
> *is féagh do leabhar dá lár.*

[The literary (i.e. written) language whose thrust is not self-evident or succinct and the noble reading aloud – for ardent judges and bards, they are the keys for opening locks.

Memorise the old testimonies of the sages and you will guide each assembly well – you will not meet with disgrace or shame – and look to your book for their basis.]

It is the social status of the new written versions of the *Táin* that is all-important, drawn in as they now are, to the new aspirations of a social compact between clerics and kings in the eleventh and twelfth centuries.

Marking Up the Text

Finally then, it remains to follow through on the consequences of placing the *Táin* firmly within the cultural ambit of the written word. Evidence has not been forthcoming on the audience implications of this for Irish sagas as we have them.[77] Do clerics control the audience as well as the text in the period? An examination of M's text in LU may provide some clues. M disposes his text in a masterly and thoroughly professional fashion, and his system of headings and sense of transition between narrative blocks is revealing. The text begins (p. 55) with a major ornamented capital T. The segregation of the preface (ll. 1–134) from the rest of the narrative is done by barred titles and an *incipit* notice.[78] From there to the Boyhood Deeds segment (ll. 135–397) there are 262 lines; taken together this makes a chunk of 395 lines. The *Macgnímrada* are introduced by a central boxed heading and run from l. 398 to l. 824, a length of 426 lines.[79] The next clearly marked segment, beginning at l. 2072, is marked by a large ornamental capital, as at the beginning, and has a heading between columns: *In Carpat serda 7 in Breslech Mor Maige Muirthemne inso*. This leaves a passage of 1257 lines within which there are no clear reading directives, such as large capitals or double-marked headings, to mark segments. Also to be taken into account are the interpolations from H (at ll. 1545–1712 and ll. 1904–95).[80] How are we to understand the periodization of the narrative for these thousand or so lines? Succeeding the first interpolation, on M's new page 73 (l. 1714), there is a listing of Cú Chulainn's feats in three barred columns. If this is taken as marking a radical pause in the narrative, and accounting for H's contributions, this section would then yield 719 and 307 lines respectively. Again, if one were to further divide the 719-line section, one might look for an appropriate break at about l. 1300. Segmenting the text here would suggest that we take the end of the *rosc* variant piece and the fight with Etarcomal around l. 1287 as a major break: this is not an unreasonable suggestion, as it is also the first of the fully articulated single combats where the heroic code is fully explored.[81] M's heading here, centred towards the end of 68a, would give two sections of 257 and 460 lines respectively.[82] Finally, at l. 2524 M again uses a large ornamental capital F to begin *Foídis Medb*, the last words written by M that now remain. Whatever episode M intended did not survive here, as H rewrites the heading in the left margin as *Comrac Maind* and contributes his own tale in the remaining half page of text in LU. But this again yields us a section of 452 lines. We thus have a text from M marked up in sections of 395, 426, 719 (460+257), 307, 452 lines respectively.[83]

Granted I am assuming here that M has a number of codes at his disposal to indicate major segmentation – large capitals, boxed headings, breaks for lists and summaries, etc. – and the number of lines in each segment makes for fairly small reading units.[84] Granted too, there are severe pressures on M to accommodate the huge variety in rehtorical amplification in his received textual model. But I believe the reading segmentation of the saga is a case worth making, even if only speculatively. It places the text squarely in a textual community where there is limited access to literacy but in which literacy has immense status value, as witness the intense sense of fidelity, whether real or fictionalized, to other versions. Just as the earlier hagiographical traditions were now yielding to *Vitae* of native saints broken down into reading segments for the recreation of monastic communities, so saga texts for reading could, like the *Chanson de Roland* in the Osteney cleric's manuscript, find a congenial home in Clonmacnoise in a monastery so richly endowed by successive kings of Connacht.[85]

3 A Scribe and His *Táin*:
The H Interpolations in *Táin Bó Cúailnge*

Is scíth mo chrob on scríbainn
ní dígainn mo glé géroll;
sceithid mo phenn gulbán cáelda
dig ndáelda do dub glégorm.

Bruinnid srúaim n-ecna ndedairn
as mo láim degduinn desmais;
doirtid a dig for duilinn
do dub in chuilinn chnesglais.

Sínim mo phenn mbec mbraenach
tar áenach lebar lísgoll
gan scor, fri selba ségann,
dían scíth mo chrob on scríbonn.

[Weary my clenched hand from writing,
my sharp, full nib always ready,
in streams from my fine-beaked pen
the dusky ink draught deepest dark.

Steady, the streams of wisdom spring
from my dark and crafty hand,
pouring out on the writing page
black ink from the glossy holly.

Small wet pen in hand I master
crowds of wondrous books;

work without end, so great my heritage –
hence this claw, crippled from writing.]

Twelfth-century poem attributed to St Columba

Branching Out

The question of the interrelationship of recensions and manuscript versions of medieval Irish saga texts remains a primary preoccupation for
scholars.[1] Chapter 2 concentrated on a limited micro-textual segment –
how the opening of the tale is crafted – as part of a discussion of genre
identification. Levels and degrees of control in the transmission process has also been a key issue, and is a particularly complex matter in
the textual history of *Táin Bó Cuailnge*, where Recension I of that text
shows so many and such varied signs of reworking over a long period
of time. I now want to re-pose the question in a way that will allow us
to track the issue of the writer as encoder/decoder over a more
expanded textual field.

Γ   The changes made by scribe 'H' to the earliest extant collection of
saga texts, that of *Lebor na hUidre* (LU), altered the character of that
great codex – whether for better or worse is a debatable issue.[2] His
work has been much studied and considerable debate has ensued as to
his identity and editorial purpose.[3] The most recent contribution is
from Gearóid Mac Eoin, who has courageously assigned to H a local
habitation and a name, presenting him as a member of the Úa Maol
Chonaire family, associated with the area around Cluain Bolcáin, the
later family seat in Co. Roscommon that was to remain an important
literary centre for the rest of the Middle Ages.[4]

Γ   Mac Eoin's suggestion has important implications for the dating of
H's contribution to U. But in a more general way his discussion has had
the effect of creating the sense of a real person behind the traditional
cipher, and thus casting H himself into higher relief than before. It again
raises issues concerning degrees of authorship and textual engagement
on the part of Irish scribes, and their reading communities, with the
materials that they transmit. The substantial and radical interventions
of H in the texts of LU afford an unrivalled opportunity to examine a
specific example of medieval Irish textual productivity. By analysing the
work of H one may thus attempt the exercise of reading Irish saga texts
synchronically at the level on which they are processed and transmitted
at a specific place and time and by specific individuals.

My critical reading in this chapter aims to engage the text with full recognisance of that individuated site of productivity. Obviously, appropriate attention must also be paid to the text's diachronic history – to do so is the common convention of Irish scholarly practice.[5] But a diachronic reading – that is, an engagement in textual dissection which aims to isolate and identify 'original' layers or date-coded strata – becomes here the necessary and subordinated adjunct to an informed assessment of a particular productive node in the text's historic temporality.[6] By taking a such a synchronic test case – here, the total effect of H's editorial presentation of his text of the *Táin Bó Cúailnge* – one may begin to see at close reading range the nature of the medieval Irish writerly compact itself; one may observe this compact as it operated in the matter of the contextual choices made and the options explored by one reader, 'H,' in order to transmit to a specific set of other readers in his cultural group his own literary insights. It would thus, of course, be anachronistic to view this as an isolated textual project where the writing subject, H, re-composes a saga or reshapes a whole book for his own personal aesthetic satisfaction. The writerly compact involves a scholarly deference both to the authoritative status of the texts at his disposal and also to the assemblage of shared cultural values in his proximate readerly circle. Thus in any evaluation of H's significance one must continuously bear in mind the constitution of tradition and the cultural profile of the textual audience.

So, with this in mind, it seems in order to take a fresh look at H's contributions to the complex textual evolution of *Táin Bó Cuailnge*. Of necessity, and not least because it is so deeply implicated in the crucial aspect of the opening rhetorical stratagems of Recension I (U) of the saga, I begin with, and pay particular attention to, the verse prophecy delivered by the woman poet Fedelm; the poem, supplied by H, serves as the device that constitutes the major framing device of this version of the narrative.[7] But first, for the sake of convenience, I will list H's major interpolations in order:

H in LU and Its Táin

I   55b–56a, on an erasure: the poem *Atchíu fer find firfes cles*, spoken
     by Fedelm, *'banfhili do Chonnachtaib'* (woman poet to the Connacht-
     men), as she is described by M.

II   71a–72b, an intercalated leaf containing a number of incidents; an
     additional incident is added to 70b on an erasure.

III 75a–76b, a smaller intercalated leaf with an erasure on 74b contain-
     ing the beginning of the interpolation. On 76b the erased(?) mate-
     rial from 74b is rewritten and rhetorically embellished to fill up the
     space.[8]
IV   82b, twenty-one lines written in an erased space.
V   78a, last five lines of the poem, *Éli Loga*, on an erasure.

In the introduction to her edition of Recension I, O'Rahilly goes a
long way in her explication of these contributions of H in the text.
While she is sceptical of the relative value of H's additions and
changes, she does show some of their more positive features. She
points to some thematic parallels between H and scenes in Recensions
II and III: for example, in the matter of scenes that have no equivalence
elsewhere in the *Táin* tradition, the treachery of Ailill and Medb in H
mirrors scenes of deception by Ailill in II and the treachery of Medb in
III. She claims for H some powers of invention in writing up connec-
tive passages and in creating entirely new ones. She also suggests that
there is one compelling consideration prompting, if not entirely
explaining, the radical if somewhat muddled additions of H. Noting
that most of the additions anticipate material represented later in
YBL's continuation of the saga, she suggests that H's work is connected to the possibility that the main scribes of LU may never have
had access to any more of the saga than the manuscript now contains.
What O'Rahilly characterizes as M's abrupt break-off in mid-page
(82b) after writing a title and the opening two words of the next incident represents LU's faulty textual possession of the *Táin*.[9]

O'Rahilly's account of H's activities assumes that H was attempting
to farce LU (AM), the in-house reading manuscript at his disposal,
with materials drawn from an alternative version and supplemented
by some minor contributions of his own.[10] But that is not to say that in
assigning him an enhanced role, O'Rahilly had it in mind to ascribe
any but the most rudimentary literary savoir faire or sensitivity to H
and his material. 'The H-interpolator shows little regard for the proper
sequence of events or their geographical location ... he (or his predeces-
sor) inserted the interpolations pretty much at random ...' are typical
editorial comments.[11]

The degree of originality in his contribution would, on first examination, be difficult to analyse much beyond what O'Rahilly has suggested. Nevertheless, within the broad frame of her discussion and
conclusions there remain significant critical issues of the author/audi-

ence type which I have indicated above. Ambiguity still attends the precise significance of H's work and the common scholars' terms, 'the H-interpolator' or 'the reviser'[12] leave unresolved several larger, general considerations of this kind. Thus one might ask: What is the dynamic interplay between the roles of writer, editor, and scribe exemplified in H's work?[13] How does one assess the matter of originality and/or dependence on presumed, once-existing and now lost, written *Táin* versions? How does one work through the difficulty of analysing the relationship between invention based on a learned, exclusively text-dependent idea of tradition, and a more diffuse, 'popular' sense of H's contribution? What does it owe to an assumed cultural ambience that may be open to, indeed saturated with, oral storytelling traditions even while it is committed to their absorbtion and inscription in a written record?[14] Indeed must we go outside such O'Rahilly-type assumptions about the text and ask if the latter formulation above, which attempts to frame textually the factor of 'floating oral traditions,' is necessary at all.[15] If one puts aside for a moment the question of originality of content, are there other ways of viewing the work of H that may open up for us something of his engagement with and attitude to saga narrative? With some of these questions in mind, I would like to explore the significance of H's work by paying closer attention to certain aspects of the textuality of the UH text and especially to the challenge posed by Interpolation *I*, the poem *Atchíu fer find*. In view of O'Rahilly's many illuminating comments about the other H-passages, her relative neglect of this first contribution is curious, for it is here that the surviving manuscript versions of the poem bear witness to intriguing and complex lines of manuscript interdependence.

Interpolation *I*

The context of the poem may be briefly stated: Medb and Ailill have assembled their armies and are about to set off on their enterprise, but they hold back for a favourable sign;[16] Fedelm appears and on Medb's invitation begins the process of the *imbas forosna* rite. This produces the poem, *Atchíu fer find*, some forty-six lines in a mixture of *deibide*-type metres. Because it is written by H on an erasure, both Thurneysen and O'Rahilly assume that the effect of his intervention was to erase from the written record an original *rosc*, the poetic form most appropriate to the context. The lost poem would then, in spirit, provenance, and style, be a link with what Dillon describes as the 'canonical text' of the *Táin*, most purely represented in the *roscada* sequences preserved for us by M in the passages he designated as *córugud aile* (1028 ff.).[17] The perils of seeking original or, more appropriately in this context, originary forms should by now be obvious to all contemporary readers of early Irish literary texts.[18] In this particular instance, moreover – if one is assessing the synchronic effect of the total text as it now presents itself in U – it is not really useful to foreclose critical examination of the existing substituted text by viewing its surviving, rewritten versions as a mere consolation prize for the now vanished privilege of access to an older, hence more challenging and more 'authentic,' discourse.

Granted, the context does not help the reader to forget the lure of the old; Fedelm, by the vatic cachet of her very name,[19] her striking visual impact, and her dramatic arrival on the beginning scene of the saga, represents the sum of a powerful archetype.[20] Indeed, it is the very strength of that archetype of visionary prophetess that seems to invest her message with an aura of authority, warding off scrutiny and close reading by the sacred privilege and guarantee of her presence.[21] Now as a plain syllabic poem, it nevertheless seems from its context to still carry the charge of rhapsody. It also invites such a reading by certain elements of its form: as a unitary lyric utterance eschewing narrative matter and lacking story-coded 'real' information, it seems to demand assent and suspension of critical dissection.

It is clear that the disjunctions now constituted in the texts of the saga that contain this inserted poem generated considerable textual complexity of their own for H; and this is over and above the particular trace effect of the literary context left by that which has been erased from the record. Trace evidence of that 'lack' also needed to be resynthesised in the consequent re-reading/re-inscribing. Thus the relationship between poem and context is not that of a simple raw splice with an awkward hiatus between new poem and older prose introduction.[22] Problems existed already in H's received text: after the description of Fedelm in A's hand, scribe M has rewritten the first few lines of his or A's text – in which Fedelm identifies herself – over an erasure. This identification of Fedelm as a graduate of poetry from Alba is possibly borrowed from the accounts of Scátach and Aífe in *Tochmarc Emire* and differs sharply from the identification found in Recension II. The 'authenticity' of the hieratic site is always, whatever its formulation, rhetorically constructed, and in this instance the narrative scenic surround must have undergone some rewriting to include, for example, the sophisticated *descriptio* of Fedelm herself. In chapter 6 I will describe some elements of Fedelm as a displaced and displacing figure in my discussion of the women in the text. Here, for the purposes of following H's particular strand of writerly intervention in the *Táin*, I propose to approach the scene laterally, so to speak, using the other surviving versions to stalk H: there are two full manuscript witnesses to the Recension I text of the poem – U (H) and Egerton 1782 (W) – and while the versions they present are largely similar, there are subtle differences between them in text and presentation.[23] By comparing them it may be possible to open up a critical space that will allow some additional light to fall on the scribes' understanding of their text and provide a better sense of H's distinctive contribution.[24]

Fedelm's Prophetic Words

Atchiu fer find firfes cles
co lín créchta fora chnis
lúan láith i n-airthiur a chind
óenach mbúada a thulchind.

Fail secht ngemma láith ngaile
for lár a dá imlisse
fil fuidrech fora glinni
fil leind ndeirg ndrolaig immi.

Dofil gnúis as gráto dó
dobeir mod don bancureo
duni óc is alaind dath
dofeith deilb ndracuin don chath.

Cosmail innas a gaile
fri Coin Culaind Murtheimne
nocon fhetar cúich in Cú
Culaind aasa caini clú
acht rofetursa amne
is forderg in slúagsa de.

Atchíu fer mór forsin maig
dobeir tres dona slógaib
cetri claidbini cles n-an
fil i cechtar a dá lám.

Dá gáe bolga immosbeir
cenmothá colg det i[s][25] sleg
ardaric imbert don tslúag
sain gním fris téit cach n-arm uád.

Fer i cathfhochrus bruit deirg
dobeir in cosmail cach leirg
ardaslig tar fonnad clé
cotagoin in ríastarthe
delb domárfas fair co se
a[t][26]chíu imrochlád a gné.

Ro gab toscugud don chath
mani airlestar bid brath
dóich lim iss é dobobsaig
Cú Chulaind mac Sualdaim.

Slaidfid for slúagu slána
fochiuchra for tiugára
fáicfidi leis míli cend
ní cheil in banfháith Fedelm.

Snigfid crú a cnesaib curad
do láim laich bid lánpudar
oirgfid ócu imregat fir
do clannaib Dedad meic Shin
beit cuirp cerbtha caínfit mná
la Coin na Certa atchiu-sa.

[I see a fair man who will perform weapon-feats, with a multitude of wounds on his skin. A hero's frenzy is visible on his forehead, an assembly of talents on his brow.

The seven jewels of the hero's ardour are set in each of his two pupils, his jaw is stripped back, he wears a red hooked tunic.

His face is appropriate to his status, he inflames the women with desire; a young person with a beautiful appearance, he bears a dragon shape to the battle.

He resembles, in his fury, Cú Chulainn of Murtheimne. I do not know if he be this Cú Chulainn of fair fame, but I do know this – that the army is blood-drenched by him.

I see a big man on the field who engages the army in battle. Four hacking swords he holds in each of his two hands – an amazing feat.

He assaults them with two *gae bolgae* along with a bone-hilted sword and a spear. He plies the army with them, each one is used with its own special technique.

A man in the warrior-gear of a red cloak – he appears thus in every battle; he attacks them across the left rim (of the chariot), the frenzied one cuts them down. The form in which he had revealed himself up to now, as I look his appearance changes.

He has moved to the forefront of the battle; unless heed be taken there will be destruction. Indeed, I think it is Cú Chulainn son of Súaldam who now approaches you.

He will cut down your entire army, he will destroy you in mass slaughter, you will leave a thousand heads to him – the prophetess Fedelm does not hide it from you.

Blood will spurt from the bodies of heroes, this hero's hand will do untold harm. He will kill young men, the men of Clann Dedad mac Sin will quit the scene. There will be bodies hacked to pieces, women will lament because of the Smith-Hound whom I see].[27]

The verse is scripted by H as a straight bravura performance by the character Fedelm; H introduces the poem simply with a conventional rubric for a verse passage in a narrative: *conid and asbert* (so it was then she recited, l. 66). In U then there is no deeper development of a dramatic role-playing cue between client and visionary. The sense of a dialogue frame is not as fully marked up visually in U, being represented only in the Medb/Fedelm prose introduction.[28] By contrast, W's version omits the conventional segue phrase, *conid and asbert* and the sequence thus has much more dramatic impact: *Fedelm banfaith co acca ar sluag? ... atchíu forderg atchíu ruad* [Fedelm, woman prophet how see you our host? I see it full-crimson, I see it red]. By so punctuating the poem the W scribe chooses to emphasize the dramatic rhythm of the scene and to see the poem as involving a duet of choric players. More significantly, the syllabically correct line of the question elucidates an answering metrical line in a manner that recollects numerous situations where women are involved in the vatic completion of a verse quatrain.[29] W, then, enters into the spirit of the poem as a mimesis of ritual drama, as a continuation, or rather the end product, of an ongoing dramatic process, the reconstructed *imbas forosna* rite itself.[30] In addition, the W version divides the poem in two by repeating the verse dialogue 'stage direction' halfway through: thus both halves have rhetorical integrity; they begin with *atchíu* and both comprise a sequence of description leading to a positive identification of the hero. W thus collapses distinctions between the poet narrator, who presents meta-textual action, and the enunciated prophecy itself. By so doing audience distance is cancelled and the role of the reader is substantially altered. The reader is now in the front line of emotional participation and must now re-compose this distance between himself and represented discursive process in the saga text.

Through the Glass Poem – Reflection

Before entering into detailed study of some specifics of the text of H it may be well to attempt to describe the general structure and effects of the poem, assuming that one were first to apprehend it as, in some measure, a dramatic enunciative moment in a saga where there are scenes that provide a fictive encoding of oral declamatory potential.[31] In this spirit, the introductory frame of the Medb–Fedelm question and answer sequence adds to its formal impact. The variations evident in the various versions of the poem and its discursive context offer slight but significant clues as to the poem's impact, even as they also present a blurred and unstable textual field. Stepping back to scope the text through its variants, one might say that the 'poem' is the utterance that is represented by the sum of all the manuscript witnesses. In other words, all the versions attest in different ways to the presence of a discursive artifact, a poem of a dramatic monologue type embedded in a prose context; it is the effects of this state of discourse that I will try to describe, first generally, and then more specifically as H presents the poem.

The chief characteristic of the first half of the poem is its concentration on the envisioning of the hero as a figure dominating a limited scenic field. In this respect it selects certain details from the description of Cú

Chulainn that appear elsewhere in the saga, while keeping an appropriate if minimal rhetorical decorum of describing the physical body in order, beginning with the head and torso.[32] O'Rahilly went to some trouble to avoid the obvious reading of quatrain 2c (*fuidrech fora glinni*) as one of the standard details in the description of Cú Chulainn's *riastartha*, the canine-like baring of the teeth and jaws, on the grounds that it clashed with the apparently benign aspect of the beautiful (sic UH) hero of the quatrain following. It seems an unnecessary avoidance: the rhetorical trick here is to present a hero who displays a bewilderingly protean and unstable visual facade;[33] his characteristics veer between the terrifying and the beautiful, or, in contextual terms, between the two great rhetorical prose 'runs' that occur back-to-back later in the *Táin* (ll. 2245–2366): the hero in war-frenzy and the hero at social play.[34]

Once this initial rhetorical direction is established – description as transformation and the successful negotiation of fluidity in Fedelm's act of interpretative utterance of an inner visionary voice – then other words, *delb*, *cosmail*, *gné*, *gnúis*, in these opening quatrains assume their place, yielding the effect of a carefully pointed auctorial deliberativeness in the reading and translating into significance the visual signs and behavioural markers in the performance of the envisioned hero.[35] In his outlandish physical projection of himself in *cles*, in *riastartha*, in *delb dracuin*, in *gal*, in *lúan laith*, as well as in his bewildering ability to show simultaneously a face of terror and a *gnúis gráta* (attractive face) to flutter the camp-follower women, he is recognizable to Fedelm, the professional reader and, through her, to the recipients of the poem, as being 'like' Cú Chulainn. The dramatic pace of the revelation is held in check and economically managed by the *imbas forosna* practitioner in order to achieve maximum effect. After a 'making strange' of envisioned figure in a heroic landscape, this eclectic creation of an as yet directionless 'effect of the hero' is now tentatively given a name, but a name with little resonance as yet for the Connacht part of the audience. The figure, which up to this point has simply floated in the timeless present tense of the vision, is now provisionally named and, beyond the name, is made prophetically and forcefully relevant to the rite's clients; *acht rofetursa amne/ is forderg in sluagsa de* (H, qu. 3 ef). This will be more brutally driven home in the second half of the poem by an insistent rhetoric of focused savage destruction and with the personal authority of Fedelm's own truth assertion: *slaidfid for sluagu slána,/ fochiuchra for tiugára;/ fáicfidi leis míli cend,/ ní cheil in banfháith Fedelm* (qu. 9).

This is the specific contextual import of the poem. In a more general

– one might say rhapsodic – manner one may also see the poem as the way through which both the internal actors and the responsive audience participants enter with Fedelm the liminal world of anarchic battle chaos and dehumanization, and some of that potential of terror and awe is thereby given a prefatory release into the saga. The poem may then be said to enact a liminal and initiatory ritual with respect to the reception of the text itself; it is the discursive equivalent of leaving home and entering another language, another set of emotional responses, and another world. However, given the internal logic of heroic event, the shock of alienation is necessary and is an effect to be sought. This is what warriors need and expect to hear before a battle. The threat and challenge of the poem is thus an essential part of heroic ritual posturing. Leaders look for signs, and for better or worse, the poem concentrates the heroic mind on the task ahead. Such an utterance – whether couched in the aurally disconcerting 'scrambled' discourse of the *rosc*, or more plainly as here – provides a crucial emotional key to the participants. It is a group experience which, ideally, ought to function as a shared bond among co-fighters. That the Connacht side and its leaders are incapable of creating a heroic community in this or in any other way is part of the whole story of the *Táin*.

This is by no means the only way of identifying and describing the operations of the poem. The figure of Fedelm maintains several mantic functions: I have already identified the 'search, see, and name' visionary mode.[36] The troubling *menma* of Cú Chulainn is already in the air, though it can only be sensed by Fedelm. Out of the disturbing vagueness of the blank cipher, 'redness,' Fedelm must not only construe a presence – the first section of the poem, but also a prognostication – the closing half. But prognostication is finally required to be more than descriptively and emotionally persuasive. It must reduce to two alternative utilitarian-based readings: is this expedition going to be lucky or unlucky? Fedelm would be failing in her professional duty, so to speak, if she were not to call the outcome conscientiously according to her knowledge and her brief. But if one remembers the power of the Fedelm archetype, one more detail of the poem also falls into place. She fulfils, though admittedly in a muted way, her proper mediating role; she may prophecy war but she must counsel peace.[37] Thus she offers the only possible advice: *mani airlestar bid brath* [unless one come to terms there will be destruction].[38]

Thus far I have been describing the effects of the poem as presented by H and considering the characteristics of the poem itself in a general

manner. In the case of W, the effect of visionary decipherment, drama-
tized by W's stage directions, is enhanced by the single most significant textual variant, (W, l. 12), where W reads *duine óacc anaithghnith
dath* to H's *duni óc is álaind dath*. The term *anaithghnith* is one of a number of words of similar construction, of which the most common is *ane-
targnáth*, used in early Irish literary texts to convey first impressions of
individuals coming from another world who are recognized as exotic
either from their personal appearance or their clothing.[39] Such words
convey not only a sense of the mystery but also a sense of the challenge
to decipherment that they present to the interpreter and audience of
the tale. *Dath* in this context conveys less 'complexion,' 'colour of skin'
as 'semblance.' The term as a whole, then, points to the 'reading' task
of the *imbas forosna* visionary; the individual is unknowable to the
audience, but for Fedelm the description, however difficult, must lead
to an identification and a name – especially if there is a suspicion that
there is something inhuman about the hero.

In itself, W's phrase represents no great distance between his understanding of the poem's contents and that of H. It does perhaps point to
different textual contexts out of which the two versions of the poem
emerge: *anaichnid* is the term used to introduce the great description of
Cú Chulainn's *riastartha* after his healing: *Is and so cétríastartha im Choin
Chulaind co nderna úathbásach n-ilrechtach n-ingantach n-anaichni de* [It
was then that a multiple distortion came over Cú Chulainn so that he
became terrible, many-shaped, amazing, and unrecognizable] (ll. 2245–
6); in the *Tuarascbáil Delba Con Culaind* that follows this, he is described
as going *do thaisbénad a chrotha álgin álain do mnáib 7 bantrochtaib 7
andrib 7 ingenaib 7 filedaib 7 aes dána* [to show his gentle and beautiful
form to women and ladies, to girls and maidens, to poets and men of
art] (ll. 2337–9). Why is this latter site of more significance to H? In
phrasing it in this way I am, of course, implying that, for the purposes
of a literary critical approach, one may provisionally see this variant as
a genuine innovation of H and not a received reading. The obvious
answer lies in the combination of the adjectives 'gentle' and 'lovely':
the hero is only sporadically harshly alien and he also has a human
domestic aspect. It would seem that H shows a consistent interest in
the sexual politics surrounding Cú Chulainn, whether it be in the
inclusion of an incident linking him with Findabair in Interpolation *II*,
or in bringing Medb and Cú Chulainn together in Interpolation *III*. In
one sense we might perhaps speak of a progressive misogyny in the
Táin tradition from its earliest articulation in the archaic *Conailla Medb*

midchura poem through Recension I and the H-version to Recension II.[40] But this would be to imply that H is continuing a clerical tradition. In another way, however, the H version evokes the whole sense of an active audience through whose admiring eyes the memorialization and the actualization of the fact of the hero may be mediated after the presentation of his heroic distinctiveness, his *ríastartha*. The audience then stands in for both writer and audience, for H's writerly compact itself. That audience may now be demanding that the hero be shown in more scenes involving women precisely because the audience is moving out from a purely male monastic context into a mixed context of a regional king's court with women present as a constituent element of the demand for saga entertainment. The whole question of *riastartha* textual construction and H's interest in it is a matter to which I shall return later.

It is, of course, impossible to say why, if such ever did exist, an 'original' *rosc* was scrapped by H. It may well be that the lost item never existed in this form, and that, as I have been attempting to convey above, the contextual layout of the poem and possible textual cruces in his source document were such that H felt an entirely new presentation was desirable.[41] He may also have augmented the warp-spasm/beauty contrast. The question then arises for the textual historian as to where he might have found his material. Was it already textually composed, and do W, UH, the H 1. 18 gloss, and LL represent independent witnesses to such a pre-existing syllabic poem? It is hardly likely that the poem is H's original composition and that all other versions are ultimately dependant on UH. How then do we understand the way in which the textual tradition is marked or altered creatively by H?[42] If the poem is not an original composition of H, then the clue offered by the term *álaind* admits of two variant solutions. H may be closest to the lost prototype poem on which all versions depend, but it is not necessary to posit dependance on a prototype at this specific point in the text. Alternatively, *álaind* may be seen as a creative option taken up by H, an option available to him because he already has a fluent 'map' of the text in his memory. Hence H can easily substitute one term for another in his source with respect to particular topoi – displays in the form of shape changing and sexual flaunting – to which, as we shall see, he is most attentive. H is then a close, one might almost say an obsessive, reader in that these are scenes to which he habitually returns; he is also a canny adaptor to new audience demands.

Perhaps we can also go a little way further towards fleshing out these observations and assessing the nature of H's input here by following closely his other contributions to the *Táin*. In the process a number of alternative ways of considering H's creativity will suggest themselves. For convenience, in what follows I lay out the remaining interpolations with summary detail.

Interpolation *II*

In Thurneysen's view this whole sequence is taken from an existing text of a type very similar to the *córugud aile* section that M had written in just before the point where H inserts the extra leaf. O'Rahilly took a more nuanced view; it is indeed similar in many respects to the *córugud aile* piece from M, but it is to be differentiated from it by the haphazard fashion of H's treatment of his assumed source. The incidents covered are the following:

(a) Truces are brokered by Lugaid mac Nois and Fergus mac Róich. Lugaid, a Munster prince, is also an active character in the *córugud aile* sequence that immediately precedes.

(b) *Comrac Con Culaind fri Findabair*. Maine fails and Lugaid succeeds in persuading Cú Chulainn to come and meet Findabair. He sees the deceitful substitution of the *druth* for Ailill, kills the *drúth*, and shames Findabair.

(c) *Comlond Munremair 7 Con Roí*. Munremur and Cú Roí fight inconclusively. This incident is obviously taken from a Y-type continuation, being a close copy of the stone fight between Aimirgin and Cú Roí (ll. 3393–409).

(d) *Aided na Macraide*. The boy troop from Emain Macha, under their leader Fiachna Fulech mac Fir Febe, are slain. This is doubly out of place, as it also does not fit in its alternative location in U (M), where it happens during Cú Chulainn's healing sleep (ll. 2166–75). H follows up the account with a discussion of Cú Chulainn's warp-spasm.

(e) *Bánchath Rochada*. Rochad mac Fathemain comes to to help Cú Chulainn. He is lured away and betrayed by the promise of Findabair. He undertakes not to return. The incident is found later in the Y-continuation (ll. 3347–53) near the Cú Roí episode.

(f) *Aided na Rígamus*. The seven Munster princes of the Y-continuation (here called Clann Dedad) who have also been promised Findabair in the Y-continuation (ll. 3354–67) – but not in this version – fight

Cú Chulainn. In Y, they fight their own side and cause the slaughter of Glendomain, one of the three great slaughters of the *Táin*.[43]

(g) *Aided Cáuir.* This dovetails with the ending of the episode given by M, 73a. One may also assume that the erasure area effected by H on 70b once contained the first part of this episode.

What points of significance are there to link H's interest here with the content of *Atchíu fer find*? First of all there is a general interest in warp-spasm descriptions. H introduces a generalized frenzy digression as an addendum to the incident of the death of the boy troop. The model scene of the great *riastartha* in the surviving section of U *TBC* is in M's hand, so the insertion by H of a minor warp spasm here does not fit O'Rahilly's idea that the main purpose of the latter's additions is to present material beyond what was available to U's reading community. Strictly speaking, H is correct to link the death of the boy troop and a *riastartha* here, as it was partly to avenge them later that Cú Chulainn entered into the great frenzy which resulted in the Slaughter of Breslige. But this motivational sequencing is somewhat submerged in the great sweep and flourish of this latter *riastartha* account, where the sheer richness of rhetorical artifice makes of the description a major verbal event in itself and renders any minor leftover narrative business almost irrelevant.

Here in H's addition, the *riastartha* is effectively separated from its narrative purpose and is introduced on the thinnest of excuses, a gloss on the reference made to the *lón láith* [the warrior's aura] by Ailill (ll. 1650–7):

Ar ba bés dó-som in tan no linged a lón láith ind, imréditis a t[h]raigthi iarma 7 a escata remi 7 muil a orcan fora lurgnib, 7 indala súil ina chend 7 araili fria chend anechtair. Docoised ferchend for a beólu. Nach findae bíd fair ba háthithir delc sciach 7 banna fola for cach finnu. Ní aithgnéad cóemu ná cairdiu. Cumma no slaided ríam 7 íarma. Is de sin doratsat Fir nÓl nÉcmacht in ríastartha do anm do C[h]oin C[h]ulaind.

[For it was usual with him that when his hero's flame used to rise up in him his feet would turn to the back and his thigh muscles would turn to the front and the muscles of his calves would move around to his shins; one eye would be inside his head and the other one protruding from it. A man's head would fit into his mouth. Every rib of hair on him would be as sharp as the spike of a thorn bush with a drop of blood on every hair.

He would distinguish neither loved ones nor friends. He would slash
equally before and behind him. It is for this reason that Connacht people
had given 'The *Riastartha*' as a name to Cú Chulainn.]

The references to Cú Chulainn's appearance pick up items from both
the great *riastartha* account (ll. 2250–3) and, possibly, from the Boyhood
Deeds sequence, also with the detail that in his frenzy he could not recognize friends or his own side (ll. 804–9). Twice in H's addition there is
reference to the prepositional pairing *íar* and *re*, in the second instance
in relation to his sword play. The whole description is then summed up
with a reference to the nickname '*riastartha.*' There is a strong possibility that H is thinking in etymological terms here; from the phrase *riam
is íarma* it is a brief step to another related prepositional pairing, *ria is
tar*. Rather than conceive of Cú Chulainn's sword dexterity as the ability to strike before and behind him (at friend and foe?), a technique
which makes little practical sense, one should perhaps think of a fore-
hand/backhand slashing action.[44] In this case *re is tar* or *ria is tair(i)sde*
is a reasonable bridging doublet, and thus a precise syllabic analysis
type of etymology of the Isidorean kind so dear to medieval Irish
scholars may be suggested for *riastartha.*[45] Indeed, the whole passage is
constructed around linked prepositional phrases, all working up to
this etymological invention of a nickname.

Whether the connection is made simply with *ria is-* or with a sense of
a paired and modified set of prepositions as I suggest, one can see the
mental shift that H has made. From a general interest in *riastartha* as a
visually registered phenomenon made up from two descriptive segments of *TBC* – an interest reflected in both the poem above and here in
Interpolation *II* – we can now, with this etymology, observe at closer
range H's real work of choice. When he writes, *Is de sin doratsat Fir nÓl
nÉcmacht in riastartha do anm do Coin Culaind*, since it is his addition and
his etymology, by citing *Fir nÓl nÉcmacht* as 'author' he may be inserting himself obliquely in the text. If so, he signals the scholarly mindset
of his own western-oriented and western-based learned community.[46]
Moreover, in the process he sets the specifically Ulster identity of the
hero somewhat to one side and adopts a Connacht perspective.[47] The
way Cú Chulainn 'belongs' to Ulster by kin and by place name matters
less, H is implying, to a Connacht audience than the entertainingly
'weird' aspects of this saga hero. He is then the clown, visually presented as the 'back-to-front-inside-out man,' deconstructed lexically by
the literary group as the 'prepositional man,' potentially a figure of

burlesque and most pointedly a verbal construct. Thus H interposes a distancing membrane of self-conscious textuality, and the resultant effect is to render the audience's ability to apprehend Cú Chulainn transparently as the noble hero in his warrior exultation less than straightforward. It is, in short, to discover the blocking effect of the author in the writing of H, the reader.

The second connecting point between the work of H in Interpolations *I* and *II* is the deployment of sexual themes. If we return to those incidents in *II* that are brought forward by H from the later part of a Y-type continuation, a certain rationale for their treatment in H emerges that has some bearing also on *I*. There is a persistent thread of interest in Munster figures. Lugaid mac Nois, the Munster prince, has already figured as an important mediator at the end of the *córugud aile* section of M; H preserves this role for him through incident (a) and on into (b), the newly invented meeting of Cú Chulainn and Findabair. One might ask why H is intent on bringing in early an erotic contact for Cú Chulainn, an episode that serves to deflect some of the sexual intrigue interest away from the Rochad incident later in (e). The impulse to create a scene early in the sequence in which Cú Chulainn may be seen as attractive to women picks up one note of the *Atchíu fer find* poem, but that alone is not sufficient cause. A ripple, default effect also spills over into the treatment of the Munster royal mercenaries in (f). Clumsy as some of the plotting of this sequence may be, by overloading and displacing early on the motif of sexual diplomacy with Findabair, H here achieves a certain result. The fate of the Munster princes is now not linked with Rochad because in H's new scene Findabair has not slept with him, and thus there is no question of their responding to provocative actions as overt rivals for her hand. Now, in their new H-position, they do not fight their Connacht allies for Findabair; they merely face Cú Chulainn as men and die. They exit from the text quietly with their dignity intact rather than in the big bang of one of the most deadly and ignominious battles of the *Táin*, the *Imshlige Glendomnach*.[48]

If H simplifies and alters their role in this way, his focus is also sharper in one other respect; here they are called *Clann Dedad*, and with this name the reader is brought back to one of the keynotes of the final quatrain of the Fedelm poem. Significantly, in the light of H's interest in Munster figures, the reference to the Clann Dedad does not make its way into the Recension II version of *Atchiu fer find*, though, as I have noted earlier, the piece is the only material from the H-interpolations that features in the Book of Leinster *Táin*.[49] Why the interest of a Con-

nacht *literatus* in working up a role for the men of Munster is not
shared by the LL redactor is not immediately clear.[50] H's ultimate
sources for this may well lie in a type of material, now represented by
Luccreth moccu Chiara's seventh-century poem, *Conailla Medb
míchura*, but which may once have contained much more *Táin*-type
lore of Munster relevance.[51] According to Carney the purpose of Luccreth's poem seems to be to explain why 'a people in Munster held that
they were not by origin Munster folk but had come to that province
from the neighbourhood of Tara, in comparatively recent times, the
reign of Oengus, son of Nad Froích.'[52]

At first surmise, then, it would seem that H can call on a submerged
tradition in which Munster figures played a larger role than in Recension I of the *Táin* as we now have it. But this means only that one can
discern a general textual area within which to locate the formative
influences at work on this alternative tradition, while the matter of the
intermediary levels and conduits of transmission remain obscure.
Indeed one might hazard that H's fresh emphasis on 'the matter of
Munster' may represent no deeper pool of received and progressively
augmented tradition than the fairly immediate cultural environment of
H himself. Whatever its antiquity, it represents an important critical
choice on the part of H. It re-introduces Munster as a real player in a
reworked literary landscape in a way that parallels the rise of Munster
to prominence in the late tenth century and thereafter. H's treatment of
this southern material might indeed respond to further calibration
with contemporary political events.[53] Generally, the O'Connor kings of
the late twelfth and early thirteenth centuries sought alliances with the
MacCarrthaigh of South West Munster. The arrival of a new bride has
repercussions through all performative genres.

It is possibly for this reason also that the need to rescue and present
in a prominent position the role of the Munster hero Cú Roí governs
H's inclusion and treatment of that incident. In the Y-continuation
Amairgin is the opponent to Cú Roí, ably assisted by his son Conall
Cernach. But Conall Cernach is one of the Ulster exiles, and his presence here is incongruous. Amairgin is also difficult: he is introduced as
a figure capable of trance, and hence resonates with other poetic
Amairgins in the tradition.[54] Conall Cernach is also the ancestor of the
Dál nAraide people and the Laigis. By avoiding a figure associated
with these families, particularly the Laigis, it is possible that H intends
a snub to another distinguished learned family, the Laigis Uí Crim-
thainne, associated with Terryglass and with Nuacongbála, the place

of writing of the Book of Leinster. He has instead opted for an innocuous substitute, Munremur mac Gerrgeinn, a safe Ulster stay-at-home who figures in the hosting of the Ulstermen later on in the story.

Clann Dedad is a general term for the Érainn of Munster,[55] and in the U text of *Táin Bó Flidais* H interpolates the detail that Clann Dedad, the family of Ded, was one of the three warrior races of Ireland.[56] He has in this way succeeded in shaping a text of the *Táin* so that exemplary incidents for all three warrior groupings – viz. the Gailióin, the Fir Domnainn, and the Clann Dedad – are fairly presented. Thus, he shows a consistency between his glossing procedures and his disposition of narrative. Details such as these are valuable in that they yield an image of H as possessing the ability to shape received narratives in a variety of significant ways.

In some pseudo-historical sources Déd mac Sin is interchanged with Cú Roí.[57] In H, incident (c), Cú Roí is specifically said to have come to do battle *do chobair a muintiri* (to help his people), unlike the statement of Y that he comes *do chomruc fri Coin Culaind* (to fight Cú Chulainn). The new character, Munremur, figures again briefly in Interpolation *IV* as an analogue to Mand.[58] Cú Roí, as the arch-representative of the Clann Dedad, also leaves the field in an orderly fashion, and this group of references, taken as a whole, may reflect on the choice of words in the Fedelm poem, where they are understood as a defined group: *imregat fir/do c[h]lannaib Dedad meic Shin.* O'Rahilly translated this as, 'the men of Clann Dedad meic Sin will flee,' but 'flee' seems a rather stretched meaning for the verb in question, *imm-téit.* 'The men of Clann Dedad will leave (i.e. will exit quietly my text),' gives a fairer picture of the manner in which H has presented his Munster figures. The phrase from the poem also anticipates in a general way the behaviour of the Munster contingent in the final battle, where their action is also a matter of a dignified retreat: *Lotar didiu in Gaileóin 7 na Muimnich* [The Leinstermen and the Munstermen left] (ll. 4108–9).

But in more specifically literary terms the conclusion of the Cú Roí incident (c) allows us to see further into H the craftsman's general attitude to his material. In suggesting that Cú Roí acts to safeguard his own people, H is actually following closely the phrasing of the Nad Crantail episode just before in U. Here Medb suggests either Cú Roi or Nad Crantail as a fitting opponent to Cú Chulainn: *Boí fer di muintir Con Ruí isin phupaill. 'Ní therga Cú Roí,' or se. 'Is leor leiss dodeochaid dia muintir and* [One of Cú Roí's people was in the tent. 'Cú Roí will not come,' he said, 'he thinks enough of his people have gone there already'] (ll. 1398–1400). H's insertion of Cú Roí at this point thus makes perfectly good sense and shows H as nicely sensitive in yet another register to the verbal echo effects of the narrative which he is following and presenting. The incident ends inconclusively with the following comment:

> Dogníat córai íarom Munremur 7 Cú Roí 7 téit Cú Ruí dia thig 7 Munremur do Emain Macha. Ocus ní thánic Munremur co lá in chatha. Ní thánic dano Cú Ruí co comrac Fir Diad.

> [Then Munremur and Cú Roí made peace and Cú Roí went to his house and Munremar went to Emain Macha. Munremur did not come until the day of the battle. Cú Roí, moreover, did not come until the fight with Ferdiad] (ll. 1622–5).

Here H corresponds less to the profile of a professional storyteller than he does to the figure of a professional handler of texts. The persons of Cú Roí and Munremur are viewed not so much as actors in a dramatic narrative but as figures in a textual order. Having been disturbed from their original place in the source text, they must now be returned to it. Thus Munremur is returned to his position in the Muster Roll of the Ulstermen and Cú Roí to a point in the narrative soon after (and not before) Cú Chulainn's fight with Fer Diad.[59] O'Rahilly, following the story line and pursuing her theme of H's weak grasp of narrative linear chronology, objected that he does not return for some 250 lines after Fer Diad.[60] He actually makes his next appearance, strictly speaking, not in a narrative incident but in a list, Dinda na Tána (ll. 3154–60), which is given *immediately* after the fight with Fer Diad.[61]

Interpolation III (on an intercalated leaf)

(a) The women gather to look at Cú Chulainn as he prepares to fight Lóch. This continues an incident already begun by M (ll. 1904–9).
(b) Cú Chulainn is attacked by *fían* bands (ll. 1910–17).
(c) There is a meeting with Medb and an attempted ambush. Cú Chulainn chants a martial poem (ll. 1918–74).
(d) The fight with Lóch is completed (ll. 1975–95).

This interpolation is carefully integrated into the text, but in content it is a less substantial piece of work than Interpolation *II* as it contains only one major new episode, the tryst with Medb at Focherd. O'Rahilly has suggested that to the interpolator it may have formed a parallel with the deceitful encounter between Cú Chulainn and Findabair and Ailill in Interpolation *II*.[62] She points out, moreover, that U's text was already disturbed at this point by what is probably an interpolation (ll.1884–1903) from a later incident in which women climb on their menfolk's shoulders to catch a glimpse of the hero in his *diallait óenaigh* (festival garb). She also suggests that it is M's reference to another version of feats done at Áth nGrencha (alternatively Áth Tarteisc) that gives H the opportunity to add some material here.

Two elements are noticeable in H's addition. First, he is content to continue the episode as it has been first established by M, an episode that gives prominence to the women's role in the presence of, and in engagement with, the hero. It is the *banchuire* as a whole that acts here, forming a kind of mocking and taunting chorus against which the figures of Medb and Findabair and their actions may be set. Thus the effect of the women as a group on the hero and he on them at the scene of battle is signalled here, just as it was in the Fedelm poem.[63] It is as if M's description of the womenfolk, already sited in a disturbed textual zone of remaking, galvanizes H to creativity; he expands on his theme in the only available way, by creating a meeting between Cú Chulainn and Medb, one of the two designated female actors left on the Connacht side whom he has not yet used.

How H Made a Poem

H's creative competitiveness is also aroused in one other respect here, namely his interest in etymologies of a particular kind. At l. 1778 Fer Báeth is dismissed by M.

> 'Ná téig, a Fhir Báith, co n-aicther in fríthi fónúar-sa.'
> 'Tochra úait,' ar Fer Báeth. Focheird Cú Chulaind in sleig n-íarom i ndegaid Fir Baíth co n-érrmadair áth a dá chúlad co ndeochaid fora beólo sair co torchair tara aiss issa nglend.
> 'Focherd sin ém!' or Fer Báeth. Is de atá Focherd Murthemne.
> Nó iss é Fiacha asrubairt: 'Is beóda do fheocherd indiu, a C[h]ú Chulaind,' or sé. Conid de attá Foc[h]erd Murthemne.
> Atbail fo chétóir Fer Báeth isinn glind. Is de atá Glend Fir Báith.
> Co cloth ní, Fergus co n-epert:
>
> 'A Fhir Baíth is báeth do fhecht

'sin magin i tá do fert
rosiacht coll do chombár and
is crichid hi Cróen Chorand.

F[r]íthi ainmnigther a n-ard
co bráth bid Cróenach i mMuirthemniu
ó 'ndiu bid Focherd a ainm
ind airm i torcha(i)r, a Fhir,' a Fhir Baíth 7c

['Don't go, Fer Báeth, until you see the discovery I have made.' 'Throw it
here,' said Fer Báeth. Cú Chulainn then threw the spear after Fer Báeth so
that it struck him in the nape of the neck and went out through his mouth
and he fell backwards in the valley. 'That was a throw indeed!' said Fer
Báeth. From this comes Focherd Muirthemne. Or else it is Fiacha who
said: 'Your wounding throw is lively (reading *beócherd*) today, Cú Chulainn,' he said. Hence Focherd Muirthemne. Fer Báeth dropped dead in
the valley. Hence comes the Valley of Fer Báeth. A thing was heard, and
Fergus recited:

'O Fer Báeth your expedition was foolish, on the ground where your
grave is. Ruin reached your valley there and an end in Cróen Corand.

Fríthi the hill is called, Cróenach will always be on the level(?); Focherd
will be its name from now on, the place (i.e. the hill) where you fell, O Fer
(Báeth).']

Here we have no less than three different etymological glosses and
three different witnesses – Fer Báeth, Fiacha, Fergus – to the place
name involving the person and the action, viz. Glenn Fir Báith, Fríthi,
Focherd.[64] But there are also a number of problems with the two-quat-
rain poem ascribed to Fergus, and this confuses the sequence considerably.[65] Given the incorporation into the poem of what may have been a
gloss – *Muirthemne*, in M's exemplar – it may be that H recognized
these problems of poetic jumble in the Fergus poem and thought he
could easily improve on this in his section by offering a more rhetorically charged poem than the simple *deibide* of his reading text; this new
poem would incorporate the two-syllable etymology of Focherd in a
more memorable fashion, and in a way that we are coming to recognize is H's preferred style:

Fó mo cherd laéchdachta .i. maith
benaim béimend ágmara
for slóg síabra sorchaidi.
Certaim ág fri ilshlúagaib
im díth erred anglondach
sceó Medbi 7 Ailella.
Altai drochrúin derchoblid
gossa dubrúin banmassa
cengait celga úargossa
fri ág erred anglonnach
congeib dagrúin degmessa
oc fir dia ndich dagarliud .i. aca mbí degbríathar
im anglonna fó.

['Outstanding is my warrior art (occupation?); I strike terrible blows on
an enchanted bright host; I wage war against many hosts involving the
destruction of champions, even Medb and Ailill. Evil counsels of great
import are hatched, deeds of a sinister plot, woman-alluring. Fierce cold
treacheries advance to destroy brave warriors. He takes judicious good
counsel from a man who can well advise[66] concerning heroic deeds'
(ll. 1952–64).

At first inspection, this poem is well constructed and appropriately
designed. In metrical form it presents itself as an archaic piece, with H
supplying his own glosses on the supposedly difficult words. Its rhetorical elements are correctly in place, yet do not obscure the meaning:
the lines are heptasyllabic with tri-syllabic end-words; it is liberally
ornamented with alliteration (nine out of thirteen lines show regular
alliteration, with two examples of alliteration across the line and stress
barrier). In addition, there is a tight lexical design: out of forty-seven
words, twenty-four are part of a word or syllable repetition scheme: *Fó/
fó, cherd/ certaim, slóg/ ilshluagaib, ág /ág/ágmara, erred andglonnach/ erred
anglonnach, drochrúin/ dubrúin/ dagrúin, gossa/ uargossa, banmassa/ degmessa, dagarliud/ dagrúin, dith/ dich.* Yet it is precisely this narrow and
repetitive lexical band which makes the poem suspect; it carries no
flaws of age or obscurity and thus it may well be freshly composed on
the model of older and similar *roscada.* If, then, it may well be H's own,
how does it compare with his other work?

The first effect of the H-poem is to create a disjunction between the etymological source of the place name as just determined by an act in the narrative – the action described by the verb *focherd* – and the simple signalling of its one-on-one relevance to the scene of the act, henceforth to be re-named 'Focherd.' With H's poem, *cerd* has now moved out of its grammatical confines as a verb form denoting the specific narrative action of 'casting' that has gone before and has become the term for skill or art in general. The function of a poetic intervention at this point has changed from the purposes it serves in the M narrative; from a simple etymological one-on-one jingle in *deibide* we now have a poem which projects an aura of archaic authority. Cú Chulainn proclaims his warrior art, he displays himself verbally. At this moment linear action is suspended so that the audience may step inside Cú Chulainn's consciousness and view a minor apotheosis of the hero from the inside; we take on his own measure of himself as he speaks in the throes of warrior exultation. Within the confines of the poem, the audience can also step back from the action and view some major themes of the saga in condensed terms: here are offered the energy of Cú Chulainn, the awesome impact of violence in war, the treachery of the enemy – especially in the plotting involving fools manipulated by women – and the need for advisors and right judgment. H has once again presented a poem the construction of which depends on the constant need to recapitulate the whole sweep of the saga and present it in a space within which something other than simple fidelity to narrative sequencing concerns can be rehearsed.

There is, however, an added dimension to H's work; *cerd* in the poem has now become, poetically, the word signifying art or skill in general. The note after the poem draws attention to the superior etymological contribution his poem has made by offering a better 'author' for the place name and its meaning: Cú Chulainn. Because it is his own composition, however, the collapsing of internal and external 'author,' such as we have seen already in the Fir Ól nÉcmacht interpolation, means that the attention and the praise is ultimately directed towards H himself:

Combad de sin dano rod lil a n-ainm as Focherd dond inud .i. 'fo' 'cerd' .i. maith in cherd gascid do necmaic do Choin Culaind and sin.

[It is from this (i.e. *cerd*, the double object, Cú Chulainn's action, and more grammatically proximate, the poem itself, the form in which the feat has been poetically memorialised), then, that the name Focherd stuck to the place, that is *fó cerd*, meaning, good was the warrior skill that happened to Cú Chulainn there.]

But it is also possible that H intends to frame the poetic utterance of Cú Chulainn in a specific way: with the simple substitution of the equivalents *cerd* and *dán*, the first line of the poem, *Fó .i. maith mo cherd laéchdachta*, echoes a well-known segment of the gnomic text *Senbríathra Fithail*. Here the good life of the scholar is contrasted with the dubious fate of the man of war:

[Maith] *dán ecna*
dogní rig do bocht.
Dogní anrath do essirt.
D. sochenel do docheniul
D. gaeth do baeth.
Maith a tossach.
Ferr a dered.
Airmitnech issin chentur.
Logmar issind altur.
Ni dercointech fri dered .i. fri tabairt nime dó

Doilig dán laechdacht.
Ni erdairc. 7 is dergna a dúi
Gnimuch duthain a suí.
IT etradaig a bí.
IT iffernaig a mmairb.
Nir thimna athair da mac.
Mairg dianid dán laechdacht.,

[Good the profession of learning, it makes a king of a poor man, it makes a great man of a vagabond, it ennobles the lower classes, it makes the foolish wise. Good its origin, better its end, respected in this world, rewarded in the world beyond; he is not despairing of the end, that is in the matter of getting heaven. Miserable the profession of arms, it is not respectable; its worst are churlish and without honour, its best are active without any joy; alive they are fornicators, dead they belong to hell. The fathers bequeath nothing to sons. Woe to him whose profession is arms!][67]

This section of the gnomic tract is frequently found separated from its context and circulating as an independent and popular piece.[68] When

H's poem is contextualized against the background of this well-known item, the ironic framing H brings to his addition is clear. As a literary man his commitment to a full-blown model of military ideology is less than complete; indeed the yawning gap between the two discursive statements – of H and of *Senbríathra Fithail* – is patently impossible to bridge. We cannot know with certainty that H was aware of this item of social criticism, which seems to have enjoyed wide circulation; if a relationship can be posited between it and the H poem, it forces a rereading of *Fó mo cherd laéchdachta* that can be seen to undermine radically the traditional sentiments of the heroic model itself through the very formulation by which it is being proposed.

Moreover, this determination of H to intervene in the text at precisely this point and to mark the saga with his specific literary stamp at the scene of *Focherd* is rather carefully signalled in his handling of the surrounding text; in the middle of his construction of the Medb encounter some lines before, he shows himself particularly interested in this place name to the exclusion of others at this point.[69] It is perhaps also significant that Interpolation *II* begins in the middle of the incident *Aided Redg Cáinte*, where there are a number of suggestive bridges to the later Focherd material. For example, there is listed, some lines just before H begins: *Iar tiachtain iarom geogain firu Crochine* [corrected to *Croiniche* by M] *.i. Focherda. Fiche fer focherd de.* [Having arrived then, he killed the men of Cróenech .i. Focherd; he cast twenty men from him].

It may be, then, that the incident of the fourteen men at Focherd as given by H is not entirely his invention. There are traces of an incident of groups, of variously five or perhaps fourteen treacherous men at the end of the fight with Lóch where M summarizes:

Is hé sin Cóicsius Focherda 7 Cóicer Óengoirt. Nó is cóic lá déc iss ed ro boí Cú Chulaind hi Focheird, conid de atá Cóicnas Focherda isin Tána.

[That is the five ranks (the lamentation?) at Focherd and the five of Oengort. Or it is a fortnight that Cú Chulainn was at Focherd, and it is from that one has 'the Fiveness of Focherd' in the *Táin*] (ll. 2033–6)

At this point in the tale the chronology of the narrative is quite disturbed, as the linked incidents of Lóch, the Mórrígan and the healing of Lúg do not occur in coherent sequence. Thus at the end of the segment on the healing of the Mórrígan, M again inserts a killing of fourteen men in a grouping of five, six, and three (ll. 2057–66).[70]

In considering H's 'invention,' in this incident one may say that he was attempting to dislocate the name Focherd from a specific association with any one particular incident and to turn it into a textual site in which he could pursue some of his own literary interests. He makes of Focherd a powerful icon for a more generalized summary of a series of successful encounters. The significance is now coded into a well-fashioned and appropriate poem that focuses on Cú Chulainn and his heroic transformations but which also, as we have seen, works to subvert the language of heroic process from the perspective of the professional learned man.

H, Crafty with Words

Leaving these larger issues of H's deeper designs aside for a moment, however, what I should like to mark at this point is the most striking aspect of H's working methods: he seems to take special delight in highlighting and creating disjunctive syllabic etymologies. Other examples that might be added are either a feature of H's own work at this stage of the saga or mark his interested commentary on his reading text, M. Consider the following from the fight with Lóch (ll. 1979–81):

> Ó tháinic íarom do shaigid ind atha, bibsat (bidbsat Y, bidgsat C) ind fhir na bu tairis. 'Biaid tart eisc sund indiu,' ol Gabrán fili. Is de atá Áth Darteisc (Tarteisc YC) 7 Tír Mór Darteisc (Tarteisc YC) ó shin forsin phurt sin.

> [When he came to the ford the men drove the cattle through it. 'There will a thirst for water (or "drying up of," "a muddying of") water here today,' said Gabrán the poet. It is from this that Áth Tarteisc and Tir Mór Tarteisc derive as names for that place.]

The text of Y shows that H is expanding here an incident that he had erased in M to make room for the interpolation, and there is no way of knowing if the initial puns are in H's source text M. But in a way we have come to recognize as a typical H linguistic turn, there is, first, the same prepositional-derived type of analysis as in *riastartha*: *tairis* suggests tar(t) eis(c), and is followed by the place-name derivation from Gabrán's poetic authority, *Tarteisc*. But, in addition, H's reading suggests a third possibility by a typical H-nasalization; *Ath Darteisc = dairt eisc,* 'cattle puddle.'[71] In a similar elision process in Interpolation *IV,* the fight with Mand throws up another onomastic creation, this time spelled out in reverse order: *conid de atá Mag Mandachta .i. Mand Echta .i. écht Maind and.* I shall discuss this further below.

This latter pun works on a typical H syllabic transposition, as will be evident from the following examples. These are drawn from H's glossing activities on the M text at points where he is about to insert a substantial piece of his own work or has just finished a contribution. Thus, on 77b, at the end of *Slánugud na Mórrígna* at a place called Áth Chéit Chúile, M has: *Is and asbert Medb: 'Is cuillend dund ém guin ar muintire.' Is de atá ... Cuillend Cind Dúin ...*[72] [Then Medb said, 'It is like holly to us, then, the wounding of our people.' From this derives ... the Holly of the Head of the Fortress ...] (ll. 2070–1).[73] H glosses *cuillend .i. is col lind,* 'it is a crime to us,' and picks up one of the triad of sinister or bad luck names from the list of slain druids' wives that had just been given. The scribe of C has incorporated the gloss into his text and, on the strength of this, O'Rahilly has accepted H's gloss into her translation of the incident (182). In so doing she is in effect assuming that H is correcting M: this is not, I believe, the way in which H is to be read; he is exploring for pleasure the punning echoes in a difficult passage, rather than simply substituting a 'correct' reading for an incorrect one.

Finally, in a slightly more complicated operation there is the following wordplay in *Aided Redg Cáinte*: Redg in typical *cáinte* fashion asks Cú Chulainn for the dart which has killed Buide. He gets it in an unexpected way (ll. 1513–20):

> *Tuc dam-sa do gaí' or in cáinte. 'Acc óm,' or Cú, 'acht dabér seótu dait.' 'Nád géb-sa ón,' ar in cáinte. Gegna-som dano in cáinte úair nad fáet a targid dó, 7 asbert in cánte nad bérad a enech mani berad in cletíni. Focheird Cú Chulaind íarom in cletíne dó co lluid triana chend forstarsnu.*
>
> *'Is tolam (.i. sét talman H) in sét se (talam set sa Y, tolamh set C) ém!' ol in cánte. Is de atá Áth Tolam Sét.*

['Give me your dart,' said the satirist. 'I think not,' replied Cú (Chulainn), 'but I will give you something valuable.' 'I won't accept that,' said the satirist. So he killed the satirist because he would not take what was offered to him, for the satirist said that he would dishonour him if he did not give him the dart. So then Cú Chulainn cast the dart at him and it went right through his head. 'That's a very speedy gift!' said the satirist. From this is the name, The Ford of the Swift Gift.][74]

Here H's gloss *sét talman* 'gift of land' typically transposes the words and picks up on the legal aspect of *sét*; ironically and unusually, it is a *sét* of ground that has been given the satirist; but this unexpected grant of land to a low-life satirist is in fact his own grave. It would be reasonable to assume here that, as in the previous example, H saw the witty possibilities present in the response of Redg and could not resist stretching the reader's sense of the text.

Interpolation *IV*

The Mand episode is interesting on a number of points. O'Rahilly suggests that it is entirely H's invention (xvi–xvii) and points out how neatly H has entered his contribution by utilizing the opening words of M's broken-off piece. If this is indeed so, then the occasion is an important one in that it is the first opportunity to view H creating a scene *ex nihilo*. The results are deeply significant: as O'Rahilly notes, the description of Mand shows a familiarity with hagiographical techniques of personal description; or rather, one might rephrase this and say that H shares the same rhetorical model of encomiastic *descriptio* with the hagiographic style of the introductory passages of the Patrician *Vita Tripartita*.[75] Mand is a Connacht man, kin to the same traditional Connacht warrior grouping as that other shadowy figure of late invention, Cú Chulainn's foster brother Fer Diad, yet the figures for *comparanda* are all from Ulster. He has already dragged in one of these figures: Munremur mac Gerrcind. Unlike the usual hagiographic usage, the person described by H is not idealized; yet there is an attempt at typology of another kind. The portrait has ambitions to be somewhat more psychologically and socially nuanced than the normal run of such expositions in the *Táin*. Mand is clearly intended to be less than aristocratic in his origins and habits: *brogda ... im longud 7 im ligi, ... trebur* [rough ... in eating and sleeping ... a yokel]. The term *trebur* relates to *trebad* the specifically peaceful role of the *briugu* or professional provider of hospitality in the *túath*. He has no military role in early Irish society.[76] *Brogda*, 'landed,' has an extended meaning of 'strong' but in an non-militaristic register. As befits a participant of less than warrior status, he chooses to fight without weapons. Once again H organizes the fight around a brief warrior frenzy phase for Cú Chulainn and concludes with a punning toponym (ll. 2544–6):

> Tic a fherg niad 7 atraig a bruth míled cor trascair Mand fón corthi coro scor i mminágib. Conid de atá Mag Mandachta .i. Mand Échta .i. écht Maind and.

> [His fighter's fury came to him and his boiling warrior heat rose up and he threw Mand against the pillar and dispersed him into little pieces. Hence the name, the Plain of Mandachta, that is, Mand + Échta, that is, the death of Mand here.]

As with the term *riastartha*, H's punning habits begin with an approximate verbal likeness, here, between, *minága* (small joints) and *(Mag) Man(d)achta*, made all the more alike if one takes the elision of *d* in *Mand-* into account.[77] From there he proceeds to explain his pun and segues into the inverted word-order analysis he had offered in *tolam sét/sét talman* above with *Mand échta/ écht Maind*, and the additional pun present in the phonemic redistribution of *Mand Échta/Ma(gh) nÉchta*.[78] Again, however, the overall effect suggests a whiff of the burlesque in this heroic gesturing. Mand is blatantly a fiction, and equally blatantly non-heroic. Indeed there is a food theme running through the passage, from Mand's eating abilities to his boast that he will grind him up between his two hands, and to Láeg's reminder of struggles for the champion's portion at an Ulster feast. In addition, there may well be a further pointed reference here: the phrases *fer tailc trebur* and *trénfher tnúthach*, are close to the common expression *trebar tnúith* (greedy service). His death may also involve something more grisly than the translation above; it may denote a punishment congruent with his gross and greedy aspects: The verb *minaigid* is obviously related to *min* (break in pieces); but it can also mean 'eviscerate' (cf. *DIL sub* related *minach*, 'entrails').[79] H is playing with a heroic genre, neither able to condemn it outright nor to leave it unmarked by his scepticism.

Interpolation V

One might say that H follows a similar procedure to the poem *Fó mo cherd laéchdachda* in his addition to the *Éli Loga*, the healing chant of the god Lug (ll. 2130–5):

Ní fuil leó do nertsháegul
fer do baraind bruthaigte
co niurt for do lochtnamtib
cingith charpat comglinni
is iar sin atrai.

[They have no power over your life strength; let loose your boiling anger strongly on your flawed enemies; step into your strong chariot and after that rise up.]

The piece picks up on a significant element of its immediate context, the information from Lug that his enemies have no power over Cú Chulainn's destiny at this time; *imbir-seo féin do gním gaiscid t'óenur forsna slúagu úair ní leó atá commus t'anma don chur sa.* [Ply your own heroic deeds alone on the hosts because it is not they who have power over your soul at this time] (ll. 2183–4). It adds to this a brief recapitulation of the great *riastartha* which is about to come, concentrating this time on the rising up of Cú Chulainn in his fury to destroy the host in his chariot at *Sesrech Breslige* (ll. 2278–315).[80] That it is a composition of H may be suggested by the fact that it is added after a five-syllable line, *slig delb silsa ríut*, which offers a weak closure of a kind to the poem up to this point. H's addition shows some of the same characteristics as his other poems: an interest in the warp-spasm phenomenon and the use of these poetic interludes to provide summaries of the whole action of the saga, all laced with key heroic thematic concerns, here the idea of heroic fate. It constitutes, indeed, the wise counsel that had been envisioned for the hero in *Fó mo cherd laéchdachta*. There is also some similarity of poetic technique: the same use of word repetition in different nominal compound arrangements and semantic values, for example, *co niurt/nertshaegul, fer do/for do*; and a similar deployment of alliteration beyond the normal conventions for this type of verse, e.g. *ní* ... *nertshaegul, niurt* ... *lochtnamtib*.

Understanding H

What then are the major conclusions to be drawn from H's interpolations? Generally, I have been trying to make a case that H is rather more intelligent than the editor and commentators of Recension I have allowed. But there are several specific points to be made about the nature and significance of his various contributions. First, he is an engaged and responsive reader of his master reading copy U (AM). His favourite literary activity is the creation of syllabic etymologies which often rely for their effect on the appreciation of a pun. Indeed, our general perception of the liberal use of punning etymologies in Recension I would be very greatly reduced if H's input were discounted. Their exercise and the use of anagogical association in the description of Mand points to a scholar for whom the habits of learned ecclesiastical thought and composition are ingrained, even if at times, perhaps, lightly held. The handling of the Mand episode shows an individual who is inclined to fall back on alternative – one might say, non-traditional – saga stratagems of narrative organization when required to compose new material.

Secondly, he does not avoid the challenge of poetic interludes. He has contributed one poem, *Fó mo cherd laéchtachta* and added to another, the *Éli Loga*. He has added a crucial poem to the beginning of the saga, *Atchíu fer find*, some elements of which may be his own composition. He gives a nuanced prominence to the function of poets in the narrative and to their involvement in the action. His changes to the Cú Roí episode – viz. his omission of Aimirgin – may just possibly spring from the familiar currency of the archetypal poetic name, hence from a need to show solidarity with native Irish ecclesiastical perspectives as expressed in the various *Cána* that prohibited imposition of military duties on clerics or the learned. The bias which the term *álaind* shows in the Fedelm poem may indicate a responsiveness to the increasing role played by eulogistic poems to princes in the literary repertoire of his time. In this respect it is well to remember the 'original' context from which the *álaind* term was drawn by H:

> *Dotháet Cú Chulaind arna bárach do t[h]aidbriud in tshlóig 7 do thaisbénad a chrotha álgin álaind do mnáib 7 bantrochtaib 7 andrib 7 ingenaib 7 filedaib 7 aes dána, úair nír míad ná mass leiss in dúaburdelb druídechta tárfas dóib fair ind adaig sin reme. Is aire sin tánic do thaselbad a chrotha álgin álaind in lá sin. Álaind ém in mac tánic and sin.*

[Cú Chulainn came the next day to see the host and to show his well-born and lovely aspect to women and ladies, to girls and maidens, to poets and men of art; for he did not regard as honourable or becoming the grim and wizardly shape he had been in the night before. It was for this that he came to show his well-born and lovely face that day. Lovely, indeed, was the young lad who came there.] (ll. 2336–41)

H is responsive to the double imaging of the text here: the relations of Cú Chulainn with the women are part of the primary action of the narrative; but this supplemental reference to poets, taken from a section of the text which shows every sign of late rewriting, and the use then made of it by H, implies an increasing sense of the memorializing and hence textualizing process in the saga. The appropriate eulogistic decorum of a bardic eulogy will always involve an equal balancing of the image of the prince at war and at peace, of the fierce and the lovely.

This eulogistic context for H's choice of *álaind* and the invocation of a feminine admiring presence also carries a later medieval courtly charge: it implies a formal arena, a courtly setting in which the hero displays himself and is displayed to an audience of women who must be included in the scene, even in the incongruous context of a battlefield. Granted, the description of the beautiful hero has always been a feature of Irish saga writing generally, but here the presence of poets provides the extra contextualizing framing of the scene in the art of eulogy.[81] In this respect, the joint use by H and by Muiredach Albanach Ó Dálaigh of the anagogical method of personal description may imply a common cultural milieu against which these rhetorical genre-shiftings take place. Indeed we might place together the evidence of the Mand description with its clear coding of socially nuanced description, the social critique of the *Senbriathra Fithail*, and the poem of Muiredach Albanach Ó Dálaigh to Richard de Burgo, which contains the sketch of a rather novel advice to princes. When these vernacular items are in turn placed with the social ranking preoccupations evidenced in the *imago generalis ecclesiae* from Gilbert of Limerick's *De Statu Ecclesiae*, one might suggest a far more active self-consciousness in twelfth-century Ireland about the porousness to contemporary social codes of such literary texts as the *Táin Bó Cuailnge*.[82] The scribal perception of these sagas is as much an awareness of their adaptability as it is our often mistaken sense that they are valued because they are monumentally, timelessly, and unproblematically heroic in their cultural values. This is not a process that begins with H; indeed consciousness of social difference and rank is also presented with a biting edge in the Boyhood Deeds sequence, in the incident in which Cú Chulainn slays the smith Culann's hound. If, as has been suggested,[83] the Boyhood Deeds section is later than the body of the saga, both the latter's request to the king to lessen his feasting retinue in consideration of a smith who must live by his craft revenues alone, and the application to Culann of a bathetic rhetorical style for the lament for his hound also attest to a growing – though still admittedly slight – interest in other than purely heroic models in the changing social arena of saga.

Come Out, Come Out, H, Wherever You Are!

The question often asked about the *Táin* is, whom does the *Táin* serve? While suggestions have been made as to originary motivations, both generally thematic and historically specific,[84] only John Kelleher suggested an actual line of textual interest and transmission in proposing the Louth/Clonmacnois nexus.[85] Beyond the siting of the text in Clonmacnois, the question has not been much taken up. That the tale must undoubtedly have meant different things to different audiences separated in location and in time is self-evident. The evidence for the individual textual investment on the part of its successive medieval professional handlers, and the evidence for their textual communities, need not be obvious. Indeed it is in the very spirit of medieval Irish scholars' attitudes to their material that any shifts of interest will likely not proclaim themselves too loudly. In this respect, it seems that one of the marks of H's personal involvement in the text is to be seen in the way he advances, by the only means appropriate to him as a conserving scribe, the interests of non-Ulster groups. That he should bring forward the role of the Munster heroes in the tale and improve their profile of honour may be a matter of antiquarian professionalism, but it is also a matter of twelfth-century political reality. Less clear is his reason for supplementing what may have been a mark of Connacht learned interest – the invention of Fer Diad from the western fighting caste, the Fir Domnainn – by including the fight with Fer Diad's uncle, Mand. However we read the unheroic unpreparedness of Mand, his connections with the two other western heroes, Fer Diad and Fróech, are nevertheless unmistakable in terms of genealogical reference and – in the case of comparison with the Fróech incident – of style.

All these successive augmentations must have gone some way further in providing a more varied locus of interest in the text for western readers of the *Táin* than the form of the saga which western centres had originally received could provide. Note, however, that in the shading of the description of the *riastrad* in Interpolation *II* and in the invention of Mand, the commitment to a western readership is not fully or enthusiastically endorsed by H; ironizing distance is evident as befits, perhaps, the historical circumstances of H, his class, his ecclesiastical affiliations, and his family.

Mac Eoin has identified crucial place names in H's work in LU that suggest his family background and his close associations with Loch Cairrcin (Ardakillen Lough) near Strokestown, Co. Roscommon, and noted the close proximity of this to the lands of the Úa Maol Chonaire family in the later Middle Ages. Crannog dwellings in the lake show medieval occupation, and from the Annals record it is clear that it may have retained an original status as a royal residence site. Thus one would envisage, perhaps, a grant to this learned family of the use of O'Connor kings' demesne lands.[86] It may be because of their enjoyment of land in the prerogative of the lord that the family figures as the leading minister in the royal inauguration rites of the O'Connor kings.

One might, perhaps, add to Mac Eoin's treatment of H place names and suggest a somewhat wider region or constituency of H's interest: at the beginning of *Imram Curaig Maéle Dúin* in an H-intercalated page, the Eoganacht Ninussa is glossed by H as Eoganacht na nÁrand, and a little later beyond his intercalation as *.i. a Tuathmumain*.[87] In *Aided Nath Í* the conclusion on the poets of Connacht is added by H from a YBL type of recension, and he supplies a note on the graves of the poets from Gnó that is not picked up by later manuscript versions of this text: *.i. i n-iatur* (sic) *Conacht ita .i. Delmna Tíri da Locha*, i.e. the barony of Moycullen, Galway. The final sentence of this tract occurs only in H: *Conid senchas na relec insin*.[88] Incorporated in *Aided Echach Meic Maíreda* is the story of Lí Ban, the mermaid saint of Bangor association. An exclusively H text, it may bear the trace of H's own rewriting and his ability to call on texts from other monastic centres. At the beginning of the tale H glosses Tír Cluichi Midir as *Mag Find*. This is identified by Hogan as the Bredagh or Keogh's country, the parish of Taghmaconnell in the barony of Athlone.[89] What seems apparent from these references is an individual who has a knowledge of the environs of Connacht appropriate to a scholar who must supply material pleasing to secular patrons but who is also interested in religious texts, and who knows a number of locations on a length of the Shannon that might reasonably be considered to be in the natural constituency of Clonmacnoise.[90]

This Is Not the End

H has a claim to our appreciation in one final respect and that is in the way in which we formulate ideas about writerly continuity and influence in Irish literary tradition. In *Acallam na Senórach* there is a brief reference to the events of the Ulster saga cycle:

> *táinic ... d'Ard in Ghaiscid atuaid, frisi raidther Fochaird Muirt[h]emne, bhaili a nderna Cúchulainn in <u>foic[h]lerd gaiscid ar</u> sluaiged Tána Bó Cuailngi ...*

> [and he came ... to The Heroic Height in the north, which is called Focherd of Muirtheimne, the place where Cú Chulainn made his heroic weapon-throw on the hosting of the *Táin Bó Cuailnge* ...][91]

The wording makes it likely that the author of *Acallam na Senórach* knew the H version of the saga and adds to the other internal clues in that great compilation further evidence that this text too has a Connacht origin.[92] From here the phrase is picked up by O'Cleary's Life of Aodh Rua Ó Dómhnaill: *go Fochaird Muirtheimhne bhail i nderna an Cúchulainn ... an fhoicheird ghaisgidh.*[93] By this point in the argument one may well ask if H should not be allowed the glory due him as an essential link and an enabling voice in the self-conscious negotiation from one model of heroism to another in these two crucial phases of Irish literary and patriotic sensibility.

4 Epic Writing and Mythic Reading

'He isn't the Messiah. He's just a very naughty boy!'

Brian's mother in *The Life of Brian*

In this chapter and the next I approach by another avenue of inquiry the three intersected issues that may be deemed to constitute the textual ground of the *Táin*: oral tradition; scribal literacy traditions, with their full baggage of Irish monastic literary interests; and finally, as I have been emphasizing in the last chapter, individual invention. By reposing the issue of interpretation under the general rubric of myth and its mediations, I am also attempting, with the help of the *Táin* tradition itself, to push towards a resetting and redefining of the question of the pagan/Christian content divide in medieval Irish literature. I will read two passages – here one of the Boyhood Deeds events, and in chapter 5, the account of Cú Chulainn's healing – two passages likely to present a fair case for the presence in the text of underlying mythic values. These values may not be immediately evident on the surface of the text, if text is understood simply as a record of narrated action, but they may be assumed to exist in the text as a mythic deposit.[1] My focus is still on the written word, but I now want to leave it more open for consideration as a complex, fabricated item of tradition, whose reception nevertheless remains responsive to the values offered by social custom and changing social reality. Hence a reading of the passages in question under the rubric of myth will necessarily view them from a wider and deeper concept of the repository and the usages of culture than the idea of a purely textual tradition alone.[2]

The Introduction indicated the main lines along which run Irish scholarly enquiry into mythic values in Irish saga. Before entering into a more detailed discussion it may be helpful to keep distinct some specific ideas on myth, as these serve in turn to guide my reading. First, myth may never be decanted cleanly from the form of its telling; many discursive genres can be implicated in myth, each delivering it according to its own generic norms. Second – and this, though simple, bears repeating – myth is not simply a pleasing fabulation, however ill- or well-structured; rather, anthropologists have taught us that myth always has a vital social referent. Third, even where a structuralist method is used to analyse mythic discourse, a method that relies on assembling the greatest possible number of tellings, this does not mean that an end-transformative or essentialist notion of a myth's function is the goal to be arrived at: the interest of the myth, the object of scrutiny, is not the distillation of myth as the typical intellectual product of 'the savage mind,' but rather the process, 'the myth at work.' It will also help to bear in mind changes in the way in which scholars have constructed medieval cultural conditions, from an older traditionally imagined state of single-audience oral communality towards a model which I would urge – that of mixed cultural elites and nucleated reading communities.

I prefer then to keep the idea of myth simple and text-focused. I begin with the simple definition, influenced mainly by ideas from Loraux: myth as the re-play of the imaginary at any given stage of the usage of narrative by a participating culture community.[3] This formulation seems to me to preserve the validity of the textual witness, and at the same time it indicates that the mythic text will always carry a performative function which may, with the text, change over time. Gregory Nagy has suggested that myth in the strictest Homeric usage of the term *muthoi*, as contrasted with *logos*, may be seen as yet another type of speech act; although one cannot simply apply the same fundamental terms of mythic discourse as this to the Irish material, there is a real sense in which a consideration of myth can bring its receptors closer to the idea that they are in the presence of power-infused discourse that speaks to and moves its hearers in important ways.[4] Finally, in handling the text in this way, one more important contrastive factor must be borne in mind. There is myth and there is mythology. What appears in the Irish literary record – and this certainly the case with the *Táin Bó Cúailnge* – is more properly described as mythology – that is, as myth always already worked over, and, as such, subject to several degrees of internal exegesis, categorization, and rationalization by medieval Irish *literati*.[5]

These latter two ways of reading 'mythic' writing are not necessarily antithetic to each other, nor does a move to the latter mode invalidate mythic discourse and yield us a deconstructed pile of mere mythic fragments. As Gregory Nagy has pointed out in a parallel context, in discussing the way in which the contrastive pair *mythos* and *epe* function as registers in Homeric epic, 'the social occasion for epic [read here "Irish heroic narrative"] may be destabilized or even lost but the genre can compensate or even recreate it.'[6] Thus, for example, we may not have in the Boyhood Deeds section of the *Táin* a *direct* window on, much less a direct narrative of, Irish rituals of warrior initiation, but we are nonetheless enabled to glimpse such a structure, refracted through the recuperative powers of the text, as it might be have been grounded and projected imaginatively in a given social reality.

The passage I discuss in this chapter is a lesser scene from the Boyhood Deeds episodes in Recension I: the raid on Emain Macha by Eógan Mac Durthacht's men. (In chapter 5, I again approach the question of myth and concentrate on the healing visit made to the hero by his divine father Lug mac Ethlenn, ll. 481–523.)[7] As I examine these passages I shall ground my views with reference to a number of myth criticism traditions. By using all means possible to discover and to focus attention on the multiplicity of potential codes which are partially or wholly realized – or, indeed, at times suppressed – one may come to a more fully nuanced understanding of the play of what one may tentatively call mythic operations in the saga and its traditions.

In this chapter I shall argue that within the generally accepted reading of the Boyhood Deeds as descriptive of initiatory rituals generally, the chosen episode of Eógan Mac Durthacht's raid fulfils a further and quite precise function. Its inclusion as a fully functional part of a well-thought-out narrative program is, in my view, amply justified from a number of perspectives. Thus there is a need to examine again Cecile O'Rahilly's arguments, viz. that this episode was not part of the 'original' text and represents an innovation and an interference in Recension I.[8] In such a state of relative textual supplementarity it is possible to see its history of composition and re-composition as being directed with a certain rhetorical exemplary attention to its meaning; this means that there is no need to admit or exclude this textual item from a narrative of social transformation judged on the criterion of 'originality' alone.

In the Lug incident discussed in chapter 5, it may well be that the issue of Cú Chulainn and his divine paternity has an implied subtext from which any discussion of the scene should begin.[9] In the Cú Chulainn tradition, if not in the text, there are two other-world fathers: Lug and Sualtaim.[10] By privileging the Lug strand of divine paternity, a key genealogical connection of Cú Chulainn with Fergus is lost, the role of Sualtaim displaced and rendered confusing, and something of the oldest levels of the plot obscured. Thus ideas of paternity set in the context of kin-relations may have played key roles in the idea of the intervention of the god, but these are now subdued. In addition, by analysing the mythic construction of the Lug scene itself, as well as the actors in the scene, one may bring into relief changing aspects of the role of this divinity in early Irish texts.[11]

Before examining these matters in detail, however, it will be necessary to study the contextual placement of each one in the *Táin* narrative tradition in order to see more clearly the degree of scribal confidence, hesitation, or improvisation which attends their transtextual scribal reception and transmission. Only by paying attention to the way in which these scenes are set in and marked off from their surrounding narrative in the two earliest recensions can reasonable inferences be made about the weight of significance that each segment may be assumed to bear. Thus I pay particular attention to the entrance and exit stratagems of both the Eógan Mac Durthacht Raid segment and the telling of 'The Coming of Lug,' in terms of their larger distinctive narrative frames: The Boyhood Deeds (*Macgnímrada*) and Murthemne's Great Slaughter (*Breslech Mór Maige Murthemne*) respectively.

Textual Status of the Macgnimrada

As Cecile O'Rahilly has pointed out, there are obvious differences between Recensions I and II in the presentation of the *Macgnímrada* as a whole. In both versions the *Macgnímrada* forms a very special and ambitious narrative project, namely, the insertion and strategic grouping of tales from the hero's past into the narrative time of the main action. The whole Boyhood Deeds section occurs as a major break in the forward narrative line of the saga; it follows the incident where the armies are blocked by Cú Chulainn's sinister shaft, planted in the ford, bearing the severed heads of the Connacht advance scouts (ll. 330–55). It is prefaced in both Recensions by a passage in which Fergus' authority as a privileged speaker for Cú Chulainn is established by his recital of a prose rhapsody on the heroic qualities of the young hero. It is here, at this latter point in Recension I, that the practice of subtitling resumes after the initial separation of the opening scenes from the body of the narrative action by the general label, *In scél iar n-urd inso sís*. (ll. 134–5)[12] Fergus's praise of Cú Chulainn, as represented by the common tradition in both recensions, also seems to have generated an additional reprise of the praise topos in Recension II.[13] In this version too Fergus is given a number of visionary interventions in rhapsodic prose and verse in praise of Cú Chulainn.[14]

In Recension II the Boyhood Deeds contains only three untitled stories: Cú Chulainn's arrival in Emain Macha, the killing of Culann's hound, and the taking up of arms as a preparation for a raid across the borders of the province (ll. 738–1217). It has a frame title, *Incipiunt macgnímrada Con Culaind*, and the conclusion relegates the segment firmly as part of the prefatory matter of the narrative: *Conid innisin do macgnímaib Con Culaind sin for Táin Bó Cúalnge, ocus remthús in sceóil 7 na sliged 7 imthechta in tshlúaig a Crúachain connici sin. In scél fodessin is ní and fodechtsa.* Recension I contains four additional stories – three of which have separate headings in U – that come directly after the first tale (ll. 398–824). The whole segment shows some manuscript difference in entitulation: U has *Na macgnímrada inso sís* (The boyhood deeds here below), while W omits *sís* and Y gives *macerda conculaind so* (Cú Chulainn's boyhood feats here) in the margin. Lacking directive *sís* in U's favoured formula type, *innso sís*, the headings in the other manuscripts are removed somewhat from a scribal working reality as directives for copying and reading down the page; in them, a more active reading-oriented sense prevails, with textual chapter headings copied as part of the reader's text rather than as direct metatextual guidance to a text handler. It is worth going into details of textual management for the Boyhood Deeds at this point, since the organizing codes can reveal much about the attitudes and resources of the several scribes at the moment of writing, and may help to distinguish their input from the (commonly shared?) marks of the unknown shapers of the tradition before them. There is variation between the manuscripts of Recension I in the matter of choices for the titles for episodes; U has a much heavier scoring than Y or even W.[15] Thus U as a whole, and even more so UH, have a much clearer agenda of textual micro-management than any other version.

The additional four tales in Recension I follow the first and make up a group of five tales narrated by Fergus. This heightened presence of Fergus as narrator, and his role in the generation of the Boyhood Deeds as meaningful narration, will be discussed further towards the end of this chapter. The remaining two tales are narrated by two other exiles who were originally, in the story of the Birth of Cú Chulainn, listed as among his foster fathers.[16] At the end of the group of five tales, Fergus concludes his recital with a formulaic summation designed to alarm his listeners. Apart from this clustering, each of the three 'primary' tales end with variations on the same formula in both Recensions. The relationship between the two sets of formulae can be observed by matching their first occurrence in both:

I	II
'Fer dorigni inna gníma sin inrapatar lán[a] (lana W, slana Y) a c[h]óic blíadna	'Mac bec doringni in gním sain icind choic mblíadan iarna brith coro scart maccu na curad 7 na cathmíled ar dorus a llis 7 a ndúnaid fadessin,
nírbo machtad (cé no thísed co hor cocríche, 7 om. Y)	nocorb éicen machta nó ingantus de ciano thísed co hor cocríchi,
cé no éisged (foisced Y) a cinnu don cethroir ucut.'	gana thescad gabail cethri mbend, gana marbad fer nó dís nó triur nó cethrur in am indat slána .xvii. bliadna de for _Táin Bó Cúalnga_.'

[I. 'A man who was able to do these deeds when he was five years old, what wonder that he [would come to the border region here] and cut off the four mens' heads?'] (ll. 537–9)

[II. 'A young boy who did these deeds five years after he was born and overthrew the sons of warriors and fighters at the very portal of their own residence and their fort, there ought not to be any wonder or amazement that he should come to the border region and cut a four-pronged shaft and kill one, two, three or four men when he is full seventeen years old in _The Cattle-raid of Cooley_.'] (ll. 814–19)

The means of contrasting past and present actions in the formula of Recension II, formatted in a typical alliterative and repetitive style, is smooth and insistent. Each Ulster witness steps up to his narrative task and acquits himself with the same formula; there is no avoiding the intent of conjunction, contrast, and progression between each of the three boyhood deeds in turn and the present evidence of the border killings. The result is a more orderly narrative but a somewhat flat effect; the connection between past deed and present action is a two-dimensional one. Recension I makes the analogue by less forced and more economic means – indeed, Y's omission of the border reference tightens the formula even more.[17]

The Eógan mac Durthacht incident

Cecile O'Rahilly considered the three-story Boyhood Deeds form to be probably the original shape of this section of the saga; she doubted that the powers of invention of Recension II were up to re-editing a larger compass of tales so drastically.[18] This may well be so. Her observations, however, do not lead to any clarification on the form of the collection in the earlier version and how it might be decoded.[19] I do not think that the idea that they are newly appearing tales in Recension I, and thus suspect of innovation, is an initial barrier to a mythic reading of any one of them. Cultural products at all times can be presumed to have an organic relationship with the society that produces them. So it is not only what the editor considers the originary form of the Boyhood Deeds that can presume formal value and hence a privileged relationship to a workable mythic paradigm; I assume that the story of Eógan mac Durthacht's raid can indeed bear a measure of significance. By first identifying all the narrative patterns and motifs that suggest themselves in the incident, we may then hope to better understand what deeper compulsions might have led the tradition-shapers of Recension I to opt for an extended model of this distinctive segment of the saga.

> Cath Eógain meic Derthacht fri Conchobar inso
> 'Boí immisse chatha eter Ultu 7 Eógan mac nDur[th]acht. Tíagait Ulaid don chath. Fácabar-som inna chotlud. Maiti for Ultu. Fácabar Conchobar 7 Cúscraid Mend Macha 7 sochaide mór olchena. Dofúsci-seom a ngol. Sínithi iarom co mmemdatar in dá liic ro bátár immi. Hi fíadnaise Bricriu ucut dorónad,' ol Fergus. 'Atraig cath la sodain. Cotricim-se fris i ndorus ind lis 7 me athgaíte.
> 'Fuit! Dia do bethu, a popa Fergus,' ol sé. 'Cate Conc[h]obar?'
> 'Ní etar-sa,' ol mé.
> Téit as íarom. Ba dorcha ind adaig. Fóbair a n-ármach. Co n-acca ara chind in fer 7 leth a chind fair 7 leth fir aile ar a muin.

*'Congna lem, a Chú Chulaind,' ol sé. 'Rom-bíth 7 tucus leth mo bráthar ar mo
muin. Beir síst lim.'*

'Ní bér,' ol sé.

*La sodain focheirt in n-aire dó. Focheird-som de. Immasínithar dóib. Doscarthar
Cú Chulaind. Co cuala ní, in [m]boidb dinib collaib.*

'Olc damnae laích fil and fo chossaib aurdragg!'

*La sodain fónérig Cú Chulaind 7 benaid a chend de cosind luirg áne 7 gabaid
immá[i]n líathráite ríam [de, Y, W] dar in mag.*

'In fail mo phopa Conchobar isind ármaig se?'

*Frisgair side dó. Téit chuci conid n-acca issin c[h]lud, ro boí ind úir imbi do cach
leth día díc[h]lith.*

'Cid día tánac isin ármag,' ol Conchobar, 'co ndeochais úathbás and?'

*Tanócaib asin chlud la sodain. Ni thurcébad sesser linni di t[h]rénfheraib Ulad ní
ba chalma.*

*'Tair reond don tig ucut,' ar Conchobar, 'co ndernai tenid dam and.' Ataí-seom
thenid móir do.*

'Maith didiu,' or Conchobar. 'Díanom thísad mucc fhonaithe robadam béo.'

'Rag-sa conda tuc,' ar Cú Chulaind.

*Téit ass íarom. Co n-accai in fer ocond fhulucht i mmedón ind fheda, indara lám
dó cona gaisciud inti, in lám n-aill oc funi in tuircc. Ba mór a úathmaire ind fhir.
Fanópair-som arapa 7 dobeir a chend 7 a muicc laiss. Loingid Conchobar iar sin
in torc.*

'Tíagam diar tig,' or Conchobar.

*Condrecat fri Cúscraid mac Conchobair. Bátár dano tromgona fair-side. Do-beir
Cú Chulaind for a muin. Dollotár íarom a tríur co hEmain Macha.*

[Eógan mac Durthacht's battle with Conchobar here.]
There was an outbreak of fighting between the Ulstermen and Eógan mac
nDurthacht. The Ulstermen go to battle. They left him asleep. The Ulstermen are defeated. Left behind on the field were Conchobar, Cuscraid
Mend Macha, and many more besides. Their wailing wakened him. Then
he stretched himself so that the two flagstones around him broke. He did
that in the presence of Bricriu here said Fergus. Then he got up. I met him
at the entrance to the enclosure and I sorely wounded.

'Hello, what is this, friend Fergus?' he said. 'Where is Conchobar?'

'I do not know,' I replied.

Then off he goes. The night was pitch-black. He heads for the battlefield.
There appeared before him a man with only half his head and half
another man on his back.

'Help me, Cú Chulainn,' he said. 'I have been wounded and I am bringing away half of my brother on my back. Give me a hand.'[20]

'I will not,' said he.

With that he threw the bundle at him. He threw it back. They tussled together. Cú Chulainn gets thrown. Then was heard a thing, i.e. the War-Goddess from among the bodies.

'Poor makings of a warrior there that lies down under the feet of ghouls!' At that Cú Chulainn got up, struck off the fellow's head with his hurley and went along the battlefield playing ball with it.

'Is my master Conchobar on this battlefield?'

He answered him. He goes in his direction until he sees him in a ditch and the earth was piled up around him on all sides to hide him.

'Why have you come on the battlefield?' asked Conchobar. 'Is it to learn what mortal terror is?'

Then he lifted him up out of the ditch. Six of the most stalwart of us Ulster warriors could not have done it.

'Come with me to that house yonder,' said Conchobar, 'and make a fire for me there.'

He lit a big fire for him.

'That is good,' said Conchobar. 'Now if only roast pig could be brought to me, I would be restored to life.'

'I will go and get it,' said Cú Chulainn.

Out he went then. He saw a man at a cooking pit in the middle of a wood; in one hand he held his weapons, with the other he was roasting a pig. The man was very terrifying. Nevertheless he attacked him and took from him both his head and his pig. Then Conchobair dined on the pig.

'Let us head for our own house,' said Conchobar. They met with Cuscraid, Conchobar's son. He was grievously wounded. Cú Chulainn took him on his back. And thus the three returned to Emain Macha.']
(ll. 481–539)

I believe that the addition of the extra incidents in Recension I can be seen to complement the general significance of the Boyhood Deeds as a distinctive part of the whole saga narrative. This arrangement presents a more nuanced access to the meaning of the entire segment under-stood as an incremental education in role responsibility on the part of the hero. The shift from three sharply delineated and very different sto-ries, as in Recension II, to the lengthier narrative exposition in Recen-sion I also reveals a literary sensitivity to the question of generic category. We now have in Recension I an amplified 'Childhood' narra-tive within the narrative of 'Boyhood,' as if an awareness of genre

typology itself triggers and licenses its amplification. I shall return to
this aspect of narrative, as describing a process of incremental social-
ization over time, when I discuss more specific aspects of warrior
nomenclature later in this chapter. Now I turn to the more basic issue
of the scene of the narrative and how a sense of strategic space is
worked out in the sequence.

From Playing Field to Killing Field

Already in the first incident common to all versions – the arrival of Cú
Chulainn in Emain Macha – there is a division of enactment space into
interior and exterior, in this instance, the playing field and the palace.[21]
The implications of that division, the boundaries and ambiguous interstices that each location implies, the transgressive possibilities, and
more specifically, the *agon* of the young hero's progressive negotiation
and enlargement of meaningful space are essentially what is explored
and expanded in the version of Recension I. Cú Chulainn's transitions
are not easy: his wildness and his incrementally socialized self are frequently at odds; they must, in each incident, be presented and placed
in dynamic relation with each other. Thus there are aspectual as well as
sequential and accumulative pressures on the narrative. Control of the
young hero's aggression against the boy troop is achieved only with
difficulty and is always in danger of breaking down despite repeated
intervention by Conchobar and Fergus. The extra tales in Recension I
contribute to that sense of tension and struggle for control. For example, even the basic and natural function of sleep must be renegotiated
for a hero who possesses such innate and natural wildness (ll. 257–69).
This hero does not sleep until a verisimilitude of wildness and the hard
life of the wild raider, the flat stone bed, is brought indoors and his vol-
atile humours balanced by leveling the sleeping space. Even with that
compromise of inside/outside, his civility must be consciously willed
and assumed every morning, and those who share domestic space
with him are still in danger from his liminal moment of confusion
between sleeping and waking. The imaginative act required to understand this hero is one of seeing the fictive space he occupies mirror his
inner psychic space.

   The real interest of the Eógan mac Durthacht raid story, in its turn, in
the expanded sequence, is that it takes this inside/outside matrix,
expands its spatial range and uses it to introduce the hero to wider
issues than aggression as play. Within a warrior-initiation structure it

enacts the stages of alienation and re-integration, and also makes a statement about the necessary equilibrium between a condition of civic order and a condition of war. The underlying myth of initiation which covers the whole Boyhood Deeds segment would also dictate that such an incident be handled in a specific way: night raids, inversions, and horror mark the process of young warrior initiation by way of a common Indo-European cultural poetics. In such a night-time raid, appropriate to the *fian* phase of an Irish culture hero, Cú Chulainn is tested for the first time in real battle conditions; the conclusions are significant.[22]

'The Tale in Order Here!'

As the scene begins, the context is sketched rapidly: the Ulstermen are beaten in battle and in full retreat, their king apparently left for dead on the field. The house space of the hero is somewhat compromised, however: the presence of the disreputable Bricriu, as house mentor and as someone who is not involved in the battle, strikes a warning note; the boy will do well to begin by clearing this morally unsound place.[23] His first introduction to war on leaving the domestic precinct is one of horror by way of direct sensual assault: the groans of wounded men and the sight of mutilated bodies. The negative reaction of the young boy to the grisly encounter with the wounded man who carries his own brother and his refusal to help is in character, since up to now he has typically not listened to a request that implies subservience to any other but the king. However, in this tale he will, by way of contrast, go on to accept the load of the king and his wounded son as an honourable burden.

Thus, ideals of social service, hierarchically organized, are fairly clearly exemplified in the narrative. But there is more to it than straightforward exemplarity on the level of a tale used as communicator of desirable social behaviour. The cultural poetics of warrior initiation constructs the narrative in specific ways: as a night raid, the scene is one of inversion and transgression and it is precisely the horror of the dark unclean that constitutes the theatre of meaning. The encounter with the walking wounded deconstructs humans at war into two unsustainable halves. The brothers, twinned in their split condition constitute a paradox; linked and unnaturally unitary as they now are, one half-headed and one half-bodied, they can no longer be reconstituted as normal integrals. That they speak at all represents a challenge and a danger: they are already in the world of the shameful dead, and to consort with them is to risk being taken with them to their shadowy world beyond the human.[24] The throwing of the half body at the hero is a deliberate effort to engage him through physical contact in the polluted world of the dead.

How close the hero comes to being annihilated without being fully aware of it can be seen from the actual engagement with the two. The first wrestling bout does not go well for Cú Chulainn; he is thrown down and the voice that speaks from the heap of bodies is the embodiment of war terror itself, the goddess Bodb. Her words clearly imply the testing status of the incident: he is judged as an *olc damnae laích* – a bad candidate for warrior status – if he can be brought down so easily by terror and her ghastly acolytes. Cú Chulainn, however, subverts the curse of war terror by reverting back to his childish comportment. He exploits the liminal ambiguities of his own status between that of child and adult by transforming the dispatch of his adversary into a game. He beheads him with his hurley and then, using the head as his ball, plays his way through his first experience of the battlefield. It is a stratagem that protects Cú Chulainn but also limits his understanding; insouciance is not enough. The further and more serious testing of his mettle swings back into focus with the first words the king addresses to him after being found: 'Why did you come to the battlefield? To experience deadly terror there?' The concept of terror, *úathbás*, will not just be overcome by the hero; he will also internalize it as he himself becomes in turn an agent of terror.[25] The term is subsequently used of Cú Chulainn himself in a sequence later in the saga – *In Carpat Serda 7 in Breslech Mór Maige Muirtheimne* – in a set of formal, rhetorically marked passages that describe the battle cry and the great warp spasm of the hero (Recension I, ll. 2087, 2245).

Under the protecting sign of childishness, a psychological state that is, however, becoming an increasingly threadbare resource as the story unfolds, he searches for the king as a child might call for a parent in the dark. His discovery of Conchobar imposes another kind of test on the boy and the simplicity of narrative style here recuperates well Cú Chulainn's own untroubled perspective. He accepts Conchobar's strange behaviour totally and there is no auctorial shading that might signal the oddity, indeed the transgressive nature, of the scene. The king is hiding in an earthen pit or ditch, almost covered by earth. Has he fled the fight and thus lost the battle for his people? And if so, is this not one of the occasions under Irish law where a king loses his honour price completely and automatically becomes an unkinged recreant?[26] Is it prudence that has driven him to this spot or cowardice? In order for the episode to overcome these embarrassments and function smoothly we must consider a third option: to see it as a deliberately structured symbolic enactment. The king is in a sense ritually dead and buried, and Cú Chulainn's rescue is a kind of salvific visit to the netherworld. The rescue is not just a physically heroic thrusting of the king back on his feet again; it is a virtual raid on the otherworld, where not only is the king rescued but, in typically Irish archetypal story pattern, the nourishment of the other world, fire and the food cauldron, are carried off as well. I will return presently to the theoretical implications of this register of symbolic reading; suffice here to note that the means by which the king is 'saved' contains a final testing of the hero in the form of the fearsome warrior roasting the pig (again the note of terror, *úathmaire*, is applied to this figure), and a kind of miniature saga subgenre of 'The Successful Hero's Return' is generated. However, though Cú Chulainn is still the actor in the narrative, his deeds are now entirely in the register of service to the king and the nature of his exploits is now viewed from this perspective. Indeed loyalty to the king also extends to his family as, in a neat reversal of his early refusal to carry the wounded brothers, he carries both the king and the king's son back with him as honourable burdens to Emain Macha. So, a fairly informed reading of the passage would yield something like the above sample commentary as a first level of reading.

How Irish Scribes Read, or, Is There a Myth in This Class?

Over and above these symbolic actions, there are a number of discursive codes and heuristic issues pertaining to mythic discourse which could be further explored for this tale. For McCone the overarching and validating model for a native Irish narrative – conceptualized as 'the heroic biography of Cú Chulainn'– is clerical and lies within the matrix of a Christian master narrative program, which alone is capable of encoding its base material authoritatively on the level of truth.[27] From this perspective, and especially for Cú Chulainn, aspects of the hero's narrative should be regularly responsive to Christian typology.[28] Thus one might suggest that the Boyhood Deeds in general take their generic form from the prior Christian category of the Infancy Gospels, particularly *The Gospel of Thomas*, a text known and translated early in Irish literary circles.[29] If this were so, then it could provide a model for an episode in the narrative in the Recension I version that seems insistently repetitive and yet uncertainly deployed. In the first account of the hero's arrival in Emain Macha, he knocks out fifty boys (ll. 435–6) . When it is made clear to him that this is not acceptable behaviour, Cú Chulainn assumes responsibility for them; he goes out with the king to where they have fallen on the playing field (l. 450); there they are revived and given back to the custody of their foster parents (l. 456). This motif is repeated in a second brief tale in Recension I (*Aided na macraide*), but this time the boys are left truly dead. In *The Gospel of Thomas,* on three occasions Jesus in anger kills some of his playmates and is then rebuked by the crowd and his father Joseph. In the last incident he briefly revives the boy Zeno who attests to Jesus' non-culpability.[30] In the saga the replication of the incident, once in the arrival scene and again in *Aided na Macraide,* may show that the 'author' of these incidents is uncertain as to how to play this topic in the light of some confusion – carried over from the apocryphal model – about showing vengeful responses from the boy hero Christ/Cú Chulainn. In general, one may say that the Infancy Gospels are interested in presenting the childhood deeds of Jesus – at play, with his parents, etc. – as prefigurations of his adult deeds. Only in the cycle of Cú Chulainn tales and in the Finn tales is there any attempt to describe heroic Irish childhoods in this way. But does this mean that the impulse to rework the Cú Chulainn dossier derives from the Infancy Gospels? To suggest that the Boyhood Deeds sequence is modeled as an Infancy Gospel narrative for Cú Chulainn involves a rather strained reading and applying it does little for a reader's ability to decode the scene.

In a similar fashion one might ask whether Christian hagiography in general, itself owing much to the Gospel narratives of Christ's deeds, might have contributed something to the understanding of the Boyhood Deeds as a defined narrative sub-genre in Recension I. The episodic miscellany form and style of some Irish hagiographical narratives may be an influence. Thus one finds in Recension I the tags *fecht n-and ... fecht n-aile* (once, another time) that are also characteristic of Irish hagiography. Similarly, the stone bed of Cú Chulainn is an ascetic motif found in Lives of Irish saints. The development of Brigidine hagiography also offers a useful site of comparison. The Old Irish *Life of Brigid* offers, to a far greater degree than accounts of other saints in their youth, a coherent narrative program of 'Girlhood Deeds' of a clearly initiatory nature.[31] But here it is much more likely that by the time this Life was written in its present form, the influence was most likely to have been from saga to hagiography rather than vice versa.

One might conclude this review of possible Christian modeling with a final possible typological association: it is perhaps most suggestive of all to see a Harrowing of Hell model for this narrative of a hero who rescues his adopted father and his son along lines I have sketched out above.[32] On the whole, however, my brief examination of possible Christian frames has been disappointing in that it has not yielded anything of singular value for this present narrative. However, I shall return to the question again in the next chapter where the Christian underpinnings to more markedly mythic segments of the text begin to assume a much greater significance.

From a Tale to a Myth

In posing the question of myth construction and decoding in Irish narratives, two approaches have been tried with some success in the past twenty years of saga commentary. McCone has shown that it is useful to start from a Proppian perspective if one wishes to consider myth from a structuralist point of view.[33] Thus, following the model of Propp's tale analysis by functions, there are basically three operations in the night-raid narrative. Apart from the hero's setting forth and return, three tests of the hero have a certain symmetry of their own: overcoming the doomed man with the corpse, finding the king, and responding to the king's test by overcoming the fearsome man with the pig. These scenes or functions are not unique and recur elsewhere in Irish saga. For example, two of these functions are also aligned together in the saga *Togail Bruidne Da Derga*.[34] Here, in an atmosphere of general otherworldly terror, a test involving a hideous figure, Mac Caille, with a burnt but living pig is revealed as a fatal *gess* for King Conaire. Nothing but evil befalls this king hero after he meets Mac Caille and his awful partner, and in a fairly obvious way they are omens of a royal death.[35] At the end of the saga, trapped as he is in the fateful house, Conaire asks his desperate defenders to abandon their defence and bring him a drink of water. His champion Mac Cecht responds but the water comes back too late for the king. Mac Cecht then tries to save the king's son by carrying him from the battle but cannot do so. However, he does succeed in rescuing the king's head and body and brings them back for honourable burial in Tara. It is clear, then, that we are here dealing with traditional motifs from the

common saga repertoire that can be utilized variously in tales for specific purposes.[36]

But to take the reading of tale as myth on the level of Proppian functions beyond the immediate contextuality of literary construction,
towards its illocutionary and actantial potential, there should also be a
recognizable social contextuality and end purpose to the narrative.
Here, one may turn to the early Irish legal corpus to discover whether
there might be an approximate answering social context governed by
custom or law. McCone has pointed out, in the case of the early saga
Echtra Nerai, that there is a legal precedent governing the challenge of
fear of the shameful dead, and moreover that there is a legal text that
actually cites this tale; the precedent formula is *gell fri saigid n-omna* 'a
pledge for facing fear.'[37] Just as the tale of Nera referred to above finds
an immediate validation in a legal formula (*gell fri saigid n-omna*), so
too, the whole *Táin* episode here may well have been appreciated as a
well-recognized social scenario or legal conundrum for an early Irish
audience. Early Irish law gives as two of the seven major situations
that might concern a champion, the occasions of *tabuirt i úathbás* and
tabairt a hár-maig ['bringing out of terror,' and 'bringing from a field of
slaughter']. The full text reads:

> *Atait secht n-aire ruanada la Feine ata comdilse do cach richt: tabairt foidb fir do
> tuit a re, tabairt o ro-domain, tabairt a uathbas, tabairt tar trethan, tabairt a teine,
> tabuirt a har-maig, turchlu a suainemnad seol formna [?].*[38]

[There are seven burdens of a champion among the Féni that become
equally his property: taking spoils from a man who has fallen in battle,
taking from a great depth, taking in a terrifying situation, taking across a
stormy sea, taking from fire, taking from a field of slaughter, what is given
for a rigged sailing ship (?)]

The legal focus here is, as is most frequently the case, on the recompense, or what is due a person of a particular class in a specific context.
Nevertheless, the assumption is that only a champion, one inured to
danger, would be expected to put himself in jeopardy like this and that
he thus richly deserves the recompense directly related to the feat. The
legal rubric would then provide some bridge between saga action and
underlying actual social custom, especially as the term *aire* ('burden') is
also consciously deployed in the saga incident. Legal sanction for certain heroic feats would thus constitute the ground and primary mean-

ing of the whole episode – if, indeed, one could be sure that the legal list is not itself dependent on a literary saga tradition. Whichever type of 'document' is to be the validating one, it may be fairly stated that the question of textual meanings in this narrative segment is interdependent with a set of Irish social constructs, articulated explicitly as social praxis in legal discourse and implicitly as narrative function in saga text.[39] The idea of the legal *aire* remains, however, on the level of the symbolic: Cú Chulainn does not 'own' the king after his act of bravery; he merely moves into a new and necessary relationship of *ruanad* to the king by the fact of his carrying him off as his 'burden.'

This fairly narrow but rigorous focus on the reading of myth as a projection of social process approaches a second, more general line of myth enquiry that has been demonstrably useful in Irish scholarly analyses. Tomás Ó Cathasaigh has built on earlier work by Van Hamel, Lord Raglan, and others to advance the idea of 'exemplary myth' and the 'exemplary hero.'[40] Myth in this sense can be used to validate, transform, or even establish social custom. It can also be exemplary in the systemic sense of laying down a grid of action that happens in mythic time, and thus provides an exemplary blueprint for heroic action in the historic human time of saga heroes. This latter systemic approach has more relevance to the understanding of the relationship of divine father and human hero in the following chapter, and I will postpone such a discussion till then. It is the former, the registering of social custom and the role of myth as normative discourse, that occupies me here.

Words and Actions: Reading Then and Now

There is a also a line of scholarly commentary that sees ritualized transition from one social state to another, on the lines of the Van Gennep model of liminal process, as relevant to the *Táin*. Anthropological analysis on these lines has been applied to the Boyhood Deeds as a whole from Georges Dumézil on.[41] That perspective should, I believe, be sharpened even more. It seems that Recension I has better preserved some of the technical vocabulary of social transition in that only in this version do we find an attempt to utilize the term *gillae* as a precise and meaningful part of the terminology of moving from one social phase into another. According to *DIL* the term's most fundamental meaning is to designate 'a youth of an age to bear arms.' In the YBL version of *Cormac's Glossary* the related term, *gillacht*, is defined as one of an ordered set of *colomna aís .i. aimsera aís*: '.i. naoidenacht 7 macdacht, gillacht 7 óglachas, sendatu 7 diblideta.'[42] [Columns of life, that is periods of life, e.g., childhood and boyhood, youth and young warriorship, old age and decrepitude.] Both narrators of the youthful exploits, Fergus and Conall Cernach, distinguish the stages of the young hero's actions by restricting the term *gilla* to those incidents that happen after the tale of his arrival at Emain Macha and his acceptance by the royal household. In the first incident, he is simply called *mac*; curiously, the king is called *óclaech* – a sort of *primus inter pares* – in the keenly observed atmosphere of the military school of Emain Macha over which he presides. In the final episode of the hero's taking up of arms and patrolling the border in a chariot, Cathbad the druid uses the term *óclaech* of a graduand candidate for arms; but Cú Chulainn is addressed as *gilla* by the king who has seen him step out of line in order to advance himself precociously up the ladder of heroic achievement.

Recension II knows none of these distinctions and uses *mac bec*, with *gilla bec* twice as a simple synonym for *mac bec*. Seeing the shape of a clear and formal vocabulary of transition in use in Recension I helps to ground more securely the function of these tales as narratives of liminal and transitional experience – hence tales that satisfy an essential criterion for myth as a narration that markedly expresses social structures. Curiously, the Eógan mac Durthacht episode contains no marked referential term for Cú Chulainn except for the challenging reference to the *olc damna laíc* (bad *makings of a warrior*) by the war goddess. Is this story then out of character with the others in the expanded Boyhood Deeds sequence of Recension I? There is evidence that it has been retooled for the occasion it occupies in the overall agenda of the saga, and not all manuscript witnesses convey it quite similarly.[43] More 'primitive' aspects of Irish prose narrative are clearly displayed in this tale: simple – even minimalist – sentence structure, paratactic juxtaposition of sentences, and direct speech with laconic and undeveloped dialogue. However, this has been integrated into the general narrative flow by the foregrounding of Fergus as the narrator's voice. There is considerable sophistication in the switching back and forth between Fergus as the narrator's voice and the extra-narrative voice of Fergus in the action of the main-frame saga. A switch can sometimes happen in a very compressed syntactic space, as in the following: '*Hi fíadnaise Bricriu ucut do rónad,*' ol Fergus ... '*Cotricim-se fris i ndorus ind lis 7 mé athgaíte.*' The relation of the Boyhood Deeds segment to the larger narrative is an issue that is more properly of literary significance, however, and I will deal with this aspect of the narrative after all myth-related issues have been discussed.

Reading Now

Up to now I have deployed various usages of the term 'myth' in order to enlarge the zone of meaning of these micro-narratives on the level of their functionality. Most of these usages have already been utilized with insight by other scholars in the explication of Irish sagas. In one of his most accessible treatments of the structural method of myth analysis, *The Story of Asdiwal*, Lévi-Strauss makes the distinction 'between two aspects of the construction of a myth: the sequences and the schemata.'[44] The narrative sequences, the actions that can be organized on a Proppian model, are the content, the melody line, so to speak; the schemata are the counterpoint, the sets of dynamic oppositions that punctuate a mythic narrative at every turn. Perhaps the richest yield of meaning for a contemporary general reader of Irish saga is to be located here; and in invoking these I rejoin the early simple reading of the piece that I used at the beginning of this analysis. The possible sets of 'structuralist' vertical contrastive pairs for the Eógan mac Durthacht episode under discussion would certainly include the following: king/rebel, warrior/child, night/battle, darkness/fire, house/field, house/tomb, broken bodies/whole bodies, humans/spirits, dead human body/dead animal, raw flesh/cooked flesh, eating/killing, strangers/friends, father/son, male/female, lying down/standing up, aimless wandering/directed movement, chaos/order, safety/danger, innocence/knowledge.

All of these contrastive pairs bear on the significance of violent action itself, with its bias towards psychic and physical degeneration and death. These are opposed by the cultural, social constructs that are called into play to avert this outcome. Domestic values of home, feasting, and natural kindred ties are now appropriated to social kinship, as service in a re-established social hierarchy; all these are re-enacted and reasserted through the agon of the warrior at the very site where he mediates these oppositions: his own body. The originary natural unity of the brother enemy pair at the beginning is shown to be a merely mechanical model of split and polluted bodies. It is rejected at the end of the tale in favour of a bodily triadic unity that is both naturally *and* socially constructed: Cú Chulainn as the son of his *popa*, as socially constructed, the *garmac*, the sister's son, the loyal servitor. It is as such that he sustains the natural kindred pair, Conchobar and his natural son, Cúscrach.[45] The drama of progression here is close to Mary Douglas's ideas of pollution: 'The symbolism of the body's boundaries is used ... to express danger to community boundaries ... Concepts of pollution ... work to keep the limits of society intact through their symbolic enactment in the boundaries of the body.'[46] In this sense then, Cú Chulainn engages with pollution, but on his own warrior terms and, in so doing, earns the moral authority to reconstitute and revivify as 'natural' the endangered social order.

Playing War Games

To touch the half-life of bodies on the way to death is to be infected by them, to be distracted from life and brought down to annihilation and the world of the spectral dead. Paradoxically, it is Cú Chulainn's own childishness and his cleverness which can parry these negative miasmas by interpreting them as game and by interposing between himself and their power the idea of play as deflection. The 'tag game' that becomes the 'hurling game' represents in little the way in which humans can enact 'as if' spaces to bring them safely through crises. On the level of a saving ritual, the significance of staging games was never richer in Irish narrative than it is in this text: on the battlefield 'hide and seek' becomes 'playing dead,' 'playing house,' becomes a playful riff on the royal inauguration ritual of 'carrying the king,' and by these successive stagings the king and the status quo are restored.[47]

A complex saga such as the *Táin* partakes with epic in the enterprise of establishing overarching discursive structures within which specific speech acts or performative acts of the hero and the social collectivity together can be enacted.[48] The Boyhood Deeds is one such marked segment. It is a set of tales within the tale, a faceted myth reflecting on its enclosing narrative. Here, in the speech acts of the opening mini-tale of the boy's arrival at the king's court, is enacted Cú Chulainn's legal outwitting of the king in the matter of a solemn contract of protection; the boy outmaneuvers Conchobar, shows up the king's legal negligence, and takes control of the boy-troop.[49] Here another story facet shows the formal renaming of the hero receiving its power from the hound-killing, hound-substituting acts of Cú Chulainn; the boy's transformative deed arises directly from his claim of exemption from royal attendance duties and the king's act of negligence in forgetting that he was coming later to the feast of Culann the smith. Here again the hero outmanoeuvers druid, king, and warrior mentors to seize the right – again through a verbal sleight of hand – to bear arms, to ride a chariot, and to raid beyond the border in a process that ends when a rite of illegal alienation is transformed into a rite of integration; seizing this day ensures that his glory will live forever and be the benchmark against which all other fame will be measured. Finally, here too, in the Eógan Mac Durthacht incident, the hero passes a fundamental and *specifically-named* legal test of warriors, *Tabuirt i úathbás*, the conquest of fear and the victory over the world of the dead.

Myth Rejoins Epic

The enjambement of this marked narrative segment with the larger narrative is fascinating to view and necessary to understand if one wishes to appreciate the relationship of marked tales and main action that sustains the saga as a whole structure. It also structures my sense of how myth is created as a specially marked category of saga writing, where old forms are validated but where there is nothing archaic or primitive about the ability of writing to continue to create mythic discourse. In Recension I, Ailill decides that the armies will rest and eat after the setback of the forbidding branch spiked with human heads. He calls for entertainment for the armies and somewhat unluckily traps himself by insisting that Fergus tell him some Ulster heroic tales: *ní do imt[h]echtaib 7 airscélaib in c[h]eniúil cosa tíagam* [something of the adventures and famous tales of the people we are approaching] (ll. 358–9).[50] In the suggested frame of an entertainment, the terms of reference here are not purely informational and pragmatic but rather have an unmistakable performative shading. Recension I intensifies this shading by giving what is in essence an auctorial, or at least scribal directive: *Is and trá adfessa dóib imt[h]echta Con Culaind* [Then was told to them 'The Adventures of Cú Chulainn'] (l. 360).[51] The effect of this metatextual intervention is to identify in a formal way the status of the Boyhood Deeds episodes as a discrete verbal performance with a real audience, a performance that generically will consist of a narrative with multiple incidents and a chorus of storytelling performers. The storytelling is set up as social entertainment, both in the internal logic of the narrative and in its external auctorial labeling as a literary work: *Imthechta Con Culaind*. The stories are told in the traditional entertainment setting of a royal meal, even if the venue has shifted from palace to campground. In Recension I, Fergus's narrator role is enhanced by the greater number of the tales he tells and by the way in which he intervenes actively in the body of the telling. His manipulation of his audience is patent: by the use of the vocative demonstrative *uccut*, in the technically incorrect citation of Bricriu as a witness, as cited above, and, above all, by the trapping of Ailill into the foolish admiration reflected in his audience response: *rofes robo dor[n]d níad 7 ba ríg rúanada* ['I knew it was the fist of a warrior and the arm of a champion.'] (l. 467).[52]

It is also a speech act performance organized around a formal principle of verbal efficacy. As such, the verbal performance of the Boyhood Deeds is already anticipated by the segue into it – the guessing game of 'Who's there?' – between Ailill and Fergus, which serves to negotiate the transfer between it and the larger narrative (ll. 361–73). The guessing game wrong-foots and confuses all prior concepts of Ulster heroic display and reputation that the Connacht side might have held. As Fergus goes on to build up the awesome figure of Cú Chulainn before the eyes of Ailill and Medb in the formal genre of a boasting run in heightened prose, they are at a loss to categorize him. Is he *fer* or *gilla* (Ailill, ll. 374–5) or, as Medb contemptuously says, is he but *áes ingini macdacht* [age of a teenage girl], as yet incapable of male action [*ní thángatár a fhergníma beus*] (ll. 394–5)? As speech acts, the episodes of the Boyhood Deeds are essentially charm-like in their structure: as Cú Chulainn was then, even more so is he now, and the longer the string of applied incidents, the more effective the spell to terrify and rout the enemy will be. Particularly effective as charm is the Eógan mac Durthacht episode: a tale of horror told in the dark, full with mangled bodies and with the dread war goddess, present already in the saga and already radically disturbing men's ability to perform on the field of battle. It is a tale that carries a warning: even though the king be disabled (as Conchobar is now in Emain Macha) you will still not prevail against a side that has such a hero fighting for it.

As if conscious of the ritualistic nature of the preceding narrative segments, the transition from Boyhood Deeds to a resumption of the cattle raid narrative is negotiated in a complex and somewhat awkward way. It is not easy to move from a relatively self-contained and heightened narrative enclosure back to the general narrative. In this case, awareness that the previous matter of the *geis* of the ogam-marked branch which had forced a stop to the action is unresolved causes an iterative ripple effect where the major action resumes. The *geis* is duplicated and augmented, this time with a whole tree (ll. 825–

32). Even with this incremental stratagem there is awkward repetition, as O'Rahilly has noted.[53] At Medb's entreaty, Fergus intervenes, requiring a chariot to negotiate the tree bole (ll. 341–5). After the Boyhood Deeds segment, the same request from Medb generates a single combat scene between Cú Chulainn and Fráech, which all scholars agree is a later interpolation (ll. 833–57). Finally, after the Fráech episode, Fergus leaps across the blockade; the effective cue is given but in a sentence that loses any efficacy it might have as a narrative marker by being mis-set as a heading to a miscellaneous sequence of minor incidents (l. 858).

Recension II marks the end of the segment with a formal closure in the shape of an immediate reference to the Boyhood Deeds in the context of the whole saga followed by a top-down listing of the titles of segments – preface, route, adventures of the host – thus far: *Conid innisin do macgnímaib Con Culaind sin for Táin Bó Cúalng, ocus remthúus in sceóil 7 na sliged 7 imthechta in tshluaig a Crúachain connici sin* (ll. 1214–16).[54] This kind of closure means that the master plot line can once again proceed, unencumbered by any need to explain unfinished business that went before. But the most significant change to the Boyhood Deeds narrative between Recensions I and II may well be a simple name switch in the roster of narrators of the deeds. In LL Conall Cernach's name does not occur among the list of narrators. The change may seem minor but its significance takes us back to the crucial issue of scribes' engagement in the narratives that they work with. As Uáitéar Mac Gearailt has shown, the Book of Leinster version of *Cath Ruis na Ríg* gives a major role to Conall Cernach, and he argues plausibly that this marks an intervention into saga transmission by the scribe of this section of the manuscript himself.[55] As one of the Úa Cremthainn family who took their genealogy back to this hero, the scribe of LL would be concerned to show him in the best possible light, as he did positively in *Cath Ruis na Ríg* by giving him a major part of the action. Something similar may be happening here. The scribe may have been unwilling to acknowledge that Conall Cernach may have fought on the side of the Connacht men in the service of Medb, whom the author of Recension II seems to regard with a consistent repugnance. By substituting another warrior narrator for Conall Cernach, the scribe keeps the heroic integrity of his own heroic ancestor intact.

What we have come back to, then, in this final view of my sample 'mythic' text, is the principle of the centrality of the scribe in this investigation. Whatever critical code we use to open up the discourse of the

Táin, it must finally come back to the issue of the scribes as the primary witnesses of their own literary tradition. I have already explored this issue in detail in chapter 3. In chapter 5 I explore other facets of mythic language, using a part of the narrative that is a good deal more complex in the range of its literary ambition.

5 Myth to Epic: The Coming of a God

CHRISTY *impressively*: With that the sun came out between the cloud and the hill, and it shining green in my face. 'God have mercy on your soul,' says he, lifting a scythe. 'Or on your own,' says I, raising the loy.
SUSAN: That's a grand story.
HONOR: He tells it lovely.

J.M. Synge, *The Playboy of the Western World*

Epic Forms

In chapter 4 I used the redaction of the Boyhood Deeds segment to introduce some possible approaches and to explore several facets of the mythic proposition. In my discussion of this early sequence in the *Táin* saga the emphasis was on specific aspects of the marriage of narrative and mythic discourse. Two strands of scholarly work set the scene for exploring the question: the nature of exemplary myth and the presence of implicit ritual acts of heroic initiation. As background to the latter, the work of McCone went a long way in elucidating both the ideological aspects of heroic initiation in early Ireland and its congruence with other Indo-European examples;[1] Ó Cathasaigh showed also how ideas of exemplary myth might have formed satisfying literary patterns in other sagas.[2] What I wished to track in chapter 4 is the way this plays out in a more strictly textual context, where a developmental model of a heroic initiation myth is projected in the discursive stratagems of the encoders vis-à-vis their fictive narrators and their protagonists, and, in turn, their audiences.[3] From there, I reconstructed the significant social actions and identified their constituent speech acts.

This led into the question of identifying games and sites for 'acting out,' and, in particular, the analysis of those further speech acts of competition and dominance that centre around Fergus and serve to position audience and narrator. It was also important to examine the linkage of this section of the saga with its immediate narrative context because such bridging of the gap between two markedly different levels of enunciation is patently a matter of individual literary effort on the part of the different textual recensors; consequently, the seams between can tell us much about the literary construction of the larger narrative from its smaller, discrete constitutive units.

Myth then, in certain restricted forms of the term, may well be a tool 'good to work with' as an approach to aspects of the *Táin* narrative in that, in telling the tales of the hero's transformation into a model of supra-human precocity, what is perceived as significant in the attitudes and even the rituals of surrounding social institutions can, by this discursive means, be privileged and highlighted.

But the Boyhood Deeds segment is not the only initiatory or transformative discursive structure in the saga. Indeed, if we accept in that instance that deeply embedded initiatory practices provide a valid underlying frame, not just for describing a hero's relations to his environment on the general level of social ideology, but also for providing an answering rhetorical means to a proper discursive display mode – a means for showing the results of his transformation in a verbally iconic fashion – then it seems logical to search for such frames elsewhere in the text. When I speak of display mode I have in mind the patently ostensive, non-narrative aspects of the climactic ending of the final Boyhood Deeds tale, Cú Chulainn's adventures on the border patrol:

> *Dogníth són íarom. Conrig Cú Chulaind inna ésse 7 tecmalla in t-ara inna heónu. Conreraig Cú Chulaind íar sin inna heónu di thétaib 7 refedaib in c[h]arpait.* <u>*Conid samlaid sin luid do Emain Macha: dam allaid i ndíaid a charpait 7 íall gésse oc folúamain úassa 7 trí cind inna c[h]larput.*</u> *Recait iar sin co Emain. 'Carptech dorét far ndochum,' ol in dercaid i nEmain Macha.*

[That was done then. Cú Chulainn fastened the reins and the charioteer collected the birds. Then Cú Chulainn tied on the birds using the cords and bindings of the chariot. *In this manner it was that they went to Emain Macha: a wild deer behind his chariot, a flock of wild birds fluttering around it, and three severed heads in his chariot.* Then they got to Emain. 'A chariot drives towards you!' said the watchman in Emain Macha.] (ll. 797–803)[4]

There are further important aesthetic implications here for the entire saga. A balancing of the entire narrative structure of the *Táin* around the theme of the investiture of the hero may be suggested as the over-arching plan of the whole work. The struggle between two warring territorial groups for the bull of Cúailnge constitutes the force behind the main narrative action in geographical and spatial terms. More specifically, however, the narrative thematics of the saga revolve around the hero as warrior, as marked by and projected in a pattern of initiation and display. This is manifested most acutely in what follows the drama of his wounding, the event which brings on the healing visit of his divine father. The double scenes which are played out there of terror and beauty – the night-time scenario, the arming of warrior and chariot, his great battle fury, the slaughter he inflicts, and the self-display of the festively dressed hero to the women the morning after – answer to the same schema as that offered in the last story of the Boyhood Deeds (ll. 794–821). It is not insignificant to its importance that the scene of the healing by Lug occurs at the centre of the work, both textually and spatially.[5] It may be seen as rehearsing again in a major key what had already been structured in the Boyhood Deeds: namely, the idea of the warrior as initiate, as candidate for the reception of divine energy. This energy is conferred in a scene marked by privacy and intimacy but the gifts bestowed are those in which the whole complex array of society necessarily takes an acute interest, in that this heroic power is to be invested in the hero's social role as defender of the tribal territory.

In the discussion that follows I will take this position as my given starting point while I go on to analyse the constituent and more specifically textual aspects of the saga account. In staging the coming of Lug in this way I do not wish to downplay what is perhaps the most important literary aspect of the whole scene – its epic ambition. Indeed the epic coding of the scene is a fundamental part of its myth-making on a number of levels. Brent Miles has proposed to read the entire sequence as a unit, running from the night-time position taken up by Cú Chulainn at Lerga and his uttering of a warrior's cry straight through to his revenge for the boy troop and his great warp spasm (ll. 2072–334); Miles sees this sequence as being influenced in a number of direct and circuitous ways by Classical epic models, beginning with the *Iliad*.[6] His analysis of this passage in the *Táin* is exciting and the evidence he adduces to support his claim is impressive and convincing. However, he does not comment on the healing scene and the question of the theomachy. This makes it all the more imperative to ascertain its place in the classicizing rewriting of the *Táin* in this period. From Miles's perspective, the cry of Cú Chulainn and his view of the enemy fires at ll. 2076–87 begins the epic classicizing, and from there the creators of the saga moved to the arming of the hero as their next point of classicizing interest. Such an approach would leave the healing scene isolated, and consequently I posit a different but complementary line of construction for this crucial encounter. Indeed, it is precisely Miles's work in isolating the related classical epic scene followed by the composer of the *Breslech* episode that highlights all the more the need to account for the major insertion of Lug in the story.

Incidentally, in working on this section of the tale one is struck by the fact that this attempt to raise the discursive nature of the *Táin* to an epic level seems to have been a project abandoned in time along the way. The combat with Fer Diad, which may well be the next major section of the tale to receive special literary treatment, is writing in a quite different fashion. Here a mixed prosi-metrum style is selected with extensive verse dialogue that allows greater access to the discursive individual emotional states of the two heroes, even switching speakers in the middle of a poem.[7] In other words, literary styles are already beginning to favour the narrative formatting of the up and coming Fenian 'ballad' tales.

The *topos* of 'The Coming of Lug' occupies as prestigious a position in the *Táin* as it does in Irish literary tradition generally; it is the manner in which 'The Coming of Lug' in the *Táin* plays against the grain of Lug's traditional acclaim that interests me here.[8] Contrary to expectations, the arrival of the god takes place quietly in a scene already full of heroic clamour and marked by the lurid chiaroscuro of darkness, fire, and unquiet. Later, the god also leaves silently, in a textual fog, so to speak, as one sees no real attempt made to create any bridge between this act of great moment and the next stage of the narrative. Even before exiting from his narrative, Lug recesses himself in order, as he specifically states, that the subsequent glory of the restored hero be all the more marked by his having fought alone and by having maintained his heroic singularity as a unique badge. What I am mainly interested in here is to explore the discursive resources available, in order to be able to meet the challenge of 'writing in a god,' to the particular *Táin* man of art who is responsible for rewriting this scene.

In the main narrative the transfer of heroic energy is structured as occurring between Lug and Cú Chulainn in the episode where Lug heals Cú Chulainn (ll. 2073–2184). Lug sends him into a restorative sleep and chants a martial poem to him which is simultaneously a healing lullaby and a warrior incitement. He then fights in his place while the hero is in his therapeutic sleep. Several hints prepare the scene ahead of time for Lug's major entry into the saga and create a linkage with the earlier initiatory scenes of the Boyhood Deeds. Successive *Táin* scribes have prefigured his presence there in the earlier initiatory segment. Cú Chulainn's reckoning of the army from his vantage point at Áth Grencha is compared by scribe M – with some exaggeration and inaccuracy – to the great reckoning made by Lug in the *Cath Maige Tuired*.[9] The actual telling of the Boyhood Deeds also takes place at this site; it is glossed by H as Lug's ancient domain, *fri Cnogba atúaid* [north of Knowth].[10] Such a deliberate reference to the proximity of Lug's traditional residence to the site of 'The Boyhood Deeds' performance is a way of associating this entire early sequence with the patronage of Lug.

So one might posit that the newer 'true' narrative hinge of the *Táin*, as we have it in Recension I, is the encounter between Cú Chulainn and his divine father/mentor. It is the linkage set up between the two poles, first the initiatory, and then the culminatory act of transference, which constitute the entire saga as an act of showing 'the triumph of the hero.' Can it be further posited that there are other related symmetries operative in the narrative arrangement? For example, the series of single combats in the first half may, roughly speaking, be seen to function as prelude and contrast for the great apotheosis of total and irresistible heroic force exemplified in the massed actions of the latter, post-Lug half of the story? Thus the superhuman heroic energy vested in Cú Chulainn by right of divine parentage is but imperfectly realized in the first half of the narrative. As Medb had defined him earlier, he does suffer wounding, he has but a human body, and the physical wear and tear of the single combats does eventually wear him down.[11]

It may also be that scribe H's perceptions of necessary adjustments to the narrative as he found it are correct in that by bringing forward to the first part of the story some of the later single encounters he is responding to that deeper structural pattern of partial and full initiation.[12] There is also common agreement among scholars that the most elaborate of the single combat encounters in the post-healing phase of the saga, the fight with Fer Diad, is a later composition and may be derived from the fight with Lóch, which properly falls in the first half. Thus an earlier ascending scale may be assumed to have been augmented and superimposed, with the defining single encounter – this time between perfectly matched equals, Cú Chulainn and Lóch, bound by the ties of initiatory foster-brotherhood – placed just at the point of divine interventions.

It is also important to note that an alternative and perhaps older local scenario for the healing of Cú Chulainn exists in fragmentary form in the second half of the narrative as we have it. He is brought to bathe, for example, in the healing rivers of Cooley (ll. 3149–50), and through much of the latter part of the action, where Cú Chulainn ceases to be the main focus of attention and some care is given to the recovering Ulster side, he is obviously still in an invalid state and is absent from all but the last phases of the final great battle.[13] It would seem then that the narrative originally had a vignette on the wounding and healing of the hero, which was then written up as the healing by the god, and which was later augmented by further wounding from the fight with Ferdiad. Surprisingly, the hero is also formally enumerated in the great muster of the Ulstermen where he is referred to as *Cú Chulaind mac Soaltaim a sídaib* [Cú Chulainn, son of Sualtaim, of the fairy dwellings] (l. 3860).[14] The ambiguity of this nomenclature is startling in that his earthly patronymic, son of Sualdam, is yoked with a patrilocal reference, 'from the fairy mounds,' which pertains to Lug, or rather to Cú Chulainn himself as the son of an other-world figure. It is then a title under some strain and is only appropriate for the hero after his investiture by his divine father.[15]

Heroic Crisis, Childish Cries

The scene of crisis which prefaces Lug's intervention opens in a world marked out as a liminal zone. It is in the inverted no-man's-land of the battlefield at the ford, weakened by the triplicate powers of his death-goddess adversary the Morrígain, and in the lurid light of the night-time battlefield, that Cú Chulainn comes to the extremity of his human resources. Finally acknowledging to himself his crisis of displacement and lying exhausted on the grave-mound at Lerga, he calls out for help. He requires a messenger to tell his earthly lord and mentor Conchobhar that he can no longer hold the line:

M'óenurán dam ar étib
sech nís n-étaim nís léicim
atú ar trathaib úaraib
m'óenurán ar iltúathaib.

Apraid nech fri Conchobar
cía domissed níbo rom
rucsat Meic Mágach a mbú
conda randsat etarru.

Ro bíi cosnom im óenchend
acht nád lassa nach óenc[h]rand
día mbetis a dó nó a trí
lasfaitis a n-aithinni.

Bec nárom nítsat ind fhir
ar imad comlaind óenfhir
ní rubaim níth n-erred n-án
immar atú m'óenurán.

[I am here alone against the hosts. I can neither hold them back nor let them go. In the cold watches I am alone against many peoples.

Let someone tell Conchobar – should he come to me it could not be too soon. The sons of Mágu have carried off their share of cattle, are even now dividing them.

One single person could be opposed but a single log does not catch fire. If there be two or three of them, however, then their kindlings will blaze up. The men have almost overcome me, because of the number of my single combats. I cannot do battle against famous warriors in the condition I am in here, all alone.] (ll. 2007–23)

The consequent visitation of his divine father Lug confers definitively on Cú Chulainn the most extreme form of the mark of warrior caste identity, irresistible battle fury or, in a term exclusively reserved for Cú Chulainn, *riastartha*. This supreme manifestation of heroic energy will be formalized within an answering, elaborate description which subsumes this fury into an account of the arming of the hero, his chariot, his festive self-display, and his great rout of his enemies. It is rendered in a prose marked with high epic stylistic ambition, which, in writerly terms, is clearly the climax of the entire saga.[16] The idiom of a transference – here healing and irresistible energy – from a higher power by which apotheosis is achieved shares many features with the idiom of poetic inspiration that is, as noted in chapter 2, invented to explain the survival of the *Táin* itself: the technique of prostration, of mantic sleep in the sacred place, the grave-mound and the invocation

of the absent mentor figure, here the father god.[17] Through the powers
of Lug, Cú Chulainn is reconstituted with a new-found strength and,
thus fortified, he displays himself in a double showing: first as a fearsome figure to the armies in the mass slaughter of Sesrech Breslige, and
then, in all his festival finery, to the women. In this double manifestation of terror and beauty he recapitulates in himself the form of the earliest account of 'the Showing of the Hero': that contained in the
prophecy of Fedelm at the beginning of the saga (ll. 63–113).

The Climax in Its Textual Environment

From this rapid sketch and from the perspective that the healing scene
is a moment of deep significance for the entire narrative, I now examine in greater detail the staging of Lug's visitation. For it would be
pointless to assert the ritualized, even iconic, importance of the scene
without understanding the literary stratagems by which it is staged.

> *Ro gabsat trá cethri choíced Hérend dúnad 7 lonngport isin Breslig Móir i*
> *mMaig Murthemne, 7 ro láiset a n-ernail búair 7 braite seocho fodess hi Clithar*
> *Bó Ulad. Gabais Cú Chulaind icond fhert i lLercaib i comfocus dóib, 7 ataís a ara*
> *tenid dó tráth nóna na haidchi sin .i. Lóeg mac Ríangabra. Itchonnairc-seom úad*
> *grístatinem na n-arm nglanórda úas chind cethri cóiced nÉrend re funiud néllma*
> *nóna. Dofánic ferg 7 luinni mór ic aicsin in tslóig re hilar a bidbad [7] re himad a*
> *námat. Ro gab a dá shleig 7 a scíath 7 a chlaideb. Crothis a scíath 7 cresaigis a*
> *shlega 7 bertnaigis a chlaidem, 7 dobert a srem caurad asa brágit coro recratar*
> *bánánaig 7 boccánaig 7 geiniti glinni 7 demna aeóir re úathgráin na gáre dosber-*
> *tatar ar aird. Cordas mesc ind Némain forsin tslóg. Dollotar i n-armgrith cethri*
> *chóiced Érend im rennaib a sleg 7 a n-arm fodessin co n-erbaltatar cét láech díb do*
> *úathbas 7 cridenes ar lár in dúnaid 7 in longphairt in n-aidchi sin.*
>
> > *Dia mbaí Láeg and con-acca ní, in óenfer dar fíartharsna in dúnaid fer nÉrend*
> > *anairtúaid cach ndíriuch ina dochum.*
>
> > *'Óenfher sund chucund inossa a Chúcán,' or Láeg.*
>
> > *'Cinnas fir and sin?' or Cú Chulainn.*
>
> > *'Ní handsa. Fer caín mór and dano. Berrad lethan laiss. Folt casbude fair. Brat*
> > *úanide i forcipol immi. Cassán gelairgit isin brot úassa bruinne. Léne de shról ríg*
> > *fo dergindliud do dergór i custul fri gelcnes co glúnib dó. Dubscíath co calath-*
> > *búaili findruni fair. Sleg cóicrind ina láim. Foga fogablaigi inna fharrad. Ingnad*
> > *ém reb 7 ábairt 7 adabair dogní, acht ní saig nech fair 7 ní saig-seom for nech feib*
> > *nachas faiced nech hé.'*
>
> > *'Is fír sin a daltán,' for sé. 'Cia dom chartib síthchaire-sa sein dom airchiseacht-*

sa dáig ar bíth foretatar-som in t-imned már inam fhuil-sea m'óenur i n-agid
cethri n-ollchóiced nÉrend ar 'Táin Bó Cúalngi' don chur sa.'

  Ba fír ém do Choin Chulaind anní hísin. A nad-ránic in t-óclách airm i mbói
Cú Chulainn, argládais 7 airchissis de.

  'Ferda sin, a Chú Chulaind,'ar sé.

  'Ní mór side etir,'for Cú Chulaind.

  'Dabér-sa dano cobair dait,'ar in t-óclách.

  'Cía tai-siu eter?'or Cú Chulaind.

  'Iss messe do athair a ssídib .i. Lug mac Ethlend.'

  'It tromda dano na fuli form-sa. Ba héim dam mo íc.'

  'Cotail-siu sin bic, a Chú Chulaind,'or in t-óclách, 'do throm-thort[h]im cot-
ulta hicond ferta Lerga co cend teóra láa 7 teóra n-aidchi, 7 firfat-sa forsna slógaib
in n-airet sin.'

  Canaid a chéle fordord dó, contuli friss co n-accae nách crecht and ropo glan.

  Is and asbert Lug:

[Then the four provinces of Ireland pitched camp and bivouacked at
Breslech Mór in Mag Muirthemne. They sent on their haul of cows and
plunder ahead of them south to Clithar Bó Ulad. Cú Chulainn took up
position at the grave-mound at Lerga near to them. His charioteer Láeg
Mac Ríangabra, lit a fire the evening of that night. From his position Cú
Chulainn saw the flickering reflection of the bright gold armoury over the
heads of the of the four provinces of Ireland from the [red] sunset clouds.
Anger and rage seized him seeing that host, from the multitude of his foes
and the number of his enemies. He grabbed his two spears and his shield
and sword. He shook the shield, brandished the spears and swung his
sword and uttered a hero's yell deep in his throat. With that the goblins
and spectres and sprites of the glen, and the demons of the air howled
back for sheer terror of the impact of his screaming. And the madness of
Némain filled the host. And the hosts of Ireland made such a clatter of
arms with the points of their own spears and weapons that a hundred
warriors died of fear and terror in the middle of the encampment that
night.

  While Láeg was there he saw a thing – a lone man coming straight
towards him from the northeast right through the Irishmen's encampment.

  'A lone man coming towards us, little Cú,'said Láeg.

  'What kind of man is that?' said Cú Chulainn.

  'Easy. He is a lovely and tall man. His hair spreads out, yellow and curl-
ing. He has a green mantle in folds around him, with a brooch of bright

silver fastening it at the breast. Over his fair skin he wears a tunic of royal satin inset with red-gold bands that reaches to his knees. He has a dark shield with a hard boss of beaten bronze. In his hand is a five-pointed spear and he has also a forked javelin. The moves, the tricks and the plays he makes are amazing; no one accosts him, however, and he challenges no one – it is as if they cannot see him.'

'That is true, my lad,'said he. 'That is one of my friends from the fairy dwellings come to console me, for they can tell the great straits I'm in, alone as I am at this time against the four great provinces of Ireland on the cattle raid of Cúailnge.'

It was indeed true what Cú Chulainn said. When the warrior came to where Cú Chulainn was he saluted him and comforted him.

'That is manly,'said he.

'Hardly that,' said Cú Chulainn.

'I will help you,' said the warrior.

'Who might you be?' asked Cú Chulainn.

'I am your father from the fairy mounds, Lug mac Ethlend.'

'The wounds I bear are heavy. I need to be healed.'

'Sleep now for a while, Cú Chulainn,' said the warrior, your deep swoon of sleep at the grave-mound at Lerga for three days and three nights, and I will fight against the armies during all that time.'

Then he chanted a man's song to him and put him to sleep until he saw that every single one of his wounds was healed.

It was then that Lug sang.] (ll. 2076–113)

Initial difficulties are presented by the shifting state of the text at this point. The wounding and healing of the hero take place at a point of compositional overlap, so that there is a flurry of minor discrepancies between the textual witnesses for both recensions, which renders the hermeneutical task more difficult. Within Recension I it is at this point that H chooses to insert a major interpolation in U, just before the crucial scene (ll. 1904–95). C also faces difficulties; the version of the hero's poem from Recension II is placed just after the death of Lóch. In U, following a pattern noted earlier, headings for the single combat scenes preceding this section are given, but in Y they do not receive titles and in W and C they are much scantier. Similarly, there is no title in Y to the first act of the drama of wounding and healing, the arrival of the Morrígain. One might conclude from this that the less the text is scored as in Y, the farther one is from a consciousness of rewriting and conscious textual adjustments. In other words, the awkwardness in U may well be a signal of closer proximity to the anxieties of text-in-process, while Y understands the text as canonical and given. For this reason it is always instructive to pay close attention to the operations of the U scribes.

As noted above, the scene proper is part of a larger and apparently purposeful rewriting and inflating of this section of the saga in an epic register; the style reaches its greatest rhetorical splendour when the hero reawakens after his healing. Thus the reconceptualization of the entire section as an exercise in a high epic style best describes the most triumphalist part of the sequence, the topic of 'the Arming of the Hero' (ll. 2185–315). The discursive issues behind the wounding and healing scenes may well have also been influenced by self-conscious 'epic' concerns, as noted below, but it is the other registers deployed here that now need to be analysed.

One of the first things to observe, then, is the manner in which the entire scene is embedded in the ongoing action; indeed this textual site is a virtual palimpsest of inscription and re-inscription. Much of the richness of the scene is edited out of the LL version. There Cú Chulainn's poem is dislodged from its place in Recension I and inserted after the death of Lóch, probably in the interests of logicality. The LL poem itself is clearly secondary and developed from the form in Recension I. It expands on points made in the first poem and a flabby, unfocused sequence of verses is the result. More significantly, as we shall see below, the coded *MARB* ('dead') from the first letter of each stanza, as in Recension I, is lost and with it the cue for the main influence behind such a poem. The coming of Lug in LL involves no structured moment of personal revelation as the verbal exchange between Lug and the hero is omitted. The incantation of Lug is omitted entirely. These slippages in LL are fairly evident and in what follows I am assuming that the Recension I version is the more useful one to work with.

The Wounding

Cú Chulainn's wounding is itself complex and is composed in three stages of vulnerability: (a) the difficult fight with his foster-brother Lóch and with Lóch's brother (ll. 1875–1995); (b) the fight with the Morrígain (ll. 1845–71, 1982–2005, 2038–54) and, also implicated in this, the presence of Medb and the women (ll. 1887–98); (c) the stampede of the cattle.[18] These are not discrete motifs but rather are interlaced together in the narrative – whether accidentally or deliberately is hard

to tell. Complicating the task of any reader of this section in Recension
I is the manner in which the intrusion of H further complicates the picture; H intercalates a single page, 75–76, which draws out considerably
the fight with Lóch. In addition, Y breaks off after the healing of the
Morrígain and only resumes in the middle of the great set piece on the
arming of the hero.

The Death Goddess

Of the three woundings, the most significant in terms of its obvious
mythic associations is the Morrígain episode. The cattle (c) are closely
connected to the other world if we are to credit the background context
provided by the smaller foretales to the great saga – *Echtrae Nerai*[19] and
Táin Bó Regamna[20] – and are clearly, from these contexts, a proprietary
obsession of the goddess herself.[21] The encounter with the Morrígain
as it appears in Recension I shows signs of expansion beyond its original scope and is itself shaped by the wounding/healing thematics of
the entire section. As the entire sequence raises important questions
about the manner in which elements of the saga are constructed, I will
first consider this in some detail. This sequence provides a useful illus-
tration of how successive textual layerings and over-layerings in the
writing of the segment also create a corresponding palimpsest of
meaning.

The first part – the arrival and threats of the Morrígain – was considered by Thurneysen to be the work of the B contributor and by
O'Rahilly to be entirely the work of the LU compiler, hence a very late
addition to the saga.[22] The Recension I account is very close to the telling of the same incident in the tale *Táin Bó Regamna*. The question of
which account of the arrival of the Morrígain is dependent on which
has been raised by Rolf Baumgarten.[23] He argues that in *Táin Bó
Regamna* the correct form of the threat issued by the goddess is: *'Is oc
didin do báis-siu atáu-sa ocus bía,' olsi* ['I am and I shall be bringing about
your death,' said she].[24] Deriving *didin* from the verb *do-feid* (leading,
bringing about) and reading *báis* as 'death' instead of the preterite of
the substantive verb *attá* provides a smooth reading which demonstrates that the hostility of the Morrígain is fundamental and is of a
piece with her prophecy of his future death on the cattle raid. The goddess turns this threat to his life into a formal magical proposition by
linking it specifically with the coming of age of the Connacht bull calf
in her possession. The quarrel then develops into a question of her

power and her three shape-shifting threats to come against him in the *Táin* in order to bring about his death. These threats are met by counterboasts formally uttered by the hero: 'I swear by the god the Ulstermen swear by that I will wound you in the ribs, eyes, legs, etc.' Each is followed by a qualifying 'unless' formula, 'unless you leave me alone.' This formula differs significantly from what is found in the redaction of this same passage in the *Táin*, as we shall presently see. Thus there is every reason to think, with Baumgarten, that the error shown by the Egerton text of *Táin Bó Regamna* – reading *diden* (bringing about) as *do dídin* (your protection) – is the source of the love/hate proposition to the hero with which the goddess enters the scene of action in *Táin Bó Cúailnge*.

From one literary context to another, then, the theme of the goddess implacably hostile to the hero is recast. The demonic temptress morphs from the primitive flitting and shape-shifting crow-goddess of *Táin Bó Regamna* into the more romantic but nonetheless malignly marked figure of the *puella senex* of the *Táin*. The change is not surprising; it is within the range of the *topos* and, in a saga that goes out of its way to emphasize the hero's sexual attractiveness, the change fits well. In *Táin Bó Regamna* the encounter between hero and goddess is left inconclusive, pointing to a future doom not actually encompassed by the tale itself. The dialogue exchange between the two also develops a significant new detail in the *Táin Bó Cúailnge*: here the hero's countercurse formula is changed from a simple, 'unless you leave me alone,' and brought into the dynamic frame of binary opposition: the goddess is threatened with maiming in return for her cursing of the hero unless he counters the curse with a blessing (*bia fónd anim sin coro secha bráth bennachtan fort*, ll. 1861ff.). The word *bennacht* and possibly the concept itself is, of course, a Christian borrowing and the subsequent scene of blessing and healing involves an interesting over-compensation in the gloss that attempts to bring it back to the fictive pagan context: *'Bid slán doduc!' ol Cú Culaind. 'Bennacht dé 7 andé fort!' ol sé. Déi leó-som in t-áes cumachta, andéi immorro in t-áes trebtha.* ['Health to the giver!' said Cú Chulainn. 'The blessing of god and ungod on you!' he said. Their gods were the powerful ones and their ungods were the farming ones] (ll. 2043–5).[25]

From this digressive look at the Regamain tale one can better appreciate the variant structuring of the scene in the major saga. But though this presumes that *Táin Bó Regamna* is an earlier text than our present text of Recension I, it clearly never stood alone as a free-standing saga text. Its very structure of uttered future threats that are intended to be played out in the bigger *Táin* marks it as a composition designed to serve the interests of the larger work.[26] The Morrígain's triplicate wounding, her associations with healing milk, and the manner in which she tricks Cú Chulainn into healing her aligns her with the cunning of supernatural raptors in Irish folklore generally and is also reflected elsewhere in Irish saga material.[27] The fight with Lóch is complicated by her intervention. Indeed there are serpentine features to Lóch also; he is twice said to have a horned skin which renders him invulnerable. This is not the only dislocation of normal narrative order: the mutual wounding and healing of Cú Chulainn and the Morrígain is interrupted by his '*M'óenurán*' poem, a move that puzzled later handlers of the text. But layering in here the cry for help as prelude to his healing from Lug serves to signal the turning, which this rewriting of the scene effects, away from the problematic trap of false healing by the death goddess and her cow and towards the benign healing by a more acceptable pagan sovereign figure, Lug.[28]

The *Clamor*

In his crisis of vulnerability Cú Chulainn resorts to a direct appeal for help in the poem '*M'óenurán dam ar étib*,' The verse is neither in the archaic metric style nor marked as of special note (that is, with *r.*) in the manuscripts. Moreover, it bears some signs that what is expressed here may have displaced and suppressed a pre-existing textual form: a syllabic poem of which only the opening line, *ní airciú a n-átha la linni*, survives leaving only a trace in the anticipatory mark, *7 rla*. '*M'óenurán dam ar étib*' is also displaced from its regular Recension I place in C. The underlying model for the poem is the idea of *clamor*, in the simple form of a warning cry, a stratagem resorted to at other points in the narrative by Cú Chulainn's father, Sualtaim, at his son's insistence: *Fir gontair, mná brattar, baí agthar!* [Men are wounded, women snatched, cattle driven off!] (ll. 3410–53, passim).[29] The *clamor* is traditionally the recourse of those without power and it is in this idiom of human vulnerability that Cú Chulainn's cry for help is delivered.[30] The reader comes closer to the inner workings and emotional frailties of the saga hero here than at any other point in the narrative. The play of meaning that emerges for this poem when it is read in an intertextual context must now be considered.

All the Lonely People

What is of particular interest is the formulaic quality of the opening line. Its closest analogue is the opening lines of the Old Irish religious poem *M'aenarán dam isa sliab*, with which it shares the device of a *dúnad* on the words *m'áen/m'óenuran*.[31] This poem is somewhat unusual in that at least three very different versions of it survive, attesting perhaps to its continuous and popular use as a prayer through the entire medieval period.[32] It is incorporated into Manus O'Donnell's *Betha Colaim Cille* and it is possible, as Carney suggests, that the second recension of the poem was the product of a collecting and revising project undertaken in preparation for the planned new Life of the saint.[33] The circumstances of the poem's utterance as given in the O'Donnell *Life* are reminiscent of one of the oldest providential scenes in Irish hagiography: the escape of Patrick from his enemies and the recital of Patrick's *Lorica* poem.[34] There is some incidental resemblance to the present *Táin* poem context in the hagiographical model: the forces of the hostile ruler massed in waiting, the motif of invisibility, and the fact of the poem's invocation as protective spell countering the evil palpable around the hero.[35]

I would like to go into some of the details of the pseudo-Columban poem here in order to map out one large controlling idea that is clearly evident in the religious verses but also lurking below the surface of the treatment of the epic hero's vulnerability. There is the obvious consonance between the opening lines: behind the *Táin* piece is the shadow of the punning doublet, *étaib/shétaib* [hosts/ways]. Whether we take *étaib* as his massed enemies or the cattle milling about, the ghost of a religious line lies behind as a benign presence. The whole context of Cú Chulainn's predicament is his fear of collapsing into the terror of the liminal unknown – now become tangible in the sinister other-worldly aggression of the female Morrígain – and the disconcerting psychic confusion of having to fight his magically endowed double, his foster-brother, Lóch. It is against such terrors, especially the major category of the spells of women, worldly or other-worldly, that the Christian poems are directed.[36] In these Christian poems one touches on two types of interrelated terror: outside the known domestic space the individual is prey to the alien and other-worldly forces which civilization consigns to the margins. The destabilizing and raptorial forces of the other world remained a continuous concern in Irish tradition with many examples in Irish folkloric belief even down to recent times. The sinister forces that await the individual once he steps outside the borders of the tribe are parallelled by the Christian soul's experience of the perils awaiting the newly departed soul in the world beyond the body as the soul moves through the cosmic zones of hell/heaven. Ultimately, of course, it is this model of the other-world space beset by demonic forces at every stage that lies behind the medieval doctrine of the seven deadly sins.[37]

When Lug first arrives on the scene he is identified by Láeg as an *óenfer* (l. 2090), a lone man. Cú Chulainn in turn identifies himself as *m'óenur* (l. 2102). As Lug exits the text he again emphasises the term *óenur* (l. 2183) with respect to the hero, this time ratifying a transformed Cú Chulainn in his utterly unique status as the paramount hero, and so providing a lexically themed closure to the whole incident that began with Cú Chulainn's anguished cry: *m'óenurán dam*. In this register of aloneness the key term by which Cú Chulainn identifies himself is this *óenurán*. The word *óenurán* itself, it may be noted, seems to have a specific range of usage. Its best-known occurrence is probably as the first line of the attractive monastic poem, *M'óenurán im aireclán*.[38] I here list examples – not necessarily complete – of the term in order to be able to draw some conclusions about its semantic range as used in the Cú Chulainn *clamor*.

(a) The monastic poem above: *M'óenurán im aireclán/ cen duinnén im gnáis*. The several *án*-type diminutives of the first quatrain in this so-called hermit poem mark it as a monastic devotional *jeu d'esprit*, and there is a well-developed riff on the word *óenurán* covering the final two stanzas after the first *dúnad*, with the word itself providing the closure.[39]

(b) What may be its earliest occurrence is in the Bangor-related text of *Aided Echach Meic Maireda*, in a poem uttered by the heroine, the mermaid saint Li Ban[42] (*LU*, ll. 2925–3134). In a context that is not fully explained for this tale Li Ban is turned into a mermaid following the creation of Loch nEachach and finally seeks baptism from St Comgall's community in Bangor. In her poem there is some use of diminutives and a stanza describing her ordeals in the lake after being cut off from her own kin begins: *M'óenurán im rommra ro* [I am all alone in my great expanse of waters] (*LU*, l. 3105). Carney dates the text as after the seventh century but before 800.[40]

(c) The term also occurs in the poem to the Virgin Mary by Blathmac, dated ca. 750 by Carney:[41] *sirsan dot mac – dígrais dál, ron-ailt-siu a oenurán* [happy for your son – great the occasion – whom you reared alone] (ll.720–1).[42] The specific context here is the contrast between the memory of the humble childhood of Christ reared by his mother with no paternal kindred, and his present post-crucifixion victory as he brings back from hell to heaven the whole human family as his household.

(d) What is probably the most appealing use of the term comes from the early ninth-century poem on the monastic scholar's cat, *Messe ocus Pangur bán*. In a poem rich in self-reflection on his own intellectual and monastic life, the monk envisages Pangur's life as both in harmony with and contrasted to his own: *Cia beimmi a-min nach ré / ní derban cách a chéle: / maith la cechtar nár a dán; / subaigthius a óenurán* [Though we are like this together at all times, neither of us impedes the other. Each of us loves his craft, in our separate solitudes we delight in our skills].[43] This is probably the most sophisticated use of the term in the list so far. A basic monastic usage of *óenurán* as human solitude and absence from kin is presumed and is then combined with a compensatory relationship of man and animal living in a site of realized redemption, harmonizing nature and culture in friendship and understanding, close, and yet separate by virtue of difference of species.

(e) A story concerning Cormac mac Airt and Ciarnat with whom he falls in love. This incurs the jealousy of his wife Ethne. Forced to grind corn with a quern like a slave, Ciarnat is marvellously helped by Cormac's provisioning her with a mill: *Tairrustair uirri in rí rán / ina tigh na háenarán / co rus-toirrcestar fo leth / íar sin co nár fét robleth* [The great king came upon her in her house, all alone as she was; and he made her pregnant and she was not able to grind corn after it].[44]

(f) In a lighter vein there is the random quatrain from the Middle-Irish metrical tract: *Ní fetar / cia lassa fífea Etán; / acht ro-fetar Etán bán / nicon fhífea a hoenurán* [I don't know who will sleep with Etan; but the fair Etan know this well – she is not about to sleep alone].[45] The light touch here should not obscure for us the fact that this reference to a woman pursuing her desires independently stays within the register of a socially marginal and unprotected state.

(g) Here one might also add the pieces linked by a common phrase in the traditions on the mad King Suibhne, once in a piece dated from the ninth century and again reused in the twelfth-century saga,

Buile Suibhne: The Adventures of Suibhne Geilt.[46] In the early poem attributed to Suibhne Geilt the first line, *Mairiuclán hi Túaim Inbir*, is glossed with the phrase *barr eidhin*. This piece, with its rhyming diminutives, obviously belongs to a monastic devotional milieu; the note is struck of the solitary person, kinless by choice, of one who though alone admits no barriers between himself and the con-templative's cosmic vision of a creator. The phrase is incorporated again into the setting of the twelfth-century saga in a context heavy with kin-based issues.[47] Suibhne's sister's son, Loingsechán, in an attempt to lure the mad king back to his senses and his home and station lies to him and tells him his family is dead. In the scene leading to this, Suibhne's reaction includes a recognition of who he is, and the need to acknowledge his sin and do penance for it: *Do chath rod, / a Dhé nimhe, ní ma lott, / Bá Suibhne Geilt m'ainm iar sin, / mh'aonar dhamh a mbarr eidhin* [Unluckily did I go to a fierce battle, God of heaven. After it I was called Suibhne the Grazer, alone as I am on top of an ivy clump] (ll. 565–9). He pities his own isolation, the hardships he has endured and the constant lack of sleep in his new life of abjection. Some of Suibhne's comments on the so-called tragic news from Loingsechán also recall the context of the Cú Chu-lainn piece. His stoic use of proverbs echoes their use in the *Táin*: *adúdh re hénoires* [trying to create fire from one brand] (l. 835), ech-oes Cú Chulainn's cry on the note of *óen*: *ro bíi cosnom im óenchend / acht nád lassa nach óenchrand*. Similarly, Suibhne's *as dorn im dhiaidh* [it is a fist around smoke] (l. 838), recalls *is gat im gainem na im grian* [it is a withe around sand or sunlight] (l. 3462), of one of the LL poems in the 'Fight with Ferdiad' episode.[48] To sum up the Suibhne evidence: though the exact term *óenurán*, marked by the devotional diminutive, is not found in the Suibhne tradition there are traces of a similar contextual understanding of the state of aloneness as one finds for the rest of the samples. More significantly, perhaps, the use of proverbial *vanitas vanitatum* sayings brings Suibhne and Cú Chulainn together in the dead zone of abnegation, of heroic loss of confidence in their previous confidently held selves.

It is evident that certain types of people experience aloneness as a specifically marked state in early Irish traditions. Some of the lonely ones are women faced with the burden of raising a child alone without conventional marriage or kin supports. Other women like Li Ban suffer the loss of kindred and suffer displacement of space or state of being.

Lonely male figures are ascetics who have placed themselves beyond their kindred for the love of God, or individuals, such as Suibhne or Li Ban, who have lost their place in the civilized world. If one were to characterize the usage of the word *oénurán* in monastic tradition one might say that it occurs as an item in a terminology of vulnerability and liminality which is itself bounded by the larger frame of reference of Christian abnegation and trust expressiveness. The idiom of pathos summoned for Cú Chulainn's heroic aloneness comes about because much of what he suffers – bodily harm, deprivation, lack of sleep etc. – can be parallelled in Christian asceticism. Finally, and this is the key to a reading of Cú Chulainn's poem as a re-formed Christian one, is the acrostic that informs its structure. As I note above, the first letters of the four quatrains taken together read **M-A-R-B**, thus unmistakably linking this poem to the devotional poem associated with a hermit Marbán and his half-brother King Guaire.[49] Scholars agree that this Marbán is an entirely fictitious creation owing his existence to the metonymic quality of his name as appropriate to a religious ascetic. This same King Gúaire, one recalls, is associated with a developing myth of the *Táin* transmission. But though the Cú Chulainn poem echoes the monastic voice it is quite to be expected that in the interests of saga decorum significant elements are lacking or suppressed. Cú Chulainn is not 'dead' in quite the same way that a hermit or dependent woman would consider themselves 'dead,' as without the claim to a legitimating socially active presence. The dimension of trust in a providential Christian deity is not expressly voiced in the *Táin* saga; instead, it is deflected into an alternate and substitute construct appropriate to epic, the compassionate helper as pagan god.

Providence versus Fate

It is well to dwell an instant on the distance travelled in this scene from the image of the confident young hero who had earlier famously declared: *'Acht ropo airderc-sa, maith lim cenco beind acht óenlá for domun'* ['Provided I am famous, I do not care if I be but one day on earth!'] (ll. 640–1). That paradigmatic heroic self-assertion serves as an index of heroic completeness: a short life precludes any opportunity to open up the issue of existence as complex or problematic in any way. One of the facilitating mindsets of such a heroic articulation is the idea of fate which, despite, or perhaps because of, the long tradition of unreflecting heroic response to death, has never seemed to loom large in a consideration of Irish heroic behaviour. Paradoxically, it is Cú Chulainn's experience of weakness that opens his story up to issues of destiny. By returning to the first Columban item mentioned above, the poem 'M'áenurán dam isa sliab' one can see more clearly how to reconstruct a heroic thematics of destiny for the Táin scene, a thematics that would lead on from the very clearly articulated occasion of the young Cú Chulainn's statement on seeking glory over old age. The whole poem is a little meditation on fate and destiny, of which one quatrain in particular is of interest to us here:

In laech reanas a c[h]neas mbán
isin áth fri galus ngúr
ní nesu do éc, cid baeth,
indás dun gaeth bís ar cúl

[The warrior who utterly expends his beautiful body
in the ford against fierce aggression,
Though he be reckless, death is no nearer to him
than it is to the coward in the rear.][50]

It is indeed tempting to think of the exemplary 'young warrior at the ford' as none other than Cú Chulainn himself, and the envisaged scene as representing his dilemma at this juncture in the narrative, but of course we have no way of knowing if there is a real relationship of influence between the two pieces or, indeed, which poem may have influenced the other; the use of the baeth, gaeth rhyme in the religious poem implies something of a critical distancing from the business of making brave. Yet the issue of Cú Chulainn's destiny is certainly more real at this point in the saga than at any other. I argued above for accepting Baumgarten's emendation in the Táin Bó Regamna text so as to read the words of the Morrígain as, 'I am and shall be encompassing your death,' and taking this as the source of the malign goddess scenes in the Táin. Here too, the shadow of other clearer forms – in this case, the curse of the death goddess as a given, a potent and unwavering force of pagan destiny – suggests itself powerfully to the reader who rethinks this scene reinforced by that harsher older reading. So, Cú Chulainn, the culturally informed reader of signs knows and enters this scene already a marked man. But under certain limits fate can be countered by a higher and more powerful divine speaker. Hence, in the concluding words of Lug to his son he denies the Morrígain's reading its effectiveness, resets the heroic destiny clock and assures the hero: *'Acht imbir-seo féin do gním gascid t'óenur forsna slúaga úair ní leó atá commus t'anma don chur sa'* ['but inflict your warrior deeds, you alone, on the armies, because it is not with them that the power over your life resides at this time'] (ll. 2182–4).[51]

In the Name of the Father/God

Help, as the audience knows, comes to Cú Chulainn, following his *clamor*, not from Ulster where he seeks it through a deployment of interpellation of the father/mentor Conchobar, but from the other world. And it now remains to analyse the various elements – divine and human – of this second half of the diptych. First, one notes the manner of Lug's arrival on the scene of action. Cú Chulainn's power cry, his *srem caurad* which prefaces it, is by this stage no more than a kind of lower-scale reflex of the original effect of his *riastarthae* powers. Its echo produces an eruption of miscellaneous non-human types of terrifying other-worldly responses; *coro recratár bánánaig 7 boccánaig 7 geniti glinni 7 demna aeóir re úathgráin na gára dosbertatár ar aird* [and the spectres and spirits, the demons of the glens and the demons of the air gave back the cry with the sheer terror of the cry that he gave forth] (ll. 2083–4).[52] The effect is to reiterate the power of the death goddess at this time: *Cordas mesc in Nemain forsin tslog* [The Neman attacked the host] (l. 2085). Formless terror is again shaping itself as in the first night scene of the Boyhood Deeds sequence, itself, we remember, a tale of the dark told in the dark. Doubleness and chaotic indefinition is further rendered by the arrangement of the day/night sequencing. As day ends the lurid scene is backlit by the rays of the setting sun and the isolation of the hero is expressed by placing him in the small circle of light afforded by Láeg's campfire. In contrast to this melodramatic positioning and the pervasive horror of the war goddess, the arrival of Lug is marked by no such pyrotechnics.[53] He is invisible to the armies, though his appearance follows an accepted formula for describing an other-world apparition: *'ni saig nech fair 7 ní saig-seom for nech feib nachas faiced nech hé'* ['no one approaches him and he makes for no one as if no one could see him'] (ll. 2097–8). Lug is 'textually neutral' in that there is nothing in the description of his appearance – green mantle, silver brooch – to mark him as anything other than ordinary. He is not even identified specifically by Cú Chulainn, that excellent reader of his own saga: *'cia dom chartibh síthc[h]aire-sa sein dom airchiseacht-sa ... ar*

Táin Bó Cúalng _don chur sa'_ [one of my other-worldly friends come to lament me on the _Táin Bó Cúailnge_ at this time] (ll. 2099–100).[54] Indeed the narrator himself moves into the scene to comment at this point by re-echoing Cú Chulainn's _Is fír sin_ with _Ba fír ém do Choin Chulaind anní hísin_ [That was a true statement of Cú Chulainn's] (l. 2103). We are thus guided into a mode of suspended disbelief as the delicate process of staging a god is re-enacted. By what means does the narrator then move into the major epic mode of theophany?

The Field Doctor

Lug comes as a healing god, and though his intervention has other aspects this is his primary function. There exists a fair amount of commentary on the question of the Celtic reflexes of presumed Indo-European tripartite healing systems.[55] In this vein the Irish example of healing most commonly cited is that of the incident of Dían Cécht and his son in the saga, _Cath Maige Tuired_.[56] In that text much care is taken to assign specific tasks and to identify specific characteristics to the various members of the divine race, the _Tuatha Dé_. There, however, Lug is not assigned a healing role. How, then, is one to understand Lug's healing here?

If we reach for consonant Indo-European features, several models suggest themselves, the obvious one being that already cited – the triple healing pattern where medical ministration by word, wound probing, and herbs are aligned with the three complementary classes of an Indo-European social grouping. Thus Lug accomplishes all three types of healing together here: he puts healing herbs in the wounds as a third-function figure, he tents the wounds as in military surgical healing, and, as sovereign figure par excellence, he heals by therapeutic word. It is difficult to proceed beyond this general pattern, however, and it is rather the double structure of call and help that interests me here. If one begins to consider classical epic influences, such as might have been available to Irish storytellers, then the benign help afforded by Apollo to Hercules assumes importance. But more specifically, there is in fact a clear classical epic occasion where a wounded warrior appeals to a god and receives the consequent healing visit of that god. In the _Iliad_ Hector is indeed visited by Apollo when he lies exhausted after battle. Apollo rouses him to fight again and promises that he himself will go before him and fight with him.[57] More nearly alike is a relatively minor figure in the _Iliad_, Glaucos, who lying wounded, cries out to Apollo:

O lord, heal this wound,
Lull me my pains, put vigour in me! Let me
shout to my Lykians, move them into combat!
Let me give battle for the dead man here.[58]

Apollo hears him, 'cutting his pain, making the dark blood dry on his deep wound then filled his heart with valour' (l. 528). In an epic context, this is a classic expression of Apollonian healing following the model of supplicant/answering god as we seek to find it in the *Táin*.

Though, as I note above, the healing worked by Lug in the *Táin* can indeed be made to answer the Indo-European formula as described by Puhvel and others, it must also be noted that the dominant healing motif is incubatory here, thus bringing us closer to the actual major praxis of late Antique and Celtic Apollonian and especially Aesculapian modes of healing. Sleeping in a place that is the sanctuary of the god and receiving a therapeutic communication with the god is not too far from the sleep in the vicinity of a sacred place or a necropolis. It is also a common visionary experiential motif in Irish saga in general and there is no reason to set aside the literary evidence for the custom. The locus of Cú Chulainn's vision and incubatory healing is designated as an ancient grave, a *fert,* and the appearance of Lug from his other-world dwelling nearby, the *síd*, encourages thinking of the two terms as identical.

Are we to assume then as sufficient explanation for the scene a general equivalence of Lug and a Celticized healing Apollo through the route of conscious epic rewriting? This would be to separate it stylistically from the first half of the supplication/healing diptych which seems to be basically Christian in its underlying rhetorical mode. I believe that one can suggest a possible route of transmission whereby a Christianized version of the Apollonian/Aesculapian archetype might have found a place in this imagining of a healing god.

We know that the Celtic Apollonian shrines of Gaul and Britain continued to attract clients beyond the Christian period, even perhaps as late as the sixth century in Gaul.[59] These may have, in some measure, inhibited the growth of the cult of Aesculapius, though a consideration of the layout of such healing complexes shows that the healing procedures must have had many aspects such incubation, bathing, and supplication in common. We also know that the cult of the healing Apollo was easily assimilated with native Celtic healing divinities of a more diffuse type. The evidence for the continuance of incubatory practices at Apollonian healing centres, as well as Asculapian shrines, in Celto-

Roman Britain is less well attested than in Gaul. There are, however, votive inscriptions from a number of British sites.[60] Further, as Aline Rousselle has pointed out in the case of the shrine of Saint Martin of Tours, we cannot really separate in terms of general praxis or social function the healing practises of Christian and pagan shrines.[61] Carl Hauck has also used the evidence from the Germanic barbarian gold bracteates of the pre-conversion period to demonstrate the intrusive and almost universal use in the Germanic world of the healing iconography of Aesculapius employed by the élites as protective amulet.[62] He has further shown the iconography of Aesculapius spilling over into the Christian iconography of the Merovingian period and providing a model for the image of the *Christus medicus*.[63]

The *topos* of the comparison of Christ to both Asculapius and Apollo is extremely common in the Latin West and the image of the *Christus medicus* is frequently deployed.[64] By the fourth century the extreme and immediate hostility to Asculapius had abated and the image of the *Christus medicus* had a general application in the plan of salvation as the enemy of the devil. As Ambrose expressed it: 'If we have been in the power of the devil, we are no longer. We have found shelter with the Physician. He has healed our former wounds ...'[65] In both patristic excursus, in the work of Augustine, Ambrose, and Jerome, and in the evidence of popular religious practice, there was an insistence on the dual nature of healing whether spiritual or physical, viz. the need for the suppliant's cry along with the intervention of the divine healer. A fair example of popular usage is demonstrated by the wording of the Timgad inscription from North Africa: *Bonis bene et gaudete Petrus et Lazarus; petere summo de Rege, subvenire tibi ... rogo te Domine suvveni Christe tu solus medicus sanctis et poenitentibus amare manibus et pedibus Deum* [Good to the good, rejoice; Peter and Lazarus; ask of (?) the high king to come and help (?) you ... I beseech you Lord, Christ, come to my aid; you alone are the doctor to holy ones and sinners; love (?) God with hands and with feet].[66] The popular and scriptural base for this is found in the use of the Psalms themselves as protective devices. In this spirit Augustine, in his sermons, returned repeatedly to the theme of Christ the physician. Indeed much of Augustine's use of the Passion in the Sermons as illustrating the heroic competence of *Christus medicus* is structurally devised as formulae of sympathetic magic:

> Relieve my deep wound after thy great mercy: the wound I have is deep, but in the Almighty I take refuge; I would despair of my own so deadly wound, unless I could find such a good Physician.[67]

What was I, unless Thou didst heal? Where was I lying, unless Thou didst come to me ? Indeed with a huge wound I was endangered but my wound itself cried out for the Almighty Physician.

In the *Soliloquia,* a text known and glossed in the circle of Eriugena and his fellow Irishmen, there is the following: *satis mihi sunt vulnera mea, quae ut sanentur, pene quotiidianis fletibus Deum rogare* (my wounds are such that to heal them I must beseech God daily with tears).[68] Early Irish devotional texts, in particular the witness of hagiography, is markedly thin on evidence for popular cults of healing associated with holy figures or places.[69] So one must perforce look at slightly different types of healing for comparably structured scenes.

Patrick, a Father behind Fathers

A more direct site of reference for Cú Chulainn's healing is the strange account in St Patrick's *Confession* of his being assailed by demonic forces in the transitional phase of his early conversion. After a night-time ordeal during which the demon takes away all his physical strength he is finally relieved by calling out to a syncretic Helios/Elijah/Helias and by being touched by the first rays of the rising sun:

> *Eadem vero nocte eram dormiens et fortiter temptavit me Satanas, quod memor ero quamdiu fuero in hoc corpore, et cecidit super me veluti saxum ingens et nihil membrorum meorum praevalens. Sed unde me venit ignaro in spiritu ut Heliam vocarem? Et inter haec vidi in caelum solem oriri et dum clamarem 'Heliam, Heliam' uiribus meis, ecce splendor solis illius decidit super me et statim discussit a me omnem gravitudinem, et credo quod a Christo Domino meo subventus sum et spiritus eius iam tunc clamabat pro me.*

[That same night I was asleep and Satan tried/tempted? me severely, and its memory will remain with me as long as I live. He fell on me like a huge boulder and all the parts of my body were powerless. But from whence did there come to me, ignorant in spiritual things as I was, the idea that I should call on Helias? And as that was happening I saw the sun rising in the sky, as I was calling, Helia! Helia! with all my strength, and behold the splendour of that sun fell on me and immediately all the oppression left me. And I believe that it was from Christ, the Lord, that my help came and that it was his spirit in me that cried out for me.][70]

The passage has been much discussed and its editor, Ludwig Bieler, while accepting as relevant to this account the widespread patristic equivalence of Helios and Elijah, discounted the idea that Patrick himself was fully aware of the connection.[71] He also rejected as arbitrary the suggestions that it is to be connected with the cry of Christ on the cross in the Passion narratives of Matthew and Mark.[72] In so doing, he failed to see the rhetorical function of this passage in Patrick's autobiography. The language is deliberately indeterminate and liminal so as to reflect dramatically Patrick's own consciousness at this period of his life. He has turned to God, and God has rescued him, but he is still in the process of distancing himself from his surrounding pagan environment. He is as yet unlettered in his faith, hence that faith still reflects the flawed nature of his experience and environment hitherto. In that sense, it is proper that the shadows of the Old Testament and even pagan paradigms are his only resources, not just considered separately but in the very form of syncretic inchoateness in which Patrick projects them in this retrospective work. His separation from his pagan environment as a specific process or *rite de passage*, both physical and mental, is rendered dramatically in a series of exemplary incidents at this point in the *Confession*; the incident of his prostration and ordeal at the hands of diabolical forces serves to illustrate the rightness of his abiding trust in a Spirit who guides and transforms his own imperfect and instinctual devotional language born of solitude and deprivation. That the dual cry, *Heliam, Heliam*, happens to reflect the dual cry, *Eli, Eli*, of Christ on the cross, and that it also calls up a dramatic confrontation between the benign solar forces and the malign powers of night, merely shows how Patrick intends us to be aware of the manner in which his own self was balanced at the edge of two worlds and two belief systems at this point in his life.[73]

In discussing this passage it may be well to consider how this motif from the *Confessions* fared in the subsequent Patrician Lives. In Muirchú's Life the passage is tidied up somewhat and does not reflect the original's patent attempt to reconstruct and reflect the confused nature of Patrick's own thought processes as he remembered the scene.[74] In Colgan's *Trias Thaumaturges* the scene is rendered as one of exclusively spiritual significance; it is the prophet Elijah who is the ministering helper and there is something of the original's acknowledgment of the weight and importance of the scene to Patrick himself.[75] In the varying versions of the *Vita Tertia* the scene is even further released, so to speak, from the confining structure of Patrick's thoughts and is rendered dramatic, with Helias and the demonic visitor as actors in the event:

> *Fortiter temptauit eum sathanas, et cecidit diabolus super eum tribus diebus et tribus noctibus, et oppressit eum grauitate saxi ingentis, ita ut nichil membrorum suorum posset mouere. Tunc Patricius uocauit Heliam bina uoce in adiutorium. Venitque Helias et liberauit eum. Dixitque ad eum diabolus: 'Ab hac die non habeo potestatem in te usque ad diem mortis tue' Statimque ortus est ei sol et splendor et eiecit ab eo omnem torporem et grauitatem et omnes caliginum tenebras, et restitute sunt ei uires eius.*[76]

> [Satan tempted him greatly, and the devil lay on him for the space of three days and three nights weighing him down with the rock of a huge weight, so that he could not move a limb. Then Patrick invoked Helias twice for help. And Helias came and freed him. And the devil said to him: 'From this day I have no power over you until the day of your death.' Suddenly the sun rose in its splendour and cast from him all torpor and oppression and all the darkness of the night, and all his energies were restored to him.]

Here I have quoted the version of this Life where the speech of the devil is at its most evolved. Note that it is also approaching closer still to the sentiments of fate expressed by Lug in the *Táin* when he assures Cú Chulainn that the Morrígain's assemblage of hostile manifestations cannot hurt him on this occasion as his fated time is not yet come.

What is also of interest here in the context of a discussion of powers of healing is the title of Lug's healing poem in Recension I: *Éli Loga*. In treating the word *Éli* the *DIL* editors seem to accept that the term in the *Táin* might have something to do with the invocation in Patrick's *Confessions* but they do not specify.[77] They also, however, link *ele* (salve) with *éli*, though the glossary tradition derives this latter term quite correctly from the Greek *elon* and the Latin *oleum*. Two terms and two concepts of healing, both linguistically separate, are synthesised here: on the one hand there is the idea of a healing word process in conjunction with a ritual act, the application of a physical unction; on the other, a healing through the power of particular words alone, whether rendered strange and multivalent through being foreign and exotic, or rendered magical because they have been used before in a sacred or empowering context. Christ's double '*Eli, Eli*' becomes the *Éli* of Lug and, as an aspect however awkwardly conjoined with the *Táin* healing scene, answers to the requirements of a healing ritual in the world of the *Táin* scribes.[78]

Parallel usages also exist which may flesh out the idea of ritual healing. In the St Gall Incantations, dated eight to ninth century, there is a charm against a spike that states: *Arnoib briathraib rolabrustar crist assa chroich diuscart dím an delg* [By the sacred words that Christ spoke on his cross remove from us this spike].[79] Though we cannot be sure that the charm refers to the *'Eli, Eli'* utterance, it is likely to be so as the use of exotic naming techniques and languages is the common mark of charm language efficiency. Elsewhere from the same period, in the Stowe Missal Spells against a thorn, we have as an alternative to the words of Christ, the healing power of the sun's brightness: *líi grene frisben att, benith galar* [May the sun's brightness attack the swelling; may it strike the sickness].[80] Wounds, then, can occur in a heroic or an ordinary domestic context, and both can be seen to be addressed by the same healing techniques, whether pagan or Christian, or ideally now, a mixture of both.

Many of the rhapsodic elements of Lug's *for-/fer-dord* remain opaque.[81] Its title, however, suggests its anchorage in a Christianized syncretic complex for which we have some evidence in the documents of Irish Christian tradition. And I think it must be conceded that, attractive as the Lug/Apollo Indo-European syncresis is – even mediated through an Aesculapian model of institutional healing in the world of the late empire – it is still necessary to posit a more proximate conduit for the typology of a destroying spirit/healing god duo. One aspect of that process might reasonably be exemplified by the Patrician *Confessio* dossier, itself deriving much of its metaphoric power from the syncretic possibilities available to Late Antique Christianity in a way I have described above. Such an exemplar would have been accessible to a Christian monastic culture and may well have supplied a lead for the recreation of the visitation of the native god, that most numinous of moments in an imagined pagan – indeed, epic – time past.

At Last, a Father!

Being a god is, however, only one of Lug's roles here. There is a romantic – as opposed to an epic – troping to Cú Chulainn's story. It is also a tale of the son who through adventure, bitter experience, and testing of the self, finds his true father who has been absent since his conception. The exchanges between the hero and the divine father are replete with a tenderness and, indeed, tentativeness absent from the tone registers of the saga up to this point. This switch to another register is first indicated by the charioteer Láeg, who spots the single man approaching them, moving as if on another plane straight through the opposing army. He addresses his hero for the first and only time as *a Chúcán* [little Hound]. As the Irish grammatical glosses on Priscian's Grammar note, this diminutive form of address is proper when addressing youngsters and is to be understood as a part of a register of affection.[82] Indeed the whole scene is framed on this note: when Cú Chulainn expresses sorrow for the death of the boy troop while he slept, Lug consoles him and addresses him with this same affectionate vocative. Again there is a low-level set of puns and allusions surrounding the first verbal exchange of the whole scene: Lug's *ferda sin*, can be read as 'that is excellent,' or 'that is manly.' O'Rahilly favoured the first reading, but if I am correct in seeing a far greater sense of language subversion in the saga than has hitherto been acknowledged, then the call to protocols of male recognitions is also key in the exchange.[83] Cú Chulainn's modest response *Ni mór side etir* is obviously a surface disclaimer to the compliment of manliness/excellence and registers emphatically how completely his splendid heroic isolation has changed from the triumphal poem of a few incidents back: *Fó mo cheard láechdachta*. He is now at his lowest and most vulnerable. When the offer of assistance comes, Cú Chulainn does not reject it: he does not assume that help means either military assistance or nuisance distraction as he did with the offer of his earthly father earlier; he merely asks who his mysterious visitor is.

Lug's response should normally be a moment of high drama, but the revelation of paternity opens up for Cú Chulainn no responding joy or glory. From his reaction to the revelation it is clear that Cú Chulainn's trajectory of thought is leading him into a state of regression such that his new-found state of sonship is itself elided at the very moment of discovery. What he seems to acknowledge most is his own broken body and the possibility that the visitor – writ small in his consciousness as father, writ large as magician as he originally surmised – might help if he should ask humbly for healing. The mutually chanted *ferdord* (man-chant) assumes greater importance for its ability to suggest a mediating term between maleness as fused genetic bond and maleness as structured subordination and mutuality, whether of son to father in a legal sense or adolescent to powerful mentor. It does seem, nevertheless, that some residual sense of sonship and dream of the father's presence surfaces in Cú Chulainn and remains as a kind of lingering residue. When he awakens, healed of his wounds, he begs Lug to remain with him and fight by his side. It is as if the return of the father conjures up a prelapsarian dream of gendered sameness and perfect parity between the young hero and the newly discovered parent. But the Oedipal laws of father-son fissure are pitilessly enforced. Lug counters by invoking a solitary state of heroism where the rules of glory cannot allow parity of heroic action, even between father and son. One must succeed the other; the two may not act as one. With the hero we, the spectators to the drama, are returned from the brief sojourn in a tender other world and thrust out again to face the scene of battle.

Conclusions

Thus is acknowledged dramatically the essential duality of Irish thinking about the other world. With few exceptions the denizens of the other world are evil and demonic to the Christian inheritors of older pagan tradition. Offers of help from such as the Morrígain must be exposed as illusory and deadly. The fairest of faces can conceal the devil himself.[84] If Lug was not already benignly configured in Irish tradition, he would have had to be reinvented as he is here. The *Táin* 'myth' of Lug is distinctive; it is created for the purpose of countering on the level of secular epic the evil of a world above the human, registered entirely under the rubric of feminized demonism. Lug is the necessary male counterweight and the honourable exception to a malign 'other' domain.

Lévi-Strauss has spoken eloquently of the problems of history construction, of the 'fraudulent outlines' whereby the organiser of history purports to find alleged seamless historical continuities and definition.[85] Such 'fraudulent outlines' serve, in his view, as a product of 'abstraction,' of a means of escape from the basic terror in historical consciousness, the 'threat of infinite regress.' Such a model might also extend to the discursive segment which I have been analysing here, where one may observe the reconstruction of linear time sequences in the establishment of a human-divine genealogy. Spatial relations between this world and the next also serve to dramatize interactions between the characters in the staging of the constructed myth. We the present readers, no more than the medieval audience, will never know if the wounded suppliant/healing god scenario is intrinsic to the story of the *Táin* from the beginning and how 'natural' it would be for a saga writer to envisage Lug in such role. From what the text can tell us, a new divine paternal myth of Lug seems to have supplanted an older or more local one of Sualtaim as the 'father from the *síd*.' Neither will we ever know if and how this scene might witness as a reflex to an originary context of Indo-European Apollonian archetype or as a rewrite on classical models. What we do know is that it problematizes the naive idea of a native myth and, in so doing, raises further questions on how one handles sources and analogues. Something has been emplotted or fixed in the oldest surviving narrative of the *Táin* as we have it. How old it is may be questioned. But the 'fraudulent' outline of the Christain *topos* may indeed have served its reconstructive purpose and have saved those who received the *Táin*, now and in the past, from the fear of infinite regress into a directionless and speculative Celtic hall-of-mirrors past.

6 The Invention of Women in the *Táin*

Cathal mc Finguine, rí Herend, moritur, de quo Mór Muman dixit:
>*In tImblech*
>>*Ro sáer Ailbe dia bachail,*
>
>*is óen ina erdarcus*
>>*A úr dar étan Cathail.**

[Cathal mac Finguine, king of Ireland dies, of whom Mór of Munster said:
>Emly,
>>made great by Ailbhe's staff
>
>its one and only fame is now
>>its clay on Cathal's brow.]

Annals of Inisfallen, 742

Getting Sharp

One of the standard deconstructionist operations is to take whatever binary opposition that is deemed to dominate any given text and reverse it. This seems particularly apposite to a discussion of the way issues of gender shape narratives. As Roberta Krueger has remarked concerning French medieval romances, 'in the world of chivalric honor, the masculine hero is constructed in opposition to woman, upon whose objectification his honor depends.'[1] Staking out the

---

*An editor's note to these lines reads: 'As the ascription to [the woman] *Mór* Muman (+632) is an anachronism, Meyer suggests that *Fer* Muman, a poet of the 8th or 9th century, was the composer.' My comment: Cheated again!

domain of the feminine by reversing this process is a worthwhile operation in itself; it may have the additional benefit of being one of the best ways of gaining a perspective on the peculiarities of the fortress masculine. Clearly any breach in the stronghold of hegemonic male discourse in the saga must try to break women's cover and reposition them through a process of reading by indirection. In thinking about the form this chapter should take and how to make a fresh entry into the discourse of the feminine as it pertains to Irish saga tradition in general and the *Táin* in particular, it may prove useful to preface my analysis by sketching in some of the critical lines in the current feminist agenda in medieval literature; this will allow the reader to follow more clearly the trajectory of my rhetoric on the issue of how women are written into the *Táin*. But it must be emphasized again that the focus of this chapter is on the language of women rather than on the way in which that language refracts the historical reality of Irish women's lives in the past.

How to Make a Woman

I begin then, with some apologies for rather obvious statements, from the premise that behind an agenda such as the textual 'invention' of women lie the much wider issues of the ways in which culture is now conceptualized and the various modes of its articulation. It seems that current critical thought has designated two approaches as highly significant, both for what they have contributed to the study of women in the Middle Ages and also for the flaws inherent in the two perspectives. The first can be described as the structuralist/feminist view as it is used to describe the operations of the feminine in the record of the medieval past, a past in which can be included – by way of extension or analogy in this instance – early Irish culture. This approach, in the way that it often frames and situates a discourse about women in a mode of liminal process, makes use of the anthropological work of Victor Turner, and behind him of Arnold van Gennep, and is best exemplified in medieval studies by Caroline Bynum's enormously influential work on medieval women mystics, their discourse and praxis.[2] In Irish Studies a correspondingly influential literary study in this liminal mode is Nagy's *The Wisdom of the Outlaw*, a work I have used with profit earlier in this volume. Nagy's analysis concentrates on Fenian lore but he also looks, albeit incidentally, at the liminality of women by treating it as a subset of a dominant type, the Fenian social pattern.

In the structuralist or binary model, the feminine achieves the level of visibility in culture by being posited as existing in dialectal tension with the patriarchy. Thus a number of formulations and critical languages are made available from this perspective.[3] The feminine is defined as 'other,' as 'frame,' as 'non-representability,' as 'periphery' to the male agenda of self-justifying, signifying action, and hence of the central cultural modes of valorization.[4] In such terms of reference women are constituted as 'that which is other than culture,' as the site of undifferentiated nature, as the zone of the abject.[5] Thus for those who explore the idiom of the heroic, the general proposition is advanced that it is in the various acts that separate the male from the realm of the maternal that culture is founded and constituted.

This first approach is joined by the long-standing tradition of mythological criticism in Celtic scholarly writings which has framed the question of feminine presence in saga from the point of view of the sovereignty goddess model.[6] Here too, the ritual and discursive operations of culture are largely unproblematic: culture is always already there to be replicated but hardly to be (re)-invented, let alone radically changed or seriously contested.[7] In many ways a disruptive tension is most evident when the image which women characters are supposed to portray is most insistent: one is forced to look here for the rebound, the echo effect, where the over-determined figure so mythically construed begins to display the strain, and begins to look as if she may undermine or subvert the discourse into which she is forced. The stereotype of the goddess has remained, until lately, the dominant approach to the presence of the feminine in the *Táin*, though we are now beginning to see some interesting re-evaluations of the whole methodology of viewing women. Patricia Kelly has advanced an extremely interesting line of argument which analyses the actions of Medb in the *Táin* and, by turning the sovereignty principle argument around, succeeds in deconstructing it.[8] Recently too, Joanne Findon has circumvented the mythological approach and achieved some interesting results by concentrating on the position of women characters and their roles in narrative.[9]

From the mainline structuralist perspectives, valuable as they are, culture and the feminine in culture are essentialized. And a large question still looms. How, within this critical language, is one to factor in historical process? How does one see others – or as here, how did saga makers see the feminine – as historically constituted? The language of the sovereignty goddess could possibly be de-essentialized: one way would be to look outwards from her configuration to the social construction of the group and to the play of power and hegemonic voice in medieval Irish regional politics; but rarely is this path utilized as it might be to arrive at a dynamic model of historical change or of the part played by women in the historical process.[10] The exception to the difficulty of matching historical process to theory here is Máire Herbert's article on Irish sacred marriage considered as a transformation from metaphor to metonymy following a Barthesian line of argument.[11]

In a social constructionist view where the self figures as a way of speaking about social patterning, the figure of the feminine also tends to blur, dissolve, and retreat into a cipher, a metaphor for society and power.[12] In addition, there is still a tendency in Irish Studies to flatten historical difference by organizing insights around what one might call the great transformational models in Irish scholarship: the orality/literacy moment and the paganism/Christianity transition are two such powerful models that militate against diachronic or historicist readings of the feminine in texts.

Thus the important agenda of bringing these saga texts under more precise historical scrutiny, from the perspective of the women in the texts, has only just begun to be addressed and, as I have outlined above, it has proved difficult in several ways to insert the issue of the feminine into the historicist agenda.[13] Legal codes have been quarried in an attempt to read women more accurately into early Irish society and Irish saga texts; scholars such as Ó Corráin and Máirín Ní Dhonnchadha[14] may be said to be exploring the ways in which one might establish a developmental model in the discussion of women and their social definition over time even where the atemporal bias of written legal discourse in early Ireland militates against such a reading.[15]

The Words to Say Them

Here I want to press a little further into this matter of construing women in early Irish texts. Against the background of the major question of how women are read as historically constituted, I want to begin at a first stage of the premise by suggesting ways in which one might begin to explore the manner in which women are *textually* constituted in the *Táin*. Some well-known post-structuralist observations of Dominic LaCapra on the interpretative problem of history posed by the methodological contrast between great books and the archive will help to set up the argument:

> The archive as fetish is a literal substitute for the 'reality' of the past which is always already lost for the historian. When it is fetishized, the archive is more than the repository of traces of the past which may be used in its inferential reconstruction. It is a stand-in for the past that brings the mystified experience of the thing itself – an experience that is always open to question when one deals with writing and inscriptions.[16]

The contrast between the putative great canonical text and the fragmented archive is not the part of this statement that is useful for my purposes here; the condition of the textual entity, the *Táin*, works against one's seeing it as a fully realized canonical work. But the idea – insofar as it suggests opening up a concealed question – of a fissive and palimpsestic test such as the *Tain* as fetish and as stand-in may be conjured with to some purpose, if not with the pejorative deployment of the idea of the fetish which the historian in LaCapra possibly intends. There is really no such thing as the totally meaningful, totally illuminated reading, and any reader – even of a text defined as canonical, that is, a 'projected,' intentionally realized, artful, literary work – will always be guilty of the operations of the fetish in that all reading will be forced to carry undigested lumps of writing, where text will continue to baffle and the resultant reading will be necessarily as yet wholly literal, iterative and deferred. This is not a refusal on the readers' part to surrender all to the idea of the master narrative, transformed as great book. It is rather to compound two things: the refusal of the reader to acquiesce to an over-facile interpretation, and a wish to maintain a zone of pleasure around a work that comes to its contemporary reading site after a long and difficult trajectory. In this sense, the gapped, impaired, and intriguing reading that a scarred and fissured text demands has been honestly earned and is an honest part of its story.[17]

The mystification of the text need not be seen as a frustration of literary plenitude, as opposed to its troubling aspects when applied to historical enquiry: it constitutes its very condition and, if I shift the emphasis of LaCapra's phrase slightly, may be said to constitute the very site of all literary critical work. One further aspect of the *Táin* as archival fetish – that is, as a text stopping short of the canonical, and always liable to slip away from our integrative critical efforts – is the fact of its open-endedness and multiplicity; one is drawn to the site of mystification by its condition of interrupted integration and its imperfect replication, by the fact that there are several texts of the *Táin*. Not being a 'great book,' the text offers more surfaces, more entrances, in a Barthesian sense, to gain access by.[18] By paying particular attention to the shifts between the versions one can open up a useful space in that mystification. What can be said is still nothing completely cohesive as befits a lack of cohesion in the text: what one is voicing is merely one's sense of the pathways between and behind writing. These are some of the problematic entities to be negotiated in the construing of the feminine in the *Táin*. The position of women in the versions of the saga mirrors some of the frailty of the *Táin* textual archive itself. That some of these feminine textual sites may be contestatory and conflictual is, thus, to be expected: that some appearances of women in the text are provisional, textually frail and vulnerable to erasure, is thus easily imaginable in the cultural coding of a text such as the *Táin*. As with the thematics of other chapters in my study, finding women necessitates an approach that considers the two main recensions and marks their difference. It also means that I take for granted the excellent analyses that other scholars have made of the background and characteristics of Medb, the only dominant woman in the text. In chapter 1 I noted the reasons why I see Medb as a thoroughly modern queen for the twelfth century; I thereby demote her discourse from a hieratic goddess condition or even the parodic language of misogynists, to that of a more immediately innovating and threatening force in the social status quo.

Desperately Seeking Fedelm

Let us begin with a non-controversial view of the feminine in the text. Most scholars would place as central to its agenda the articulation of a preoccupation with heroic male militaristic behaviour and would locate the world of the feminine as tangential or in opposition to this. I take first a fairly simple example of the difficult articulation of the feminine in the interstices between versions. Towards the beginning of the narrative, Cú Chulainn and his father Sualtaim are lying in wait for the armies as they move across the central plains of Meath; the location in the environs of Kells is precisely given – indeed, updated by the *M* interpolator as Crossa Caíl. We begin with a refracted, dissipated sense of military action which, because of the flashbacks and the shifting of scenes from one side to the other without an actual meeting of the two, is as yet weak in the incidence of actual high heroics; but the glossing at least gives some confidence that the contributors to *LU* have focussed their attention on the narrative at this point. Cú Chulainn sends Sualtaim on an intelligence mission to Ulster, which, as we know, will be frustrating in that Ulster cannot or will not respond to the threat at the borders. In the meantime, he himself must, he says, go to keep a date he made with Fedelm Noíchroide. Though Cú Chulainn has a hunch (*menma*) that the armies are close he has other pressing business:

> Isim écen-sa techt i ndáil Fedelme Noíchride–.i. i ndáil a hinailte boí i comair Con Culaind i ndormainecht (.1. fo clith H, .1. hi clith W)–dim glinniu fadéin dochóid friae)

['I must go to keep an assignation with Fedelm Noíchride' – he/it means, to visit her servant girl who was secretly Cú Chulainn's concubine – 'to fulfil my own pledge which I gave her'] (Recension I, ll. 522–5).

The trace of glossing is quite clear here and some adjustments already seem to have been made to the appearance of a woman in the surviving text; The redactors of Recension I are aware of a problem and they are trying to avoid it. How is one to understand the hesitation? Fedelm Foltcháem, the daughter of Conchobar mac Nessa and the wife of Cairpre Nia Fer is a woman of some significance to early genealogical pseudo-history.[19] The greatest expansion of her role and characteristics occurs in *Fled Bricrend* where she is curiously cast as wife of the Ulster hero Loegaire Buadach. There she is praised *ar febas do chrotha 7 do chéille 7 do chenéoil* [for the excellence of your form, your intellect and your good birth], a judgment to which she herself assents; after all she belongs to the highest social level, being the product of a socially approved aristocratic marriage of a virginal mother, the equal of her husband in highest rank. Do the narrators know their saga tradition well enough to know that Fedelm is a woman already confusingly deployed in a number of ways in saga and learned historical tradition, wife either to an Ulster warrior or a Leinster king who was also, as here, credited as reigning at Tara? It may be for the sake of literary, if not ethical, propriety that the scribe sends Cú Chulainn whoring off after a lesser target, a target that would not so substantially raise questions about the treatment of the literary or historical substratum to the text. Or it may also be that a socio-ethical displacement/emendation is felt to be necessary as the woman in question is socially high-caste; however Medb herself, the only other woman in the *Táin* of equal rank with Fedelm, may behave, it is not proper for Cú Chulainn himself to display such socially disruptive promiscuity. Hence, a maid-servant will do.

Whatever the case may be, there is a further reworking in the LL text which places the sexual encounter in a different light:

'Am écen-sa tocht i n-herus inalta Feidlmthi Noíchruthaige fodess co Temraig ram glinni fodessin co matin.' 'Mairgg théit ón ám,' ar Sualtaim, 7 Ulaid do lécud fo chossaib a namat 7 a n-echtrand ar thecht i comdáil n-óenmná.' 'Amm écen-sa trá techt, dáig meni digius, gúigfitir dála fer 7 fírfaitir briathra ban.'

['I must go south to Tara to fulfil my own given pledge to meet Fedelm Noíchruthach's servant girl with whom I made a date till tomorrow morning.' 'Woe to him who goes thus,' said Sualtaim 'and leaves the Ulstermen to be trampled underfoot by their enemies and by outlanders for the sake of going on a date with any woman!' 'I must go, however, for unless I do, men's contracts will be falsified and women's words verified.'] (ll. 439–55)

Even if the LL author makes it quite clear what he wishes Cú Chulainn to enunciate here by providing him with a neat summation formula, there still seems to be an over-determination of meaning. There are two ways of reading this, and they are not entirely in accord with each other. Cú Chulainn's precise enunciation of the rationale for his choice reads like a conventional heroic gesture of mastery and control; a hero must keep his word and must not run the risk of being publicly embarrassed or compromised subsequently by the public reproach of a woman.[20] But Cú Chulainn is in the process of making an error of judgment here, and one must attend also to the fact that these words are also the formulation of the LL author as he himself responds to the textual given of the scene. Equally then, this elegant formula functions as an over-emphatic enunciation of a world imagined upside-down on the level of the encoder; a world where women might actually control the agenda of meaningful conduct reflects the author's own fearful perception of an overly feminized milieu.

In LU Cú Chulainn continues after his love night to display a provocative casualness, sleeping late and having a nice bath: *Nípu moch*

didiu dolluid Cú Chulaind aṣa bandáil. Anais co foilc 7 co fothraic. [Cú Chulainn dallied late at his amorous assignation. He stayed around for his
wash and his bath] (ll. 313–4). He sees quickly, however, the strategic
mistake he has made and expresses regret that he should have been
detained elsewhere: *'Ni má lodmar dó' ol Cúchulaind, 'ná mertamar Ultu.
Ro leicsem slóg forru can airfhius.'* ['Going there means we betrayed the
men of Ulster!' cried Cú Chulainn. 'We have let the enemy army loose
on them unawares'] (ll. 315–6). Betrayal is perhaps a rather strong
word to use in this context but here it stands as a plain judgment on a
simple dereliction of duty as Cú Chulainn understands it.

In LL, on the other hand, the moral is made explicit:

*'Amae, a phopae Láeig,' ar Cú Chulaind. 'Ní ma lodmar dar mbandáil arráir. Is
ed is lugu condric ó neoch bís i cocrích éigim nó iachtad nó urfhócra nó a rád cia
thic 'sin sligid ní tharnic úan do rád. Lotadar fir Hérend sechund i crích nUlad.'
Forairngert-sa duit-sin, a Chú Chulaind, sain' ar Láag, 'cia dóchuadais it bandáil
co ragad méla a mac samla fort.'*

['Alas my friend Láeg,' said Cú Chulainn, 'our date with a woman last
night has turned out badly. The least that one who is guarding a border
can do is to give a warning cry or shout or alarm or announce who goes
the road. We failed to announce it. The men of Ireland have gone past us
into Ulster.' 'I foretold that for you, Cú Chulainn,' said Láeg, 'that if you
went to your appointment with a woman, such a disgrace would come on
you.'] (ll. 532–9)

The iterative and obsessive structure of Cú Chulainn's reaction reflects
rather well the sense of severe unease with which the LL author seeks
to invest this occasion. It marks in LL – but not in Recension I – the
definitive end of Cú Chulainn's sexual activity on the *Táin*, and though
the sphere of his actions are defined rather modestly at this stage as
that of watcher at the border, a definite turn in the action is now being
engineered in both versions through the agency of a heroic sexual
encounter.

But it is also obvious that, whatever the function of the sexual
encounter between Cú Chulainn and Fedelm and her women here,
both Recensions have more important work for this meeting beyond
the merely sexual. It is primarily a device for exploiting political and
genealogical networks available for the Ulster side. Fedelm is here the

wife of Cairpre Nia Fer, daughter of Conchobhar and mother of the juvenile Erc who, as a little clone of Cú Chulainn himself, will eventually come on the Ulster hosting in spite of his royal Tara/Leinster father (Recension I, ll. 3815–38, LL, ll. 4535–59). His coming is strategically placed at the end of the *Toichem na mBuiden* sequence, and Fergus there declares, using appropriate bovine imagery, that the addition of the men of Tara and the presence of the little boy will be the decisive factor in the eventual victory of Ulster (ll. 3815–38.)[21]

For the saga's redactors and their learned milieu Fedelm's story carries the message of the usefulness of dynastic intermarriages in the fostering of alliances, and the effectiveness of the avunculate system from the point of view of maternal kin. In addition, we have in LL the information that Medb's hand had once been sought by Cairpre Nia Fer but that she had refused him in favour of his brother Ailill. Thus it suggests some potential drama in the decision of Erc to come into the battle on the side of his mother's kin, considering that Ailill is his paternal uncle. The whole narrative thread involving Fedelm is thus made to have its beginnings in the ambiguous moment in Irish pseudo-history when control of the midlands is posited as a difficult period of interregnal indeterminacy. The narrative returns again to this important area and the final great events, the hosting of the men of Ulster and the ensuing battle, are placed here. In this way an incident which, on the surface, reads as an example of simple misogyny, serves as a device to focus the *Táin* narrative on the politics of Tara and the high kingship. The *Táin* is anchored in its proper 'historical' context as part of a greater historical continuum. By showing the favoured inside track to the kingship of Tara enjoyed by the family of Conchobar, the texts also provide a potent traditional image of perennial political meaning to the redactors of both recensions as the successive campaigns for paramount kingship in their own lifetimes are mounted by families from across the Shannon. Thus Cú Chulainn's sexual diplomacy here can be read against the grain of the general misogyny of both recensions and emerge as a *felix culpa*, a connecting link with an appropriate epic surround. On this level the slip of Cú Chulainn into dangerous sexual distraction can survive even its sharpest articulation in LL.

Taken on its own the lapidary nature of the phrase, *gúigfitir dála fir 7 fírfaitir briathra ban,* and the apparent ease with which the LL narrator can reach for such a neat formula, provides a fairly simple example of a heroic misogynist rewriting and this general drift in the changes between versions is of a type to have been noticed by scholars who have commented on the anti-feminine agenda of the second Recension.[22] Generally, these variations exemplify the ability, born of long and easeful literary use, of the saga idiom to transform itself without effort into a story of women and their dangers.

Losing Findabair, Finding Fer Diad

I want to move now from the site of this Fedelm in the text to consider, in what is purely discursive terms, the most elaborate example of the heroic misogynist theme as it is rewritten by LL. Here a genre that is normally proper to women's enunciatory domain is co-opted by male figures. This occurs in the greatly reworked section containing the story of Fer Diad (LL, ll. 2606–3596, Recension I, ll. 2567–3142). At some point in the textual history of the *Táin* a section with a new hero, Fer Diad, unique to this saga, is introduced. He is bribed by Medb and Ailill to fight Cú Chulainn; although they have once been foster-brothers together in their military training under Scátach in Alba, Fer Diad proceeds to renounce his old bond with Cú Chulainn and, after a series of fierce single-combat fights, is finally slain treacherously by him. I am concerned here with the language and the social performance of grieving enacted by Cú Chulainn on the death of his friend.[23] In Recension I the rhetoric of heroic lament remains a passionate articulation on a relatively small scale (one poem of nine stanzas: ll. 3101–42) of grief for the loss of a heroic friendship. In Recension II this is expanded on a number of different rhetorical registers. First comes a dialogue poem between Cú Chulainn and his charioteer (ll. 3386–410) in which the hero is unwilling to absorb the fact that he has achieved the greatest victory of his career; then comes a sequence of lamentation proper couched in a series of rhetorics (ll. 3414–34). Next come verse sequences: the language is primarily specular and retrospective in ll. 3440–59, with an important coda, *Findabair inge[n] Medba* (ll. 3460–65);[24] this is followed by the stripping of the body and leads into the poem, *Dursan a eó óir*, which picks up on material from Recension I; finally come two further sequences, *A Fhir Diad is truag in dál* and *Cluchi cách, gaíne cách*. The idiom is still specular here: the body of the fallen hero – rendered passive but no less beautiful and no less heroic, signed as it is by heroic markings in death – is literally opened to view and displayed as flawed by its secondary marking, the wearing of the *eó ór*, Findabair's golden brooch and the shaming wound.

Indeed, the lamentation sequences, in their effort to reinstate Fer

Diad into a heroic male company whose ranks he has been deceived into deserting, takes both the co-option and abjection of women and the specular intentions of the incident onto another register of discursive significance. Part of the lament sequence indicated above, that beginning, '*maith a Fhir Diad, ba dursan dait nech dind fhiallaigh rafhitir mo chertgnímrada'* [Well, Fer Diad, a pity that it was not of the company who knew my deeds of valour] (ll. 3416–7) uses *rosc* material from the earlier death tale of Cú Chulainn himself.[25] In that tale, however, such a language is spoken about Cú Chulainn by his wife Emir and constitutes a kind of woman's reproach that Ulster male heroic bonding had not been capable of ensuring her husband's safety. Here such a desired heroic companionship is envisaged as the tragically lacking antidote to the poisonous company and words of women: *Dáig ni adiartaís ind fhir sein de fhessaib ná dúilib ná dálib ná briathraib brécingill ban cendfhind Connacht.* [For these men did not follow the messages or desires or love meetings or the deceptive words of the blonde women of Connacht] (ll. 3424–5).[26]

This type of prosody may be marked off as proper to women's lament and in LL it is taken out of a woman's mouth and put into a man's. In these laments for Fer Diad, not only is this ritual role of the mourning woman taken up by Cú Chulainn himself, but the space for a traditional feminine discursive role and loving gaze is also explicitly denied:

Findabair inge[n] Medba,
gé beith d'fhebas a delba
is gat im ganem ná im grían
a taidbsiu duit-siu, a Fhir Diad

[Though Finnabair, Medb's daughter be surpassingly beautiful in figure, her appearing to you now is as useless a gesture as fastening a withe around sand or gravel.] (ll. 3460–4)[27]

In this radically curtailed space where no room is allowed either for the tropes of desire for the beautiful woman whose love will cure or for the traditional feminine role of lamenting fallen heroes, Finnabair herself is totally silenced; her visible presence reduced to a shade, and her only answerable response is suicide. Even the wild mother of the sons of Nechta Scéne, who is given a brief walk-on lamenting role in Recension I (ll. 755–6), is not to be found in LL. Also removed from the register of mourning behaviour, with the suppression of the entire Fráech episode in this Recension, are the elegant other-worldly ladies in green gowns who are seen bending over the body of the dead hero, Fráech, in an archetypal gesture of lamentation (Recension I, ll. 855–6). Women's laments are here stifled and replaced by a male-authored discourse. As Sheila Murnahan has put it with respect to Greek epic and women's lamentation: 'Lamentation threatens to undermine the *kleos*-conferring function of epic because it stresses the suffering caused by heroic death rather than the glory won by it.'[28]

What more does this denial of a woman's place in a heroic social schema tells us about the deeper cultural structuring of gender in the discursive world of early Irish saga? In the mourning language of Cú Chulainn there is a movement of return to origins, of return to the Edenic space of heroic innocence. In his laments Alba is the place where the heroic twins, mentored and protected by the fierce mother Scátach with a gendered identity unproblematically bivalent, could enact without anxiety games of mutual deference, heroic play, and heroic love. Moreover, the Fer Diad episode in the *Táin* seems to have developed a literary life of its own from a series of earlier encounters with foster-brothers all bribed to fight Cú Chulainn by being promised Finnabair. Of these, Lóch shares two features with Fer Diad: their horn skin and the manner of their death, being pierced through the anus by the *gae bolga*.[29]

One may here see the really terrifying aspect of death for these heroes: the greatest debasement of the male-gendered heroic person occurs at this node; the idea of the death of the hero is an enactment of a type of sexual assault that feminizes the defeated male. Furthermore, if Lóch and Fer Diad are mirrors of each other, then the placement of Lóch's death in the narrative may also be congruous with the strong emphasis on the danger of women and of being made womanly in the death of Fer Diad. At one stage of their fight Lóch is actually getting the better of Cú Chulainn and places him in a dangerously vulnerable female position: *co mboí fáen fortarsna isin áth ina ligu* [so that he was prostrate, belly-up across the ford] (ll. 1984–5). The fight with Lóch takes place in the context of excessive and confusing attention paid to Cú Chulainn by women: he must survive women's interference in the battle stratagems, Medb's curious but hostile gaze, and, above all, the love/hate attraction/aggression of the protean Morrígain. From all this he is saved by the fatherly, supernatural intervention of his father

Lug. The scene of his healing is replete with a language of male reinforcement: *ferda sin a Chú Chulaind ..., canaid a chéle ferdord dó*; Male terror of the devouring female is, then, a fundamental aspect of the language of heroic misogyny in that it seems to be associated with deep anxiety about the instabilities in male gendering and the creation of stable, adult identities for the hero.

Re-placing Fedelm

I would like to return for a moment to the earlier scene of Fedelm, as a way of exploring other issues associated with gender and discourse. Despite the difficulties involved in picking a way through the contradictory genealogical information available for Fedelm Noíchride, her incorporation into the fabric of the narrative by the LL author does not involve any very complex readings of women in the text. What is of interest, however, is the placing of her story in Recension I. It may be that this Fedelm receives her license to enter the text through a possible displacement of another – Fedelm, the visionary, whose disturbing eulogy of Cú Chulainn, present but not standard in all versions, dominates, in its ultimate placement, the opening segment of the LU narrative (ll. 29–112). At ll. 222–5, Cú Chulainn declares his intention to visit the Tara Fedelm, and at ll. 301–8 the scribe M of LU notes that other versions put Fedelm's prophetic vision here; immediately following this, Cú Chulainn returns from his rendezvous. In between this going and returning is the incident with the withe, which is a duplicated scene.[30] One could suspect here that the Fedelm female prophecy was removed from its original spot in order to accommodate the development of a purely male-dialogued mantic performance by Fergus and the druids. The identity of this prophetic Fedelm carries a much higher charge of discursive significance, however, than the (possibly reduced?) Tara lady has; moreover, for a figure that has such an important hieratic role to play in the *Táin*, her presentation is curiously tentative.[31]

Fedelm is two very different people in LU and LL. In LU she is an armed female figure from Alba, a reflex of the woman warrior Scátach in her ability to perform the latter's prophetic rite of the *imbas forosnae*; she was originally sited close to the borders of Ulster and hence has a stronger adversarial connection with prophesying defeat for Connacht. In LL she is on Connacht ground; she seems even more gratuitous there, considering that Medb's visit to the druids to sway the outcome is more strongly developed in this version. As an other-world female messenger from the fairy mound of Crúachu Fedelm functions much as Aoibheall, the tutelary goddess of the Uí Bhríain, does in a similar scene in the early twelfth-century *Cogadh Gaedhel re Gallaib* when she appears before the armies of Brian Bóruma in the mustering of the Dál gCais before the battle of Clontarf.[32] In LU Fedelm suddenly appears when Medb's charioteer turns the chariot to the right in order to negate the sense of foreboding introduced by Medb's dark comment on the curses which will attend her expedition. Fedelm, then, realized in a half-romantic, half-magically formulaic way (*co n-accatar*), is the sign being sought. She carries both the feminine symbol of skilled competence in her hand, a *claideb corthaire* [a weaver's beam] and also a set of weapons. O'Rahilly has suggested that the description which follows, identifying her as an armed girl in a chariot, may be somewhat *ad hoc* in its invention: *gaisced* [arms] out of place and added from misunderstood association with the *claideb corthaire* above, and both chariot and *gaisced* thrown in for good measure at the end of the description.[33] In both versions, allowing for the expected embellishments of Recension II, the rhetorical run of exotic description is designed to designate 'otherness.'[34] In LL her appearance is secondary to the druidic consultation which Medb in her chariot undertakes: she appears suddenly in front of Medb's returning chariot and actually weaves a fringe in a classical symbol of destiny; Fedelm's 'sword' is actually a weaver's beam and there is no mention of primitive poetic rites of *imbas for-osnae* as in LU. Rather, the text speaks of *tairngire 7 remfhástine*.

In both versions, then, Fedelm is 'fixed' or invented by an unstable set of references. In LU, she can very easily fit into a liminalist reading of the feminine, replicating in an unstable female mode aspects of Scátach and even of Cú Chulainn himself. In this sense, the term *macdacht* supplies a crucial negotiatory term which serves to hold the gendered meaning and function of the whole scene in place. The word, even if derived from Indo-European **maga-*, and hence essentially the same word as the English *maiden* and thus an exclusive female designation in origin, may also have been affected by the *macc* [boy]- root and hence is available for an interesting range of cross-gender play.[35] She is mounted in her own chariot rather than appearing suddenly from the side of Medb's. Having wheels is an important sign of prestige and Recension II, by weakening Fedelm's presence, embellishes considerably the idea of a mounted Medb.

Woman Talk

What is said on this occasion and how it is said is, however, crucial to the flow of the narrative in other ways. The interpolated prophecy poem of H is not a perfect fit and the *rosc* .r.-marking is inappropriate to the metrical form. In chapter 3 I discussed the poem and its significance; here I want to signal the discursive effect of the exchanges between Medb and Fedelm before the poem begins. In their formally planned dialogue they act out together the *imbas for-osnae* rite in the form of a query-and-response structure leading up to the moment when the prophecy begins to flow. The repeated question *Fedelm banfháith, co acci ar slúag* and the answer *Atchíu forderg, atchíu rúad* can both be viewed as seven-syllable lines with end rhyme.[36] The forms negotiate the rite in planned bouts of cooperation and contestation that segue between ritual, dramatic, and, one might also add, illocutionary modes of utterance.[37] But what is to be noted here is the gendered nature of the phenomenon itself. The entire archaic and pagan divination scene is managed and administered by women alone.

Women are frequently seen making verse in Irish saga; a typical scenario is the game of completing quatrains as a form of conjuration. A *locus classicus* is found in the tenth-century tale *Fingal Rónáin*, where the treacherous stepmother, by completing a suggestive quatrain, gets the king's son killed by his own father's jealousy.[38] In the reduced scope of a two-line verse exchange Medb and Fedelm begin their ritual complicity. Between them they call up the figure of Cú Chulainn, and the verse itself – though it is not rhapsodic in form – is organized along typical divinatory principles. The hero is described much as he will be further on in the text, in the great account of the arming and the frenzy of the warrior after his healing by Lug (*Recension I*, ll. 2185–334); there is in the prophecy, as in the later description, a progression from the benign, sexually attractive display of the hero to his terrifying *riastarthe* phase and his wholesale slaughter of his enemies at the battle of Sesrech Breslige.

But there is a further aspect to this rhetoric which I now want to signal in particular. One woman, Fedelm, is here 'constructed' visually and rhetorically both as a figure of another woman, Scátach, and as the warrior Cú Chulainn himself: as women here recreate iconic heroic men in speech, and approach conditions of gender detachment, is there any indication that in Irish saga tradition one might find a special form of discourse approaching the status of a distinct feminine rhetoric shared between women?[39] In other words, what is the space allowed for women who speak and create marked discursive sequences together, even if only to call up men? Is there a distinct textual domain of women who utter together? Let us look at a few promising contexts here.

The first example comes from the *Táin Bó Fróich* saga at the point in the tale when Fróech is bringing back the branch of berries from the danger-filled pool; the narrative is interrupted in order that Findabair's speech on Fróech's beauty, cast as a discourse of repetition and rendered formulaic in the memory of the retelling, may be inserted: *Ba ed íarum aithesc Findabrach, nach álaind ad.chíd, ba háildiu lee Fróech.* [This was the utterance of Findabair afterwards, anyone lovely that she would ever see (she would say) that Fróech was more beautiful to her].[40] In this instance we have a specific manipulation of discourse so that the narrator may signal and fix the impact of the scene into a freeze-frame mode by transposing a rhetorical sequence from a presumed future elegiac discourse of Findabair's about Fróech. Findabair makes two discursive halves of herself. In this sense Findabair herself may be said to be used by the narrator as the authority whereby Findabair evokes Fróech and calls him up at a time when he himself will no longer be there to be witness to the truth of the assertion.[41] Findabair thus is doubled, as the young girl in her pride joins with the old woman she will become, in asserting the prerogative to continue to utter her lover precisely because she once publicly tried to assert her right to love him and failed.[42] The twinned nature of the poetic moment is tragic precisely because lament is a woman's last chance to speak with effect and is yet always already beyond the point of responsive communication.

Similarly, in the famous passage in *Longes Mac nUislenn*, one might say that Derdriu and Lebarcham, the female satirist, between them 'call up' Naoise first in a colour-coded wish for a lover from Derdriu and then in his identification by Lebarcham:[43]

'Ro-pad inmain óen-fher forsa.mbetis na tri dath ucut .i. in folt amal in fiach ocus in grúad amal in fuil ocus in corp amal in snechta.'
'Orddan ocus tocad duit!' ar in Lebarcham. 'Ni cían úait. Atá is'taig it arrad .i. Noísi mac Usnig.'
'Ni-pam slán-sa ám,' ol-si, 'conid.n-accur-saide.'

['Beloved would be that particular man who would have the three colours yonder – that is hair like the raven, a cheek like blood and a body like snow.' 'May you have honour and good fortune!' said Lebarcham, 'He is not far from you. He is inside here and near you, Noisiu son of Uisliu.' 'I can't live,' she replied, 'unless I see him.']

A final example comes from *Fled Bricrend*.[44] In the flyting of the women that forms the frame of the story, Emir produces a speech in praise of Cú Chulainn in terms that are close in some essential *riastarthae* respects to the prophecy of Fedelm:

> crithir fola for a crund
> cobur fola for a claidiub
> caín forondar a chorp hi crú
> créchta ina chaíncnis
> álta ina thoeb liss
> caín feid a rosc rochéim inna chend síar
> caín fualaing fuither glaini sair
> sírderg a sella
> ógderg a fonnaid
> fordeirg a fortgae ...
> co rrici mo chelese Coin Chulaind
> cro don glésin samlaitir (cf. Eg. samlithir)

[drop of blood on his spear-shaft, foam of blood on his sword; beautifully is his body reddened with blood, wounds in his lovely body, wounds in his sides; beautifully does he turn his eye back into his head, beautifully does he stretch out his jawbone; full red his eyes, clear red his chariot wheels, deep red his chariot cushions ... compared with my husband Cú Chulainn, others are like blue compared to red]

Here what is interesting is to see the manner in which Emir's words echo the meta-discourse and the prophecy of Fedelm in the *Táin* (LU, ll. 50–113). Both speak in counterpoint to the enunciative presence of other women. As Fedelm creates the heroic icon of Cú Chulainn out of the fundamental element 'red,' out of spilled blood, wounds, and clothing, interweaving it with the dual beauty/terror effect of heroic sexual and destructive energies, so too Emir grounds her image of the hero in the same element. In both women's speeches the hero is also beautiful because of the heroic red display of his body and his warrior trappings; indeed one might say, looking to Findabair's description of Fróech and Deirdriu's projection of their ideal lover, that 'red' marks fundamentally the display of the hero in the specular words of women every bit as much as it does those of men.[45]

There is an obvious question lurking at this stage of my argument which must be addressed. To what degree is the language of heroic misogyny in saga generally, and the *Táin* in particular, influenced by an ecclesiastical tradition of anti-feminist rhetoric? To some extent this has already been considered by others, but it is not a question about which it is easy to be dogmatic.[46] Indeed the language of misogyny seems to be so deeply endemic that, unless there is specific verbal correspondence or citation evident in a saga text, it seems hopeless to attempt to make a distinction. However, that early Irish *literati* might be able to conceive of women having an analogical grid of their own, independent of men, is certainly aided by the existence of a system of typology governing saintly women in Irish ecclesiastical thinking. In a successful transposition of the social articulation of the avunculate in devotional terms, it was natural to see linked feminine chains of analogy: for example, Íte in relation to Brigid (The Brigid of Munster), Brigid (the Mary of the Gáel), in relation to Mary, and both as substitute mothers in relationship to Christ.[47] That this ecclesiastical patterning of a feminine line of authoritative acting can also be transposed, in a learned context, to secular tradition is evident from a reference in *Cormac's Glossary*:

> *Búanand mumi na fían .i. bé nAnand ar chosmaile diblínaib. Amail robo máthair déa indí Anu, sic Búanand quasi mater erat na fían. Aliter Buanond .i. daghmathair, in buan as bon .i. dindi as bonum, ut dicitur genitur buan o ambuan .i. maith o ulc. A n-and fil isinni is Buannand issed fil isinne is Annand .i. mathair deorum*

> [Buanand, foster-mother of the fíana, that is *bé nAnand* because of the similarity between them; just as Anu was the mother of the gods, so Búanand was as a mother to the fíana. Otherwise, Buanand, that is, the good mother; the *buan* from bon[um] .i. from that which is good, as it is said, 'good derives from not-good': i. good from evil; from the [negative] *an(d)* that is in it, i.e. Buannand, what is there is Annand .i. mother of the gods.][48]

Nagy uses a liminalist argument to gloss this female figure: 'it would seem that Bodbmall, Búanann, and Scáthach are all multiforms of a supernatural martial foster-mother figure who appear in various contexts.'[49] While this formulation is valid in its terms, Cormac's wording and his way of arriving at a decoding would also indicate that, if one is searching for specific sources for this analogical facility, ecclesiastical typology and inverse etymology of the *lucus a non lucendo* type are the discursive models here, with the additional sting in the tail that a female deity carrying a 'good' (*bonum*) lexical mark must surely have to be be turned on her head to be valid.

When a Man Meets a Woman

Thus far I have examined the operations of three models which have informed scholarly critical language about women in the *Táin*: the language of liminality with respect to Fedelm, the language of misogyny, always associated in this saga with Medb, and finally, the language of typology. All three can with some effort be taken apart to see through the verbal operations whereby language against women is constructed. Now I want to turn to another incident for which the terminology of the goddess has been insistently invoked to provide a rationale and context. Here some feminist critical ideas on body language and women may supply alternative ways of looking at meaning in the work as it is mediated by the two first recensions. The exemplifying passage is the famous incident at the close of the LL version (ll. 4821–51) where Medb, by stopping to urinate, checks Cú Chulainn's harrying of the armies as they attempt to cross the Shannon. She creates three rivers and a placename. In Recension I, Medb's request for protection seems simple and unnuanced and has no reference to urinating. The closest analogue in this version of the *Táin* would be the ruses by which the Morrígain wins healing and a blessing from the unwitting hero (Recension I, ll. 2039–55). But there the Morrígain scene is part of the epic rewrite of this section of the saga, and is much more elaborately developed than the incident in question here involving Medb and the hero. In LL, on the other hand, the gesture of urination seems closer to the topos of the humiliated ruler in battle who demands an inappropriate and incongruous request of the champion, thus further complicating the outcome of the conflict.

Why does the scandalous incident of the queens's urination occur here in LL and what is its significance? There is indeed a scene of Medb relieving herself in Recension I, but it occurs much earlier (ll. 2866–75). As Fer Diad is setting out, full of foreboding, to his last fatal encounter with Cú Chulainn, he turns back one last time to bid farewell to his comrades in arms.

'A gille,' for Fer Diad, 'ní cóir i ndénmait, dula cen celebrad do fheraib hÉrenn. Impó dúnd agaid na n-ech 7 in charpait for feraib hÉrind.' Ro impó in gilla aiged na n-ech 7 in charpait for t[h]ri fri feraib hÉrenn. Is and do-rala Medb ic sriblad a fúail for urlár in pupaill. 'In cotlud do Ailill inossa?' or Medb. 'Nad ed ámh,' ar Ailill. 'In cluine do c[h]liamain núa ac celebrad duit?' 'An ed dogní-som ón?' ar Ailill. 'Is ed écin,' for Medb. 'Ac luigim- se a luigend mo t[h]úath ná tic arna cosaib cétna chucaib-si fer dogní in celebrad út.' 'Ar aba ina tairtemar dá deighc[h]leamnas didiu' or Ailill, 'acht co táethsad Cú Chulaind lais, fó linn cémad comhtuitim dóib. Ane robad ferrdi lind Fer Diad do thérnom.'

['My lad,' said Fer Diad, 'it is not right for us to go without bidding farewell to the men of Ireland. Turn back the horses and chariot to face the men of Ireland.' Three times the charioteer turned horses and chariot to face the men of Ireland. Medb was urinating on the floor of the tent. 'Is Ailill asleep now?' asked Medb. 'No indeed,' said Ailill. 'Do you hear your new son-in-law bidding you farewell?' 'Is that what he is doing?' asked Ailill. 'It is indeed,' said Medb. 'But I swear by my people's oath that he who is so bidding you farewell will not return to you on his own feet.' 'Because of what we have gained by this marriage,' said Ailill, 'we care not if both of them fall, provided that Cú Chulainn is killed by him. But indeed we should be the better pleased if Fer Diad escaped.'] (ll. 2862–75, trans. O'Rahilly)

The incident is well constructed as a cynical play of misunderstanding between the characters involved: for Fer Diad, all his premonitions tell him that death awaits him; the heroic challenger is lonely, and the emotional need to construct a ritual of heroic and dignified leave-taking is behind his gestures. Medb, with her casually obscene physical frankness trivializes the elegiac attitudinizing of Fer Diad. Her gesture is lewd as it relates to Fer Diad, a sexual display which is inappropriate to the mother of the bride on the morning after his agreement to marry with the daughter but before he has enjoyed sexual intimacy with her. At the same time the gesture is domestic as it relates to the interior scene with Ailill, a casual conversation of spouses between conjugal bed and privy. The heroic import of Fer Diad's gestures is also denied and misappropriated; it is now cruelly and egotistically misread as the deference due from the new matrilocal son-in-law, who, as such, will always be socially degraded by Irish social convention. Thus the urination scene is well integrated into the narrative of Recension I at this point and – be it noted – entirely absent from LL.

We will never know how the urination theme figured in the narrative of any proto-*Táin* but there is perhaps a reason why the LL author saw an opportunity in the incident for an appropriate action to finish out the closing scenes. In all recensions there is a sentence immediately after the final derrière-exposing halt of Medb which, in turn, gives rise to the sharpest articulation of the most famous of all anti-feminist statements in the *Táin* tradition: *is bésad do cach graig remitét láir, ro gata, rotbrada, rofeither a moín hi tóin mná misrairleastair* [that is the usual thing for a herd led by a mare. Their wealth is robbed, despoiled and locked up in the backside of the woman who led them astray] (Recension I, ll. 4123–4). Traces of real anti-Medb hostility are already there, occurring even in the very early *Conailla Medb míchuru*:[50] The preceding statement in question is: '*Correcad lochta 7 folachta sund indiu, a Fherguis,*' ar *sí*. O'Rahilly has provided only a very tentative translation of this phrase – 'Men and lesser men meet here today, Fergus,' taking *locht* to mean 'group of individuals' – and she indicated that she felt it was some kind of proverbial phrase, the import of which is not now clear. One might also read *locht* as 'defect,' hence the notion of the expedition as well and truly messed up. A more pointed, or at least alternative, reading might begin with *folochta*, 'cooking pits' and note the common usage of *locht* as the contents of the cooking vessel, thus yielding a variation on the 'fat is in the fire' (fat and fire coming together) idea. This has the advantage of bringing us closer to two terms through which we might access the scene of Medb's urination. Besides *fulachtad*, 'cooking,' DIL lists *fulachtad*, 'bloodletting'; in addition, the common phrase, *fulacht fian/fiadh* describes various obvious pits or significant small-scale features of landscape; there is also the literary term *fulacht na Morrígna*. Both these usages provide a context within which one might see certain bridges in the *f+V+l-* root variations of this word cluster that might have activated punning possibilities for the LL redactor. Was it this, as much as confusion about female bodily functions of menstruation/urination, that nudged the redactor to regroup the topos of urination here rather than leave it in the place where it occurs in Recension I?

Scholars who have commented on this scene have been struck by the occurrence of scenes similar to Irish saga in the Scandinavian *Edda* tradition, where incidents of women who urinate/menstruate rivers also occur and where the hero overcomes them and stops the flow with a well-aimed stone to the vulva.[51] Motz, in discussing the river-crossing, giantess-defeating journey of Thor, argues against Clunies Ross that water holds no specific connection with femininity in Germanic folklore, literature, or myth, while at the same time asserting that the Irish tales where this motif occurs are cosmogonic and may even have been borrowed into Old Norse where, presumably, such connections are forthwith lost.[52] Bowen was in no doubt that there was a significant cluster of such motifs in Irish tradition which lend weight to his conclusion that, for this incident in *LL*, one should look to the mythology of the sovereignty goddess for a satisfactory explanation.[53] As he put it with splendid flourish: 'Mythology retains its power over the tradition and here it has fought invention to a standstill.'[54]

One may indeed be helped to a richer reading of the scene by resorting to these types of mythological operations but not in quite the same terms that Bowen utilized. It is certainly useful to follow him a little further, along the path of the contextual narrative materials which he assembled, and turn to the tale of Lugaid and Derbforgaill.

Laa and didiu i nderiud gemrid. Snechta mór and. Doniat na fir corthe mór don tsnechtu. 'Tabram ar mún isin coirthe dús cia as sia ragas ind. In ben o ría triit isí as ferr congaib úan.' Ni roacht didiu uadib. Congairther Derbforgaill uadaib. Nir bo áill or nir bo baeth. Téit arai forsin corthe. Roselaig uade co talam. 'Dia fessatar trá ind fir so ní congrádaigfider i fail na óinmná. Gatair a súile assa cind 7 a srona 7 a da nó 7 a trilis. Ní ba soaccobraite ón.'Dognither a pianad amlaid sin 7 berair iartain da tig.

[On a certain day at the end of winter there was deep snow. The men make a great pillar of snow. The women went up to the pillar. This was what they got up to; 'Let us urinate on the pillars to see whose urine will penetrate deepest. The woman who penetrates it through and through is the most sexually powerful of us.' However they were not able to penetrate it. Derbhforgaill was called by them. She did not like it because she was not a lewd woman. She went up on the snow mound and it gushed out of her right down through to the ground. 'If the men knew about this no one would be desired compared to this one. Let her eyes be taken out of her head and her nose, two ears and hair (var. the flesh of her buttocks). She won't be attractive then!' She was tortured like this and then brought back to her own house].[55]

Bowen has noted the various sexual components of this 'gruesome' little tale, the phallic mound and the variants, *ergaire* and *congaib* which involve the phraseology of sexual abilities in a fairly literal sense. He concludes: 'Just as the phallic myth depends on the notion that a man's potency is reflected in actual genital size, the corresponding female myth, as we see it here, measures a woman's sexual power by the capacity of her 'inner' space, with the bladder undoubtedly serving as an analogue for the vagina and uterus. All of this makes the relevance of river and urine symbolism to the figure of the fertility-sovereignty-war goddess a little clearer.'[56]

In this cruel little tale issues of sexuality are inescapable. But whether one is justified in linking Derbforgaill to the mythological complex as described by Bowen is doubtful. Myth, if present, must, as I propose in chapter 4, meet some standard of social conduct clearly articulated in a formal discursive way. Instead it may be more useful to consider that what is at issue here is the way gender games are played out. One might begin then with the proposition that the underlying game is one of imitating male contestation; after all, it is the men who first make the pillar, and the women only play when the men have grown tired of the novelty. Male children playing inauguration games on a playground mound is attested elsewhere in the literature, in the elegy by a Mac an Bhaird poet for his patron fallen in the Battle of Down.[57] In the list of boyhood feats in the *Mellbretha* [Sports Judgments] legal text, two items are listed side by side, *corthe críche* and *tochailt trebán*.[58] Binchy considered these to mean, 'rounders' (running round a marking pillar?) and 'building sandcastles' respectively. Sayers suggested a tentative reading of *trebán* as *srebán*, giving 'the excavating of streamlets.'[59]

It is at least possible to interpret this in the most obvious way, as a boys' pissing competition. If this is so, the imitation game of the women makes more sense here. It is a case of women who will be boys, and the possibility suggests itself that for early Irish cultural discourse, the site of gender itself can be viewed as a cultural possession which is available for manipulation in a number of ludic, even parodic and contestatory ways. It also seems to me that commentators carry their own cultural baggage with them to the process of interpretation; Bowen reads an essentially male myth of female sexuality into the tale when he speaks of a woman's sexual power measured by the capacity of her inner space; Bitel, on the other hand, reads a 1970s women's myth, also reassuring to men, observing that a woman who can control urination has well-developed vaginal muscles).[60] One might explore further, as Bitel attempted to do, early medieval theories of the female body by referring to Jacquart and Thomasset's work on medieval ideas of sexuality and the body and Laqueur's claim that early medieval societies assumed a one-body idea of sexuality:[61] thus, the close mimicry of men's games here by women is enabled by the concept of the unity of all bodily fluids and the homology between sexual parts.

The violent rejection by the other women of Derbforgaill, the woman who can melt snow like a man, ultimately rests as much on the heat as the amount of the urine.[62] With her Galenic humours, theories of heat as the prerogative of male bodies and moisture of women's, are confounded; Derbforgaill is dangerous, both as the woman from outside the group and also as the woman with the subversive body who might be capable of both giving and experiencing pleasures in sex in ways that usurp a long-standing male prerogative and disturb the standard of gender by which women themselves collectively orient their gender identity. Arbitrary violence directed against women is summarily punished, as is appropriate in a post-*Cáin Adamnáin* world, by the heroic custodians of social morality, but one suspects that there is particular satisfaction resonating in that tale from the revenge killing of all the guilty women. Nancy Partner's comment apropos the conflicting appeal and alienation we feel when confronted with medieval stories involving women comes to mind here: 'Sexuality may be cruel but gender can be mean.'[63]

Bearing this in mind I would like to return to the pissing scene in the LL *Táin*. Medb's act is caught in the process of textual transformation. Drawn to this spot in the text by the punning assocciations of *folacht/ fualacht/fual/fuil*, the scene compromises all involved. As Medb is presented, she endangers the army by her delay. Her request for time out is phrased in the same fashion as the request of Conchobar in the incident of the fight with Eógan mac Durthacht's raiders in the Boyhood Deeds segment of the narrative: there Conchobar also presents an ambivalent reading, an apparently ignominious picture of an unheroic sovereign. It too also contains the same formula of heroic physical frustration – male hunger, female satiety: *Dianom thísad mucc fonaithe robadam béo* [If only a roast pig were to come to me I should live] (LU, l. 513) and *nída béo-sa meni shiblur-sa m'fhúal úaim* [I won't live if I can't relieve myself] (LL, ll. 4828–9).

The name of the game here is not so much a slippage into a mytho-logical mode appropriate to an old sovereignty goddess but rather a gender performance to confound the male hero. It is, in effect, the same game of gender assertion played with the same result by the women of the *polis* of Emhain Macha in the Boyhood Deeds sequence, when they bare their breasts to the berserk boy.[64] By actions like these women project a direct language of the body that can stop a male-directed action dead in its tracks. It is a category of feminine discourse which can be deployed *in extremis*. It is a part of the experience of the femi-nine which stands right at the border of culture, and by responding to it men are led into a dangerous zone where their rigorous control over their own culturally gendered behaviour is in danger of being con-founded.

Only [Female] Fools and Horses

To discuss the effect of the differing narrative recensions by trying to map the analogical movements of playing on and across gender boundaries is to come close to the rules of the game of male initiation as recoverable in the various parts of the Indo-European spectrum.[65] Indeed, one might cite one more gendered example from the *Táin* materials relevant to this. During Cú Chulainn's fight with Fer Diad, Cú Chulainn urges his friend *ná bris chíg* (literally, 'do not break a breast, LL, l. 3046). O'Brien linked this breast metaphor for the friend-ship bond with the strange custom, *sugere mammellas*, of the Irish raid-ers who, in his *Confessio*, agree to transport Patrick back to Britain thereby asserting the evidence of male bonding built around rituals of deliberate sexual queering.[66]

But if gender inversion games are part of the display and relational repertoire deployed by males in early Ireland, then, in an analogous though more limited way, it seems that they are available to women also. For a brief moment here Medb reclaims the bogus difference of misogyny by re-inventing the embarrassment of urination as a strata-gem to force Cú Chulainn to observe restraint. By his refraining from injuring her in her moment of staged vulnerability the armies are enabled to cross the Shannon under protection. Like a cunning female animal who resorts to body-decoy stratagems to protect her young,

Medb has turned both sexual and gender difference back on men to good effect.

It is a brilliant piece of body language improvisation but it is probably in the medieval Irish nature of things that the moment is not sustained. The seasoned male professionals take over the management of the retreat and proceed, in male backlash fashion, to wrestle back control of the cultural agenda by redefining with a damning animal metaphor their default-mode sense of the feminine:

> 'Feib theit echraid láir rena serrgraig i crích n-aneóil gan chend cundraid ná comairle rempo, is amlaid testa in slúag sa indiu.'

> [As when a mare goes before her troup of foals into unknown territory, with no leader to guide and advise them, that is how this army has been beaten today.] (LL, ll. 4849–51)[67]

Obviously to have a woman on top is to be without a social head (*gan cenn*). Even at this juncture, however, I think it is still worthwhile to lay open this master statement – which is also an ironic but damning self-indictment of Fergus' own role as guide and advisor – to a reader's scrutiny, and to point out the obvious. In the long history of the Indo-European domestication of the horse, mares are the normal leaders of horse herds and young stallions are expelled from the group nucleus.[68] Mares do not go crazy and lead their dependants into danger in mating season. We should not believe the assertions of what is not just because they are uttered by failed heroes, rogue bulls, or dogs in the manger (to mix up the saga's metaphors a little). Herds led by mares are the rule not the exception, they cannot seriously be made to represent a world upside down no matter how much men try. In short, the gender argument has not been closed in spite of what the men say.

I also like to think that in this, as in many other ways we have already encountered, certain effects were aimed at by our various scribal witnesses to Irish saga creativity: intent as they were on the game of words, they do not neglect to show that actions can also speak. By following through and re-thinking some of these actions as they articulate twisted motives on the level of gendered bodies, their commitment to the values of narrative that perennially fascinated them is clear. By creating such open-ended texts they ensured that the book would remain open after them and that the endless tale of how to play a woman would go on.

How it did play on is illustrated neatly by an incident in the medieval compilation of Fenian tales *Acallam na Senórach*. At one point in this narrative Patrick and Caílte arrive at a place called the fort of Medb and the usual question on the place-name derivation is asked. Caílte replies:

'In é seo ro ba baile bunaid di?' ar Patraic. 'Ní hé úm,' ar Caílte, 'acht fa lith laithe na sámna ticed dácallaim a druad 7 a filed ann dús cid ra biad ar maith nó ar saith in bliadain sin di, 7 is amlaid ticed si, ina náe cairpthib ann .i. nae carpait roimpe 7 náe carpait ina diaid 7 nae carpait cechtar do dib leithib di.' 'Créd má ndenad sí sin?' ar Patraic. 'Na roised braenscoid na conaire 7 glomarchind na hechraidi, 7 nach salchadais na dechealta nuaglana.' Ádhbur subhach sin!' ar Patraic.[69]

['Was this the place where she dwelled?' asked Patrick. 'No indeed,' said Caílte, 'but on the festival of Samain she came here to converse with her druids and her poets to learn what good or evil might happen to her that year. This is how she would arrive, in a group of nine chariots, with nine chariots before, nine chariots following and nine at either side.' 'Why did she do that?' asked Patrick. 'So that the muddy water of the path might not reach the bridle-bits of the horses and soil her new clean robes.' 'That is a silly business!' said Patrick.][70]

The origin of this piece of information is to be found only in a scribal note to an incident in the *Tain* as recorded in LU, telling us that the armies of Connaught prepare to make camp the first night of their campaign, at Loch Carrcín. Queen Medb arrives with her nine chariots and the scribe Maelmuire adds she always traveled like this lest the dust of the armies soil her clothes.[71] Patrick's reaction to the tale is sharply ironic: that is *subhach*, 'amusing,' comical, or even 'wanton' being the range of this word. It is a precious and rare moment in Irish literary tradition where we can actually see a literary judgment being passed by one text on another, in this case the most famous of all Irish sagas, the *Táin*. Patrick, or as I think, the Patrician clerical author of the *Acallam* as we have it, is on the one hand asserting the primacy of *his* heroes and *his* narrative, but he is also giving notice: women of the caliber of Medb, the wayward, promiscuous, amoral queen of Connacht of the older generation of saga, will no longer be quite as welcome on this new literary stage, where the cycle of Finn and the Fenians is now being quarried by ecclesiastic reform authors to display all the right social mores. Another, more amenable paradigm of feminine sweetness and decorum is now taking her place.

7 The Sense of an Ending

This is the public disclosure of the inquiry of Herodotus of Thurii, so that the events of men will not become faded with time and that great and marvelous deeds, some performed by Hellenes, and some by barbarians, will not lose their fame especially what caused them to wage war with each other. The learned men of the Persians say that the Phoenicians were the cause of the disagreement ...

Herodotus 1.1

What It Was All About

'Beginnings are always troublesome and conclusions are the weak point of most authors.'[1] George Eliot's professional observation as to beginnings has been borne out by the difficulties observed in the *Táin* narrative as its successive handlers have attempted to set it in motion. The strength or weakness of the saga's conclusion must now be considered. Or rather, to change the idiom – because this study does not operate with the Victorian certainties available to Eliot – one needs to consider the ways in which a dialectic of closure and openness affects the *Táin* ending. The study of ending as closure directs a reading of the end as given over to ideas about the (re-)establishment of order, while the view of any ending as open-ended remains more attractive to the contemporary reader: it allows for the thematization of problems attendant on the way a text ends, and becomes a way to reposition the author/encoder vis-à-vis his narrative. Reading for closure after Foucault can also mean that one is aware of the extratextual contingencies of narrative: the order that comes with closure may not be a natural category; rather it is imposed by the realities of power.[2] It is with these considerations in mind I turn to the concluding segment of the saga.

Ostensibly, the end of the *Táin* is taken up with the story of the final moments of the two bulls. But for the two human sides of this quarrel the end presents a kind of stasis, where the action as it dies down throws up paradoxical internal perspectives on what might constitute a desired end. Each side gets its due. From the Connacht point of view their rulers emerge safely from battle and they do carry away the prize bull, so in that sense, for them a successful '*táin*' has been accomplished and completed. But the reader knows that this obfuscates some of the assumptions of the narrative up till now, because the regional affiliation of the hero had demanded that his be the privileged point of view. From the Ulster side their warriors are, indeed, victorious and they push their foes back across the Shannon in disarray. They have the satisfaction of an aftermath, of seeing the *crech* taken by their opponents dissipate and come to nothing in the fight of the bulls. Complicating the ending further in Recension I is the overview of the narrator, who imposes his own kind of epilogue. Peace is established with specific terms and remains in place for seven years.

A happy-ever-after note? Hardly. Such a time frame comes uncomfortably close to the idea of the periodic malign enchantment that afflicts the Ulstermen, the 'lack' which was the essential condition with which the story began.[3] Evil does not work on a progressive time model; it is, rather, cyclic, and will never be decisively banished. Thus a positive outcome is to be understood as temporizing, and no hero can rest secure in his fame. This kind of end is never simply the end: it remains permanently locked into the open-endedness of what will happen next time.

Issues that are, properly speaking, extratextual to the work also intrude – indeed, the end is precisely where they may be expected to reassert a pull on the narrative. Ó Riain's interpretation of the historical context of the saga as referring to events in the first decade or so of the ninth century suggests that it may be well to compare its end with the summation of the Annals' account of a decisive battle in this period of rivalry between Connacht and Ulster:[4]

Slogud Muirgessa m. Tomaltaig co Connachtaibh la Conchobur m. nDonnchada co rici Thir in Oenaigh, 7 fugerunt repente post tres noctes, 7 migrauit Aedh m. Neill in ob[u]iam eorum 7 combussit terminos Midi eorumque fuga capris 7 hinulis simulata est

[A hosting of Muirgius son of Tomaltach, with the Connachtmen, [led] by Conchobur son of Donnchad as far as Tír ind Aenaig,[5] and they fled suddenly after a period of three nights. And Aed son of Niall marched against them and burned the borders of Mide; and their flight was compared to that of (herds) of goats and deer] (*Annals of Ulster,* sub anno 808)

As far as annalistic recording of such battles goes in the period this is quite an elaborate narrative treatment. In the language of the Annals the term for a hosting, *slógad*, is one of the earliest of military terms to be deployed in the vernacular; as in sagas, the term refers strictly to the assemblage and march of an armed force and there is a real sense in the above notice that the encounter is a great to-do about very little. The mixed armed assembly of the aggressors is the main act; no king dies, no army is shattered, heroics become bathetic, and the possibilities for literary play are evident. The likeness to the *Táin* is obvious. The main point of similarity is the curious *topos* in the annalistic entry on the flight of the Connacht forces being like the flight of a herd. The Annals do not normally use (heroic?) similes in this way. A denigrating allusion to goats and deer is not too far removed from the *Táin* rout of the Connacht armies and the humiliating bestial language of mares and herds gone astray that is applied to them by Fergus. Thus a certain stylistic congruence between the two genres is perceptible here and, in my view, strengthens Ó Riain's case for a significant connection between historical event and answering literary text. As a literary issue, the logical conclusion of raising the question of the congruence of annalistic and epic mentalities is to suggest that ideas of closure in the *Táin* may share in the necessary sense of deferred closure of the annalist; the saga/annal closure is always provisional at best, always remains open to the sense of time as an ongoing, reversible process, and so the sense of an ending, outside of a Christian vision of finite time and clear end, cannot help but be artificial.

I turn now to explore the issues of closure in the text from other intra-narratological perspectives, in particular the relationship between the two early recensions. From the point of view of an Irish saga typology of narremes, we are left with two narrative lines that require closure: the cattle-raid and the rout. The two are interconnected insofar as the fight of the bulls might be said to constitute a kind of augural duel which decides an otherwise ambiguous outcome. Both cattle and rout are linked to the two perspectives on the action, Connacht's and

Ulster's. Again, there are substantial shifts between the two Recensions in the manner in which their respective closure is accomplished. The end in Recension II has received most attention because its well-known Latin colophon has provided a kind of culture shock to readers who, having enjoyed the entire tale, are brought up short by the critical judgment of the scribe who considers the whole work to be a mere 'entertainment for fools.' In sketching some of the ways in which the ending is charted I will inevitably have to retake this judgment into consideration. But, as expressed in the Introduction, to allow it to over-shadow the real literary satisfactions to be derived from the final stages and to give it too much authority as a retrospective on the entire achievement of the work itself, would be to acquiesce too easily in a misplaced reverence for the master reader in the past and to forget that one of the challenges of this study is to help to renew and free up the pleasure of the text for ourselves, the contemporary readers.

Staging the End

Some aspects of the gendered and misogynist content of these conclud-ing scenes have just been addressed in chapter 6. I have already described how simmering tensions between Medb and Fergus give a particular tone of misogyny to the final acts of the story. There, reading like a feminist, I suggest that in this instance Medb's feminine body-language trick actually works to a good end and saves the armies as they cross the Shannon. Fergus, however, takes up this same language of the body in a way that animalizes women negatively. It is here that Recension II begins to display a blurring of the dialogic clarity that is maintained in Recension I. YBL has clear speaker markers:

> *is and asbert Meadb fri Fergus: Correcad lochta 7 fulachta sund indiu a Fhergais*
> *ar sí. Is bésad, ol Fergus, do cach graig remitét láir, rotgata, rotbrata, rotfeither a*
> *moín hi tóin mná misrairleastair.*

> [It was then that Medb said to Fergus, 'Camp confusions have come on us
> here today, O Fergus.' 'Such is what happens to every stud led by a mare,'
> Fergus replied, 'They are robbed, they are taken, and their substance is
> destroyed on the backside of a woman of bad counsel.'] (ll. 4121–4)

In Recension II, however, the variant text implies that Fergus is respon-sible for all this direct speech, as he is the only designated speaker.[6] In fact in the spatial imaging of the narrative in LL Fergus and Medb seem to be envisaged as being in two different places: Fergus is doing his militarily correct task of counting the survivors, while Medb is in Cruachain arranging the spectacle of the bull fight, something she had long desired to see. Much of the fury which Fergus displays as he lashes out at Medb in both versions is, of course, a pent-up frustration with the manner in which his own battle exultation and his heroic dynamism could not be displayed at all in the mass conflict. Now in the dying moments of the tale he deflects his violence – both verbal and physical – on the orders of beings below him, women and animals.

This is, in fact a crucial shift of register and a language of devaluation dominates the choice of rhetorical stratagems for the ensuing ending; it is particularly clear in Recension I. In Recension II, there is an inevitable drift back to a habit of embellishment suitable to the period in which it was written, so that the narrative elements that constitute the ending have become less focused. But before closing in on the specifically narratological issues implicated in the staging of the end by both versions, I need to deal with the major building block of the ending, the fight of the bulls themselves.

Scholars have suggested that the bulls in the narrative function as mythological beasts, and in one sense this would provide a much neater sense of total narrative closure.[7] Their mythological status is assumed from the *Táin* foretale which locates the origin of the bulls in a series of human to animal transformations, beginning with a pair of quarrelling pig keepers.[8] This would throw up a number of interpretative options: the ongoing and unresolved quarrel in the foretale would imply that the two were meant to close out the main tale with their mutual self-destruction; the regional rivalry reflected in the original falling out forms an appropriate backdrop generally for the nature of the war in the main saga. The usefulness of this approach is limited, however, and the whole point of the foretale seems to be as a self-contained unit which effects a transition between an earlier 'mythical' time with a primeval Edenic vision of Ireland as a place of harmony and its eventual fall into the historic war time of saga; the transition being represented by the sequence of human to animal transformations. It functions as a frame tale but little of its resonance carries beyond.

Some of the formal characteristics of the final scene of the two bulls may, however, best be isolated by intertextual comparison of another, generic, kind. I find it useful to compare it with the ending of the more blatantly satiric *Scéla Mucce Meic Dathó* (The Story of Mac Datho's Pig) in order to emphasize the structures and the formulaic aspects of the mode of mock-heroic rhetoric which imbues this tale of the final fate of the bulls.[9] The saga *Scéla Mucce Mic Dathó* tells the story of a feast with a quarrel between the heroes of Ulster and Connacht over Ailbhe, the hound of their Leinster host, Mac Dathó. After a vigorous boasting contest between the provincial heroes for the right to claim the champion's portion of the festive meat, general mayhem ensues when Mac Dathó releases the hound in order to see which side the beast will choose.[10] The dog not only chooses Ulster but, with heroic intensity, attacks Medb and Ailill's chariot and is the cause of the Connachtmen being routed. The charioteer Fer Loga kills and dismembers the hound, but his canine fame lives on in that his body parts are the source of place names along the route northwards. In an even more farcical coda, Fer Loga in turn hijacks king Conchobar's chariot, seizing him from the rear in a compromising (dog like?) embrace and shames the king into granting him his wish – a year in Emain Macha with all the girls of the palace singing love songs to him.[11] After the year is up he returns with a gift of two horses from Conchobar and, presumably, all are satisfied.

Goodnight, Sweet Calf ...

From this summary the points of similarity with the *Táin* ending are apparent. There is a quasi-mythological touch to the manner in which new place names are created by the dismembered body of the (divine?) animal in each text. In both texts there is a referee and an audience for their struggle: Mac Dathó of *Scéla Mucce* in one, Fergus, with a refereeing doublet Bricriu, in the other. The basic shift to parody is made by treating the dog like a hero in his own right and endowing him with a sudden patriotic loyalty to his people of choice, Ulster.[12] The bull is also rendered comic by being treated like a heroic single-combat player. He is goaded into action by the taunts of Fergus, who reminds him that his honour is bound up with his own people, the Ulstermen (Recension I, ll. 4136–7). Another parodic element is the presence of a figure of ridicule introduced suddenly at this stage of the saga as if in witness to the sudden loss of the register of heroic seriousness: in one it is Fer Loga, in the other, Bricriu, whose unheroic character is a standard feature of Irish saga.[13] From the point of view of Fergus, defeat is especially bitter, and one of the discursive modes whereby defeat is registered is this swift and savage descent into parody. The line between being great and simply feeling ridiculous is a very fine one.

But the most significant aspect of the two narratives is that they share the element of the game of chance, of deciding a quarrel on the basis of an animal's choice. In the *Táin*, Recension I, this is represented as follows: *Dolodar iar sin ina slóig dia guin. Ni léig Fergus acht a thecht leth bud mellach lais. Is iarsin doascain dochum a thíri.* [The host made to kill him (i.e., the Donn Cúailnge after he appears from the lake contest with the dismembered body of Finnbennach impaled on his horns), but Fergus would only allow that he be let go wherever seemed good to him. It was then that he turned towards his own land (i.e., Ulster)] (ll. 4143–5).[14]

Granted the brisk and parodic nature of the closing style, there is much, nevertheless, that is also elegiac about the death of the bull and it is evident that some care has been taken to structure his last days. His route home is organized in a movement of threes: the three drinks he has on the way, the disposal of the three parts of his rival's body, which he has brought up from the lake, and finally, the sequence of three actions on the way: the bellowing at Kells, the butting of the hill Étan Tairb, and the digging of a ditch at Gort mBúraig. The aetiological work of the bull on this journey is correctly planned along a discernible route and, in this sense, is impressive if hastily filled in; the place names that embody his deeds and constitute the record of his dismemberments seem, for the most part, to have these names already before he inscribes his deed on them. It is almost as if the sense of an ending brings with it an answering rhetoric which plays narrative at double the normal speed. Bricriu only figures briefly in the narrative of the bulls. His story is an extra-*Táin* narrative, an incident outside the frame of the present tale. Recension II, however, allows the whole story: Fergus had quarreled with him the year before the *Táin* began and had buried a chessman to the depth of the piece in his head. Recension I mentions his convalescent status only in passing; it as if here his death, through being trampled by the bulls, is a matter of so little consequence and his weakened and non-combatant state is not worth commenting on, so great is the need to tell this tale of the bulls in one grand narrative run.

Recension II by contrast, while it remains generally close to Recension I, develops its ending in a much more relaxed, more embellished, and anecdotal narrative style. There is a certain amount of secondary writing blurring the clean outlines from the beginning of the operation of the ending. Medb gathers the men of Ireland to watch the bulls, but before we are told why, they happen to start fighting. Recension I specifies and nails by an etymology the place of combat: *co comarnic fri Findbennach hi Tarbga hi Muig Aií .i. targuba nó tarbgleó. Roí Dedond a chétainm in c[h]nuic sin* [he met Finnbennach in combat in Tarbga in Mag Aí, that is Bull lament or Bull battle. The former name of the hill was Roí Dedond] (ll. 4125–7). LL brings up the tale of the two bulls on a larger scale, and into sharper focus: the invader bull seeing the lovely unknown land for the first time, issuing a challenge with his roar, and being responded to equally heroically by the Connacht bull. The fight is suspenseful, with advantage changing from one side to the other. The role of referee is described explicitly and a full account is given of Bricriu's ambiguous warrior status and untrustworthy character. The circumstances of his death by trampling are fully explained: he is standing in a pit between the bulls. But the citation of Bricriu is paradoxical on a number of levels; normally his part in saga action is at the beginning of a saga where his provocative and challenging behaviour initiates, rather than terminates, a story. In addition, any story he figures in will carry a charge of parody. In this instance Bricriu could be said to function as the supplement of parody, the esential code switcher to this narrative mode. The parodic normally implies the imposition of critical distance from the object-text and, as such, seems to me to function here as a way for the author/encoder to close down the fiction. It is, then, one of the most important off-switches that the redactors have at their disposal.

The bulls themselves take on a classic *riastarthae* distortion of eyes, cheeks and nostrils, embellished by simile and LL's characteristic runs of alliteration. Later, when goaded and slapped (in suitable heroic sublime mode by the huge spear of Cormac Cond Longas) Donn Cúailnge recovers, but one notes that, though he is given human understanding in LL's version, the clear structure of auspicious choice of direction is no longer present in the narrative as it was for Recension I. Where YBL had characterized the bull's choice as a matter of auspices and ritual: *Níp sén* [This was not auspicious], LL's rewriting loses all sense of this: *Nirap sét suthain suachnid dún in sét sa* [This is not likely to be any item/ journey of great and lasting value to us] (ll. 4886–7).[15] Fergus's bombastic ringmaster response is also appropriate to the heroic rewriting but adds little of apparent relevance to that resolution of human conflict one expects of an ending, unless reassigning the language of Recension I, 'Ulster's spoils of victory' word, *coscur*, to the brown bull is considered significant:

'Maith a fhiru,' bar Fergus, 'léicid a óenur más é in Findbennach Aí fhail and, 7 más é in Dond Cúalnge, léicid a choscor leis. Natiur-sa bréthir is bec i ndernad imna tarbaib i farrad na ndingéntar innossa.'

['So, men,' said Fergus, 'if it is the Finnbennach of Mag Aí leave him alone, and if it is the Donn of Cooley let him have his victory. Upon my word, little is the bullfighting we have seen compared with what will be done now.'] (ll. 4897–90)

With the dismemberment of the bulls in LL, generic rewriting of another kind intervenes. It is brave indeed to assign a new etymology to Cruachain.[16] It is possible that there is a shade of Leinster *dindshenchas* bias interposing itself here, a borrowing from the place-name lore of the cattle horns associated with the fortress of Almhu, the legendary home of Finn mac Cumhail.[17] And it is possible that the change of focus in the dismemberment place names reflects also a new Leinster bias as well. The most daring of these new names is the etymology and double citation of Dublin: *Ra chuir a chlíathaig uad go Dublind rissa rátter Áth Cliath* [he tossed the rib-cage from him as far as Dublin which is called the Ford of the Hurdles/Rib-cage] (ll. 4908–9).[18] This would fit with the status of the Book of Leinster itself as having special associations with the career of Art mac Murchadha, the contemporary and ill-fated king of Leinster.[19]

Ends and Means, Storytellers and Scribes

In different and unexpected ways the two Recensions approach the fact of the end with separate perspectives. Despite the speed with which Recension I wraps up its work, it does present the façade, style, and structure, of a true ending:

Do géni Ailill 7 Medb córae fri Ultu 7 fri Coin Culaind. Secht mblíadna iar sin ní roibi guin duine eturru i nn-Érind. Anaid Findabair la Coin Culaind 7 tíagaid Con[n]achta dia tír 7 tíagaid Ulaid do Emain Macha cona mórchoscar.

[Ailill and Medb came to an arrangement with the Ulsermen and with Cú Chulainn. For seven years after that there was not a single person wounded in Ireland. Findabair remained with Cú Chulainn, the Connachtmen returned to their territory and the Ulstermen came back victoriously to Emain Macha.] (ll. 4157–end)

The positive result of the war is a true and stable period of peace agreed on by the parties. There is no more raiding out of province by the Connacht men and the Ulaid are free to enjoy the re-invigorated royal centre of Emain Macha. With this, in the last lines of the saga, a return is forced to Cú Chulainn and the matter of Ulster. Recension I is keen to keep in the foreground the figure of the hero Cú Chulainn. Peace must be separately negotiated with him and his terms agreed upon. The price is Findabair, and here some warning bells begin to ring: something is off here. Most scholars find it difficult to see this as anything other than a major blunder, since the unfortunate girl had been supposedly finished off by Cú Chulainn earlier in the story (ll. 1569–1605). But for this earlier scene Interpolator H is the sole witness, and even he does not make it explicit that she is in fact killed rather than merely humiliated, so perhaps there some space for excuse.[20]

But there is more to come: O'Rahilly notes that for the ending sentence there is a striking similarity of wording between the end of the *Táin* in Recension I and the tale, *Fled Bricrend 7 Longes Mac nDúil Dermait*. Kaarina Hollo has examined this tale and has suggested that it must have been written in Clonmacnois some time in the ninth century, after 835, the date when Kelleher suggested that the *Táin* came to Clonmacnois.[21] She has further claimed that the work actually borrows heavily from the *Táin*.[22] However, there are indications that the relationship goes the other way.[23] To misplace a Findabair while thinking all the while of a Finnchóem is hardly accidental and signifies a kind of studied nonchalance: an ending is an ending is any old ending ... an auctorial gesture whose only likeness is the whack on the rump of the bull; let randomness decide.

What is of serious general interest here, however, is what such borrowing reveals about saga production generally. An ending for the *Táin* has been fashioned in a quite complex way: out of a saga that itself shows every evidence of having been composed in the Shannon region by someone who was already *au fait* with Ulster saga texts. The impression this leaves us with is one of intense creative activity in more than one scribal centre. One witnesses, in a fairly short space of time, the phenomenon of the Ulster saga going global, so to speak. Thus, whatever a modern reader's opinion of the literary merits of this closure, it marks a key creative moment in generic tradition building.

Scribe-Speak

In the two recensions the scribes themselves appear to bring down the curtain to their respective narratives. In Recension 1 the exceptional coda *FINIT AMEN* appears in large letters. The effect is to gesture towards the termination of the writing act that produced the saga and to register a scribe's own satisfaction with the worthy finishing off provided by an adequate ending that may well be of his own devising. Paradoxically, it is Recension II that provides no literary buttressing of the end – the narrative as such ends abruptly with the death of the bull. Instead there are attempts to flag the narrative's course by emphasizing the fact of closure in technical terms. There are in fact three notices of the end closing out the LL text: for convenience I list them here:

> *Gorop a hús 7 a imthúsa 7 a deired na Tánad gonici sein*

> [This is the beginning, the development of the narrative and the ending of the *Táin* to this point.]

> *Bendacht ar cech óen mebraigfes go hindraic Táin amlaid seo 7 ná tuillfe cruth aile furri*

> [A blessing on everyone who will study the *Táin* exactly like this and who will not add any other form to it.]

> *Sed ego qui scripsi hanc historiam aut verius fabulam quibusdam fidem in hac historia aut fabula non accommodo. Quaedan enim ibi sunt praestrigia demonum, quaedam autem figmenta poetica, quaedam similia uero, qaedam non, quaedam ad delectationem stultorum.*

> [But I who have written this *historia* or rather *fabula*, do not give credence to the various incidents related in it. For some things in it are the deceptions of demons, others poetic forms; some are probable, others improbable; while others are for the amusement of thick-witted folk.]

Before I discuss the issues raised by these two last items I want to note briefly the first, an in-character *finit* flourish of the author. This is clearly of the same order of narrative flagging as is found in the early stages of the text; it balances the term *remthús* used at l. 1215.[24] The other two have received most attention and have been discussed most recently with great sensitivity by Nagy, Ó Néill and Poppe. Joseph Nagy has suggested that the balance represented by the double colophon, one in the vernacular and traditional, the other in Latin and highly condemnatory of the saga, perfectly reflects the creative tensions between a traditional orality on the one hand and a scholarly milieu that values the written word on the other.[25] Pádraig Ó Néill makes the most useful suggestion that the two colophons represent the work of author and scribe respectively. He goes on to discuss the classical and ecclesiastical tradition behind the use of such words as *historia, fabula, figmenta poetica, ad delectationem*.[26] Erich Poppe, who perforce writes on the matter with no reference to Ó Néill's work, emphasizes the Augustinian heritage of the LL formulation: 'the literary theories implied in the colophon result from the application of the textual analysis which *Grammatica* teaches.'[27]

The most crucial medieval terms used to define and analyse narrative, inherited from the classical world, are *narratio* and *fabula*.[28] Discussion of the ethical and proprietal problems raised by the relation of these two terms to the central truth or reality they are deemed to serve is, on the whole, standardized through the entire medieval period, and they are accepted as derivative of their Ciceronian formulation in the *Rhetorica Ad Herennium*, and *De Inventione*. *Narratio* is a subset of the category *inventio* and a primarily legal rhetorical context underlies all Cicero's observations:

> *Narratio* is an expression of events that have occurred or are supposed to have occurred. There are three kinds: one which contains only the case and the whole reason for the dispute; a second in which a digression is made for the purpose of attacking somebody or of making a comparison or of amusing the audience in a way not incongruous with the business in hand, or for amplification; the third kind wholly unconnected with public issues, and recited or written solely for amusement, provides training at the same time. It is divided into two classes:
>
> 1 Concerned with events:
>
>   (a) *fabula*, or narrative in which events are not true and have no verisimilitude;
>
>   (b) *historia*, or account of actual occurrences remote from our own age;
>
>   (c) *argumentum*, or fictitious narrative which might nevertheless have occurred.
>
> 2 One concerned with persons, in which not only the events but also the conversation and mental attitudes of the persons is shown. This form of

narrative should possess great vivacity, resulting from changes in fortune, contrast of characters, severity, gentleness, hope, fear, suspicion desire, dissimulation, delusion, pity, sudden change in fortune, disaster, sudden pleasure, happy endings to the story. But these embellishments must be drawn from what will be later said about the rules of style.[29]

In this double-faceted account, narration is envisaged as not quite independent of the actual realia of a courtroom performance, but yet reaching close to the kind of free status of performative entertainment of a typically Roman kind.[30] For the rest, narration is divided, in a fashion that remains standard through all the Middle Ages, on a truth/falsity scale. Here *historia* does not necessarily occupy the privileged primary position on the scale of acceptable generators of *narratio*. Irish learned tradition, to which the transmission of the *Táin* belongs, values the work of *historia* in the strict sense of the term, and the scribes of Recension I, at any rate, were quite prepared to accord the *Táin* the sort of analysis and version-sifting proper to the work of the historian.[31] However, in the neo-Platonic traditions of late Antiquity, traditions which Irish scholars such as Eriugena later reworked, and in the revival of these traditions in the twelfth century,[32] the value of *fabula* has undergone something of a rehabilitation. The influential discussion here was the definition of fable as *narratio fabulosa* in Macrobius' commentary on the *Dream of Scipio*.

> Fables serve two purposes: either to gratify the ear or to encourage the reader to do good works ... [The latter] are divided into two types. In the first both the setting and the plot are fictitious, as in the fables of Aesop, famous for his exquisite imagination. The second rests on a solid foundation of truth, which is treated in a fictitious style. This is called the fabulous narrative [*narratio fabulosa*] as distinct from the ordinary [Aesopian] *fabula*.[33]

It is this latter kind which, even when it involves pagan gods and questionable acts, is amenable to the veil of allegory. In the LL colophon the categorization of some *fabula/historia* as being for the delight of fools would seem to fit the first Macrobian category of the more purely imaginary, non-useful fictions. But if the LL scribe is conservative on these matters he should not be seen as dismissing secular literary traditions or their subject matter entirely. He would probably place himself in the same position as his English contemporary William of Malmesbury, who expresses these same doubts as to the manner of scoring native traditions on the truth/fable balance sheet with reference to Arthur: *Hic est Artur. de quo Britonum nugae hodieque delirant, dignus plane quem non fallaces somniarent fabulae sed ueraces predicarent historiae.* [It is of this Arthur that the Britons fondly tell so many tales, even to the present day, a man worthy to be celebrated, not by false and dreaming fable, but by reliable history.][34]

High-Brow/Low-Brow

In Irish vernacular tradition the issue of popular credulity (*ad delectandum stultorum*) on the fact/fiction grid is voiced for the first time by the author of the genealogical compilation in Rawlinson B 502, a work normally dated to the early ninth century, possibly the work of Cormac mac Cuileannáin himself. The terms are set according to an oral/written, foolish/wise split:

> *Imprudens Scottorum gens, rerum suarum obliuiscens, acta quasi inaudita sine nullo modo facta uendicat, quoniam minus tribuere litteris aliquid operum suorum percurrat, et ob hoc genealogias Scotigenae gentis litteris tribuam*[35]

> [The foolish Irish race forgetting its own (traditions), gives credence to deeds that are unbelievable and not at all factual, with the result that it neglects to commit to writing anything of its own deeds. This is why I commit genealogies of the Irish race to writing.]

In the pseudo-historical traditions of *Lebor Gabhála* concerns about the relative status of truth and fable is a familiar concept and is used especially in those sections that deal with the *Tuatha Dé Danann*.[36] Perhaps the most pertinent comments are those in the poem on the arrival of the Tuatha Dé, where the poet Eochu ua Flainn makes a rather shaky case on the one hand for rejecting fabulous traditions for their pagan dangers, and on the other, for accepting them as true if they can be seen to have passed through a filter of Christianized tradition-shaping. From the same period of the eleventh to the twelfth century comes the story of Tuirell Bicrenn and his children, where the following clear statement is made:

> *Fírinde ocus faiblend fuar*
> *hi sencusaib na sáersluag*

is don faibliudh shemhglicc sith.
ro.glen inn eric, etsid.

[Truth and fable have I found in the lore of the learned; it is to artful, other-world fable that the tale of the *éraic* pertains. Listen!][37]

Here one is clearly in the zone of acceptable fable; even when it is clearly fabulous it is nevertheless artful, ingenious – showing off the talents of its author – and useful. It is also interesting to speculate on what the colophon writer has in mind as *figmenta poetica* or *praestrigia demonum*. Ó Néill suggests that the first carries a pejorative meaning and refers to the classical authors' handling of classical mythology, but this judgment might more properly apply to the second.[38] On the Irish context of the second term one is also on surer ground. John Carey has pointed out the similarities between the colophon's reference to demonic delusions and the matter of the colophon to the tale *Serglige Con Culainn*:[39]

Conid taibsiu admillti do Choin Chulaind la háes sídi sin. Ar ba mór in cumachta demnach ria cretim. 7 ba hé a méit co cathaigtis co corptha na demna frisna doínib 7 co taisféntais aíbniusa 7 díamairi doib. Amal no betis co marthanach is amlaid no creteá doib. Conid frisna taidbsib sin atberat na haneólaig síde 7 áes síde

[That is 'The Destroying Apparition from the People of the *Síd* to Cú Chulainn.' For great was the power of demons before the faith. It was so great that demons in corporeal form used to tempt humans and they would show them delightful and secret things. As they seemed to be mortals they were believed in. That is why ignorant folk call such apparitions 'fairy' and 'people of the *síd*' (the fairy mound).] (LU, ll. 4034–9)[40]

It is clear that a major preoccupation here is the belief in the ability of the *síd* to present not just lies as truth but most especially as sexually seductive visions; these visionary apparitions are of the kind one may assume from the context of *Serglige Con Culainn*, *Acallam na Senórach* and other lateish texts involving fairy women.

Underlying these comments from the learned clerics, then, lies a concern about what is being circulated on a popular level, a level on which they would like to assert control. The anxiety about the credulity of the *anéolaig* is notable in the last passage. Thus a primary focus of the LL scribe's distaste for *praestrigia demonum* would likely have been the belief that the Morrígain's shape-shifting is really capable of harming the hero.[41] No doubt this figure flourished on the level of popular belief as the *bean sí*, the Bodb, or war goddess as death-bringer, or the fairy woman who can seduce young men. The Morrígain, as I have been reading her, is all of these and so would have been the prime focus in the narrative for a churchman's concern. All in all and taken as a whole, I would tend to give a more positive shading to the colophon than Ó Néill does. Rather than a religious statement of blanket hostility I see, on balance, a real exercise in critical analysis by rhetorical category with some applications to current pastoral concerns. I concur with him in pointing up these interests in rhetoric.

As Carey points out, however, some of the negative judgments of scribes on secular literature are counterbalanced by much more positive endorsements, as when the commentator in *Scél na Fír Flatha* speaks of wondrous apparitions to princes as benign rather than demonic visitations.[42] I suspect that there may have been a window for such positive endorsements for the work of poets in particular periods. One such, for example, would be the cultural milieu of *Cormac's Glossary* at the end of the ninth century.[43] Here the story given under the entry *prull* clearly shows a considerable interest in making male transformational other-world visitants a vital part of the ongoing debate about the poetic process.[44] Another is in the second half of the twelfth century. As *Acallam na Senórach* makes clear, there is considerable debate and social anxiety in the period about clarification of sexual roles and numerous attempts to control active folkloric beliefs in the power of demonic forces to influence daily life.[45] If a literary critique is to be mounted in this period for a text such as the *Táin*, it will reflect a revitalized debate on the truth content of literary works on a high clerical level of concern, and it will also reflect the growing pastoral concerns of the century which extends the control of the church into the round of daily life.

But the ultimate significance of the double colophon is surely that, in an explicit and sophisticated way, one may see a scribal input into the LL *Táin* that distantiates so clearly the work of scribe and the work of composer. There was obviously a felt need to tone down the exuberance and textual excesses of the earlier version/s. This, scholars agree, is one of the demonstrable literary intentions of the LL-version composer. As author he is clearly pleased with his production and promotes it vigorously. That he did not go quite far enough for the taste of one clerical reader of the resultant text is suggested by the reaction of the LL scribe. This does not obscure the fact, however, that he and the composer had a roughly similar attitude as to content. Amusingly, the colophon as written shows a suspended *n* written suprascript in the phrase *non accomodo*. Belief and scepticism run dangerously close and one might say that the energy of the saga itself almost succeeded in overwriting their best effort to keep up the official front. It proved impossible to toss out figures such as the Morrígain, and the attempt to rewrite Medb in Recension II had the perverse effect of making the narrative more entertaining still. For the resistance of the saga itself, and for the presence on the ground of consumers of foolish tales, future readers must be grateful.

The Tale of Fergus: Calling Cattle (exiles) Home

If the story of the bulls makes one way of ending the saga, it also significant to note that, at the moment when the curtain goes down on all the characters for the last time, it is Fergus to whom the task of closing down the spectacle is assigned, both as human actor and as commentator. His acts and words are marked by a rhetoric of savage belittlement. The dehumanizing of Medb is followed by a devaluation of the bull as well. Granted his words to the bull can be taken as a form of friendly fellow-hero incitement but, as I noted above, the form of his invective also manages to deny the very act of divination that he had just set up for the beast: *co n-imbert slait iarna sethnaig. 'Níp sén ... in sengamain troitech sa* [he dealt him a whack on the ribs. 'This brawling old calf was no sign of good luck to us'] (ll. 4134–6).[46]

There is something deeper here in the relationship between Fergus and the animal than simply a display of heroic bad temper on the part of Fergus. As he speaks with loathing to the 'old quarrelsome calf' he seems to connect in his language of revilement and in the spectacle of a wounded and degraded sexual behemoth with an image of his own state. He too has spent most of the saga in the Connacht camp with his warrior and sexual powers severely compromised. He too has turned against the earth and the hills in furious impotence. He too has felt the agonizing urges to strike a blow for his own people. The bull, who returns to his own herding grounds to be amongst his own cows, is a figure who succeeds in getting what Fergus knows he will never have, and what many an Ulsterman since dreamed of: an exile's return and *bás i gcríoch Ulad*.[47] But if the Connacht side does not get the bull in the end, a kind of partisan justice is rendered inside the world of the saga itself in that a major consolation is developed in the learned traditions of Connacht in later times. The battle was lost but the culture war was ultimately won. Possession of Fergus the exile's grave yielded possession of the saga. And so the cultural pearl of great price is a monopoly of western cultural figures and centres for all the rest of the Middle Ages. For their guardianship grateful thanks is due.

The Tale Beyond the Telling

Finally, then, the whole story of the saga becomes a story where heroic pride yields the stage to the abjection of the men of letters, the men of no action.[48] It is the classic Indo-European formula of exchange, *do ut des*, all over again, this time released from its social constraints in order to provide an access to our own literary, latter-day ken. In the *agon* shared between hero and scribe in the *Táin* I find I understand in a new way what Yeats's final great poem 'Cuchulainn Comforted' seems to be saying:

> A man that had six mortal wounds, a man
> Violent and famous, strode among the dead;
> Eyes stared out of branches and were gone.
>
> Then certain Shrouds that muttered head to head
> Came and were gone. He leant upon a tree
> As though to meditate on wounds and blood.
>
> A Shroud that seemed to have authority
> Among those bird-like things came, and let fall
> A bundle of linen. Shrouds by two and three
>
> Came creeping up because the man was still.
> And thereupon that linen-carrier said:
> 'Your life can grow much sweeter if you will
>
> 'Obey our ancient rule and make a shroud;
> Mainly because of what we only know
> The rattle of these arms makes us afraid.
>
> 'We thread the needle's eyes, and all we do

All must together do.' That done, the man
Took up the nearest and began to sew.

'Now we must sing and sing the best we can,
But first you must be told our character:
convicted cowards all, by kindred slain

'Or driven from home and left to die in fear.'
They sang but had not human tunes nor words,
Though all was done in common as before;

They had changed their throats and had the throats of birds.[49]

The polarity and the deadly flow between deeds and the words to say
them is ceaseless. The hero's desired end is glorious and violent death.
But so used is our western tradition to tracking his subsequent fame
among the living and to taking the process of commemoration for
granted that we neglect to follow the hero in his lonely journey beyond
the grave. Here is a remarkable Yeatsian attempt to stall and slow
down the heroic death process and to look behind the mirror. Here is
the hero stripped, isolated, and alone, unable to reconstruct or maintain any semblance of his former overpowering identity. For Yeats, the
Irish hero's death goes through radical abjection on the way to being
thrust back again into the human mind. The sweetness of the singing
and the re-clothing depends on the collusion of the hero, the slow coming into his ken the view of the necessary other side, the abject non-
heroes, the recorders of the dead. The immortality of the singing bird is
the wrought epic text that passes, in a process of laborious stitchery
and reconstitution, through many hands until it finally can become in
its written form a singing artifact of eternity. If Cú Chulainn is the
'show' hero of the *Táin* then, in a Yeatsian sense, Fergus has long been
recognized by the professionals in *Táin* tradition as their truer hero. It
seems that it is only he who can hear and answer to the unheroicness
in himself and so begin the process of weaving a telling and a text that
continues to fascinate its readers and continues to dominate the Irish
heroic agenda down to our own day.

Epilogue: Their Bodies, Ourselves

'Now I must leave, and my blessing on you, people of the *síd*. There is a meeting of the men of Ireland in Tara at the end of the year, and I must go there to converse with my comrade and joint-fosterling, Oisín, son of Finn, and also because I am summoned by Patrick, the Adze-Head who ordered me to go tell the nobles of the men of Ireland, all assembled there, of the exploits and the great deeds of valor and prowess of the *Fían* and of Finn mac Cumaill, and of the men of Ireland as well, so that the scholars and the sages may preserve the tales that we tell them until the end of time.' 'Here is some help for you from us,' said Bé. 'What help might that be?' asked Caílte. 'A drink that we give you to take to Tara for the remembrance of lore, so that you may be able to recall at will every cataract or river or estuary that you meet, along with its attendant battles and combats.' 'That is the help of friends and of a true family!' said Caílte.

Acallam na Senórach (Tales of the Elders of Ireland), ll. 7250–62

It may have struck readers as odd that this entire volume has been skewed, biased even, against a straightforward investigation of the main show attraction of Irish sagas generally and the *Táin* in particular. Where is the spectator/reader deference and awe in the face of the scenes of heroic display in which heroes do precisely what they are supposed to do – fight and go on fighting to the death?[1] Without treating this aspect of the heroic compact, of the way heroes are finally serious because they take on the burden of facing death, one is in danger of subverting too deeply the reading agenda and misreading their identities; of only seeing the bombastic *miles gloriosus* and being blind to the dignity of the figures who, despite their verbal swagger and their cumbersome self-regard, challenge death for the communities to which they belong. On a lesser but no more persistent level of fidelity to the matter of the Irish sagas, the audience for this genre must have valued the violence for its vicarious performative thrills. So, how flawed is my reading if, time and time again in the previous chapters, I have deferred and deflected into textual issues and their attendant textual pleasures what should have been a central zone of direct impact of the narrative?

Granted, this is an area that has not been quite neglected: I have explored heroics on a social and psychic level throughout in the memorialization of heroes, and the initiation and hardening up of the young adolescent as he faces his adult phase as a fighting man in chapters 4 and 5. Other scholars have already explored the realm of contestatory maleness in action.[2] Indeed, there is a whole sub-literature which deals with such aspects of epic and saga generally as heroic performative discourse, the relation of hero to his society, and the codes of the fair fight.[3] Nevertheless it seems both logical and fair to acknowledge that by my reformulating and rereading this narrative of fighting, as constituted by the *Táin*, I might be, in a certain sense, playing it false; by colluding with the text itself and emptying it out by means of objectifying and ironising strategies am I retreating from the sense of chaos, pain, and terror at the heart of a warrior's experience? How else, then, could it be done?

Perhaps the proper moment is here, at the end of my study, to address something of the impact of the narrative of violence in a direct way. In their own coding heroes value the singular death; their exits are personally stamped in a way that compensates powerfully for any ethical qualms about the act of killing or being killed. This operates on the level of a generalized culture of individual memorialization of the kind I described in chapter 1. If killing on this level offers a a ratification of the heroic self, then also being killed does not entirely empty out heroic identities thus constructed from collusive acts of violence. The rules and rituals are known and no one is entirely a victim. To a contemporary audience, however, violence is properly repugnant on a level of the real, even as, paradoxically, it is tolerated and even sought after in popular culture, crime fiction, in both documentary and fictional television police shows, in virtual reality video games, to give just a few examples. What has provoked a massive cultural aversion in the past thirty years or so is rather the site of mass deaths and atrocities. In mass killing grounds that appear on news programming one is forced as never before to look at victims, and here the impact of violence yields its most saturated kind of horror to a contemporary sensibility.[4]

Here then is where I would like to consider this question of dying violently, and to test one final time the engagements a contemporary reader might make with the resonances of the genre of saga writing to which the *Táin* belongs. This demands an opening up of the text one more time at the point where readers would all agree violence goes truly wild and the full destructive impact of the hero is most apparent. This is the moment when a recovered Cú Chulainn, in his most martial profile, yet charges the whole army:

Is and so focheird torandchless cét 7 torandchless dá chét 7 torandchless trí cét 7 torandchless cethri cét, 7 tarrasair aice for torandchless cúic cét, uair nírbo fhuráil less in comlín sin to thotim leiss ina chétchumscli 7 ina chét-chomling catha for cethri chóiced Hérend. Ocus dothóet ass fón cumma sin dinsaigid a námat 7 dobretha a charpat morthimchull cethri n-ollchóiced nÉrend ammaig anechtair, 7 dosbert fóbairt bidbad fo bidbadaib foraib 7 dobreth seól trom fora charpat 7 dollotar rotha íarnaidi in charpait hi talmain, corbo leór do dún 7 do daingen feib dollotar rotha íarnidi in charpait i talmain, uair is cumma atrachtatar cluid 7 cairthe 7 carrce 7 táthleca 7 murgrían in talman aird i n-aird frisna rothaib íarndaidib súas sell sechtair. Is aire focheird in circul m[b]odba sin mórthimcull cethri n-ollchóiced nÉrend ammaig anechtair arná teichtis úad 7 ná scaíltís immi coros tairsed fri tendta fri tarrachtain na macraide forro. Ocus dothóet isin cath innond ar medón 7 fáilgis fálbaigi móra do chollaib a bidbad mórthimc[h]oll in tshlóig ammaig ammaig anechtair fo thrí 7 dobert fóbairt bidbad fo bidbadaib forro co torchratar bond fri bond 7 méde fri méde, ba sí tiget ind árbaig. Dosrimchell aridisi fa thrí in cruth sin co farcaib cossair sessir impu fá mórtimchull .i. bond trir fri méde trír fó chaird timchill immon dúnad. Condid Sesrech Breslige a ainm issin Táin ... Deich ríg ar secht fichtib ríg ro bí Cú Culaind i mBresslig Móir Maigi Murthemni. Dírime immorro olchena di chonaib 7 echaib 7 mnáib 7 maccaib 7 mindaínib 7 drabarshlóg, ar nír érno in tres fer do fheraib Hérend cen chnáim lessi nó lethchind nó lethshúil do brisiud nó cen bithanim tria bithu betha. Ocus dothóet úadib iar sin iar tabairt in tress sin forro, cen fhuligud cen fhordercad fair féin ná fora gillu ná for ech dia echaib.

[It was here that Cú Chulainn performed the thunderfeats of one hundred, of two hundred of three hundred and of four hundred. And he stopped at the thunderfeat of five hundred because he considered that to be a sufficient number to fall by his hand in his first onslaught and his

first attacking encounter against the four provinces of Ireland. And he
went forth in that manner to attack his enemies and drove his chariot
around the four great provinces of Ireland and he attacked them with
implacable wrath and he drove his chariot furiously and the iron wheels
dug into the ground so that they cast up the size of a fort or a fortress the
way the wheels went into the ground; so that it was like dykes and stone
pillars and boulders, flags and gravel had been raised up on high around
about all the provinces of Ireland such did the iron wheels dig up after
them. He made this Bodb-like circle all around the four great provinces of
Ireland so that they could not flee from him nor scatter on him until he
had straitened them in revenge for the deaths of the boy troop of Ulster.
And he went in to battle them right in the centre and three times he threw
up a great wall of bodies around them. And with the fury of foe on foes
they were felled, sole to sole and headless neck to headless neck, such was
the mass slaughtering. Again he encircled them in this way so that he
made a sixfold slaughter on them in this fashion, heel to headless neck in
lines all around in the death 'fortress.' So this is its name in the *Táin*, 'The
Sixfold Slaughter' ... Seven score and ten kings did Cú Chulainn slay in
the Battle of Breslech Már in Mag Murthemne; countless moreover the
number of hounds and horses, women and youths, lesser folk and common folk. For not one man in three of the men of Ireland escaped without
his hipbone broken, or the side of his head smashed or the eye in his head
or without a nickname for maiming ever after. But he himself left the field
after that attack on them without a wound or a mark on himself, his charioteer, or either of his two horses.] (Recension I, ll. 2292–334)

This must be allowed to speak for itself, first, as raw killing data. Yet,
even as one absorbs this recitation of wanton destruction of human
beings one cannot help but notice the paradox: indeed, the passage
vividly describes in all its gory bodily detail the act of mass killing; but
even as the killing is enacted, the rage for order goes on, not one step
behind but pace for pace. The corpses are formally arranged in death,
marked by their hero's head-taking – hence identifiable as his war trophy – and in a tri-vallate circle, as if to create a ghastly mirror of living
habitation; the body ramparts include not only fighting men but full
retinues as well, common folk, women, children, horses and dogs – in
short, the full complement of the households of the living arranged
here in death. The *Breslech* is a totalizing image of war visited out of the
blue; it appears in the text as a striking contrast to the individualizing

combats in which Cú Chulainn has participated in from the early half of the narrative.

It is part of the rewritten sequence in which Lug heals the hero and thus reinvigorated, arms himself, becomes distorted by fury and goes out to fight his enemies en masse.[5] As part of the partial transformation to epic of Irish saga the literary process requires, to put it crudely, a high body count.

We the reader/audience know that here, as elsewhere, it is all words or, more specifically here, a combination of rhetorical and mathematical ostentation; we acknowledge as skilled readers that it this exuberance, where language aims at high epic style, rather than a middle style of event-based narrative unfolding, that moves this scene forward. But even as the purple prose itself, with waves of hyperbole piling on hyperbole, conveys the fury of violent action flaring up in the text, it quickly climaxes, transforms, and then dies down again, leaving only the more leisurely recapitulative ground rhythms of naming and numbering to play the narrative onward to its end. And even within the verbal rush that frames the killing ground scene, death is apprehended at the point where it is already passing into posthumous order. The text hastens to create a figure of bodies arranged, not scattered in a landscape; the process is one of textual memorialization, of a gathering up and naming of the dead – not for the sake of the individuals slaughtered – though names are given, their only value is symbolic, ciphers of the extent of the killing – but from the magisterial visual overview of the vicarious victor-enunciator himself, who, before he puts names to maimed bodies, marvels first at the formal design created by the destroying hero. Thus in important ways the experience of death is diverted by an aesthetic that chooses to ignore its bitterness and terror for the individual in favour of the creation of a mark in the landscape; that mark is crafted like a house and we are hard put to hold its reality as a mass grave in our consciousness.[6] There is a fundamental irony here: the more elaborate the words to speak death become, the more the experience of death itself recedes and the horror becomes, finally in the literal meaning of the word, unspeakable.[7]

Scholars have long debated whether it is legitimate to use insular textual witnesses to validate aspects of continental Celtic social and ritual practice, particularly as regards the question of continuity in heroic custom. Jackson's famous 'window on the Iron Age' approach to the *Táin* has by now been firmly closed by Mallory.[8] Opening up windows

will, however, always remain just as irresistible a habit to some as shut-
ting them is to other scholars. Thus the formal arrangement of headless
bodies in a bounded enclosure calls to mind the equine and human
long-bone altars made from the defeated army by the victors at the Belgic sanctuary site of Ribemont-sur-Ancre.[9] What the saga text seems to
do is to compress into one action the complex and long-drawn-out process of creating a Celtic trophy of the kind demonstrably present at the
Belgic site excavated by Brunaux.[10]

It is for illustrative reasons such as this, but above all for the betray-
als and failings of textuality itself as registered in the sequence above,
that one is forced to contextualize and to try to restore human feeling
to this scene by looking to other Celtic killing grounds for answering
rites. Recently, in a rescue excavation at Gondole, near Clermont-
Ferrant, archaeologists uncovered a mass grave which they have suggested may be part of the fallout from Caesar's siege of Alesia (see
frontispiece).[11] Eight human males and eight horses are laid out in
death. There are no weapons or grave goods and the cause of death has
yet to be worked out: as the excavation goes on, they are proving to be
not isolated cases. Archaeologists who have commented on the find
have noted the proximity of Alesia, but there is no real evidence that
the burial is of actual siege victims from Caesar's time. To associate
them with material evidence of post-battle human sacrifice from north-
ern heroic cult sanctuaries such as Gournay or Ribemont sur Ancre is
equally conjectural until more forensic work is done.[12]

The presence of the horses laid out in order is a trigger that, paradoxically, makes unavoidable the managed humanity of the buried
men and the biological fact of death. The two rows of four horses are
completed by the two rows of men, each with an arm over the other's
shoulder, in a way that implicates a sense of human solidarity and also
links the fate of one group with the other socially under the rubric of
the *equites* class. Horses and humans are laid down in order side by
side. What makes the body design particularly poignant is the fact that
on the bottom level there are in fact three warriors; the fourth, next to
the horse cadaver, is an adolescent boy whose whole head is tucked
under the arm of the man in front of him so that the head lies on his
companion's belly area. It is a simple protective gesture of deeply moving pathos. Emotionally, the adolescent protected by the arm of the
older warrior calls up archaic images of heroic initiation and warrior
mentoring. Viewing the scene after a journey through the *Táin* will
invite us back there to a fundamental relationship, the divine father

Lug and his son Cú Chulainn, and to the drama of bodily vulnerability played out at the very centre of that heroic experience which I tried to describe in such terms in chapter 5. Even as the viewer in our time gazes on the photographic reproduction of the sight, the eye begins to seek ameliorating design on a visual as well as an emotional level. Visually the skeletons form patterns in the surrounding earth: the bones are like a fine lattice, a repeating pattern worked with the white of rib cages and long bones to a lacy fineness. Ideas of order, and not just chronological distancing from events in the past, govern in greater or lesser degree our response to these mass killings that would, in a contemporary context, come to us in a more fraught and chaotic manner and strike us with despair at their irrationality.

This places the question of the seriousness of death in a heroically-articulated society in a different order of things from our harrowed responses to contemporary gross inhumanity and violence. But what accounts for the difference in my emotional response between the two heroic sites I have invoked: one textual, the other revealed by the archaeologist (or should I say the developer)? Perhaps it is quite simple: for better or worse, the text cannot stop speaking, cannot help itself as it endlessly shapes and re-composes its narrative trajectory because it has work to do; it needs to move beyond such scenes, even the very gravest, and to push towards the end. The limits of the *Táin's* fictional condition is here. Pity whether in epic or in tragedy is a managed response. The other Celtic mass grave, however, speaking a language of presence in silence, engages more fully on a human level because it does not talk back in any easily accessible register of discourse. In the textual site it is only the shaping and crafting of words that matter, and any pretense that some historical reality lies behind the existence of the victims is not even entertained. They are simply the 'other' to the hero, and as such, always already obliterated and dumb in the heroic mode of scoping violence. In the zone of this Gaulish grave historical issues will certainly matter in the future as scholars try to reconstitute the facts of the case; but as yet such facts that would divert and distract the gaze of the viewer barely register. The need to gather the evidence of these lives lived, which reveal themselves here so openly in death, will presently become the only ethical and scholarly position for the next stage of the enquiry. But this stage here provides a hiatus and a pause – as yet unlinked to a certain knowledge and its consequent responsibilities. Here and most eloquently, deprived as they still are of a master narrative, of partisan sympathies and historical rationalizations, long buried and forgotten bodies thrust themselves into the human mind again. But the element of communication outwards to us is absent. They are unshakeably Other: if finally they speak it is only to utter themselves, to themselves, and as we view them as they never thought to be seen, they seem to draw together away from us into a community of themselves.

Notes

Introduction

1 In what follows I use mainly Cecile O'Rahilly's edition of Recension I; *Táin Bó Cúailnge: Recension I* (Dublin, 1976). This publication appeared after her edition of Recension II, and thus much of her introduction for this recension contains material germane to the textual status of Recension I. She qualifies Rudolf Thurneysen's ideas of two written sources lying behind Recension I by proposing that considerations of oral composition might better account for doublet incidents and other repetitions; cf. R. Thurneysen, *Die irische Helden- und Königsage* (Berlin, 1921), passim. O'Rahilly's Introduction to Recension I shows a further slight development of her ideas on the nature of its composition away from oral epic theories; in her discussion of the contributions of scribe H in particular, she demonstrates the usefulness of a sensitive textual approach to recovering the compositional concerns of H. Nevertheless, her edition of Recension I is somewhat flawed in a minor way by an overriding concern for how this version fits in with all the others. This leads her to emend more frequently than would be appropriate if one were really to view the text purely on its own terms.

2 O'Rahilly, *Táin Bó Cúailnge from the Book of Leinster* (Dublin, 1967).

3 The main recensions are treated by O'Rahilly, *TBC II*, xiv–xvi. There are two other recensions. One is a fragmentary form found in two manuscripts, BL Egerton MS BL 93 and MS Trinity College Dublin H 2 17; ed. Rudolf Thurneysen, 'Táin Bó Cuailnge nach H. 2. 17,' *Zeitschrift für celtische Philologie* 8 (1912), 538–54; ed. Max Nettlau, 'The Fragment of the *Táin Bó Cuailnge* in MS Egerton 93,' *Revue celtique* 14 (1893), 254–6, 15 (1894), 62–78, 198–208. The other is RIA MS C vi 3, ed. C. O'Rahilly, *The Stowe Version of Táin Bó Cuailnge* (Dublin, 1961).

4 This phrase, taken from Seamus Heaney's 'Station Island' (*Station Island* [London, 1984], 93), is part of Joyce's message to the poet to keep him away from the too heavily rutted path of 'big Irish-issues' poetry.

5 Within this framing, the Greimas actantial model of sender/object/receiver and helper/subject/opponent has proved to be of such continuing usefulness as to be almost a given of these kinds of textual analyses. The terminology of 'enunciation' and 'represented enunciation,' narrated time versus the time of the narration, was first discussed by Émile Benveniste, *Problèmes de linguistique générale*, 2 vols (Paris, 1966–74), vol. 1, 251–66, vol. 2, 67–88. See also Gérard Genette, *Figures III* (Paris, 1972); 71–88, 122–30 and Paul Ricoeur, *Temps et récit II. La configuration dans le récit de fiction* (Paris, 1984), 113–30. For the deployment of the term 'decoder,' see Umberto Eco, *The Role of the Reader: Explorations in the Semiotics of Texts* (Bloomington, 1979); for critiques of Eco's position, see Michael Riffaterre, 'The Interpretant in Literary Semiotics,' in *Reading Eco: An Anthology*, ed. Rocco Capozzi (Bloomington, 1977), 173–84; and Scott Simpkins, *Literary Semiotics: A Critical Approach* (Lanham, MD, and Oxford, 2001), 57–86.

6 A.-J. Greimas, *Structured Semantics: An Attempt at a Method*, trans. D. McDowell et al. (Lincoln, NE, 1983).

7 For example, in chapter 4 I suggest that the scribe H in LU also produced other Cú Chulainn pieces – most notably the long version of *Verba Scáthaige* – writing in the style and spirit of his interventions in the text of the *Táin*.

8 Here I paraphrase the excellent exposition of Francois Rastier, *Meaning and Textuality*, trans. Frank Collins and Paul Perron (Toronto, 1997; first pub. 1989), 28.

9 Umberto Eco, *The Limits of Interpretation* (Bloomington, 1990), 260.

10 Rastier, *Meaning*, 27–32.

11 Jonathan Culler, 'In Defence of Overinterpretation,' in *Interpretation and Overinterpretation*, with Umberto Eco, Richard Rorty, and Christine Brook-Rose, ed. Stefan Collini (Cambridge, 1992), 122–3.

12 This phrase was overheard on a Dublin bus, spoken by a senior citizen, a fan of the robust game of Gaelic football, describing the lesser excitements of his first view of soccer.

13 For play and its related term, pleasure, I am most guided by the critical spirit of Roland Barthes; his most influential work has been *S/Z: An Essay*, trans. Richard Miller (New York, 1974; first published 1970). This was followed by *The Pleasure of the Text*, trans. R. Miller (New York, 1975; first published 1973). I first attempted a Barthesian reading of an Irish text in 'The Heroic Word: On the Reading of Early Irish Sagas,' in *The Celtic Consciousness*, ed. Robert O'Driscoll (Portlaoise, 1981), 155–61. Barthes's early

Mythologies is relevant here also, especially to my point on the projection of Cú Chulainn into the position of the essential Irish arch-hero.

14 The formative text here is Benedict Anderson, *Imagined Communities: Reflections on the Origin and Spread of Nationalism*, rev. ed. (London, 1991). Some of its implications have been articulated using a Gramsci model by David Cairns and Shaun Richards, *Writing Ireland: Colonialism, Nationalism and Culture* (Manchester, 1988). For some observations on the formative role of the Cú Chulainn myth on Irish nationalism, see Declan Kiberd, *Inventing Ireland: The Literature of the Modern Nation* (Cambridge, MA., 1995), 196–238.

15 The Cú Chulainn myth has once again shifted valency in a post-modern Ireland; typical is Paul Muldoon's mischievous take on his own 'family values' rude awakening to a post-modern world: 'It was now too late, as I crouched with Cuchulainn and Emer, / to feel anything much but nausea / as again and again S– cast about for an artery' ('Yarrow,' *Paul Muldoon Poems, 1968–1998* (New York, 2001), 380.

16 Barthes, 'Textual Analysis: Poe's "Valdemar,"' in *Modern Criticism and Theory*, ed. David Lodge (London, 1988), 174.

17 Translation with minor change from Cecile O'Rahilly, *Táin Bó Cúalnge from the Book of Leinster* (Dublin, 1967), 272. I examine this codicil in detail in chapter 7.

18 On medieval criteria for literary pleasure, see Glending Olson, *Literature as Recreation in the Later Middle Ages* (Ithaca and London, 1982), especially chapter 1, 'Medieval Attitudes to Medieval Pleasure,' 19–38.

19 Chartier, 'Texts, Printing, Readings,' in *The New Cultural History*, ed. Lynn Hunt (Berkeley, 1989), 161.

20 I have found the work of Andrew Taylor most insightful on the issue of the material support of the text. His recent book appeared just in time for me to note that he shares a number of key concerns with me, not just on the reception of medieval texts but also on the need to establish the presence of the 'desiring' reader; *Textual Situations; Three Medieval Manuscripts and Their Readers* (Philadelphia, 2002), chap. 5, 'The Text as Fetish,' 197–208.

21 This phrase comes from Samuel Ferguson's tract, 'A Dialogue between the Head and the Heart of an Irish Protestant,' *Dublin University Magazine* 2, no. 11 (November 1833), 592.

22 W. Sayers, 'Fergus and the Cosmogonic Sword,' *History of Religions* 25 (1985), 30–56.

23 For a most helpful exposition and discussion of various approaches to myth taken by Irish scholarship in the modern period see Kim McCone, *Pagan Past and Christian Present*, chap. 3, '"Pagan" Myth and Christian " History"' (Maynooth, 1990), 54–66.

24 Dumézil, *Mythe et épopée*, 2 vols (Paris, 1971).

25 Alwyn Rees and Brinley Rees, *Celtic Heritage* (London, 1961).

26 P. Mac Cana, *Celtic Mythology* (London, 1975); 'Aspects of the Theme of King and Goddess in Early Irish Literature,' *Études celtiques* 7 (1955–6), 356–413, 8 (1958–9), 58–65.

27 Arnold Van Gennep, *The Rites of Passage* (London, 1960); Emile Durkheim's work on kinship and the social functionalism of primitive belief, *The Elementary Forms of Religious Life* (London, 1957); Durkheim's students were Marie Sjoesdedt-Lanval, who wrote *Dieux et héros des Celtes* (Paris, 1940), and Marcel Mauss, whose work *Essais sur le don* continues to be immensely influential (trans., *The Gift: Form and Function of Exchange in Archaic Societies* [New York, 1954]); after Durkheim, B. Malinoski, *The Sexual Life of Savages*, 3rd ed. (London, 1932), and A.R. Radcliffe-Brown, *Structure and Function in Primitive Society* (New York, 1952) were most influential.

28 Claude Lévi-Strauss, *Structural Anthropology* (New York, 1963).

29 See the important article of A.-J. Greimas, 'La description de la signification et la mythologie comparée,' *L'Homme* (Sept.–Dec. 1963), 51–66; usefully collected as 'Comparative Mythology,' in *On Meaning: Selective Writings on Semiotic Theory*, trans. Paul J. Perron and Frank. H. Collins, Theory and History of Literature 38 (Minneapolis, 1987), 3–18.

30 Victor Turner, *The Ritual Process* (London, 1969); Clifford Geertz, *The Interpretation of Cultures: Structure and Anti-structure* (New York, 1973).

31 This is the position of Claude Lévi-Strauss, 'The Story of Asdiwal,' in *The Structural Study of Myth and Totemism*, ed. Edmund Leach (London, 1968), 1–48.

32 See R. Barthes, *Mythologies* (Paris, 1957).

33 See McCone on Lévi-Strauss, *Pagan Past and Christian Present* (Maynooth, 1990), 61–3.

34 Ó Cathasaigh, *The Heroic Biography of Cormac mac Airt* (Dublin, 1977); 'Cath Maige Tuired as Exemplary Myth,' in *Folia Gadelica: Essays Presented to R.A. Breatnach*, ed. Pádraig de Brún et al. (Cork, 1983), 1–19. See most particularly his 'Mythology in *Táin Bó Cúailnge*,' in *Studien zur Táin Bó Cúailnge*, ed. Hildegard L.C. Tristram, Scriptoralia 52 (Tübingen, 1993), 114–32. See also Elizabeth Gray, '*Cath Maige Tuired*: Myth and Structure,' *Éigse* 18 (1981), 183–209; 19 (1983), 230–62.

35 Mac Cana, *Celtic Mythology*, 58; 'Mythology in Early Irish Literature,' in *The Celtic Consciousness*, ed. Robert O'Driscoll (Portlaoise, 1981), 143–54; '*Regnum* and *Sacerdotium*: Notes on Irish Tradition,' *Proceedings of the British Academy* 65 (1979), 443–75.

36 McCone, *Pagan Past*, 107–28.

37 'Discourse' as a critical term can be relatively neutral – simply a type of lin-guistic use associated with a corresponding type of social practice. How-ever, post-Foucauldian theorists would advise caution about the term, seeing it as the systematic ordering of society in a way that validates the authority of certain institutions, behaviours, values, and identities at the expense of others. Such a discursive system embodies rules or expectations and is powerful enough to be nearly invisible from within the system. For a convenient summary of the importance of this Foucauldian use of the term for a post-colonial theorist such as Edward Said, see *A Reader's Guide to Contemporary Literary Theory,* ed. Raman Selden, Peter Widdowson, and Peter Brooker, 4th ed. (New York, 1997), 223–5.

38 Lincoln, *Theorizing Myth: Narrative, Ideology, and Scholarship* (Chicago and London, 1999), 147. I am wholly in agreement with Lincoln on this issue; it is, however, a pity that he chose as his example Recension II of the *Táin* and con-fuses it with material found only in Recension I. His seven-step protocol for the study of myth is one of the most useful analyses of the need to consider the narrator's direction of the agenda in a politicized manner; ibid. 150–1.

39 McCone, *Pagan Past*, 18–28.

40 See Donnchadh Ó Corráin, 'Historical Need and Literary Narrative,' *Pro-ceedings of the 7th International Congress of Celtic Studies*, 141–58.

41 Cecile O'Rahilly, *Táin Bó Cúailnge: Recension I*, xviii.

42 Jacques Derrida, 'Structure, Sign, and Play in the Discourse of the Human Sciences,' in *Writing and Difference*, trans. Alan Bass (Chicago, 1978), 278–94. For an interesting discussion of these ideas as they pertain to medieval his-tory, see Gabrielle Spiegel, *The Past as Text: The Theory and Practice of Medi-eval Historiography* (Baltimore and London, 1997), 33–5.

43 The most courageous recent attempt to posit early literary layers of the text is from P.L. Henry, '*Táin* Roscada: Discussion and Edition,' *Zeitschrift für celtische Philologie* 47 (1995), 32–75.

44 I am conscious here of the key Derridean concept of *différence*, the denial of the transcendental signifier, where it is precisely the absence of a centre that marks for Derrida the beginning of discourse: *Writing and Difference*, passim. It warns that a descriptive language of 'cores' and 'origins' is neces-sarily always provisional.

45 See also Calvert Watkins, *How to Kill a Dragon* (Ithaca, NY, 1999); Bruce Lin-coln, *Priests, Warriors and Cattle: A Study in the Ecology of Religions* (Berkeley, 1981); Lincoln, *Myth Cosmos and Society: Indo-European Themes of Creation and Destruction* (Cambridge, MA, and London, 1986).

46 Walter Burkert, *Structure and History in Greek Mythology and Ritual* (Berkeley and Los Angeles, 1979), chap. 4, 78–98.

47 Ibid., 96.
48 Pádraig Ó Riain, 'A Study of the Irish Legend of the Wild Man,' *Éigse* 14 (1972), 179–206; Joseph F. Nagy, *The Wisdom of the Outlaw: The Boyhood Deeds of Finn in Gaelic Narrative Tradition* (Berkeley, 1985); Kim McCone, 'Were-wolves, *Cyclopes, Díberga* and *Fíanna*: Juvenile Delinquincy in Early Ireland,' *Cambridge Medieval Celtic Studies* 12 (1986), 1–22.
49 Pierre Vidal-Naquet, 'The Black Hunter and the Origin of the Athenian *Ephebia*,' revised version in *The Black Hunter: Forms of Thought and Forms of Society in the Greek World*, trans. Andrew Szegedy-Maszak (Baltimore and London, 1986), 106–28.
50 In this case, for Dumézil, through what is for him an untypical non-Indo-European analogy of Australian aboriginal behaviour: *The Destiny of the Warrior*, trans. Alf Hiltebeitel (Chicago, 1970), 1–33, 161–4.
51 John Kelleher, 'The *Táin* and the Annals,' *Ériu* 22 (1971), 107–27; Pádraig Ó Riain, 'The *Táin*: A Clue to its Origins,' in *Ulidia: Proceedings of the First International Conference on the Ulster Cycle of Tales, Belfast 1994*, ed. James P. Mallory and Gerard Stockman (Belfast, 1994), 31–8.
52 James Carney, 'The History of Early Irish Literature: The State of Research,' in *Proceedings of the Sixth International Congress of Celtic Studies*, ed. G. Mac Éoin (Dublin, 1983); Joan Radner, '"Fury Destroys the World": Historical Strategy in Ireland's Ulster Epic,' *Mankind Quarterly* 23 (1982), 41–60.
53 A useful summary and bibliography of Tristram's work is provided by her 'What Is the Purpose of *Táin Bó Cúailnge?*' in *Ulidia*, 11–23 and the entries under Tristram in the bibliography to this collection. An important contribution from Tristram, 'Mimesis and Diegesis in the Cattle Raid of Cuailnge,' which takes contemporary literary critiques into account, is found in *Ildánach Ildírech: A Festschrift for Proinsias Mac Cana*, ed. John Carey et al. (Andover and Aberystwyth, 1999), 263–76.
54 Carney, 'History of Early Irish Literature.'
55 Patricia Kelly, 'The *Táin* as Literature,' in *Aspects of the Táin*, ed. J.P. Mallory (Belfast, 1992), 69–102.
56 But for a rebuttal of Ó hUiginn's work on the motif of swearing by the gods, see Calvert Watkins 'Some Celtic Phrasal Echoes,' in *Celtic Language: Celtic Culture: A Festschrift for Eric P. Hamp*, ed. A.T.E. Matonis and Daniel F. Melia (Van Nuys, CA, 1990), 47–56.
57 Ruairi Ó hUiginn, 'The Background and Development of *Táin Bó Cuailnge*,' in *Aspects of the Táin*, 26–69, at 62. See also the spirited defence of the oral aspects of the *Táin* in J. Nagy's review of this volume in *Éigse* 28 (1994–5), 183–8.
58 Jacques Derrida, 'Shibboleth,' in *Midrash and Literature*, ed. Geoffrey H.

Hartman and Sandford Budick (New Haven, 1986), 323; quoted in Gabrielle Spiegel, *The Past as Text*, 31.
59 Edward Said, 'Thoughts on Late Style,' *London Review of Books* 26, no. 15 (5 August 2004), 3–7 at 5.

1 Before Writing: Heroic Inscribing

1 See Proinsias Mac Cana, 'The Three Languages and the Three Laws,' *Studia Celtica* 5 (1970), 62–78.
2 The Old Irish tract on poets, *Bretha Nemed*, incorporates an extraordinary poem, '*Udhacht Athairne*,' which has been described as a 'charter of salvation' by its most recent editors. Here there is no doubt of the determined effort made early to preserve the role of the royal praise poet in a Christian scheme of things; see Donncha Ó Corráin, L. Breatnach, and A. Breen, 'The Laws of the Irish,' *Peritia* 3 (1984), 382–438 at 420–30.
3 Jane Stevenson 'The Beginnings of Literacy in Ireland,' *Proceedings of the Royal Irish Academy* 89 C (1989), 127–65; Anthony Harvey, 'Early Literacy in Ireland: The Evidence from Ogam,' *Cambridge Medieval Celtic Studies* 14 (1987), 1–15. The use of ogam as a monumental script complicates the early literacy picture; organized according to Latin grammatical usage and deploying what seems to be types of west Mediterranean letter forms, the script may predate the ecclesiastical use of written Latin texts in Ireland. In the context of vernacular literature its use as a special and restricted script probably results from its recognition as early and non-book writing.
4 Dáibhí Ó Cróinín, *Early Medieval Ireland, 400–1200* (London, 1995), 169–95; Timothy O'Neill, *The Irish Hand* (Portlaoise, 1984), passim; Malcolm Parkes, 'The Contribution of Insular Scribes of the Seventh and Eighth Centuries to the "Grammar of Intelligibility,"' in *Grafia e interpunzione del latine nel medioevo*, ed. A. Maierù (Rome, 1987), 1–18.
5 Marjorie O. Anderson and A.O. Anderson, *Adomnán's Life of Columba* (Edinburgh, 1961); Richard Sharpe, *Adomnán's Life of Saint Columba* (Oxford, 1998). The 'writing' thread in Colum Cille's biographical history is strengthened early by the post-Adomnán inclusion of a youthful transgressive act of writing. The famous tale of the borrowed and copied manuscript and the copyright issues that ensue, became the turning point of the saint's career. Writing shaped his 'Life.' See H.J. Lawlor, ed., 'The Cathach of St Columba,' *Proceedings of the Royal Irish Academy* C 33 (1916), 408–12.
6 Wendy Davies, 'The Latin Charter Tradition in Western Britain, Brittany and Ireland in the Early Medieval Period,' in *Ireland and Medieval Europe*,

ed. Dorothy Whitelock, R. McKitterick, and D. Dumville (London, 1982), 553–7. For a contrast between east and west in the practical/sacral conceptualization of writing, see Guglielmo Cavallo, 'Le rossignol et l'hirondelle: lire et écrire à Byzance et en Occident,' *Annales* 56 (2000), 4–5, 349–61.

7 In the view of Daniel Binchy, oral tradition is basic to the praxis and trans-mission of Irish law and custom, with writing merely the rendering of the law in a permanent form, brought about 'one might almost say by acci-dent': 'Distraint in Irish Law,' *Celtica* 10 (1973), 22. This view no longer pre-vails, as McCone, Breatnach, and others have demonstrated; Donnchadh Ó Corráin, Liam Breatnach, and Aidan Breen, 'The Laws of the Irish,' *Peritia* 3 (19), 382–438. The fourfold formula in the Preface to the *Senchus Már* as to the preservation of the law is telling: *comchuimne dá sen* [joint memory of two seniors], *tindnacul clúaise diaraili* [transmission from one ear to another], *díchetal filed* [chanting of poets], *tórmach ó recht litre, nertaid fri recht n-aicnid* [addition from written law, strengthening from the law of nature] (*Corpus Iuris Hiberniae* 346.24–347.17). Here writing has equal play with the reper-toire of orality, with respect to both content and material functioning of the legal system. It helps, of course, that the writing in question is sacred scrip-ture. In this scheme, the written witness trumps the others: *ro:dilsiged la dub in dícubus* [ink renders forfeit what is contrary to conscience]; Liam Breat-nach, 'The Ecclesiastical Element in the Old Irish Legal Tract *Cáin Fuithirbe*,' *Peritia* 5 (1986), 52.

8 Such is the context envisaged for the poem on the Airgíalla, composed ca. 700 and added to in the mid-ninth century; Kuno Meyer, ed., 'The Laud Genealogies and Tribal Histories,' *Zeitschrift für celtische Philologie* 8 (1911), 317–20.

9 For a discussion of the role of bishops, kings, clerics, and jurists in the con-ceptualization and administration of the laws, see Ó Corráin, Breatnach, and Breen, 'The Laws of the Irish,' 384–412. See also McCone, *Pagan Past*, 96–100, for the circumstances behind the creation of the preface to the *Sen-chas Már*. For related issues of literacy and power in Anglo-Saxon England, see Seth Lerer, *Literacy and Power in Anglo-Saxon England* (Lincoln, NE, 1991), passim.

10 See Damian McManus, *A Guide to Ogam* (Maynooth, 1991), for the use of ogam writing; for inscriptions on high crosses as memorializations of kings in a later period, see Peter Harbison, *The High Crosses of Ireland: An Icono-graphical and Photographic Survey*, Romisch-Germanisches Zentralmuseum, Forschunginstitut für Vor- und Frühegeschichte, Band 17, 1–3 (Bonn, 1992).

11 See Michael Herren, *The Hisperica Famina: Related Poems* (Toronto, 1992),

Introduction, passim, for the origin of the Irish *Loricae* prayers in the Mediterranean tradition of the *defixio*. See also the story of Morann's collar: for example, the epistle given him by the apostle Paul which, when worn around his neck, enabled him to give a true judgment; *Scél na Fír Flatha*, ed. Whitley Stokes, *Irische Texte* 3 (Berlin, 1891), 183–229. For the use of the Psalms in a magical tradition in the insular world, see Peter Dronke, 'Towards the Interpretation of the Leiden Love-spell,' *Cambridge Medieval Celtic Studies* 16 (1998), 61–74; see also Dan Wiley, 'The Maledictory Psalms,' *Peritia* 15 (2001), 261–79.

12 Liam Breatnach, *Uraicecht na Ríar* (Dublin, 1987), 139. The rituals of the satire itself involve the circumambulation of a whitethorn bush, reciting the satire, and holding thorns in the hand or piercing a clay likeness of the satiree with thorns; ibid., 114–15.

13 As Breatnach notes, there is an extant Old Irish example of a pre-satire poem (*trefhocal*) where the order of proceeding follows exactly the sequence of the ritual described above; Breatnach, *Uraicecht na Ríar*, 139. The poem in question is published by Howard Meroney, '*A mo comdhiu néll! Cid do-dhén fri Firu Arddae?*' *Journal of Celtic Studies* 2 (1958), 96–101. By immanent I mean that object and scribed name coalesce M the *blf* in the wooden rod is a shorthand for the three first wood nicknames of the alphabet, *beithe, luis, fern* [birch, rowan, alder].

14 For some interesting suggestions as to the class-based distribution of ogam inscriptions in Pictland, see Kathryn Forsyth, 'Literacy in Pictland,' in *Literacy in Medieval Celtic Societies*, ed. Huw Price, Cambridge Studies in Medieval Literature 33 (Cambridge, 1999), 39–61. See also Thomas Charles-Edwards, 'The Context and Uses of Literacy in Early Christian Ireland,' in *Literacy in Medieval Celtic Societies*, 62–82. In chapter 2 I give an account of the oral/writing issues around the tale of the *Táin*'s discovery.

15 For an excellent discussion of Irish place-name taxonomy, see Proinsias Mac Cana, *The Learned Tales of Medieval Ireland* (Dublin, 1980), 20–8. For a discussion of some issues surrounding place names in the *Táin*, see Kay Muhr, 'The Location of the Ulster Cycle: Part I: *Tóchustal Ulad*,' *Ulidia*, 149–58. Muhr concludes: 'My impression is that the conception of Tochustal Ulad [The Ulster Muster, which names a large number of places from which the "Ulster" muster is drawn] is old, intended to represent an all-Ulster hinterland, without reference to the plot of *TBC*, but that the passage has been gradually enlarged and drawn into service as a set piece' (157). I address the question of such lists in chapter 2.

16 Some paragraphs previously an Úalu is listed as one of six who stood their ground against Cú Chulainn and was killed (l. 909). There is some juggling

of two versions here, and the reappearance of an Úalu may be part of a transmitter's attempt to make sense of a patchily received text. I have restored the manuscript _fri_ ais for O'Rahilly's _fri[a]_ ais.

17 The play on the 'back' words may also be enhanced by the glossary tradition of another _ais_ word, which equates with _abha_, [river] in the glossary tradition; Whitley Stokes, 'O'Mulconry's Glossary,' in _Archiv für celtische Lexicographie_, 1, no. 110.

18 This classic attitude of defeat deprives the hero of his privileged male position on top.

19 _Dictionary of the Irish Language_ (_DIL_), Royal Irish Academy (Dublin, 1983) notes, under _úalann_ 3, that Meyer suggested a variant of _ualach_; Van Hamel suggests a word for sea: A.G. Van Hamel, _Immrama_ (Dublin, 1941), 114.

20 The fight with Etarcomal begins a fresh and more elaborately detailed sequence of single combats. They follow the 'other version' containing the poetic flyting between Medb, Fergus, and Ailill.

21 Carney, 'History of Early Irish Literature,' 120–30.

22 The word _etarcomal_ is not recorded in _DIL_ but similar compounds, such as _eterbreth_, _etercert_, etc., are quite common.

23 For a reading of Etarcomal based on the _comal_- aspect of his name, see Joseph Nagy, _Conversing with Angels and Ancients: Literary Myths of Medieval Ireland_ (Ithaca and London, 1987), 255–9.

24 See O'Rahilly's comments, 246. One would then assume that the man who makes the counterthrow would pick up Cú Chulainn's withe. So no matter how secret the identity of the hero, the withe enables Cú Chulainn to zoom in. Possibly the genitive form of the article, _ind_, was a dittographic error for nominative _in_, as there are two other _i-n-d-_ formations in the sentence: _i-ndead_ and _n-ind_. The resulting genitive case of _fhir_ would be a natural correction reflex. It also envisages the separation of verb and subject by _i ndead_ understood as an adverb.

25 We are not yet completely out of the wood's obscurity here. In chapter 3 I return to the problem that arises in the text at this point concerning the proper placement of the encounter with Fedelm. This is a much more important issue, in that some fundamental restructuring of the levels of enunciation is at stake.

26 Cf. Kuno Meyer, ed., _Fianaighecht_, RIA Todd Lecture Series 16 (London, 1910); Meyer, 'Finn and the Man in the Tree,' _Revue celtique_ 25 (1904), 344–9.

27 Nagy, _Wisdom_, 154–63.

28 It would take too long to list all Cú Chulainn's bodily morphing. His warp spasm phases in general are recycled and amplified by more than one tex-

tual transmitter of the saga, a witness to the fascination they exert; one would also include the descriptions of Cú Chulainn's seven-irised eyes, his false beards, his disguise with cloak and pillar, etc.

29 O'Rahilly considers this tale of Cethern to be a possible later addition to the basic narrative, *TBC I*, 282.

30 For the idea of reading heroic wounds in this manner in a *chanson de geste* context, see Eugene Vance, *Mervelous Signals: Poetics and Sign Theory in the Middle Ages* (Lincoln and London, 1986), 75–85.

31 See Philip O'Leary, 'Verbal Deceit in the Ulster Cycle,' *Éigse* 21 (1986), 16–26. 'Cú Chulainn surpasses his fellows in his use of words as much as in his use of weapons, and is perhaps even more elusive verbally than physically,' 24.

32 It is normally assumed by *Táin* scholars that textual references to *sliocht n-aile, sed secundum alios libros, augtair aile 7 libair aile,* or *iar n-arailib,* are genuine evidence for real lost alternative texts. That some of these may be fictions of scholarly scrupulosity serving to cloak creative initiatives of the textual handlers themselves must also be a distinct possibility to those whose tradition includes a pseudo-Augustine and a pseudo-Virgil. The three scribes of LU are referred to as A, M, and H.

33 By their references to older written traditions the scribes institute, in effect, a truth-assertion claim for their own activities. Claude Calame comments on Herodotus' use of *logioi andres* as legitimating under *they,* the equally implicated and ultimate Sender of the utterance. The 'I' of the scribe is constructed in and by the written words of others and is ready to distance itself when necessary; 'Herodotus: Historical Discourse or Literary Narrative,' in *The Craft of Poetic Speech in Ancient Greece,* trans. Janice Orion (Ithaca and London, 1995), 75–96.

34 See the plethora of glossing references that follow the introduction to the main action, beginning on a new page at l. 135. The reader is referred to H's personally meaningful geography, Cúil Sibrille, to a variant tradition (M) on Medb's vatic consultations, and to another variant on Fergus and his Connacht consort, Flidais (H). Cross references to other sagas are glossed at l. 335 (M), l. 379 (M), l. 594 (M), l. 703 (H).

35 The phrase is Hildegard Tristram's. See her most useful 'Latin and Latin Learning in the *Táin Bó Cúailnge,' Zeitschrift für celtische Philologie* 49–50 (1997), 847–77 at 849.

36 Towards the end of the saga in The Yellow Book of Lecan (Y) the narrative directions include more complex scene switches. For example, at l. 3410 the incident of Sualtaim's warning to the men of Ulster is introduced: *Céini dongníthea trá ina h-í-siu adchuadamar rocluinethar Súaltaim ó Ráith Súaltaim i*

*mMaig Muirrtheimne búadrugud a meic Con Culaind fri dá mac Gaile Dána 7
mac a shethar* [while those things were happening which we related Sualtaim of Rath Sualtaim in Muirtheimne Plain heard how his son Cú Chulainn had been tormented by the twelve sons of Gaile Dána and by his
sister's son]. At this point in the narrative a number of later inserts have
distorted an earlier sequence, which would have moved naturally from the
actual Gaile Dána episode at ll. 2547–66. Later, at l. 3941, scene switching is
even more explicit: *Imthúsa Ulad trá ní de leantar sund calléic. Imthús immorro
fer nÉrind ...* [The deeds of the Ulstermen are not followed for a while. The
actions of the men of Ireland, however ...].

2 Opening the *Táin Bó Cúailnge*

1 The term is Thurneysen's; cf. *Die irische Helden-und Königsage* (Berlin, 1911),
   96–244, and 'Die Überlieferung der *Táin Bó Cúailnge*,' *Zeitschrift für celtische
   Philologie* 9 (1913), 418–43. There are many more theories on the writing
   context of patronage and hence purpose for the whole manuscript, *The Book
   of Leinster*, than there are for the *Táin* text itself. For a summary of possible
   patrons and how this affects the way we view the *Táin*, see Tristam, 'The
   Purpose,' 19.
2 It is ironic that the more literary working the tale has received, the more it
   projects a naive innocence of prior textual tradition. Another example of
   this method is *Tromdám Guaire*, ed. Maud Joynt (Dublin 1931), which Seán
   Ó Coileáin, its most perceptive critic, has described as 'a literary tale
   [whose author's] primary interest is in creation not in preservation.' This
   tale also begins in a seemingly naive way: *Bai rí uasal oirdnighe ... feacht n-
   aill;* 'Ó Coileáin, The Making of *Tromdám Guaire*,' *Ériu* 28 (1977), 32–70 at 32.
3 Note the transposition: a woman *'ben'* becomes a wife *'ben'* when linked to
   the man. Is there a deliberate inversion here of the well-known passage in
   Ecclesiastes on the value of the good wife? It is the normal lesson for the
   Mass of a saintly woman not a virgin.
4 Medb's boasting (ll. 23–37); Ailill's teasing (ll. 8–10). The details of Medb's
   speech have often been used by scholars from Dumézil on to exemplify the
   theme of Medb as sovereignty goddess. But this is very much to abstract it
   from both its literary context and its actual resonance for a twelfth-century
   composer and audience. Much of the information that Medb gives about
   herself as the daughter of the high king of Ireland, as a leader of royal mercenaries, as the possessor of a province in gift absolute from her father –
   thus her self-proclaimed title *Medb Chrúachna* – hardly serves solemn goddess purposes, so thoroughly subsumed is it into the storyteller's mastery

of tone. It is a way for the author to convey necessary background informa-
tion of a traditional kind, but also of a fairly contemporary relevance, about
Medb. As a woman who is capable of paying mercenaries and whose father
acts as a *dominus terrae* in donating a province to her, she has some equiva-
lents, at least on the late twelfth- and early thirteenth-century scene as the
Annals for these years describe it and as F.J. Byrne has painted it: cf. 'The
Trembling Sod: Ireland in 1169,' in *A New History of Ireland*, vol. 2: *Medieval
Ireland, 1169–1534*, ed. Art Cosgrove (Oxford, 1987), chapter 1, 1–66. If
Medb is brazen, she is so in a thoroughly modern late twelfth-century way.

5 The use of the Old Norse coin word *penning* creates a powerful rhetorical
contrast with what we have just been treated to – a tour-de-force display of
wealth counted as goods and livestock. It makes it clear that it is the crudest
kind of status, personal wealth, that Medb has in mind.

6 Ailill's claim that he did not seek the kingdom of Leinster in deference to
the claims of his older brother is of interest. Bart Jaski has recently highlighted the significance of this principle of sibling royal succession. It possibly suits an idealizing twelfth-century context rather well; cf. *Early Irish
Kingship and Succession* (Dublin, 2001), passim. It should also be pointed out
that *pace* many commentators on this passage, Medb is not, in my opinion,
acting as a sovereignty goddess here. Indeed she is vigorously arguing the
opposite: that women can be *real* rulers – war leaders, gift-givers in their
own right, and controllers of their sexual powers – and all in a forthright,
public, and un-mythical way. In this vein, Medb's famous promise in the
Táin of the friendship of her own thighs, normally taken to be notorious
evidence for the construction of a promiscuous character, could simply be
taken out of the category of sex and into that of gender: an equivalent to the
kind of gracious access to the male body of the ruler most commonly occurring as a bardic poetic metaphor for the relation between client poet and
patron, a *fer aoinleabtha* (a man sharing the same bed as the lord – who is in
this case a woman); cf. P.A. Breatnach, 'The Chief's Poet,' *Proceedings of the
Royal Irish Academy* C 83 (1983), 40.

7 In Medb's words: *rafess ... ná tibértha ar áis [cen]co tuchta ar écin, 7 do bérthar
ón* [it was known that if he would not be given freely, he would be 'given'
by force and so shall he be] (l. 146). See O'Rahilly, *Recension I*, 278, for her
rationale for emendation. I have read for the sense here rather than for the
literal meaning.

8 Mac Cana, 'The Motif of Trivial Cause,' in *Seanchas: Studies in Early and
Medieval Irish Archaeology, History and Literature in Honour of Francis J. Byrne*,
ed. Alfred P. Smyth (Dublin, 2000), 205–211.

9 The most important resonance is, of course, an extended look at Medb, both

in the background information provided in the opening on her place in the pseudo-historical spectrum and in the significant further development of her traditional character. For the background of these, see O'Rahilly's notes on the text in Rescension II, 274–77. For an excellent account of the character development of Medb between Rescensions I and II, see Eamon Greenwood, 'Some Aspects of the Evolution of *Táin Bó Cúailnge* from TBC I to LL TBC,' *Ulidia*, 47–54 at 53–4.

10 I discuss this passage fully in chapter 3. One might note that Rescension I further de-stabilizes the idea of a beginning by questioning at a later point the proper place in the text for Fedelm's prophecy.

11 Nagy raises this point in his review of *Ulidia*, the collection of papers on the Ulster cycle: 'Depending upon the context of performance and other cultural factors, oral tradition can be remarkably "plastic" ... and even intensely interactive with a nascent or ongoing literary tradition, as ballad scholars have repeatedly shown' (*Éigse* 28 [1994–5], 183–8 at 188).

12 Obviously the term 'audience' needs more attention than this for its own sake. An audience can be anything from full presence of hearer/reader decoders to a convenient abstract term to signify only the element that structures expectations of how the story unfolds. I also circle back to this issue later in this chapter where I discuss the legend of the rediscovery of the *Táin*.

13 Only a small dividing line is used to distinguish gloss from entitulation here. Boxing of marginal subtitles and glosses is frequent in M's scribal methods.

14 *Thairsiu* is the preposition *tar* with suffixed third-person plural pronoun.

15 W presents a simplified version here: the glossing sentence *Ár ... Findabair* is omitted and the apparently redundant *Incipit ... n-urd* is also absent.

16 It is also of interest to speculate whether M is: (a) merely copying what he saw before him, (b) placing his three found notes together for convenience, or (c) actively trying to sort out a potential problem with his gloss by adding a final sentence of explanation, which he is encouraged to add because of the prior glossing. M's scribal standards are very high. I believe that he is not a mere mechanical copyist. I also believe that he has an extraordinary degree of commitment to the text, an attitude which causes him to look constantly for ways to facilitate and smooth out the task of the reader without compromising his own scholarly scrupulousness. This extends to adding textual explication as well. Hence I am inclined to choose (c) as the likely answer.

17 Traditional memory should not be entirely discounted. In my own locality, the route of Aodh Ó Néill's army going south to Kinsale was still pointed

out by the old people some four hundred years later. Whatever education, if any, they received would have been before an Irish history curriculum in the national schools.

18 Methe Togmaill and Methe nEoin are also unusual because they are 'new' place names related to a particular *Táin* incident, and this mixture of literary and actual names is not in the nature of the list at all. In both list and narrative the first place name is given as Methe Tog. Even in the main narrative (ll. 920–7) where the incidents and the naming occur there is a high degree of tentativeness about them. The vow of Cú Chulainn to smash the head of Medb occurs twice: here to cover the death of the pets, and again just before the point where the armies get to Findabair itself. This repetition is tidied up and eliminated in Recension II.

19 The distinction between Finnabair and Finnabair Cúailnge is fairly clear in the text but somewhat confused in O'Rahilly's index, 309.

20 In chapter 6, I discuss this evidence for the residual trace of another version of Cú Chulainn's healing which is now overwritten by the epic treatment of wounding and healing at the centre of the saga.

21 Note that the place name thus designated has a double; Fid Dúin is also described or named as Fid Mór and re-designated Slechtai. The Fid Mór of Cúailnge gets its final name from Fergus's misadventure with Medb in which his sword is stolen leaving the scabbard empty – hence 'The Wood of the Great Scabbard (*trúaill)*' or, by further appropriate punning, 'the Wood of Great Corruption.' Note too the attribution of the name's usage to the Ulstermen; the name is also included in Recension II as *Fid Mór i Crannaig Cúailngi*, ll. 295–6.

22 Further evidence of the short-circuiting of real geography is the intrusion of narrative action in the list: *for Slechtai selgatar* [past Slechta where they slashed (the wood)] (l. 120)

23 There are a number of places in Meath with this name; see Hogan, *Onomasticon Goedelicum* (Dublin and London, 1910), 419.

24 The only study that I am aware of is Gene Haley, 'The Topography of the Táin Bó Cúailnge,' PhD dissertation, Harvard University, 1970.

25 In Recension II, the second part of the list is much shorter and there is no reference to the Cronn river or the other rivers of Conaille Muirtheimne that anchor the list in Recension I.

26 Perhaps it is from over-familiarity that they omit any mention of crossing the Shannon, an event noted in the Recension II list.

27 M's glosses indicate a marked knowledge of the Kells area. Does this imply a connection with the monastic community of Kells?

28 For the role of place-name lore in narrative construction generally, see Rolf

Baumgarten, 'Etymological Aaetiology and Irish Tradition,' *Ériu* 61 (1990), 115–23. For the *Táin*, see Ruairi Ó hUiginn, 'The Background and Development of *Táin Bó Cúailnge*,' in *Aspects of the Táin*, 29–69; Kay Muhr, 'The Location of the Ulster Cycle, Part I: Tochostal Ulad' in *Ulidia*, 149–58. Also useful are the observations of Fr. Paul Walsh, now collected and re-edited by Nollaig Ó Muraíle as *Irish Leaders and Learning through the Ages* (Dublin, 2003), at 240–51.

29   Line 978, n. 3. For *fosdáilset in tslóig 7 adachtatár in crích hi tenid* [the army divided out and they set the district on fire], Y substitutes, superscript, after *tsloig: Erend fon coicid do chuinchid in tairb* [the Irish host divided up through the province to seek out the bull]. Y obviously feels the need to bolster the references to the bull in his version, something M does not bother with to the same degree. C even omits any reference to cattle in the list of gathered spoils (l. 979), but this may be a scribal oversight of omitting one in a group of dative plural nouns. The response of one of Medb's groups – that in spite of the mass carrying off of people and livestock, the bull still is not there – is noteworthy: *ni fil isin chóiciud etir* [he is not in the province at all]: M, with H correctional gloss, *isin chreich* [in the spoils]; *isin coicrich .i. isin crech* [in the district i.e. in the spoils], Y, C. It does seem as if M is not correct here but the fact that Y seems to adopt H's gloss is highly unusual. There is one other detail of note in this somewhat troubled passage: Y's rendering of the onomastic note *is de attá Glend nGat iarsin slicht sin* (l. 989) is probably what M had also and testifies to their clear sense that they are writing from 'another version.' H erases M's reference to *slicht* and substitutes *forsin glind sin*, thus demonstrating a fine disregard for M's scholarly scruples. For an excellent discussion of this and other issues, see Gregory Toner, 'The Ulster Cycle: Historiography or Fiction?' *Cambrian Medieval Celtic Studies* 40 (2000), 1–20, at 13–15.

30   Or three times including the rising of Glas Gatlaig (ll. 1024–6). With Cobtha added to the list of rising rivers (ll. 1018–19) the reader might justifiably claim to have gotten the point. The *slicht* that seems to be M's preferred and first version ends at l. 1029. The formal staging of the alternative event with incantatory verse belongs to M's *slicht eile*.

31   As they recapitulate at the end of this section before tackling the difficult *rosc* telling, note the double insistence on the authority of prior texts, multiple, composed, and of course, written: *augtair 7 libair aile* (ll. 1028–30). Y adds to *augtair*, the phrase, *in dana so* [of this poem], as if he was already thinking of the composition in verse that follows.

32   One may wonder whether the military connotation of the Latin phrase was

at all in the scribes' minds since they immediately go on to introduce the tale *iar n-urd*.

33 '*Titulus* to illustrate the circumstances of the psalm's recital (or composition?)'; Kuno Meyer, ed., *Hibernica Minora* (Oxford, 1894), 267.

34 J. H. Bernard and R. Atkinson, eds, *The Irish Liber Hymnorum*, 2 vols. (London, 1898), 1: 62–83.

35 *Tiumsugud*, verbal noun of *timsaigid*, hence 'bringing together, assembling, collecting.' *DIL sub timsaigid* gives exclusively a mustering or assembling meaning with no references to a literary process of creating a digest. At the beginning of Recension I variants of a different verb, *do-ec-malla*, are used throughout for this sense.

36 Note the triadic forms employed here and below. Here my presentation of the text is a little different from O'Rahilly's as I wish to emphasize the titular nature of most of this list, with the exception of the pillow conversation.

37 I follow O'Rahilly's translation for the early part of this notice, but I return to the question of its interpretation below.

38 The *DIL* citations of *remthús* are almost all related to precedence in military matters; hence, as with *tiumsugad*, there is a semantic spillover into *topoi* of battle assembly, etc.

39 For the tradition of a double preface in Irish hagiographical texts, see Jean-Michel Picard, 'Structural Patterns in Early Hiberno-Latin Hagiography,' *Peritia* 4 (1985), 67–82.

40 For a fine analysis of this phenomenon, see Máire Herbert, 'The Preface to the *Amra Choluim Cille*: A Re-appraisal,' in *Sages, Saints and Storytellers: Celtic Studies in Honour of Professor James Carney*, ed. Donnchadh Ó Corráin, Liam Breatnach, and Kim McCone, Maynooth Monographs 2 (Maynooth 1989), 67–75 at 68–9.

41 Stokes, ed., *Anecdota from Irish Manuscripts* 2: 48.6.

42 DIL 494, 173; it would, perhaps, describe M's boxed list, place names as summaries of action, rather well.

43 Cf. the reference to *a hinsce mod* in *Auricept na n-Éces*, l. 571: *is e imorro a hinnsemod a hinnsin a mud inunn* (leg. *imunn*) [this is its mode of narration, recitation in the mode of a hymn], *Amrae Coluim Cille*, *Revue celtique*, 20, 144. 20. I would suggest that this use of *innsin* is also present in the Suibne poem in the St Paul codex: *Gobbán durigni insin. Conecestar duib a stoir* [Gobbán made a telling of it so that its story may be told to you] (*Thesarus Paleohibernicus* II, 294]). There is accordingly a type of *figura etymologica* between *ecestar* <*in-fét* and its verbal noun *indisin*. In the discussion of *insce* in *Auricept na nÉces*, Priscian is cited when the term is equated with *oratio*: *oratio est ordinacio con-*

gruam, George Calder, ed. (London, 1914), ll. 3410–12. See also Patrick Sims-Williams, 'Person-switching in Celtic Panegyric: Figure or Fault?' in *Heroic Poets and Poetic Heroes*, ed. J.F. Nagy and L.E. Jones (Dublin, 2005), 315–26 at 319–20.

44 It also raises the question of LL's awareness of the matter of the correct number of Boyhood Deeds tales. I return to this issue in chapter 4.

45 I have edited the gloss and capitalized the M of *Maccerda*. There is constant hesitation about how to render the title of this part of the work in translation. It is not a complete saga, yet it stands out so clearly from all the rest that one is tempted to italicize it. *Annuas* clearly refers to layout of text on the page.

46 *Fotha*: according to Thurneysen derives from *fo-suide (= Latin *subsidium*); usually glossing *fundamentum* in a figurative sense; so 'cause, ground, reason' as in *is he tra fotha dia raibe in scel sa* (*Arch.* iii, 4.8), and O'Clery ('O'Clery's Irish Glossary,' ed. A.W.K. Miller, *Revue celtique* 4 [1880], 349–428), *fotha .i. adhbhar*.
Fagbál as vn. of *fo-gaib*, is not found in the Old Irish glosses (*DIL*), 'finding, getting, obtaining.' Other than its obvious alliterative value to the phrase, the exact meaning of this term in this context is not clear to me.
Dénum: vn. *do-gní*, here 'the act of making something'; cf. *tar hesi denmo ind libuir*, 'after writing the book,' *Sg.* 2a 7, and *tucait a denma*, 'the cause of its composition,' *Thesaurus Paleohibernicus* II, 298.27.
Tucait < do-ucc, 'cause, reason,' glossed *causa* in Ml. 58c 13. Cf. *caide loc 7 aimsear 7 perso 7 tucait din Gaedelg?* (*Auraicept na nÉces*, 36). It, like *Fotha*, can figure in titles, for example, *Tucait Innarbae na nDessi* (*LU*, l. 4335).

47 Herbert, 'The Preface,' 67–8.

48 According to the Lecan genealogies the Mascraide are descended from Fergus mac Roich (116r a 44, *Corpus Genealogiarum Hiberniae*, 279). The Laud genealogies place him in the family of the kings of Ulster (*Corpus Genealogiarum Hiberniae*, 322).

49 For an excellent discussion of the literary and historical issues surrounding this text and for this issue of the relationship of preface to main text, see Herbert, 'The Preface,' 67–9.

50 Thomas Kinsella uses the LL text (L) – *The Book of Leinster*, ed. R.I. Best et al., 6 vols (Dublin, 1954–83), vol. 5, ll. 32878–905 – in his translation of the *Táin*. Two recent editions – by Kevin Murray in *Cambrian Medieval Celtic Studies* 41 (Summer 2001), 17–24, and by John Carey in 'Varia II: The Address to Fergus's stone,' *Ériu* 51 (2000), 183–7 – provide a reasonable date of composition for L in the early ninth century. The three other versions are: BL Egerton 1782 (E), *Archiv für celtische Lexicographie*, ed. Whitley Stokes and Kuno

Meyer (Halle, 1907), 3–4; RIA D 4 2 (D), ibid. 4–6; *Tromdám Guaire* (G), ed. Maud Joynt (Dublin, 1931), 39–40. Of these, D, from Kilcormac, Co. Offaly, has received the least attention. In addition to having one of the largest and earliest collections of classical translation literature, the manuscript also contains, like LL, a series of the *Táin remhscélta*. The relationship of these pieces to each other has been well discussed by a number of scholars: James Carney, *Studies in Early Irish Literature and History* (Dublin, 1955), 166–88; Seán Ó Coileáin, 'The Making of *Tromdám Guaire*,' *Ériu* 28 (1977), 33–70; Joseph Falaky Nagy, 'Close Encounters of a Traditional Kind,' in *Celtic Folklore and Christianity: Studies in Memory of William Heist*, ed. Patrick Ford (Los Angeles, 1983), 129–49; Nagy, *Conversing with Angels*, 307–17. Ó Coileáin's article is particularly useful, and he suggests a date for *Tromdám Guaire* in the earlier part of the thirteenth century.

51 *Leg. for-gella*?

52 *Archiv für celtische Lexikographie*, 3–4.

53 Egerton 1782 shares with *Tromdám Guaire* the use of St Caillín, nephew of Senchán, as a character in the tale: cf. Meyer's fragmentary reading, l. 27, *allin naem m math- sc eiside* can confidently be read as *Callín naem mac máthar Sencháin eiside*.

54 Note that he does not really give a *fotha* unless we take the exchanges with Dáire as answering this description. I am inclined to think that the whole *comrád chind chercaille* constitutes the *fotha* and that there is then a redundant category in the list.

55 I postpone analysis of the scene itself until chapter 3.

56 First there is the incident of Fedelm and her prophecy introduced as *ro gab ic tairngire 7 remfháistine Con Culaind d'fheraib Hérend 7 doringni laíd* [she began to prophesy and to foretell Cú Chulainn to the men of Ireland and she made a lay] (ll. 232–3), and closed by the titles noted above, *tairngire 7 remfháistine*. Then there is the extra and heavily signalled soothsaying services that Medb demands: *ic iarfaigid fessa 7 fáistine 7 eólais* [looking for information, forecast and directions] (l. 310). Finally comes the extra prophecy display from Fergus: *Tánic gérmenma géribrach Con Culaind do Fhergus 7 ra ráid ra firu Hérend fatchius do dénam ... Ocus ro boí icá thairngire samlaid 7 do ringni in laíd 7 ro [fh]recair Medb* [Fergus got a keen and vibrant sense of Cuchulainn's presence and he warned the men of Ireland to be fearful ... And he was prophesying thus and he made a lay to which Medb responded] (ll. 394–9).

57 Pierre-Yves Lambert, '"Style de traduction": les traditions celtiques de textes historiques,' *Revue d'histoire des textes* 24 (1994), 375–91.

58 See McCone, *Pagan Past*, 90–106.

59 Lambert has pointed out the way in which Irish translators of Lucan's *De bello civile* used the category of prophecy frequently as a chapter heading; 'Style du tradition,' *passim*. See also Thomas Charles-Edwards on the force of *geis*, etc., in the structuring of Irish narratives; 'Geis, Prophecy, Omen, and Oath,' *Celtica* 23 (1999), 38–99. In his view, the emphasis on prophecy in Irish sagas represents a residual function of the earlier *filid*; Irish learned classes continued to see themselves mirrored in sagas as the masters of narrative because prophecy has now become a literary device and the mark, *par excellence*, of their controlling presence (98–9).

60 My analysis of this tale takes a quite different direction from that of Carey's and Murray's excellent studies ('The finding of the *Táin*'). I am concerned less with getting back to the originary form than with the diachronic marks of the use of the texts. For a further perceptive discussion of these texts, see Nagy, 'Close Encounters,' (n. 50 above). Though the LL version (L) is undeniably the earliest, I am more interested in the way in which the versions of this text afford a glimpse of how the understanding of *Táin* reception varied over time. Hence my interest in D. See also Murray's comments on L, n. 52 above.

61 Of the four versions known to me, L is the most pared down, and it is separated absolutely from the context of Senchán and king Guaire. D is obviously related to this but places the account of the finding in the context of the challenge of king and poet. Each presents two variants, one involving a group of saints and the other Senchán's son Muirgen. Each provides a poem of invocation to the grave of Fergus mac Roich. The text of D should be placed later in time than L's but it contains some interesting readings for my present purposes.

62 L also uses the form in the singular, as of a single unitary work: *Táin Bó Cúailnge, in Táin*, etc. Note that the invocatory poem has a different usage, *Bruiden Bó Cúailnge*, a form possibly chosen for its alliterative value.

63 Here I use the text from *The Book of Leinster*, and this is what I also translate. But in the notes that follow I suggest that the D version has a somewhat different sense of the invocation.

64 *Luaidtech* D. Perhaps *lóigtech* ' *logad*, 'forgiveness, remission of sin,' hence 'your stone of remission,' but although *logad* itself has occasionally *ó*, *loigtech* does not. Fergus is, by implication, a just pagan whose words may be listened to, not a damned soul whose raising from the dead would be considered as the devil's work. In three of the four versions mention is made of Fergus's great size. The saints can only hear him recite when he lies down. Already, then, he has been assimilated to the tradition of the giant revenant who tells his story from the remote past, having been resurrected by a saint.

Or else, unattested *luaidech> luad*, 'memorable.' The L text is clear: an adjectival form *<lóchet < lóch*, 'shining.'

65 *n-egnibh* D. Leg. *écnaib*, 'calamities' (*<éicen*?); or *ecnaib* 'with wisdoms' or 'with wise men.'

66 I assume that the form *im[m]anachta* represents *imb a n-achta*, with pret. pass. pl. of *aigid*, thus forming a kind of *figura etymologica*. One is then left with the obvious *immán*, 'driving'; this is Carey's view, 'Varia II,' 184.

67 *Luaithiu* D. This may be accus. pl. comparative of '*lúth*,' 'swifter,' 'fiercer,' or 'earlier'; alliteration can be restored if we read *ilaithiú* as 'in the day of.' Cf. Ml, 57^{d}13 D, *illaithiu sabbat*, but it breaks the stress rule.

68 *Bruiden* has a secondary meaning listed in *DIL*, 'fight'; *bó* D, is here the better reading.

69 Tradition has it that Colmcille's hymn *Altus Prosator* was given to Pope Gregory in return for his gifts to the church of Iona; *Liber Hymnorum*, ed. Bernard and Atkinson (London, 1898) I: 62–3, II: 140–1. Clearly the Columban hymn was considered as a hugely significant text in the Irish church from earliest times. The story may have been adapted in an Irish context from the historical gifts of *aestels* which Pope Gregory the Great gave to the English church along with copies of his *Pastoral Care* in the 590s; Cormac Bourke 'A Note on the *Delg Aidechta*,' in *Studies in the Cult of St Columba*, ed. C. Bourke (Dublin, 1997), 185–93. In 'The Finding of the *Táin*' Murray envisages an early ninth-century date for the text in L. In view of the fact that, as Ó Coileáin has shown, the introductory section of *Tromdám Guaire* borrows much from the Columban tradition of the saint's defence of poets, as seen in the Preface to the *Amrae*, perhaps one could suggest with him that the pope/saint exchange in Columban tradition suggested a similar myth of Latin/Irish exchange to the *Táin* tradition as well; cf. 'The Structure of a Literary Cycle,' *Ériu* 25 (1974), 88–125, at 90n4.

70 Ó Coileáin, 'The Making of *Tromdám Guaire*,' 47.

71 See Peter Harbison's remarks in his 'Church Reform and Irish Monastic Culture in the Twelfth Century,' *Journal of the Galway Archaeological and Historical Society* 52 (2000), 1–11, at 3–4. The other saints who figure in the *Tromdám Guaire* version (with the exception of Comgall) are midland or Shannon hinterland figures: St Brendan of Birr, St Ciaran of Saighir, St Senach, St Ruadan, and St Da Lua. Ó Coileáin has suggested a close link with the *Amrae* saint list ('The Making,' 35–6). The fact that a circuit is made of Ireland, Scotland, the Isle of Man in related Senchán tradition from *Sanas Chormaic* – but here with the novel addition of an ending in Dublin – would suggest a period when Irish poets were implicated in such a circuit, i.e. the later twelfth century, if the evidence from the career of Muiredach Alba-

nach Ó Dálaigh is anything to go by; cf. Brian Ó Cuív, 'Tradition and Innovation in Irish Literature,' *Proceedings of the British Academy* 49 (1963), 233–
62. This leaves open the question as to when the core 'Finding the *Táin*' was
first put together. The LL version, which omits the issue of kings and poets
entirely to concentrate on the relation between poet, disciples and the
nature of poetic inspiration, seems closest in spirit to the matter of Senchán
in the *Prull* entry in *Sanas Chormaic*. This would suggest to me a late ninth-
century date with some possibility that L is editing a prior version. See references in n. 52 above.

72 'Echtra Nerai,' ed. Kuno Meyer, *Revue celtique* 10 (1889), 212–28.

73 Ibid., 226.

74 See Andrew Taylor, 'Was There a Song of Roland?' *Speculum* 76, no. 1 (January 2001), 28–65, at 53–65.

75 Ibid., 63. Zumthor's theory of *mouvance* – that there is constant alternation
between oral performance and written reproduction – works better for a
medieval lyric tradition where there are self-conscious social issues governing the inclusion and transformation of popular song in romance contexts;
see his influential *Essai de poetique medievale* (Paris, 1972), 70–5. See also
Albert B. Lord, 'Perspectives on Recent Work on the Oral Traditional Formula,' *Oral Tradition* 1 (1986), 467–503; John Miles Foley, *The Singer of Tales
in Performance* (Bloomington, IN, 1995). The issue of oral formulae analysis
and Irish sagas has not loomed large because of the largely prose form of
the Irish works.

76 'An Address to a Student of Law,' ed. Máirín Ní Dhonnchadha, in *Sages*,
159–77. The quatrains quoted are nos. 4 and 5. As the editor notes, the term
oirléighean can also mean the act of interpreting – what is read is deci-
phered, read off as meaning. I have made very minor adjustments to the
editor's translation.

77 The matter of Welsh narratives and marked up texts has received careful
and sophisticated treatment from Sioned Davies, 'Written Text as Performance: The Implications for Middle Welsh Prose Narratives,' in *Literacy in
Medieval Celtic Societies*, ed. Huw Price, Cambridge Studies in Medieval
History 33 (Cambridge, 1998), 133–48.

78 I give numbers of lines in O'Rahilly's edition rather than in the manuscript;
this provides a reasonable assessment of the size of the segments.

79 The end of this section is not particularly marked in M: simply a heading
Slicht sain so (.i. sis) co aidid nÓrláím. M seems to falter somewhat here; his
writing gets larger and H pounces in adding a piece (ll. 864–7). When M
reappears he goes over into the margin; he is obviously acutely conscious
of much patching, *iar n-araili slicht*, etc., at this point in the narrative.

O'Rahilly comments that Y's note (l. 906) seems to work better than M's arrangement.

80 In my calculation of amounts of M-text I make silent provision for the fact that H has expunged, rewritten, and expanded two incidents in M.

81 For both W and U, the meeting of Cú Chulainn and Fergus, in the context of which Etarcomal is killed, is clearly important enough to warrant a label: *Aided Etarcomail* (om. W) *7 imarchor n-athisc fer nÉrend i mbeólu Fergusa.*

82 This heading is entirely M's creation; it is in neither the Y nor the C texts.

83 This adds up to 2216 lines in all. The shortfall is in the H interpolations. The length of the middle section of over 700 lines can be perhaps explained by the difficulty of rendering the *rosc* passages from f. 66 on. In this M does a superb job of marking up the text clearly, indeed providing extra marginal boxed indicators to indicate the respective speakers in addition to identifying them in the body of the text. These pages are masterly and give an almost dramatic and theatrical 'script' quality to the presentation. I get the strong impression that these marginal identifications are here to facilitate reading aloud in an animated fashion. More work on how medieval Irish manuscripts are scored for use might help us here.

84 Yet another easy way to divide the narrative would be according to M''s major capitals alone; this would give divisions at 682, 1842, 682. But there doesn't seem to be a sustained division by capitals alone.

85 For example, the three parts of the *Vita tripartita*, ed. Kathleen Mulchrone (Dublin, 1939) divide into 614, 1293, 1069 lines. The length of line of the two texts, when edited, are comparable. This might suggest reading sessions of some five to six hundred lines on a single occasion, with sections two and three divided as for separate reading units. But the whole question requires further codicological analysis.

3 A Scribe and His *Táin*

1 For a recent discussions of some of these issues, see Tomás Ó Concheannain, 'The Manuscript Tradition of *Mesca Ulad*,' *Celtica* 31 (1989), 13–30.

2 He is known as 'H' from the homiletic materials which he introduced into the volume.

3 Richard I. Best, 'Notes on the Script of Lebor na hUidre,' *Ériu* 6 (1912), 161ff; R. Thurneysen, *Die irische Helden-und Königsage bis zum siebzehnten Jahrhundert*, 236–41; R. Thurneysen, 'Die Überlieferung der Táin Bó Cúailnge,' *Zeitschrift für celtische Philologie* 9 (1913), 430–2; Hans Oskamp ed., *The Voyage of Máel Dúin* (Groningen, 1970), 3; T. Ó Concheannain, 'The Reviser of

Leabhar na hUidhre,' *Éigse* 15 (1973–4), 277–88; D.N. Dumville, '*Scéla Laí Brátha* and the Collation of Leabhar na hUidhre,' *Éigse* 16 (1975), 24–8; H. Oskamp, 'Mael Muire: Compiler or Reviser?' *Éigse* 16 (1975), 177–82; O'Rahilly, ed., *Táin Bó Cúailnge: Recension I*, x–xvii; T.Ó Concheannain, 'LL and the Date of the Reviser of LU,' *Éigse* 20 (1984); 212–25, K.H. Jackson, 'The Historical Grammar of Irish: Some Actualities and Some Desiderata,' *Proceedings of the Sixth International Congress of Celtic Studies, Galway 1979*, ed. Gearóid Mac Éoin (Galway, 1983), 1–18.

4 'The Interpolator H in *Lebor na hUidre*,' *Ulidia*, 31–9. The identification of H is based mainly on a study of some of his place-name glosses and some more doubtful loan word provenance.

5 An exception to this scholarly orthodoxy has been the series of challenging articles on later medieval Irish saga texts by Caoimhín Breatnach, now collected in C. Breatnach, *Patronage, Politics and Prose* (Maynooth, 1996).

6 See the perceptive and trenchant linguistic comments of McCone, in *Progress in Medieval Irish Studies*, ed. Kim McCone et al. (Maynooth, 1996), chap. 1, 'Prehistoric, Old and Middle Irish,' 28–39.

7 My text is that of O'Rahilly's edition of Recension I but with attention also to the manuscript itself and the diplomatic edition, *Lebor na hUidre: Book of the Dun Cow (LU)*, ed. R.I. Best and O. Bergin (Dublin, 1929).

8 This is O'Rahilly's conjecture; cf. *TBC: I*, note to ll. 1975–95, p. 266.

9 O'Rahilly, *TBC: I*, xvii–xviii. It may be significant that Egerton 1782 (W) is also a fragmentary text and is also missing the second half of the saga. The text there occupies two gatherings now containing ten and eight leaves respectively (88–97, 98–105), with a page missing at ll. 939–1028 and at ll. 1618–1710. The number of folios to a gathering in this manuscript varies a great deal from a high of fourteen plus two single leaves at the beginning of the manuscript to five in the third. The norm is ten (four out of twelve gatherings). There is evidence of wear and leaf loss after gatherings (cf. at 115 where a leaf is lost in the middle of *Togail Bruidne Da Derga*) and this is certainly what has happened in the first gathering. It seems from a rough word count that it would require more than two extra leaves to bring the text of the *Táin* up to the point where it breaks off in LU, but four leaves would bring us to approximately the same point in the text. Egerton 1782 contains two examples of a gathering of twelve and the addition of extra leaves to a gathering is also present, as I note above. If this is indeed a significant defect shared by Egerton 1782 and LU, it might point to a rather closer relationship between the two manuscripts than is commonly assumed. It would also assume a fairly shallow time frame for the dissemination of variants of an archetype shared by these two (U and W) of the

four manuscript representatives of Recension I, if indeed it can be said that H makes up matter for U with the help of a YBL-type version.

10 But see Ó Concheannain, 'LL and the Date,' for a widely different view. Ó Concheannain notes that O'Rahilly is mistaken in thinking that M breaks off in mid page at 82b; rather, H's material is written on an erasure to the end of the column.

11 O'Rahilly, *TBC: I*, xv, xvii.

12 This is the preferred term of Ó Concheannain, '*Aided Nath Í* and Uí Fhiachrach Genealogies,' *Éigse* 25 (1991), 1–27, 24.

13 The question has also been posed in a general fashion by E.W. Slotkin, 'Medieval Irish Scribes and Fixed Texts,' *Éigse*, 17 (1978–9), 437–50.

14 In O'Rahilly's early work on the text she was obviously strongly inclined to assume a living oral storytelling context for the saga or, at any rate, a text deeply marked by oral narrative techniques; *cf.* her Introduction to *Táin Bó Cúailnge from the Book of Leinster*, passim. However, she gives little attention to the question of oral tradition in her Introduction to Recension I. For some useful remarks on these issues see Tristram, 'What Is the Purpose of *Táin Bó Cúailnge*?' *Ulidia*, 11–21.

15 O'Rahilly, *TBC: I*, xii–xiii.

16 In Recension II there is apparently a need to create an entirely separate location for this incident; Medb goes to where her druid is to ask for a prophecy; on the return journey Fedelm suddenly appears, moving across the path of the chariot. For other significant differences in the manner of her presentation, see chapter 6.

17 O'Rahilly, *TBC: I*, xi. On the unreliability of taking *rosc*-type compositions as a mark of antiquity, see Liam Breatnach, 'Canon Law and Secular Law in Early Ireland: The Significance of *Bretha Nemed*,' *Peritia* 3 (1984), 439–59. For a discussion of some of these *Táin* verse sequences, see Daniel Binchy, '*Varia Hibernica*,' in *Indo-Celtica: Gedächtnisschrift für Alf Sommerfelt*, ed. H. Pilch and J. Thurow (Munich, 1972), 29–38; Johan Corthals, 'Zur Frage des mündlichen oder schriftlichen Ursprungs der Sagen *roscada*,' in *Early Irish Literature: Media and Communication / Mündlichkeit und Schriftlichkeit in der frühen irischen Literatur*, ed. Stephen N. Tranter and H.L.C. Tristram (Tubingen, 1989), 201–20; Karin Olsen 'The Cuckold's Revenge: Reconstructing Six Irish *Roscada* in *Táin Bó Cúailnge*,' *Cambrian Medieval Celtic Studies* 28 (1994), 51–69; Patrick L. Henry, '*Táin Roscada*: Discussion and Edition,' *Zeitschrift für celtische Philologie* 47 (1995), 32–74. Henry also suggests bravely that the *roscada* passage represents the form of the 'original' *Táin* and that we have here evidence of the editorial activity of Senchán Torpéist from the early seventh century in the transmutation of 'primitive' saga

material to more complex literary and poetic forms capable of encoding considerable thematic subtlety.

18 See McCone's trenchant comments in *Pagan Past*, passim. Herbert's discussion of the prefatory material to the *Amrae Choluim Cille* contains some very useful distinctions and her comments apropos the significance of the early eleventh-century preface to the *Amrae* are applicable here: '[the preface reveals] a scholarship which is dynamic rather than conservative, concerned, not with enshrining the *Amra* as a verbal icon, but with facilitating its appropriation and reception in the public as well as in the scholarly domain ... An extrinsic approach, which characterizes the writings of the period as antiquarian, needs to be replaced by an intrinsic approach'; 'The Preface to *Amra Coluim Cille*,' *Sages, Saints*, 67–75, at 75.

19 On the etymology of 'Fedelm,' see P.L. Henry, 'Interpreting the Gaulish Inscription of Chamalières,' *Études Celtiques* 21 (1984), 144–50, 49.

20 See the remarks of Michael Enright, *The Lady with the Mead Cup: Ritual, Prophecy and Lordship in the European Warband from La Tène to the Viking Age* (Dublin, 1996), 172–3.

21 For some of the ambiguous and problematic aspects of a hermeneutic of Fedelm, see my remarks in chapter 6.

22 The problem may be one of scene placement. M acknowledges that there was another option for the appearance of Fedelm (ll. 303–8). He may thus have had to redirect his own received text at this point.

23 The Egerton version has been edited by E. Windisch, '*Táin Bó Cuailnge* nach der hs. Egerton 1782,' *Zeitschrift für celtische Philologie* 9 (1913), 121–58. Incidentally, fragments of yet another *Táin* text that differs from any known text is to be found in the *Liber Hymnorum*, where it has been misidentified by the editors; *The Irish Liber Hymnorum*, ed. J.H. Bernard and R. Atkinson, 2 vols, Henry Bradshaw Society (London, 1898), 1: 186. The Fedelm poem has a number of quatrains where two extra lines have been added. The layout of quatrain 2 in W involves an extra line, *Ilar ndergmartra dogni* (not a new first line for quatrain 3 as O'Rahilly supposes). W supplies a better version of quatrain 3 with line *a* end-lined as *atchiu*, and thus providing a better rhyme with *banchuiriu*.

24 The text reproduced here is that of Best and Bergin's diplomatic edition of LU with minor corrections. In a paper delivered at the Celtic Studies Association of North America Annual Conference, 2000, Claudine Conan analysed the distinctive features of W and made a case for its preserving the earliest extant version of the poem. I am grateful to her for allowing me to read her work, which began as a paper in progress for my *Táin* seminar; I have learned much from her analysis. O'Rahilly also notes the five lines of

this poem quoted in the Dublin, Trinity College, MS H 3. 18 Glossary; 'A
Medieval Glossary,' *Ériu* 13 (1940), 71, no. 123.

25 The omission of *s* in this context is typical of H.

26 This is also a typical H slip.

27 Lines 4546–91, pp. 144–5. I have restored H's reading here of *cnis* for *cnes* in
l .2. Unless otherwise indicated all translations are my own. I have differed
from O'Rahilly's interpretation of the poem on a number of points.

28 In U, M simply notates *co acci/-a ar/in slúag* each time, the third time omitting *ar slúag*. The narrative sequence is begun by A, who also glosses the
phrase as *.i. cinnas atchí*. The layout of the text in the manuscript column
shows, however, that scribe M did in some measure respond to the prose
dialogue patterning; hence his readerly instincts were, as with W, to underline the formulaic aspects of the scene.

29 The best-known example occurs in *Sanas Chormaic*'s entry for *Prull* (*Sanas
Chormaic*, no. 1059, 90–4). The lost woman poet throws out a challenge of a
line and the mysterious companion of the poet Senchán answers, thus making public the identity of the missing woman. Cf. *Sanas Chormaic: Cormac's
Glossary*, ed. Kuno Meyer, in *Anecdota from Irish Manuscripts*, vol. 5 (Dublin,
1913).

30 For a discussion of the ritualistic aspects of the description in *Cormac's Glossary*, see J. Nagy, 'Liminality and Knowledge in Irish Tradition,' *Studia Celtica* 16–17 (1981–2), 135–43.

31 It is important to keep in mind that the premise of the fictive is assumed as
a given; that is, it is understood that Fedelm has no reality outside what is
projected as proper to her as an invented 'character.' In fact, given that the
etymology of her name is rooted in the act of seeing and is identical with
the role of woman prophet from continental Celtic usage, this caveat has
added resonance. It is in this circumscribed fictive mode that I speak of her
as 'seeing,' etc., rather than 'she is presented as "seeing."'

32 For the use of medieval rhetorical techniques in the LL *Táin*, see Dorothy
Dilts Schwartz, 'Repetition in the Book of Leinster *Táin Bó Cúailnge* and in
Neo-classical Rhetoric,' *Proceedings of the Harvard Celtic Colloquium* 4 (1984),
45–81; 'The Beautiful Women and the Warriors in the LL *TBC* and in
Twelfth-century Neo-classical Rhetoric,' ibid., 5 (1985), 128–46; 'Balance in
the Book of Leinster *Táin Bó Cúailnge* and in Neo-classical Rhetoric,' ibid., 6
(1986), 29–46; 'The Problem of Classical Influence in the Book of Leinster
Táin Bó Cuailnge: Significant Parallels with Twelfth-century Neo-classical
Rhetoric,' ibid., 6 (1986), 96–125.

33 There is a problem of faulty rhyme in W's *glaini/immi* but the rhymes in this
poem show scant regard for *deibide* regularity, and in this quatrain the *ab*

lines also show imperfect rhyme. That there might be a slippage between the two faces of Cú Chulainn, and hence, an answering instability of effect, is signalled in the poem itself; Fedelm's vision shifts through the half-qua-train even as she speaks: *delb domárfas fair co se/ a[t]chíu imrochlád a gné.*

34 The word *fuidrech* is glossed in H 3. 18, p. 625 as *fuidhre .i. ainm do lic oidhre, ut est fil oidhre for a nglaine.* If this is not an entirely pseudo-etymological gloss – though all glosses are of interest in that they represent real readers' mental habits – then one might imagine the foam on the mouth of the war-rior as a kind of hoar frost. The exaggerated language of the great *riastartha* speaks of flakes as big as a fleece issuing from the mouth of Cúchulainn (ll. 2262–3). The lines quoted in the Glossary above are of interest in that they represent yet another set of textual variants for this passage; but the Glos-sary version is manifestly closest to the text of H: *fil oidhre for a nglaine/ fil leann ndeirg ndrolaigh ime,/ do fil gnuis is gráta dó/ do beir modh do banchuireo/ duine óg is alainn dath 7 rl.*

35 There are aspects of the standard descriptions of the frenzy of Cú Chulainn that echo the question-and-answer identification format and some of the details of the great apocalyptic song of the Messianic hero in Isaiah 63:1–6; redness of clothing, aloneness in his exploits, wounded beauty, frenzy in assaulting the enemy. The passage as applied to Christ was a standard patristic excursus and became one of the most important iconic images of Christ as Saviour in the later Middle Ages.

36 This corresponds to the elements of the *imbas forosnae* rite – cf. Nora Chad-wick, 'Imbas forosnae,' *Scottish Gaelic Studies* 4 (1954), 39–64 – which Nagy would describe as shamanistic; see 'Liminality and Knowledge' and *The Wisdom of the Outlaw*, 24–7.

37 On the provocative aspects of women and the warband in a Germanic con-text, see Enright, *Lady with the Mead Cup*, 22–3, 38–68. On the peacemaking roles of women, see L.H. Sklute, 'Freothuwebbe in Old English Poetry,' *Neo-philologische Mitteilungen* 71 (1970), 534–41. For a study of female roles in Irish saga, see Phillip O'Leary, 'The Honour of Women in Early Irish Litera-ture,' *Ériu* 38 (1987), 27–44; M. Herbert, 'Celtic Heroine? The Archaeology of the Deirdre Story,' in *Gender in Irish Writing*, ed. Toni O'Brien Johnson and D. Cairns (Philadelphia, 1991), 13–22; Joanne Findon, *A Woman's Words: Emer and Female Speech in the Ulster Cycle* (Toronto, 1998), passim.

38 This seems an obvious echo of the Boyhood Deeds scene, when Cú Chu-lainn returns in a frenzy to Emhain Macha, turns his chariot to the right, and demands a fight. The watchman says: *Ardáilfe fuil laiss cach dune fil isind lis mani foichlither'* (l. 804). Thurneysen noted that this poem is the only H-interpolation that appears in Recension II. There the intertextual reference

is quite marked. The *LL* version reads: *mani faichlither bid brath*, though the wording of the return to Emain prose passage is somewhat different than in Recension I. There is, however, another relevant intertextual comparison to be made which has bearing on these lines: in Interpolation *III* the episode of the meeting between Medb and Cú Chulainn begins: *Conniacht (.i. arranic) Medb comairli dús cid dogénad fri Coin Culaind ar ba aincis mór lei an ro bíth leis día slógaib. Is í comairle arránic áes féig forúallach do chor i n-óenfhecht día shaichthin in tan ticfad i n-airis dála día accllaim-si, ar baí aires (.i. comdal) dála dissi ara bárach fri Coin Culaind do dénam sída celci fris día t[h]arrachtain* [Medb asked for advice as to what she would do about Cú Chulainn as it was a great grief to her the number of her army that was slain by him. This was the counsel she fixed on – to send a group of stout and proud men to set upon him all together when he would come to meet her in parley. For she had made an appointment to meet him the next day to make a false peace with him in order to capture him.] The belaboured emphasis on taking counsel and engaging in parley here may be a conscious working out by H of the theme represented in this element of the Fedelm prophecy. Note also the alliterative adjective string: a sign of lateness, of H's own composition, perhaps?

39 I am assuming that the W-form is a variant of *anaithnid*. Similarly, in the LL version the word is coupled with *ingantach* and thereafter becomes a common expression. For similar usages with variants of *-gnáth*, cf. *co n-accatar in mnaí i n-étuch ingnáth*, *Immram Brain* in *Immrama*, ed. A.G. Van Hamel (Dublin, 1941), 9; *co n-acca in mnaí i n-étuch anetargnáid*, 'Conle's Abenteurliche Fahrt,' *Zeitschrift für celtische Philologie* 17 (1928), 195. See also O'Rahilly's suggestion for the emendation of *animgnaid* to *anetargnaid* at l. 639 on paleographic grounds with *an-* as an intensive rather than a negative prefix; thus 'wonderful, remarkable,' *Táin Bó Cúailnge*, Rec. I, 252. I would suggest that 'distinctive, unusual' is a more appropriate translation.

40 This important witness to a seventh-century version of the war between the allies, the exiles, and Ulster was edited by K. Meyer, 'The Laud Genealogies and Tribal Histories,' *Zeitschrift für celtische Philologie* 8 (1912), 291–338. The progressive misogyny of the *Táin* I and II Recensions has been carefully documented by E. Greenwood, 'Some Aspects of the Evolution of *Táin Bó Cuailnge* from TBC I to LL TBC,' *Ulidia*, 47–54. The question of misogyny in Recension I is also addressed by P. Kelly, 'The *Táin* as Literature,' in *Aspects of the Táin*, 69–102.

41 Possible textual problems presenting themselves to H would be the extra lines represented in O'Rahilly's edition in quatrains 2 and 3; the Clann Dedad matter in the final quatrain is not found in LL.

42 The fragment quoted from H. 1. 18. seems to be of a family type closest to H's version and, as I have noted above, this is the only H interpolation utilized in LL.

43 This incident, the Slaughter of Glendomain, is also referred to in passing by M, though in what form he knew it there is no way of telling.

44 There is comparatively little work done with swords by Cú Chulainn in the *Táin*, but cf. the *táth béim* of the Boyhood Deeds (l. 787), described as a 'sticking' blow by Thurneysen, could equally appropriately be translated as a 'side,' hence 'backhand,' blow. See *DIL*, *táth*. The way in which directional aspects of wounding can be rhetorically envisioned and presented as magical, direction-oriented ability is well summed up by a passage in the Stowe version; *Ro gonadhsan cach tairsí 7 tréithi 7 séici* (as noted in *Die altirische Heldensaga Táin Bó Cúalnge nach dem Buch von Leinster*, ed. E. Windisch [Leipzig, 1905], 359 n.7). For prepositional elements in name etymologies, see the example of Loiches as *lóeg secha* in *Corpus Genealogiarum Hiberniae*, 87.

45 Later spellings of the term include *riastara*, as in the H 1 18 Glossary already cited. In *Cormac's Glossary* the term *riastarthae* is associated with *fuirseoir*, itself probably derived from Latin *parasitus*, and the glossing of *parasitaster* as *fuirserán* in the St Gallen manuscript of Priscian's Grammar may reflect an awareness of the link (cf. *Thesarus Paleohibernicus II*, p. 100): *Remm (reim B) nomen do fuirseoir fobith cach riastardae dosber for a agaid* [*Reimm* is the name of a buffoon; as every *riastarthae*, he turns before himself]. The explanation turns on *remm/reim* as prefixed *rem–* (before) or *réimm* (oblique); cf. Meyer, *Sanas Chormaic*, 95.

46 If we accept Mac Éoin's identification of H as an Ua Maol Conaire, one of a family who have moved rather recently from their older base in Westmeath, then we may say that the somewhat ironic distance implied in the Fir nÓl Écmacht reference befits a scribe writing '*in partibus infidelibus*,' as one of a family but newly arrived in the area. We might also be tempted to consider the slighting connotations that the alternative of the name as H writes it, *Fir nÓl nÉcmacht*, as 'men of weak liquor,' seems to have carried in some Irish medieval traditions at least; cf. Thurneysen, *Heldensage*, 76.

47 It is just possible that H is signalling a western, dialectal difference here; one might consider the words *riam 's iarum* as with semivowel quality arising from lenited *m*, and that this in itself might be reasonably close phonologically to a [ri:sirə], that is, close to a western *riastartha* with elided *t*. There is evidence throughout the manuscript that H consistently elides homorganic consonants; the quality of *-th/-d* is also breaking down to *h* or is elided altogether and this is most noticeable in H.

48 This is an incident with which U textual tradition seems to have difficulty. M's assertion that he knows another tradition of Cúr's death at *Imshlige Glendamnach* (ll. 1727–8), for which there is no correlation in Y, may mean that H's pairing of *Aided Cáuir* and *Aided na Rigamus* were both linked to *Imshlige Glendamnach* in his source. This makes H's isolation of the *Rigamus* episode more striking here. M's note on Cúr is not in Y.

49 Is it the inclusion of this as an extra quatrain that causes the tight fit on the manuscript page of the H-interpolation written text of the poem? But this would not entirely explain the entire rewriting; H simply adds to the *Éli Loga* poem, for example, in the middle of a column on an erasure.

50 The monastery of Terryglass, of which one of the proposed compilers of LL, Áed mac Crimthainn, was abbot, was returned from Munster control after the battle of Móin Mór in 1151. Was the omission of the role of the Munstermen in LL deliberate on the part of a Leinster scribe? Some of the same avoidance of Munster is evident in a poem, '*Sén dollotar Ulaia*' (ed. E.J. Gwynn, *Ériu* 10 [1926–8], 92–4), related to the saga *Cath Ruis na Ríg*, itself a saga probably composed in Terryglass.

51 K. Meyer, 'The Laud Genealogies,' 306–7.

52 Carney, 'The History of Early Irish Literature,' 113–30.

53 For some comments on the long-standing rivalry between Dál Cais and Síl Muiredaig at a somewhat later period, and for the way in which bardic poetry can promote a fairly even-handed view from a Connacht perspective, see B. Ó Cuív, 'A Poem of Prophecy on Ua Conchobair Kings of Connacht,' *Celtica* 21 (1989), 31–54, at 34–9. Carney, 'The History of Early Irish Litérature,' 113–30.

54 Henry has noted the slippage of focus for this incident even in *TBC 1*. The heading and the incident no longer bear any relation to each other; Henry, 'Táin roscada,' 35–6. The name itself would possibly have been best known by an Irish *literatus* as that of the mythical poet of *Lebor Gabála* tradition. But an Amairgen is credited in the Introduction to the *Dindshenchas* as the author of this work also. A poet of this name is cited in some texts of the *Cáin Fhuithirbe* as having a part in the development of this latter legal tract of Munster provenance; on this possibly historic, as opposed to fictive, literary personage, see Liam Breatnach, 'The Ecclesiastical Element in the Old-Irish Legal Tract *Cáin Fhuithirbe*,' *Peritia* 5 (1986), 44–8, and Peter Smith, 'Aimirgein Glúngel Tuir Tend: A Middle-Irish Poem on the Authors and Laws of Ireland,' *Peritia* 8 (1994), 129–36.

55 T.F. O'Rahilly, *Early Irish History and Mythology* (Dublin, 1946), 96, 156.

56 *Ba si sin in tres láechaicmi Herend .i. in Gamanrad a Hirrus Domnand 7 cland Dedad i Temair Lóchra 7 clanna Rudraige i n-Emain*, LU, ll. 1620–1.

57 Cf. O'Rahilly, *Early Irish History*, 177 n. 3.

58 See p. 93–4.

59 Such *textual* literalism may also lie behind the curious *Dá gae bolga* of the Fedelm poem. One assumes that it is generally known that Cú Chulainn had only one such weapon, but in the saga it is used twice; thus the 'two' of the poem may be thought of either as a textual misunderstanding on H's part or as a literal fidelity to the body of the saga. It hardly needed to be edited out.

60 See p. 261, note on l. 1625.

61 C. O'Rahilly has noted the unusual occurrence of such a list in the middle of a saga (xix and ibid. n.4) but such a narrative recuperation and assertion of control may have been felt to be necessary after the length and comparative novelty of the Fer Diad sequence. It signals again the essentially *textual* nature of the Irish saga tradition enterprise.

62 O'Rahilly, *TBC*, I, xiv.

63 Curiously, it is Y who adds the detail that it was the women of Munster who climbed on their menfolk's shoulders (l. 2368); C gives that dubious honour to the women of Ulster (of the exiles?).

64 For some general considerations on place-name construction in the *Táin*, see R. Ó hUiginn, 'The Background and Development of *Táin Bó Cuailnge*,' in *Aspects of the Táin*, 41–9. In quatrain 2 the b-line is hypermetrical. There may be an additional pun in the comment of Fiacha: his *feocherd* echoes a possible compound *beócherd*, meaning non-mortal blow. Cú Chulainn is in doubt as to whether his shot in anger has actually killed Fer Báeth (ll. 1802–3).

65 The formula *co cloth ní* is inappropriate to the context. The first quatrain is regular, a mix of *deibide nguilbnech* and *deibide scaílte*. The problems are mainly with the second quatrain: apart from the slip of *fithi* for *frithi*, *Muirthemniu* is plainly in error giving a hypermetrical line in b; I suggest a word beginning in *m-*, most likely *mag*, which could have been falsely expanded or glossed, leading M to write as he did. This does not, however, resolve all the difficulties.

66 The meaning is not quite clear to me here. The agent sense of *oc* seems to be a fairly late usage; if this is so, then it may be another reason to think of the poem as H's composition.

67 *The Book of Leinster*, vol. 6, ed. A. O'Sullivan (Dublin, 1983), p. 1522, ll. 46424–39; the translation is my own, and the relevant lines appear in bold type.

68 In the Colin Ireland edition of this text – *Old Irish Wisdom Attributed to Aldfrith of Northumbria: An Edition of Bríathra Flainn Fhína maic Ossu*, Medieval

and Renaissance Texts and Studies 205 (Tempa, AZ, 1999) – the recensions of the text that are in an Úa Maol Chonaire scribal tradition indicate a clear break between our poem and the rest of the gnomic material, as does also the version in BL MS 30512; see Ireland's discussion, 21–34.

69 *Is and íarom baí in chomdál i nArd Aignech frisi ráter Fóchaird indiu* [It was there the meeting was, in Art Aignech now called Fóchaird] (ll. 1938–9).

70 This does not include the named wives of the last three druids in the list. The scribe of C was alert to the connection between the details listed by M and H, as he substitutes for the fourteen men of H, *fiche gai ... marbius fiche fer Focherdi.*

71 See *DIL sub esc/eisc, esca.* The word seems to be primarily a Glossary or learned word. The possibility of yet another pun with *íasc,* 'fish thirst,' is also present.

72 This place name is already somewhat garbled; possibly it is meant to be a transformation of the name(s) already referred to some lines before as Cend Coriss or Dún Chind Coross (l. 2068). These names are themselves of doubtful standing as the manuscript variations and the alternative form would indicate. Note that it is not just *cuillend* but *cuillend dund* which is incorporated into the place name. Did Medb's original statement read *cuillend cinn dund*, and did M omit *cinn*, causing H to attempt to explain a difficult reading by bringing in the term *col*, which had already been used just before as one of the names for a druid's wife?

73 This is said after Cú Chulainn has killed more than one hundred adversaries, whether in single combat or in groups. I take the word *cuillend* as a form of the word for a holly object. *DIL* lists Meyer's entry *cuillend* ('abomination' as if deriving it from *coll*) here, but this is the only context for its citation and this meaning is supported by H's gloss alone. Granted *cuilenn,* 'holly object,' < *coll*, is normally written with a single *l* but in the associated place names it is written with double *ll*. Cú Chulainn had already killed Fer Báeth with a *sleg cuilend* (l. 1776) and Nad Crantail had used them against him (l. 1415). But it may be that *cuillend* has a figurative sense here; it is the pricks of mental torment Medb feels at the death of her *muintir*. Thus the transposition from actual to metaphoric and vicariously sympathetic wounding is the same as that in the well-known lament of Créide: *Di-connuircsi isin treus Aidne ro geghin secht ngoine deac for seglach a léiniod ... It é saigte gona súain ... Cráidid mo chride cainech,/ a Chríst cáid, a fhoraided:/ it é saigte gona suain; Early Irish Lyrics*, ed. J. Carney (Oxford, 1956), 86. The irony associated with the comment is no doubt intended in the saga text. The politicians' phrase 'I feel your pain' and the public cynicism that greets

it probably matches Medb's limited emotional range and the audience response quite well.

74 It will be observed that there is, in effect, a kind of explanatory glossing sentence in the text which excuses the actions of Cú Chulainn on the grounds that the *cáinte* is doing his typical *cáinte* routine of threatening dishonour for a refusal. On the verse formulae of *cáinte*, see McCone, 'A Tale of Two Ditties: Poet and Satirist in *Cath Maige Tuired*,' in *Sages, Saints*, 122–43, at 130.

75 O'Rahilly, note on ll. 2527–9, p. 274. The technique was also used in the mid-twelfth-century poem in honour of Muircertach mac Lochlann; ed. John O'Donovan, *Tracts Relating to Ireland*, vol. 1 (Dublin, 1841), 24–58; also cited in Donnchaadh Ó Corráin, 'Muirchertach Mac Lochlainn and the *Circuit of Ireland*,' *Seanchas*, 238–50. A fully developed example of the technique in bardic eulogy is also found in a poem of Muireadach Albanach Ó Dálaigh, *Tomhais cia mise a Mhurchaidh*, addressed to Murchadh Ó Briain. The quatrains in question are as follows:

A Chú Chulainn ar cleasaibh,/ a Osgair ar imreasain,/ a í Dhuibhne an táidhe teinn,/ ar áille ar shuirghe ar shoicheill. A Chearmaid ar chaoine nglóir,/ a mheirge dhualach dhonnshróill,/ a Ábhartaigh, a shaoir sheing,/ a chaoimh ábachtaigh fhoirteill. A Bhuidhbh Dheirg ar dheirge ngruadh,,/ a Mhannanáin ar mharcshlu-agh,/ a Mhongáin ar mhaisighe. A Mhidhir mheic an Dhaghdha/ ar ábhacht, ar urlabhra;/ id chéibh fhighigh nochan uil/ acht réim Mhidhir, a Mhurchaidh.

[O Cú Chulainn for feats! Osgar for contention! Ó Duibne of the hardy stealth, for beauty, for wooing, for liberality. O Cearmad for charm of voice! waving banner of dark satin! O Ábartach, noble and graceful! handsome, blithe and strong! O Bodhbh Dearg for redness of cheeks! Manannán for troops of horse! rich braided hair! Mongán for comeliness! O Midhir son of the Daghdha for merriment and speech! In thy curled locks is only Midhir's sway, O Murchadh.]

Osborn Bergin, *Irish Bardic Poetry*, trans. David Greene (Dublin, 1970), 110, 262. The poem goes on to list other Irish literary heroes and their attributes. Examples of this type from the Annals occur for the first time in the twelfth century.

76 On the role of the *briugu*, see F. Kelly, *A Guide to Early Irish Law* (Dublin, 1988), 36.

77 Note again a typical H elision.

78 H supplies this type of gloss elsewhere in LU; in *Aided Echach Meic Maireda*, for example, the only copy of which is that of H, he glosses the names of Lí Ban as *Muirgen .i. gein in mara. Muirgeilt .i. geilt in mara* (Best and Bergin, ll. 3060–1).

79 Cf. *crepuit medius et diffusa sunt omnia uiscera eius, .i. ruminaiged* (gloss on Acts 1, 18 in the Book of Armagh, *Thesarus Paleohibernicus*, 496).

80 On the boiling and heating metaphors of the *riastartha*, see McCone, *Pagan Past*, 171–2.

81 On the beauty of the ruler as a topos in Irish literary materials relating to kingship see McCone, ibid., 121–2.

82 Muiredach's poem, '*Créd agaibh aoidigh a gcéin*,' was edited by O. Bergin (*Irish Bardic Poetry*, 88–92). Gilbert's tract is included in J. Ussher, *Works* iv, 500–510. For a brief discussion of this tract, see A. Gwynn, 'Six Irish Papal Legates, 1101–1198,' *Irish Ecclesiastical Record* 63 (1944), 361–7; see also Michael Richter, *Seanchas*.

83 O'Rahilly, *Táin Bó Cúalnge, LL*, xvii.

84 An example of the former approach is Joan Radner, 'Fury Destroys the World,' *Mankind Quarterly* 23 (1982), 41–60; of the latter, Padraig Ó Riain, 'The *Táin*: A Clue to Its Origins,' *Ulidia*, 31–8.

85 John Kelleher, 'The *Táin* and the Annals,' *Ériu* 22 (1971), 107–27. For a cautionary note see D. Dumville, 'Ulster Heroes in the Early Irish Annals: A Caveat,' *Éigse* 17 (1977), 47–54. Dumville notes that the insertion of heroes into the annals record is late, possibly eleventh century.

86 See Kieran O'Conor, 'The Morphology of Gaelic Lordly Sites in North Connacht,' and Aidan O'Sullivan, 'Crannogs in Late Medieval Ireland,' in *Gaelic Ireland: Land, Lordship and Settlement, c. 1250–1650*, ed. Patrick J. Duffy, David Edwards, and Elizabeth Fitzpatrick (Dublin, 2001), 329–45, 397–417.

87 Best and Bergin, *LU*, 58.

88 Best and Bergin considered this to be an error, a mistaken title. In view of the fact that a poem on the graves of the Kings at Clonmacnoise is an important witness to the ongoing association of an Úa Maol Conaire with the funerary interests of Connacht dynasts and Clonmacnois – R.I. Best ed. 'The Graves of the Kings at Clonmacnois,' *Ériu* 2 (1905), 163–71 – one might speculate that a related interest, or a sense of involvement, in the creation of a dossier of graveyard poetry associated especially with the West is being shown here. It is also significant that in this same text, as Ó Concheannain has demonstrated, H seems to have manipulated the genealogical record with respect to the sons of Nath Í in order to give greater status to the Uí Dhubhda, lords of Uí Fhiachrach in North Connacht. See note 2, p. 235.

89 Cf. Edmund Hogan, *Onomasticon Goedelicon* (Dublin, 1910), *sub* Mag Find, p. 250.

90 Additional information about M's interests can also be gleaned from his glosses. He seems to have a particular interest in a locality in the vicinity of Kells; I have already referred to the gloss *Crossa Caíl* in the *Táin* (*Ulidia*, 124

n. 3). There are others: in *Serglige Con Chulaind* M glosses twice on the place-name Achall; *tulach i fil scrín Choluim Cille; ait hi fil Scrín Cholaim Cille indiu.* May we posit a Kells sojourn at some period in his life for Mael Muire? And what implications does this have for the history of the saga's textual transmission?

91 *Acallam na Senórach*, ed. W. Stokes, Irische Texte 4, Pt. 1 (Leipzig, 1900), ll. 2315–16.

92 Cf. *combid de sin dano rod lil a n-ainm ... i. maith in cherd gaiscid do necmaic do Coin Culaind and sin* (l. 1965). C, the only other manuscript witness here, substitutes *laochdachta* for H's *gaiscid.*

93 Paul Walsh, ed., *The Life of Aodh Ruadh ó Domhnaill*, part 1, Irish Texts Society, vol. 42 (London, 1948); part 2, Paul Walsh and Colm O Lochlainn, eds., *The Life of Aodh Ruadh O Domhnaill*, part 2, Irish Texts Society, vol. 45 (London, 1957), 90, 12.

4 Epic Writing and Mythic Reading

1 John Miles Foley's idea of 'immanent epic' is relevant here; *Homer's Traditional Art* (Philadelphia, 1999), 42.

2 For a recent discussion of the implications of the nexus between myth, literary genre, and social referent, see Claude Calame, *Poétique des mythes dans la Grèce antique* (Paris, 1999), 11–69.

3 Nicole Loraux, *Born of the Earth: Myth and Politics in Athens*, trans. Selina Stewart (Ithaca and London, 2000). For the idea of textual communities, see Brian Stock, *The Implications of Literacy* (Princeton, 1983), passim. Stock defines textual communities as: a literate core, a set of written legislation [here read canonical 'texts'], and a wider unlettered membership united orally under the same norm (238).

4 Gregory Nagy, *Homeric Questions* (Ithaca, NY, 1996), 114.

5 I take the contrast between myth and mythology from Marcel Detienne, *L'invention de la mythologie* (Paris, 1981). On myth in general, see J.-P. Vernant, *Mythe et société en Grèce ancienne* (Paris, 1974), trans. Janet Lloyd, 1984, 186–242.

6 Gregory Nagy, 'Epic as Genre,' in *Epic Traditions in the Contemporary World: The Poetics of Community*, ed. Margaret Beissinger, Jane Tylus, and Susanne Wofford (Berkeley, 1999), 23.

7 This passage is also taken from Rescension I.

8 Rescension I, 248. O'Rahilly notes here the very different style of the Eógan Mac Durthacht tale, but to me it does not seem to differ from the others so greatly.

9 By 'subtext' I simply mean that it is entirely possible that other texts may
    have already introduced the idea of Cú Chulainn's divine paternity. This
    differs from the *subtextus* usage of Tristram in that I do not assume the
    superior/inferior/native/learned structure that she invokes; cf. H.L.C.
    Tristram, 'The *Cattle Raid of Cuailnge* in Tension and Transition between the
    Oral and the Written, Classical Subtexts and Narrative Heritage,' in *Cul-
    tural Identity and Cultural Integration*, ed. Doris Edel (Dublin, 1996), 61–81.

10 On the legal aspects of Cú Chulainn's double paternity, see Bart Jaski, 'Cú
    Chulainn, *gormac* and *dalta* of the Ulstermen,' *Cambrian Medieval Celtic Stud-
    ies* 37 (summer 1999), 9–11.

11 For a detailed examination of the relationship between Lug and Cú Chu-
    lainn, see Elizabeth Gray, '*Cath Maige Tuired*: Myth and Structure,' *Éigse* 18
    (1981), 183–209; 19 (1983), 1–35, 230–62.

12 U, in fact, gives this title twice, W once only.

13 Recension I, ll. 374–97; Recension II, ll. 724–37.

14 Recension II, ll. 393–435, 604–27, 665–84. Curiously, a passage in alliterative
    prose in Recension II is applied both to Cú Chulainn and to Fergus (I
    underline the common elements): *in leom[leg. leoin?] letharach 7 ind* <u>bráth bid-
    bad</u> *[bráthlec] 7* <u>in bibda sochaide</u> *7 in cend costuda 7* <u>in cirriud mórsluaig</u> *7 in lám
    tidnaichti 7* <u>in chaindel adanta</u> (ll. 395–7, 657–9). The phrase *leom[an] letharach*
    and the verb *cerbaid* also occur in the homily, *Scéla Laí Brátha*, a text supplied
    by H in LU, at l. 2421. Is this another indication of the closer link of Recen-
    sion II with a H-type text of Recension I, as the sharing by both of the
    Fedelm poem would also indicate? In any case, by these additions Recen-
    sion II gives an enhanced prominence to Fergus as a speaker of marked dis-
    course by means other than the additional storytelling role given him in the
    Boyhood Deeds in Recension I.

15 The sparseness of entitulation is a general feature of Y.

16 Three of these tales are introduced by the episodic formula, *fecht n-and dano
    ... fecht n-aile dano*. The exception is the fight with Eógan mac Durthacht.
    O'Rahilly also suspected the segment on Cú Chulainn's killing of fifty of
    the boy troop of being an ill-considered addition, with a heading that also
    does duty for two subsequent incidents (or one incident and an H rewrite)
    in the saga. Exceptionally, there is no reference to Cú Chulainn by name in
    this episode.

17 The improvement in Y is probably fortuitous; a simple eye-skipping error
    from one *cé* to another *cé*.

18 O'Rahilly, Recension II, xxxv.

19 In Recension I, 248, O'Rahilly notes that in the story of the Recovery of the
    Táin, LL, ll. 32879–909, there is a list of the *remscéla* of the saga where only

the three primary stories are listed and cited as part of the *corp* (body) of the narrative. But we have no titles for these incidents in Recension II. Indeed, it is the titles in W's version that best correspond to those listed in *Do Fhaillsigud Tána Bó Cúailnge.*

20 Or 'give me quarter.'

21 The best account for Irish saga of spatial values and sign theory is Will Sayers, 'Cú Chulainn, the Heroic Imposition of Meaning on Signs, and the Revenge of the Sign,' *Incognita: International Journal for Cognitive Studies in the Humanities* 2 (1991), 79–105.

22 For further information on Cú Chulainn as *fian* and the history of this social institution in early Ireland, see McCone, *Pagan Past*, 203–32; McCone, 'Werewolves, *Cyclopes, Diberga* and *Fianna*: Juvenile Delinquency in Early Ireland,' *Cambridge Medieval Celtic Studies* 12 (1986), 1–22. For an influential Greek perspective on Indo-European warrior-initiation rituals, see Pierre Vidal-Naquet, *Le chasseur noir: formes de pensée et formes de société dans le monde grec*, trans. Andrew Szegedy-Maszak, *The Black Hunter: Forms of Thought and Forms of Society in the Greek World* (Baltimore and London, 1986), 106–28.

23 Bricriu's status as trickster figure and peace breaker remains quite consistent through the whole saga tradition.

24 A good example of the use of a dead body in the context of ritual pollution and challenge is found in the Old Irish tale *Echtra Nerai*, ed. Kuno Meyer, *Revue celtique* 10 (1899), 212–28.

25 Terror is a real concern for early Irish saga. For example, madness brought on by the disorienting effect of the battlefield is the dominant theme of the saga *Buile Suibhne*, ed. J.G. O'Keeffe, Irish Texts Society, vol. 11 (London, 1910).

26 *A guin inna dí chúlaid dano oc techiud a rroi dobber díre n-aithig dó, acht mad treo docoí* [Woundings to his poll while fleeing entails the honour price of a churl on a king, unless he (got them) going through (an enemy host)]; *Críth Gablach*, ed. Daniel Binchy (Dublin, 1979), 21, ll. 538–90.

27 McCone, *Pagan Past*, 65–83.

28 For the alignment of the Cú Chulainn and Christ biographies in the tradition of the Annals, see J.V. Kelleher, 'The *Táin* and the Annals,' *Ériu* 22 (1971), 107–27.

29 See James Carney, ed., *The Poems of Blathmac Son of Cú Brettain and the Gospel of Thomas*, Irish Texts Society, vol. 47 (London, 1964).

30 Ibid., 'The Irish Gospel of Thomas,' quatrains 8–21, 40–4.

31 *Bethu Brigte,* ed. Donnchadh Ó hAodha (Dublin, 1978), par. 10–18. The editor dates this Life as seventh to ninth century, with the vernacular elements

in question here dated to the ninth century. There the maiden Brigid takes a guide, proceeds through a wasteland area to where she is identified by heavenly fire as the holy one, and is consecrated a Christian virgin – the bishop mistakenly used the rite for the coronation of a bishop!

32 In the apocryphal *Book of Enoch* – a text known to the Irish – Adam, weakened by old age, sends his son Enoch to search for the life-preserving unction from the Tree of Life in the Garden of Eden. Enoch's way is barred but he is given a special role in the Harrowing of Hell whereby Adam, the first father, and all his sons are brought out of Hell to Paradise by Christ, the adopted son of Adam, there to be reunited with Enoch at the gates of Paradise. On the *Book of Enoch* in Ireland, see Martin McNamara, *The Apocrypha in the Irish Church* (Dublin, 1975), 24–7. For Harrowing of Hell materials in Ireland, see Dooley, 'The Gospel of Nicodemus in Ireland,' in *The Medieval Gospel of Nicodemus*. ed. Zbigniew Izydorczyk (Tempe, AZ, 1997), 361–402.

33 Vladimir Propp, *Morphology of the Folktale* (Austin, 1968), translation of 1927 Russian edition; McCone, *Pagan Past*, 59–61.

34 Eleanor Knott, ed., *Togail Bruidne Da Derga*, Medieval and Modern Irish Series 8 (Dublin, 1975).

35 The text follows immediately after the *Táin* in LU.

36 My student Connell Monette has suggested that the motif of the king's thirst is based on the story of David in Samuel II, 23:13–17.

37 *Corpus Iuris Hiberniae* 18, 20–31, quoted in McCone, *Pagan Past*, 151–2.

38 *Ancient Laws of Ireland*, vol. 5, 298.10; the translation is my own. I am uncertain of the translation of the final instance, which does not show the same formula as the first six; it may be a reference to flotsam recovery or to the champion's reward for watching for incoming ships.

39 This is not an easy matter to decide. The material in the Irish law tracts on the role of the king's champion and on rules of military engagement is scattered through the sources and there is no specific and coherent set of laws and commentaries on this subject; to a modern reader this seems a curious omission in a society that values heroic aggression.

40 Tomás Ó Cathasaigh, 'Cath Maige Tuired as Exemplary Myth,' in *Folia Gadelica: Essays Presented to R.A. Breatnach*, ed. Pádraig de Brún et al. (Cork, 1983), 1–19. See also his introduction in *The Heroic Biography of Cormac mac Airt* (Dublin, 1977). For his analysis of Cú Chulainn as exemplary sister's son see 'The Sister's Son in Early Irish Literature,' *Peritia* 5 (1986), 128–60.

41 Georges Dumézil, *The Destiny of the Warrior*, passim; Arnold Van Gennep, *The Rites of Passage*, passim. See also Victor Turner, *The Ritual Process*,

passim; J.F. Nagy, *The Wisdom of the Outlaw*, 227–30; McCone, *Pagan Past*, 185–93.

42 No. 322: 'Columns of life, that is, periods of life; that is, childhood and boy-hood, youth and young warriorship, old age and decrepitude.' Elsewhere the columns of life are said to be six in number (*LL*, ll. 24333–4). Interest-ingly, the Glossary tradition sees the final term as still related to an overall standard of armed service: cf. *Díbell ní inbrithe in bello* [*dibell*, one powerless in battle] (O'Mulconry's Glossary, 311); *ní buithe in bello* [he should not be in a battle] (ibid., 300). *Gilla* is the standard term for charioteers in the Fer Diad episode in both Recensions and is used throughout the entire saga in this sense in Recension II. As the Fer Diad episode is later than the body of the narrative in Recension I, it is obvious that the semantics of *gilla* were changing in this period.

43 There is confusion about the role of the house in the tale. Both W and Y have the phrase, *'co ndernai tenid dam and.'* *Atai-seom thenid mor do.* *'Maith didiu' or Conchobar.* U omits this and so renders the house to which they go the *lis* of Emain Macha. This may amount to no more than a scribal eye slip-page in U, but it does tighten up the story with no loss of significant mean-ing.

44 Claude Lévi-Strauss, *Structural Anthropology*, vol. 2 (1978), 161. This passage is discussed by McCone in *Pagan Past*, 62.

45 On this issue of the mythic treatment of natural gender, see Edmund Leach's structural analysis of the Creation and Fall story in *Genesis as Myth and Other Essays* (London, 1983), passim.

46 Mary Douglas, *Purity and Danger: An Analysis of the Concepts of Pollution and Taboo* (Hammondsworth, 1970), 112, 118.

47 Relevant here are the several references to games, role playing, and ritual humiliation in Irish inauguration rituals. The king becomes king by being borne up by his significant vassals and by going on the mound. See the descriptions of Irish inaugurations in Katherine Simms, *From Kings to War-Lords* (London, 1987), 20–40. One of the elegies for those killed at the battle of Down in 1260 turns inauguration ritual into the matter of children's games in the poet's description of his childish play of 'King of the Castle' with his friend Eachmarchach Ó Catháin; see 'Fearghal Og Mac an Bhaird's Poem on the Battle of Down,' ed. John O'Donovan, in *Miscellany of the Celtic Society* (Dublin, 1849), 404–15; quatrains 13–16, also cited by Simms, *Kings to War-Lords*, 23–4.

48 My formula here represents a summary of Calame's formulations, *Poétique*, chap. 1.

49 See Bart Jaski's analysis of this incident and its legal ramifications in 'Cú

Chulainn *gormac,'* 9–11. I go further than he does by seeing in their verbal exchanges a verbal legal trick of Cú Chulainn's by which he actually wrests command of the boy troop from the king.

50 *Imthechta* and *airscéla* are both literary terms in their own right.

51 Note the technical term and the title here.

52 The asthetic response of Ailill is comic in itself with its rather precious turn of phrase. Since Bricriu is someone whom the audience knows was left behind in Cruachain and whose word is notoriously unreliable, the saga audience would readily see the joke being played on Ailill.

53 Recension I, 253.

54 'Thus far concerning the Boyhood Deeds of Cú Chulainn in the *Táin Bó Cúalnge,* and the Prologue to the tale, and the route and adventures of the host from Cruachain to this.'

55 Uáitéar Mac Gearailt, '*Cath Ruis na Ríg* and Twelfth-century Literary and Oral Tradition,' *Zeitschrift für celtische Philologie* 44 (1991), 128–45.

5 Myth to Epic: The Coming of a God

1 McCone, *Pagan Past and Christian Present*, 203–32.

2 Tomás Ó Cathasaigh, '*Cath Maige Tuired* as Exemplary Myth,' 1–19.

3 The understanding that Recension I presents the initiatory transition in keyed terms, from *macc* to *gillae* and on to *óclaech*, advances the initiatory model considerably. For this chapter I will once again concentrate on Recension I.

4 My underlining indicates the textual keying of the ostensive mode. The degree to which the scene features a rhetorical saga 'run' ultimately based on a non-native narrative tradition from the Alexander legend of the griffins levitating the hero's chair, or perhaps owing something to the Biblical winged chariot of Ezekiel (1:5–11), is too complex a subject to enter into here.

5 In the printed edition the section containing the visitation of Lug runs from l. 2072 to l. 2334, while that concerning Lug himself ends at l. 2184. Assuming, as I do, that the opening of the saga in LU constitutes a valid opening for Recension I and that nothing has been accidentally lost from Recension I, then the Lug incident sits in the dead centre of the entire saga.

6 The PhD thesis of Brent Miles, 'Middle Irish Saga and Irish Neoclassicism' (University of Toronto, 2005), concerns the influence of Latin epic tradition on the *Táin*. In a paper delivered at the Harvard Celtic Studies Colloquium, October 2001, he presented a summary of his findings thus far. I am grateful to him for allowing me to cite him here.

7 There is progression in the two recensions: Recension I introduces each poem as a *laíd* or song. Recension II greatly extends the poetic content but favours instead the formula: *Is amlaid ra boí 'ga rád 7 rabert na briathra* [this is how he spoke and he pronounces these words] (ll. 3360–1, etc.).

8 I refer to the use of the topos of Lug's arrival in *Cath Maige Tuired*, ed. Elizabeth Gray, Irish Texts Society, vol. 52 (London, 1983), 38–41; this episode was obviously well known, judging from its subsequent use as a literary *exemplum*. See Gofraidh Fionn Ó Dálaigh's poem to Maurice, second Earl of Desmond, *Irish Bardic Poetry*, ed. Osborn Bergin (Dublin, 1972), 73–81, quatrains 20–42. The only aspects of the *Táin* staging that bear comparison is the dexterity displayed by Lug in the play of weapons and his ability to cross the camp boundary in a magical fashion.

9 *Is sí seo in tres árim is glicu 7 is dolgiu dorigned i nHérind .i. árim Con Culaind for feraib Hérend ar Tána 7 árim Loga for slúag Fomórach, ar cath Maigi Tured 7 árim Ingciúil for slóg Bruidni Da Dergae* [This is one of the three cleverest and most accurate calculations ever made in Ireland, viz. Cú Chulainn's counting of the men of Ireland in the *Táin*, the count of the Fomorians by Lug in *Cath Maige Tuired*, and Ingcel's count of the hosts at (*Togal*) *Bruidne Da Dergae*] (l. 327, gloss). Strictly speaking it is Lóch, not Lug, who does the counting in *Cath Maige Tuired*. The triadic formulation is probably derived from earlier Irish exegetical practice where the numeration coding of sacred tradition is a common trait. In its contemporary context, however, the formula represents an interesting way of filing saga knowledge, analogous to the Welsh triadic tendencies in 'The Tale of Branwen' in the *Mabinogi* collection.

10 *Oc Beloch Caille Móre fri Cnogba atúaid* is H's gloss on the site Áth Grena/ Áth nGabla (at Cill Mór road opposite Knowth; l. 335). Áth Grencha is the reading of the Egerton manuscript. For Cnogba as the site of Lug's residence, see Tomás Ó Cathasaig, 'The Eponym of Cnogba,' *Éigse* 23 (1989), 27–38.

11 Medb's cold response at ll. 393–5 is worth noting: *'Ní dénaim-sea báa de sin. I n-óenchorp ata-side. Fodaim guin. Ní móu gabáil, lasanní is áes ingini macdacht insin 7 ní thángatar a fhergníma beus.'* ['I don't hold that of any account, he has only a single body, he can be wounded, he can be taken. Besides, he is at the girly stage and his male strength hasn't come to him yet.']

12 I discuss the question of H's contribution in chapter 3, passim.

13 As it now stands, the latter part of the *Táin* contains a considerable body of narrative relating to wounds and healing in the later insertion of the story of Cethern's wounds (ll. 3161–327). This takes place in the company of Cú Chulainn and it constitutes another site of inactivity, the recovery tent, where, like the campfire setting, stories may be told.

14 This latter discrepancy may be telling. It may show that certain set pieces of the narrative, such as the military roll-call, have had a certain independent thematic value and a literary life of their own as rhetorical exercises in their own right. This is patently the case with the description of the chariot of Cú Chulainn and the narrative topic packaged under the title *Breslech Mór Murthemne*. I will discuss the issue of discrepancy considered as aspectual rather than sequential narrative structuring later in this chapter. For a list of references (incomplete) to Sualtaim as from the *síd*, see Kaarina Hollo, 'Cú Chulainn and Síd Truim,' *Ériu* 49 (1998), 13–22.

15 For the significance of this understanding of Cú Chulainn as liminal to Ulster, see the legal judgment offered on the killing of his son Connle in the text edited by J. O'Keeffe, 'Cuchulinn and Conlaech,' *Ériu* 1 (1904), 123–7. For a discussion of this passage, see Joanne Findon, *Women's Words*, 170–85.

16 In one way this more elaborate, simile-laden, exotically referenced and highly alliterative kind of prose can be seen as part of a natural develop-ment of Irish prose style: if the piece is, as scholars suspect, a later rewrite, then it is logical to expect that the alliterative, adjectival style will be much more evident. But it is clear that there is much more at stake here than the effect of a native literary chronology on stylistic choice. The similes, exotic details, and also the deliberate and regular effect of prose rhythms mod-elled on Latin prose cadence at the period endings in this section mark the writing as self-consciously epic on a classical pattern; it may also point to a declaimed reading, a performative context with a real audience. See espe-cially the section on the great *ríastartha*, ll. 2245–78, where the rhythmic stress of end periods is particularly marked.

17 For a discussion of the traditions of the 'Finding of the *Táin*,' see chapter 2, passim. The observation of Tertullian on the Celts' fondness for mantic sleep on the graves of the dead is well known. It occurs in the context of a discussion of magical and devilish visions: 'Nicander also reports that the Celts keep watch all night at the tombs of their heroes for the same purpose [to consult their oracles]'; *De Anima*, 57, 10 (*Patrologia Latina* 2, 794). This reported tradition may not be historically true; rather it could be a cliché of barbarian behaviour, ultimately derived from Herodotus on the Scythians – a detail which probably also suggested itself to Tertullian; he has just cited Herodotus and also the Greek historian on the Mesammones who consult oracles on the graves of their ancestors.

18 I take the confusion from the galloping cattle as a separate motif insofar as the stampede of the cattle across the ford occurs twice and provokes a spe-cific and poetically marked response from Cú Chulainn, of which only the

first line is quoted: *Ní airciu a n-átha la linni* [I cannot distinguish the fords from the pools] (l. 2003). This admission is a dangerous slippage for an individual who earlier boasted of his superlative gifts of discernment, and it represents a further stage in the hero's existential crisis. It also represents a textual option not taken up by the scribes of U.

19 Meyer, ed., 'Adventures of Nera,' *Revue celtique* 10 (1889), 212–28; 11 (1890), 210.

20 Ernst Windisch, ed., *Irische Texte* II (Leipzig, 1889), 239–56.

21 The association of divine female figures and cows is perhaps best exemplified in the name of the river/goddess Boand understood as 'Obtainer of cows' by E. Campanile, 'Old Irish *Bóand*,' *Journal of Indo-European Studies* 13 (1985), 477–9. I thank my student John McDonald for allowing me to read his article, 'The Water-Serpent, the Mother Cow and Her Calf: An Indo-European Myth and Its Poetic Formulae,' *Journal of Indo-European Studies*, forthcoming.

22 See O'Rahilly's Introduction to LL *Táin*, xxxi–xxxiii, for references to Thurneysen's argument; she attributes this passage to the LU compiler – that is, the individual who created the version now contained in LU.

23 Rolf Baumgarten, 'Varia III: A Note on *Táin Bó Regamna*,' *Ériu* 34 (1983), 189–92.

24 Ibid., 191.

25 For examples of the use of *día, dé* in a contrived pseudo-pagan context, see the discussion of Ruairí Ó hUiginn, '*Tongu do dia toinges mo thúath* and Related Expressions,' in *Sages, Saints*, 332–41 at 338. Unlike C. O'Rahilly, I am inclined to take the core phrase with *dé* as originally singular, a calque on the Latin *Benedictio Dei*. The gloss that follows could be compared with the position of the *Tuatha Dé* (the magician gods) and the *Fir Bolg* (the farmers) of *Cath Maige Tuired*. It is probably with this in mind that O'Rahilly translates the first term as 'magicians.'

26 The new beginning of Recension II could conceivably have been written up from a source that contained similar details about the bull and his owner, as in *Táin Bó Regamna*; see chapter 2, passim.

27 For example, in the tale involving Cú Chulainn and the mysterious woman at the Boyne, John Carey, 'Eithne in Gubai,' *Éigse* 28 (1994–5), 160–4; and again in the tale of Lugaid and Derbforgaill, Carl Marstrander, 'The Deaths of Lugaid and Derbforgaill,' *Ériu* 5 (1911), 201–8). For this latter saga see my new translation and commentary in the supplemental volumes of *The Field Day Anthology of Irish Writing*, ed. Angela Bourke et al. (Dublin, 2002), part 4. Violence towards female supernatural figures is a constant of Cú Chulainn's behaviour in Irish saga. There is one startling example of a *topos* like

that of Cú Chulainn and the Morrígain's mutual cursing in early modern Scottish Gaelic tradition in a waulking song that commemorates Donald, eleventh lord of Clan Ranald, who died in 1688: *Mharbh a' bhadhbh an Colla 's Ràghall ... Siod, a Rìgh, nach tigeadh ise,/ 'Sa làmh leònta 's a cas briste,/ Sireadh léigh am beul gach litreach,/ Gun aon léigh san tìr ach mise,/ 'S air mo làimh gun dèanainn misneach,/ Lùbainn cnàimh 's gun tàirninn silteach;/ 'N uair dhùininn beul do chiste,/ Chuirinn ùir air bruaich do lice.* [The Badb killed Coll and Ranald ... Would O king, that she would come,/ with her hand wounded and her leg broken,/ Seeking a leech in every port,/ And no leech in the land but I;/ By my hand, I would take courage,/ I would bend bone and draw blood;/ When I would close thy coffin's lid,/ I would pile earth on the brink of thy tomb.] Alexander Carmichael, ed. and trans., in *Carmina Gadelica: Ortha nan Gaedel*, vol. 3 (1923), 32–3.

28 Healing in battle by means of milk, such as occurs in *Cath Maige Tuired*, would, I think, be seen as a deliberately pagan motif of the forbidden food offered to idols kind. From this comes the need to play this scene in a way that disrupts its pagan symmetry of like answering to like and to intrude the first element of a new order of healing, the cry for help, in order to structure a new pivotal narrative point. On the other hand, there are examples of charms that do invoke the power of Dían Cécht, the divine leech of *Cath Maige Tuired* – as, for example, the St Gall charm against a number of ailments including weapon wounds: *ropslan. forsate. admuinur. in slanicid. foracab. Dian. Cecht. liamuintir coropslan. ani forsate* [May it be whole on which it goes. I put my trust in the salve which Dían Cécht left to his family that it may be whole that whereon it goes] (*Thesarus Paleohibernicus* II, 249). But the significance of the Dían Cécht exemplary tale of proper and improper healing in *Cath Maige Tuired* seems to be that it describes a sequence of healing that moves from the forbidden pagan and/or pristine state of the healing arts to the flawed state of healing now current in a postlapsarian, historical world of the saga author's writing.

29 It is also a note picked up again at the end of the tale, and given as Fergus's furious – if helpless – summary of the action. I use the term *clamor* in a relatively simple way, though the legal concept underlying it is a fundamental one: that acts of rapine or force must be countered by those too weak to resist them through raising an outcry. The idea comes into legal usage in Ireland concerning rape and is clearly modelled on the Levitical laws on adultery in the Old Testament: *Deuteronomy* 22:22–30. In the Frankish realms the term *clamor* is elevated to a more formal canonical sanction with its own liturgical ritual. See Lester K. Little, *Benedictine Maledictions: Liturgi-*

cal Cursing in Romanesque France (Ithaca, NY, 1993), 150–85. In Little's view the practice may have Irish origins but this is at best conjectural.

30 In the Old Irish Life of St Brigid, the bold and insistent manner in which the poor and the sick beg for help is taken as a matter of course; *Bethu Brigte*, ed. Donncha Ó hAodha (Dublin, 1987), chaps. 23, 27, 34, 36. The whole idea of the *clamor* is to utilize the only element available to those outside power, their physical selves, their voices, and their ability to interpose the scandal of their disordered bodies in a way that cannot be ignored. The medieval hymn *Salve Regina* embodies the idea of the *clamor* as the cry of the defence-less and the poor very well: *ad te clamamus, exules filii Evae; ad te suspiramus gementes et flentes.*

31 *M'aenarán dam isa sliab:* ed. James Carney in *Éigse* 2 (1940), 107–13. Carney does not date the poem specifically but he notes that on metrical grounds the quatrains from VII on are faulty. See also Carney's version with verse translation in his *Medieveal Irish Lyrics* (Port Laoise, 1967), 42–7.

32 *M'aenarán dam isa sliab:* from YBL, ed. John O'Donovan, *Miscellany of the Irish Archaeological Society*, vol. 1 (1846), 1–15; from Bodleian MS Laud 615, by Kuno Meyer, *Zeitschrift für celtische Philologie* 8 (1912), 302–3.

33 *Betha Colaim Chille: Life of Columcille*, ed. A. O'Kelleher, G. Schoepperle (Urbana, IL, 1918), 180–1; for a new translation see Brian Lacey, *Manus O'Donnell: The Life of Colum Cille* (Dublin, 1998), 99; *M'aenarán dam isa sliab:* ed. Carney, *Éigse* 2, 108–9.

34 Patrick's *Lorica* is dated to the eighth century and the first reference to the underlying incident is in the seventh-century *Life* of Muirchú; Ludwig Bieler, ed., *The Patrician Texts in the Book of Armagh* (Dublin, 1979). The most recent text, translation, and commentary is from John Carey, *King of Mysteries: Early Irish Religious Writing* (Dublin, 1998), 130–5, 277. Carey comments that the transformation of Patrick's followers into deer as a way of escaping his enemies also occurs in the *Táin* (O'Rahilly, ll. 942–5). One might also note that explicit in the Patrician prayer is a specific and extremely archai-cally worded petition that applies to Cú Chulainn's situation: protection is sought against the spells of women, *brichtu ban*. As Carey points out, the same phrase is also used in a *defixio*-type Gaulish inscription from Larzac; see Wolfgang Meid, *Gaulish Inscriptions* (Budapest, 1992), 40–6.

35 Themes and vocabulary also connect this poem with others in an Irish pro-tective prayer tradition: for example, *Sét no tíag*, ed. James Carney, *Ériu* 22 (1971), 26–9, and also the words *caingen, fíado find*, the invocation of Trinity, and the nine (ten?) choirs of angels; in general, the associations between the idea of the journey, life itself as a journey, and the safe passage of the soul at death are linkages common to much Irish devotional thinking.

36 Cú Chulainn's cry for help also bears some resemblance Psalm 21, which
   has been most associated with the suffering Messiah: 'My God, my God,
   why hast thou forsaken me? Why art thou so far from helping me and from
   the words of my roaring. O my God, I cry in the daytime but thou answer-
   est not; and in the night and am not silent ... Be not far from me for trouble
   is near; for there is none to help. Many bulls have compassed me: many
   strong bulls of Bashan have beset me round. They gape upon me with their
   mouths, as a ravening and a roaring lion ... Be not far from me, Lord: O
   thou my strength, hasten to help me. Deliver my soul from the sword; my
   darling from the power of the dog. For he hath not despised nor abhorred
   the affliction of the afflicted ; neither hath he turned his face from him; But
   when he cried unto him he heard ...'

37 See Morton Bloomfield's classic study, *The Seven Deadly Sins: An Introduction to the History of a Religious Concept with Special Reference to Medieval
   English Literature* (East Lansing, MI, 1967). For an Irish example of seven
   heavens lore, see Máire Herbert, 'The Seven Journeys of the Soul,' *Éigse* 17
   (1977), 1–12.

38 'M'óenurán im aireclán,' ed. Gerard Murphy, in *Early Irish Lyrics* (Oxford,
   1956), 18–19, 178–80. Carney has dated the poem to the eighth or ninth century on linguistic grounds. Like many comparable poems in his anthology
   Murphy has omitted stanzas that do not conform to strict metrical requirements, including two after the *dúnad* which he considers later additions.
   But it is clear that this and the prayers for a journey discussed above are
   part of a heavily used religious repertoire. Hence, for my purposes here,
   originary issues such as dating are less significant than the fact of their continuous use.

39 There may indeed be some cross-contamination between this poem and
   m'oenuran dam isa sliab; line 14a reads *ma(u)o(e)naran dam* in three manuscripts (Murphy, *Early Irish Lyrics*, 180). This seems to me to reflect a growing sense of the popularity of the *óenurán* as a key term for devotional
   poetry.

40 James Carney, 'The Dating of Early Irish Verse, 500–1100,' *Éigse* 19 (1983),
   177–216.

41 James Carney, *The Poems of Blathmac, Son of Cú Brettan*, Irish Text Society,
   vol. 47 (London, 1964).

42 Ibid., 62–3.

43 Murphy, *Early Irish Lyrics*, 2–3, 172. The poem is full of analytic and sophisticated self-reflection by way of binary oppositions between the animal and
   the man. Pangur, for example, is a young warrior candidate, pursuing his
   macdán or fighting apprenticeship. The poem is full of play on heroic terms

such as *cless, ar gressaib gal;* conversely, the cat is also bound by the liminal marks of the monastic enclosure, *fri fega fál.*

44 Edited from MS Egerton 1782 by Kuno Meyer, 'Songs and Stories from Irish Manuscripts,' 3 *Otia Merseiana* 2 (1900), 76.

45 In *Irische Texte* III, 19, 52.

46 Ed. and trans. in *Thesarus Paleohibernicus* II, 294.

47 Ed. J.G. O'Keeffe, Medieval and Modern Irish Series (Dublin, 1931). All citations are from this edition; previously edited with translation, Irish Texts Society, vol. 12 (1910) (London, 1913).

48 Cf. also in the monastic poem *'Marbán and Guaire'* the statement: *na seóid dochí as dorn im ceo* [the wealth you see is like a fistful of mist]; Kuno Meyer, ed., *King and Hermit* (London, 1901), 29. This quatrain is not included in Murphy's *Early Irish Lyrics*, 10–19.

49 Gerard Murphy, ed., *Early Irish Lyrics*, 10–19.

50 Carney, *'M'áenurán,'* 109

51 The unique nature of Lug's thwarting of the doom laid down by the Morrígain is emphasized by the repetition of the same phrase, *don chor so,* concluding both their statements at ll. 2103 and 2184.

52 Though I try to follow a certain thematic thread through the scene here, I do not wish to deny the more specifically textual complexity of the account. Thus, for example, I see the beginning of a high epic rhetoric developing in this scene of the cry, a development which, by inflating the effect of the *gáir,* works somewhat at cross purposes with the tracking of the weakness and abjection of the hero. This epic redirection is what powers the rewriting of the whole scene of *In Carpat Serda 7 in Breslech Mór Maige Murthemne.*

53 Lug comes from a northeasterly direction but it is not clear how to read this detail. *Cnogba* cannot be intended. Possibly it is a way of saying that Lug comes to the hero from the territory of the Ulaid or even from Emain Macha.

54 Here Cú Chulainn seems to misread the cues as if it were a revisiting of the scene of Fraéch's death earlier in the narrative. The other-world visitant in a green cloak is not much different visually from the ladies so dressed who carry Fróéch off to the *síd* (ll. 855–8). Cú Chulainn, it is noted here, renders himself subject to another's (Lug's) point of view in the scene and, in taking a miscue, gives voice to a misleading take on his own story. Lamentation is appropriate to the after-death condition of the hero. The move attests to psychic crisis – he is literally beside himself.

55 Jaan Puhvel, 'Mythological Reflections of Indo-European Medicine,' in G. Cardona et al., eds., *Indo-European and Indo-Europeans* (Philadelphia, 1970), 369–82; Bruce Lincoln, *Myth, Cosmos and Society: Indo-European Themes of*

Creation and Destruction (Cambridge, MA, 1986), 99–118; Calvert Watkins, *How to Kill a Dragon*, 525–44. For another perspective see Wendy Davies, 'The Place of Healing in Early Irish Society,' in *Sages, Saints*, 43–55.

56 *Cath Maige Tuired*, 32, chaps. 33–5. The 'myth' of healing in this text is a serious one in that much of the saga seems to address pressing contemporary concerns. It invites speculation on the current use of healing formulae at the time of the composition of the saga, the negative associations in the Germanic aspects of the healing charm cited and the need to assert Irish(?) Christian values in a world threatened by pagan Northmen.

57 *Iliad*, XV, 230–52. I use the translation by Robert Fitzgerald, Everyman's Library (New York, 1992), 358–9.

58 *Iliad*, XVI, 523–6; Fitzgerald, 392–3.

59 *Dieux guérisseurs en Gaule romaine*, ed. Christian Landes (Paris, 1992), 89–94, 119–25; Aline Rousselle, *Croire et guérir: la foi en Gaule dans l'antiquité tardive* (Paris, 1990).

60 See R.G. Collingwood and R.P. Wright, *The Roman Inscriptions of Britain*, vol. 1 (Oxford, 1965), 808, 1052. Most significant in terms of actual medical praxis is the Chester inscription: 'the doctor Antiochus (honours) the saviours of men pre-eminent among the immortals: Asklepios of the healing hand, Hygeia, (and) Panakeia' (*Journal of Roman Studies* 59 [1969], 235).

61 Rousselle, *Croire et guérir*, 200–80. There is no evidence that I know of to support the existence of healing centres of this type in Ireland, although the phenomenon of pagan centres becoming Christian is borne out for a number of sites. See Pádraig Ó Riain, 'Boundary Association in Early Irish Society,' *Studia Celtica* 7 (1972), 12–29.

62 Karl Hauck, *Goldbrakteaten aus Sievern: spätantike Amulett-Bilder der Saxonica und die sachsen-'Origo' bei Widukind von Corvey* (Munich, 1970). Note, however, that bracteates have a limited diffusion in Germano-Britain. They only occur in the Kentish area. Thus there can be no question of influence – merely of a common general process of pagan/Christian assimilation.

63 Ibid., passim.

64 See the discussion of *Médecins* in *Dictionnaire d'archéologie chrétienne et de liturgie*, ed. Fernand Cabrol (Paris, 1855–1937), 109–60.

65 *De Helia et ieiunio* 20. 75; ed. C. Schenkl, *Corpus Scriptorum Ecclesiasticorum Latinorum*, 32. 257.

66 *Dictionnaire d'archéologie chrétienne*, 158–60. This, it is pointed out, is a popular and possibly Donatist inscription. Its charm aspects, the example of Lazarus and Peter, the catalogue of body parts, attest to its use in popular circles. Such a North-African background, however, is also relevant to St

Augustine's fondness for the image of the *Christus medicus* in his sermons directed to a general Christian community.

67 *Ennarationes in psalmos* 50. 6, *Patrologia Latina* 36, 588.

68 *Solil.* 1, 14, *Patrologia Latina* 37, 870.

69 One suggestive healing miracle in the *Vita Columbae* may reflect a Christian way of doing what is essentially a popular healing charm; it also shows both the call and response structure of effectiveness and the obsession with the fated moment of death. Considering the use made of venerable manuscripts as miracle-working relics, and also the use made of a text (often a psalm fragment) as cure fetish, this very uncharacteristic Irish saints' miracle stands out from the rest: a North Sea cure comparable with the forbidden 'joint-to-joint' formulae of *Cath Maige Tuired*? 'Once, while Columba was living in Iona, he called to him ... one of the brethren, Lugaid ... "Make ready at once for a speedy voyage to Ireland ... Daiméne's daughter, the holy virgin Mogain, has had an accident. As she returned home from the church after the night office, she stumbled, and her hip is broken in two. Now she cries aloud and repeats my name constantly, hoping that I should bring her some comfort from the Lord." Why say more? Lugaid did as he was bidden. When he was ready to set out, Columba handed him a little pinewood box with a blessing inside it, and said: "When you arrive to visit Mogain, the blessing contained in this box should be dipped in a jar of water and then the water of blessing should be poured over her hip. Then call on the name of God and at once her hipbone will be joined and knit together and her full health restored." Then the saint went on: "Look, in your presence I write on the lid of this box the number XXIII, which is the number of years which the holy virgin will continue in this present life after her cure." All this was done as the saint foretold. (Richard Sharpe, trans., *Adomnán of Iona: Life of St Columba* [London, 1995], 158–9).

70 Ludwig Bieler, ed., *Libri Epistolarum Sancti Patricii Episcopi* (Dublin, 1952), 20.

71 See also Nagy, *Conversing with Angels*, 34–5.

72 Bieler's views are refuted by Danuta Schatzer, '"Iuvenes vestri visiones videbunt": Visions and the Literary Sources of Patrick's *Confessio*,' *Journal of Medieval Latin* 3 (1993), 169–201.

73 On Christ as the Sol Invictus, see Gaston H. Halsberghe, *The Cult of Sol Invictus* (Leiden, 1972); David Knipp, '*Christus Medicas*' in der Frühchristlichen Sarkophagskultur (Leiden, 1998).

74 Ludwig Bieler, ed., *Four Latin Lives of St Patrick*, Scriptores Latini Hibernici, vol. 8 (Dublin, 1971), 1.2.(3).

75 Ibid., chap. 28, p. 121. Columbanus uses the same images of light and darkness: *Patrologia Latina* 80, 253.

76 Ibid., chap. 17.

77 Clearly one is dealing with a term from the glossary tradition.

78 This echoes the newer roles of Cú Chulainn in a text such as *Siabarcharpat Con Culaind*, in Kuno Meyer, ed., *Anecdota from Irish Manuscripts*, vol. 3 (1910), 49–56, where the hero returns from hell to warn King Loegaire to convert to Christianity. The text is found in LU itself. In the precisely dated (1149) *Vision of Tnugdal*, Conall Cernach and Fergus mac Roich are placed as the doorkeepers to hell; the soul questions their position in the fourth place of hell when they were faithful to their old beliefs: *The Vision of Tnugdal*, trans. J.M. Picard and Y. de Pontfarcy (Dublin, 1989), 121. They provide an analogue to the placement of Enoch and Elias, who are also liminal figures – with Enoch also as a healer – at the gates of Paradise: *Stair Nicoméid: The Irish Gospel of Nicodemus*, ed. Ian Hughes, Irish Texts Society (Dublin, 1991), 44–5. Thus, in the world of the twelfth-century *Táin* old heroes are re-imagined in contexts where they had not earlier been envisaged.

79 *Thesarus Paleohibernicus*, II, 248. This is but one part of a sympathetic magic cure. It also requires that the verbal charm (as writing) be placed in butter with no water content (e.g. oil substitute?). It shares this feature with an Anglo-Saxon charm (as noted in *Thesarus Paleohibernicus*, 248, note *g*). It also seems to syncretize Christian and native invocations, invoking a pierced and wounded Christ and a metal-working Goibniu, the smith of the *Tuatha Dé*. Here I translate *delg* as spike. The reference to Christ and to Goibniu seems to justify thinking of a metal object.

80 *Thesarus Paleohibernicus*, II, 250. This charm has an actantial context also: it relies on the application of saliva and the curative power of the sun to heal the wound.

81 For a partial translation and discussion of the poem, see chapter 3.

82 *Thesarus Paleohibernicus*, II, 100. The diminutive also relates to the *-án* of *óenurán* discussed above. Childishness is another register of powerlessness.

83 Cecile O'Rahilly, 'Ferdai écin,' *Éigse* 16 (1976), 326.

84 The early poetic traditions associated with St Moling dramatize this demonic work of deception against which Christian men have to fight with discernment; cf. *Félire Óengusso Céli Dé*, ed. Whitley Stokes (London, 1905), 150–4.

85 Claude Lévi-Strauss, *Histoire du lynx* (Paris, 1991).

6 The Invention of Women in the *Táin*

1 See Roberta Krueger, *Women Readers and the Ideology of Gender in Old French Verse Romance* (Cambridge, 1993), 99.

2 Caroline Walker Bynum, *Holy Feast and Holy Fast: The Religious Significance of Food to Medieval Women* (Berkeley and Los Angeles, 1987).

3 For feminist critiques of the manner in which traditional Freudian ways of constructing sexual difference privilege masculine subjectivity, see Toril Moi, *French Feminist Thought: A Reader* (Oxford, 1987), and Judith Butler, *Gender Trouble: Feminism and the Subversion of Identity* (New York and London, 1990).

4 Luce Irigaray, *This Sex Which Is Not One*, trans. C. Porter (NY, 1985), and *Speculum of the Other Woman*, trans. G.C. Gill (Ithaca, NY, 1985), provides the most influential account of how one might subvert the Freudian structuralist view of women as objects of representation, of discourse, and of desire. Taken to its logical conclusion, the rigid division of male = subject / female = object would finally effect a complete deconstruction of women in texts. See, for example, the position of Howard Bloch in *Medieval Misogyny and the Invention of Western Romantic Love* (Chicago, 1991); see also Roger Dragonetti, *Mirage des sources: l'art du faux dans le roman médiéval* (Paris, 1987).

5 On women as boundary – the frame as well as what lies outside the frame – see Mary Douglas, *Purity and Danger*, passim. Julia Kristeva develops these ideas of the relation between women's bodies, pollution, and what she terms the syntax of the body – pollution as an element of social processes of definition of potential. See her *Powers of Horror: An Essay on Abjection*, trans. Louis S. Roudiez (New York, 1982), 56–112.

6 Tomás Ó Máille, 'Medb Cruachna.' *Zeitschrift für celtische Philologie* (1927), 129–46; Proinsias Mac Cana. 'Aspects of the Theme of King and Goddess.' *Études celtiques* 7 (1955–6), 77–114, 356–413 and 8 (1958–9), 59–65; Risteard A. Breatnach, 'The Lady and the King: A Theme in Irish Literature,' *Studies: An Irish Quarterly Review* 42 (1953), 321–6; McCone, *Pagan Past*, 109–21, 148–58.

7 Kathleen Biddick's synthesis 'Genders, Bodies, Boundaries: Technologies of the Visible,' *Speculum* 68 (1993), 389–418 – borrowed from James Clifford's *The Predicament of Culture: Twentieth-century Ethnography, Literature and Art* (Cambridge, MA, 1990), 325 – of what might constitute an essentialized theory of culture may be helpful here: 'culture is "naturalized as a coherent body that lives and dies. Culture is enduring, traditional, structural rather than contingent, syncretic, historical." Culture is a process of ordering, not of disruption.'

8 Kelly, 'The *Táin* as Literature,' 69–102.

9 Joanne Findon, *A Woman's Words: Emer and Female Speech in the Ulster Cycle* (Toronto, 1997), Introduction.

10 For an examination of a female figure caught in the process of transition, see Ann Trindade, 'Irish Gormlaith as a Sovereignty Figure,' *Études celtiques* 23 (1986), 143–6.

11 Máire Herbert, 'Goddess and King: The Sacred Marriage in Early Ireland,' in *Women and Sovereignty*, ed. Louise Fradenburg, Cosmos 7 (Edinburgh, 1992) 264–75.

12 For the most reductionist reading of possible values ascribed to women in texts, see the now famous essay 'Why Diotima Is a Woman' by David Halperin, in *Before Sexuality: The Construction of Erotic Experience in the Ancient Greek World*, ed. David Halperin, J.J. Winkler, and F. Zeitlin (Princeton, 1990), 113–51. For social constructivist ideas more generally, see the various essays collected in that volume.

13 For a careful analysis of the accords between literature and history with respect to some key feminine symbolic figures for the earlier medieval period, see Seán Ó Coileáin, 'The Making of *Tromdám Guaire*,' *Ériu* 28 (1977), 32–67.

14 Donnchadh Ó Corráin, 'Marriage in Early Ireland,' in *Marriage in Ireland*, ed. Art Cosgrove (Dublin, 1985), 5–24; Máirín Ní Dhonnchadha ed., *Cáin Adamnáin* (forthcoming); Ní Dhonnchadha '"Caillech" and Other Terms for Veiled Women in Medieval Irish Texts,' *Éigse* 28 (1994–5), 71–96.

15 McCone, *Pagan Past*, chaps. 2, 3, 6, and 8, has successfully demonstrated that a reading of sagas along the lines of Biblical typology can add considerably to an understanding of the preoccupations of the sagas. However, neither properly historicist issues nor the issue of women is a major concern of his study.

16 Dominic LaCapra, *History and Criticism* (Ithaca, NY, 1985), 92.

17 Andrew Taylor has been drawn to this statement of LaCapra's and has also responded to its troubling implications in his *Textual Situations: Three Medieval Manuscripts and Their Readers* (Philadelphia, 2002), 197–205.

18 Roland Barthes, *S/Z: An Essay*, trans. Richard Miller (New York, 1974), 5–6.

19 Cf. *Corpus genealogiarum Hiberniae*, 266. Loegaire Buadach figures in the tract *Senchas Síl Ír* (*Corpus genealogiarum Hiberniae*, 272). See also *Fled Bricrend* in *LU*, 246–77. Her soubriquet is variously given as Noíchride (nine-hearted) or Noíchrutach (nine-shaped); Bricriu's address to her in *Fled Bricrend* plays on the *Cóir Anmann* meaning (ed. W. Stokes, *Irische Texte*, vol. 3 [Berlin, 1897], 257), as *nua-chrutach* [fair of shape]; cf. *Ní lesainm dait dano Fedelm noichride ar febas do chrotha 7 do ceille 7 do ceneoil* (*LU*, ll. 8225–7). The gloss supports 'nine' rather than 'new': *noi crotha no tadbantais forri, ocus ba aildiu cach cruth araili* [she had nine shapes or appearances on her and each one was more lovely than the next].

20 On a woman's right to make an oath on her child's paternity against a single man, see *Crith Gablach*, 21, l. 535.

21 There is also significant linkage here with Fergus himself. The young boy, like Fergus before him, is drawn by overwhelming feelings of solidarity with his maternal kindred. Not only this, but the warriors who guard him and the Ulster folk as well will feel the bond of kinship; the phrase used, *ell condolba*, also appears earlier in the text for Fergus's own frustrated feelings of belonging.

22 Annie Power, 'The Common Authorship of Some Book of Leinster Texts,' *Ériu* 9 (1923), 126–8; O'Rahilly, *Táin Bó Cúailnge from the Book of Leinster*, liii–lv; Kelly, 'The *Táin* as Literature,' *Aspects*, 82–4.

23 For women's lament in general, see Margaret Alexiou, *Ritual Lament in Greek Tradition* (Cambridge, 1974); for lament in epic, see P.E. Easterling, 'Men's *kleos* and Women's *goos*: Female Voices in the *Iliad*,' *Journal of Modern Greek Studies* 9 (1991), 145–51; for Irish lament tradition, see Angela Partridge, 'Wild Men and Wailing Women,' *Éigse* 18 (1980), 25–37.

24 I use the term 'specular' to denote not simply a discourse marked by images of viewing and seeing; I also intend the extra psycho-analytic significance which, it is claimed, gendered occular language wields: the subject gazing objectifies the one gazed at.

25 *Book of Leinster*, vol 2, ll. 14256–73. This was noted by Osborn Bergin, 'Syntax of the Verb in Old Irish,' *Ériu* 13 (1925), 198–203 at 200–1.

26 Though one of them – Fergus – markedly does heed these same women.

27 Where Freudian analysis paradoxically locates the gaze of the Medusa as the moment of male empowerment, this is not a reading that feminists can endorse without question. See Sigmund Freud, 'Medusa's Head,' in *Sexuality and the Psychology of Love*, ed. Philip Rieff (New York, 1963), 212–13.

28 Shiela Murnahan, 'The Poetics of Loss in Greek Epic,' in *Epic Traditions in the Contemporary World: The Poetics of Community*, ed. Margaret Beissinger, Jane Tytlus, and Susanne Wofford (Berkeley and Los Angeles, 1999), 203–20, at 204–5.

29 This feature is not ascribed to Lóch in Recension II.

30 One could see a certain ring-symmetry in the two narrative loops involving the two placements of Fedelm's vision: (A) Fedelm and Medb, (B) assessing of armies, journey, (C) tryst of Cú Chulainn and Fedelm of Tara, (D) withe (ll. 29–300), (A)[1] Fedelm and Medb, (C)[1] tryst of Cú Chulainn and Fedelm of Tara, (B)[1] assessing of armies, (D)[1] withe (ll. 303–35).

31 Sleeping with a woman can be a very important point of access to important information about the future in Irish saga; see, for example, the encounter between the woman and the Dagda in *Cath Maige Tuired*, 48–50.

32 James Henthorn Todd, ed., *Cogadh Gaedhel re Gallaibh: The Wars of the Gaedhil with the Gaill* (London, 1867), 200; *The Annals of Loch Cé*, ed. William M. Hennessy (London, 1871) *sub anno* 1014.

33 O'Rahilly, *Recension I*, 240. If the arms and chariot are dependent on a misunderstood *cclaidem corthaire*, then this is in itself telling: a male scribe creates a male picture of the prophetess because he misunderstood the reference to an item belonging to women's work.

34 LL's description is organized around a much fuller blazon *topos*; Fedelm is described from head to foot with an exotic female body to go with the exotic face of Recension I.

35 See the entry for *macdacht* in *Lexique étymologique de l'Irlandais ancien*, *MNOP* (Paris, 1960), M-3. A perusal of a number of *mac-* compounds in *DIL* bears out the mixed gender slippage for *macdacht*. *Macdacht* itself is used of a man, *fer ... milla macdachta macanta* (*Annals of Loch Cé*, I 538. 16); *eter maccaib beccaib* (alluding to girls, *Irische Texte* i, 131. 26); *macogam .i. ogam bantorach* (*Auraicept*, l. 3163); *bó maccaem* (LL, 165bi).

36 The first line shows variants in its four repetitions: the vocative *a* is omitted after the first incidence, there is variation between the forms of the verb *acci/acca*, and U (M) does not give the whole line in the repetitions. I am also assuming liaison between *co ac-*, although this is admittedly doubtful.

37 See my early remarks on this in 'The Heroic Word: On the Reading of Early Irish Sagas,' in *The Celtic Consciousness*, 155–61.

38 *Fingal Rónáin and Other Stories*, ed. David Greene (Dublin, 1975), 6–7. Tómas Ó Cathasaigh has some very pertinent commentary on the significant role that ritualized women's verse can play in Irish saga with particular reference to *Scéla Cano meic Gartnáin* in 'The Rhetoric of *Scéla Cano Meic Gartnáin*,' in *Sages, Saints*, 239–45.

39 In a frivolous way Macbeth's witches come to mind. The Inscription of Larzac seems to imply two groups of priestly women in verbal cursing rituals with each other – a named group against the descendants of a dead Severa Tertionicna; see the collection of papers on the subject in *Le plomb magique du Larzac et les sorcières gauloises*, ed. Michel Lejeune et al., *Études celtiques* 22 (1985), 88–177. It may also be of interest that the continental Celtic name or visionary role of a Vidlmaas (= Fedelm) is also invoked in this Gaulish document. The alleged prayers of Boudicca to Astarte before her war with the Romans may also be relevant. Having read the lucky sign of the hare, Boudicca then addresses Astarte thus: 'I thank you Astarte and I call upon you as woman to woman ... as one who rules over Britons who have no knowledge of tilling the earth or working with their hands but are experts in the arts of war, and hold all things in common even their wives

and children'; Dio Cassius. *Epitome* LXII, 3; quoted in S. Ireland, *Roman Britain: A Sourcebook* (London and New York, 1996). Though it is a fanciful reconstruction by the Roman author, and though the whole is so full of cliché and classical general facts on Celtic habits, there still may be some element of reality behind it.

40 Wolfgang Meid, ed., *Die Romanze von Froech und Findabair: Táin Bó Fróich* (Innsbruck, 1970), 37.

41 I have deliberately stretched the range of *iarum* here to indicate its doubleness. It is the 'then' of the narrative moment itself – she said then that whatever lovely thing she was accustomed to see, Fráech was lovelier – but also the indefinite 'then' of all her life that stretches before Findabair; it is the moment of crisis, of feared death of the beloved, as much as the exquisite aesthetic moment, and as much also as the precise moment when she falls in love, which causes Findabair to project an elegiac mode.

42 The word *aithesc* can be used not just as 'utterance' but also in the sense of 'saying' or 'proverb.' In this sense Findabair has memorialized her lover as beauty itself.

43 Vernam Hull, ed., *Loinges mac nUislenn: The Exile of the Sons of Uisliu* (London, 1949), 45, 63. The translation is my own.

44 *The Book of Leinster*, vol. 2, 59–60, ll. 8327–46.

45 One might note here a coming together of the feminine elegiac and the blood language of heroic discourse in the death tale of Cú Chulainn, when Emir speaks of her approximation of tears of mourning and the showers of blood shed by the whole world for her hero: *Ba meite cach der no cithe co brath ba dia bithcoiniud. Ba meite cach rosc atconnairc no ciad frassaib fola* (*Book of Leinster*, vol. 2, ll. 1427–79. I take the Egerton MS variant *gle sin* in *Fled Bricrend* as representing *glesin*, 'woad,' and translate accordingly. Comparing red and blue is contrasting noble with working class.

46 McCone, *Pagan Past*, 133–5. McCone distinguishes rather carefully certain sovereignty texts that seem to him to use the theme of women's treachery. See also Kelly, 'The *Táin* as Literature,' 84–5, 97.

47 For Íte see Charles Plummer, *Vitae Sanctorum Hiberniae*, vol. 2 (Oxford, 1910), 130; for Brigid, see *Bethu Brigte*, ed. Donncha Ó hAodha (Dublin, 1978).

48 Whitley Stokes, ed., *Three Irish Glossaries* (Edinburgh, 1862), 5.

49 Nagy, *The Wisdom of the Outlaw*, 102 n.13.

50 Kuno Meyer, ed., 'The Laud Genealogies,' 291–338, at 306–7. The term attached to Medb here, *míchor*, which begins and ends the poem, means 'ill behaviour' or 'invalid contract,' and the poem later speaks of her deceitful beguilement of Fergus in the context of that bargain.

51 Margaret Clunies Ross, 'An Interpretation of the Myth of Thorr's Encounter with Geirrothr and His Daughters,' in *Speculum Norroenum: Norse Studies in Honour of Gabriel Turville-Petre*, ed. Ursula Dronke et al. (Odense, 1981), 370–91.

52 L. Motz, 'Thorr's River Crossing,' *Saga Book* 23 (1993), 469–87.

53 Charles Bowen, 'Great-bladdered Medb: Mythology and Invention in the *Táin Bó Cúailnge*,' *Éire-Ireland* 10 (1987), 14–34.

54 Ibid., 34.

55 Carl Marstrander, 'The Deaths of Lugaid and Derbforgaill,' *Ériu* 5 (1911), 201–18.

56 Bowen, 'Great-bladdered Medb,' 28.

57 Quoted in Katherine Simms, *From Kings to Warlords* (Cambridge, 1986), 23–4.

58 Daniel Binchy, ed. *'Mellbretha,' Celtica* 8 (1968), 144–54. Somehow the connotations of seaside holiday pursuits, however suggestive to Binchy, the scion of a provincial Irish merchant family, rings false as an amusement for the young bloods that the legal tract is designed for.

59 Will Sayers, 'Games, Sport and Para-military Exercise in Early Ireland,' *Aethlon: The Journal of Sport Literature* 10 (1992), 105–23.

60 Lisa M. Bitel, '"Conceived in Sins, Born in Delights": Stories of Procreation from Early Ireland,' *Journal of the History of Sexuality* 3 (1992), 181–202.

61 Thomas W. Laqueur, *Making Sex: Body and Gender from the Greeks to Freud* (Cambridge, MA, 1990), passim; Danielle Jacquart and Claude Thomasset, *Sexuality and Medicine in the Middle Ages* (Princeton and Cambridge, 1988).

62 For Cú Chulainn's ability to melt snow by body heat alone, see LL, ll. 1482–7. In trying to establish the idea that this story exemplifies the concept of gender play and thus encourages the exploration of meaning in Irish sagas along these lines, I do not wish to suggest that this is the dominant mode by which these stories achieve their results. In the story of Lugaid and Derbforgaill, a number of themes and effects come together to create a superbly-fashioned tale. I offer a new translation and commentary on this text in *The Field Day Anthology of Irish Literature*, vol. 4, ed. Angela Bourke et al. (Dublin, 2002), 204–6.

63 Nancy Partner, 'No Sex, No Gender,' *Speculum* 68 (1993), 419–44, at 439.

64 The motif is current in other cultural traditions and seems to be behaviour associated with a siege scenario: cf. Procopius's account of raising the siege of Amida by Cabades the Persian: 'Besides this some courtesans shamelessly drew up their clothing and displayed to Cabades, who was standing close by, those parts of a woman's body which it is not proper that men

should see uncovered' (*History of the Wars*, I, vii. 9). I owe this reference to my husband, Professor Alain Stoclet.

65 See McCone, *Pagan Past*, 203–32.

66 'Miscellanea Hibernica,' *Études celtiques* 3 (1946), 372–3.

67 The same sentiments had surfaced earlier in the final battle scene when Conall Cernach reproaches Fergus: *Ba ramór in bríg sin ... for túaith 7 cenél ar thóin mná drúithi* [That force is too great against (your) land and people for the sake of a woman's backside] (ll. 4068–9). I discuss this scene in chapter 7.

68 See Hänsel, Bernhard, ed., *Die Indo-Germanen und das Pferd: Akten des Internationalen interdisziplinären Kolloquiums* (Berlin, 1994), passim.

69 Ed. Whitley Stokes, *in Irische Texte*, vol. 4 (Leipzig, 1900), 110.

70 *Tales of the Elders of Ireland*, trans. Ann Dooley and Harry Roe (Oxford, 2000), 216.

71 This is the site that Mac Eoin has identified with the H redactor of LU. As I noted in chapter 3, it is also a historic royal residence of the Síl Muiredaig kings of Connacht. It is thus appropriate as a place of visitation for Medb but there may also be a certain edge expressed here towards the Ua Maoil Conaire family who received land associated with it.

7 The Sense of an Ending

1 Cited in Frank Kermode, *The Sense of an Ending* (Oxford, 1967), 174. For my purposes, Eliot's following remark is also pertinent: 'some of the fault lies in the very nature of a conclusion, which is at best a negation.'

2 See here the useful collection, *Classical Closure: Reading the End in Greek and Latin Literature*, ed. Deborah H. Roberts, Francis M. Dunn, and Don Fowler (Princeton, 1997). I have benefited from Fowler's introductory discussion where he introduces the psychoanalytic responses of the reader: 'Second Thoughts on Closure,' 3–22. Dunn's distinction between the anticlosure attitudes of poststructuralism and the critical theorists who would locate closure in the cultural system that shapes and determines literary production is also most helpful: 'Ends and Means in Euripedes' *Heracles*,' 83–111.

3 See E.M. Slotkin, '*Noínden*: Its Semantic Range,' in *Celtic Language, Celtic Culture: A Festschrift for Eric P. Hamp*, ed. A.T.E. Matonis and D.F. Melia (Van Nuys, CA, 1995), 137–50.

4 Pádraig Ó Riain, 'The *Táin*: A Clue,' 31–8.

5 Possibly a reference to the area of assembly for the Fair of Tailtiu.

6 O'Rahilly (ll. 4848–9) obscures this by preferring the readings of Stowe, restoring speaker markers from there and also from YBL.

7 Tomás Ó Cathasaigh, 'Pagan Survivals: The Evidence of Early Irish Narra-

tive,' in *Irland und Europa: die Kirche im frühen Mittelalter / Ireland and Europe: The Early Church*, ed. Michael Richter and Proinseas Ní Chatháin (Stuttgart, 1984), 291–307 at 296. See his citation here of previous treatments of the bulls.

8 The tale *De chophur in dá muccida* is edited by E. Windisch, *Irische Texte* 3, 243–7.

9 *Scéla Mucce Meic Dathó*, ed. Rudolf Thurneysen (Dublin, 1935).

10 The text emphasizes the ability of the hound to make a choice through glossing as *rus con*, 'canine intelligence,' chap. 19.

11 There is a distinctly shame-inducing factor in Fer Loga's hijacking of Conchobar's person. By seizing his head from behind one may also assume that he has caught him by the ears. Hence the gesture also replicates that of Deirdriu in *Loinges Mac nUislenn*, when she catches Noisiu by the ears and forces him to do her will.

12 The dog is endowed with intelligence, *rus con*. In Recension II much is made of the Donn Cuailnge's human understanding; he is shamed by what Cormac Cond Longas says of him because he understands human speech (ll. 4888–9).

13 The role of Bricriu in the staging of the ending and the fact that he was not present on the *Táin* hosting creates a problem. There is an inconsistency in the text of Recension I as we have it, in that Bricriu does appear in the saga to taunt Cú Chulainn at a crucial moment when he needs to be aroused (ll. 1990–1). But this is H's intervention and patently his invention and Bricriu is not mentioned at the corresponding passage in YBL.

14 Leaving the outcome to animal choice occurs most famously in Irish literary tradition in the case of St Patrick's burial; cf., *Bethu Phátraic*, 147–50. See McCone, *Pagan Past*, 246–7, for Old Testament parallels.

15 *Nirap* here is a secondary subjunctive form. I try to reflect this in my translation, as it is not clear whether the journey(?) envisaged is the *Táin* just undertaken or the bulls' final itinerary.

16 *The Metrical Dindshenchas* gives an entirely different aetiology for Cruachain. The centre is named after Crochen, the handmaiden of Étaín abducted with her by Midir, who takes them back to his *síd*, which is then given the name Cruachu; *The Metrical Dindshenchas*, ed. E. Gwynn, Royal Irish Academy Todd Lecture Series, vol. 10, part 3 (Dublin, 1913), 348–55.

17 For the etymology of Dublin as 'Ford of the rib-cage,' see *Metrical Dindshenchas*, part 3, 100–3. The ribs in question here, however, have a very different bestial origin.

18 The explanation of Port Lairge is also new.

19 See Donnchadh Ó Corráin, 'The Education of Diarmait mac Murchada,' *Ériu* 37 (1986), 78–81.

20 This is not how O'Rahilly sees it (261, note on l. 1594); she thinks rather that H's scruples forbade him to kill Findabair outright. I do not think of H as having a delicate sensibility and, in any case, Findabair is so much a part of the common baggage of Ulster and Connacht conflicts that it is more appropriate to keep her battered but alive and available to be dragged from story to story. It is a case of familiarity breeding narrative contempt. As for the distinction made between Cú Chulainn and Ulster, the land of Ulster and the land of the hero, this may well have a political significance of the kind I indicated in the Introduction.

21 E. Windisch, ed., 'Das Fest des Bricriu und die Verbannung der Mac Dúil Dermait,' *Irische Texte* 2 (1884), 164–217. There is an English translation by Kaarina Hollo, 'The Feast of Bricriu and the Exile of the Sons of Dúil Dermait,' *Emania* 10 (1992), 18–24. Hollo provides an excellent introduction to the tale in 'A Context for *Fled Bricrenn ocus Loinges Mac nDúil Dermait*,' *Ulidia*, 91–8. Kelleher's date is based on the assumption that Áedacán, abbot of Louth (who died on pilgrimage in Clonmacnois in 835) brought a copy of the saga with him. But the date of Áedacán's death is less important than the evidence the annals notice provides of a prior friendship between Louth and the midland monastery. The exchange of ideas and books may well have been going on for some time.

22 Hollo, 'A Context,' 96.

23 The heroine, Findchóem, is an integral part of the *Loinges Mac nDuil Dermait* wooing tale, much more so than the unlikely scenario of Cú Chulainn and Findabair ending up together as in the *Táin*. The return of the pair to Emain Macha with the booty is also an integral part of the plot. It has no place in our saga. The evidence which Hollo adduces to prove that the *Táin* is the earlier work turns on the unoriginal use in *Loinges Mac nDuil Dermait* of the motif, which also appears in the *Táin*, of casting upwards to pierce an enemy from above. But this is a reasonable ploy if the deviant *gae bolga* which operates in any way but straight is the weapon in question. O'Rahilly avoids the issue by claiming the *Táin* end is merely a scribal tag borrowed unreflectively by the scribe; but I can see no reason why it should be given a reserved category like this. Its function and status as closure remains very much the question and I would conclude that the borrowing goes the other way.

24 O'Rahilly's note on *hús* accepts it as a separate word from *tús* mainly on the evidence of O'Clery's Glossary (344); but, as I have noted before, this may not be an independent source.

25 Nagy, *Conversing with Angels*, 16–20.

26 Pádraig Ó Néill, 'The Latin Colophon to the *Táin Bó Cúailnge* in the Book of Leinster: A Critical View of Old Irish Literature,' *Celtica* 23 (1999), 269–75.

27 Erich Poppe, '*Grammatica, grammatic*, Augustine, and the *Táin*,' in *Ildánach, Ildírech: A Festschrift for Proinsias Mac Cana*, ed. John Carey, John T. Koch, and Pierre-Yves Lambert (Aberystwyth, 1999), 203–10, at 210.

28 In an unpublished paper, 'How Medieval Was Medieval Irish Literature?,' read to the annual conference of the Celtic Studies Association of North America at the University of California, L.A. (1987), I also invoked the context of the *Rhetorica ad Herennium* with respect to the colophon. To provide complimentary points of comparison with Ó Néill's discussion and to avoid repetition, what follows is excerpted from my paper.

29 *De Inventione*, XIX.

30 For such Roman recitals, see Florence Dupont, *The Invention of Literature: From Greek Intoxication to the Latin Book*, trans. Janet Lloyd (Baltimore and London, 1999), 152–69.

31 Gregory Toner discusses these issues in his excellent article, 'The Ulster Cycle: Historiography or Fiction?' *Cambrian Medieval Celtic Studies* 40 (2000), 1–20.

32 There is evidence of Irish interest in such matters in the twelfth century as evident by the manuscript of Chalcidius' translation and commentary on the *Timaeus* with Irish glosses from Glendalough: P. Ó Néill, 'An Irishman at Chartres in the Twelfth Century: The Evidence of Oxford, Bodleian Library, MS Auct. F. 15,' *Ériu* 48 (1997) 1–35. The twelfth-century neo-Platonists, following on an exegetical tradition of allegorical reading inherited partly from Antiquity, but mainly from the praxis of patristic sacred exegesis, were also quite happy to treat pagan classical narratives as *integumenta* and to read profound cosmological meanings into them. Allegory was a developing genre in this period in Ireland. As yet, however, there is no study of the uses of allegory in medieval Irish works.

33 William H. Stahl, ed. and trans., *Commentary on the Dream of Scipio* (New York, 1952), 84–5, chaps. 7 and 9.

34 *Gesta Regum Anglorum: The History of the English Kings*, ed. R.A.B. Mynors, completed by R.M. Thomson and M. Winterbottom (Oxford, 1998), 1: 26.

35 Michael O'Brien, ed., *Corpus Genealogiarum Hiberniae*, vol. 1 (Dublin, 1962), 192. The manuscripts offer a variety of different readings, and I have not followed O'Brien's editorial choices in all respects.

36 H.M.V. McAlister, ed., *Lebor Gabhála Érenn: The Book of Invasions of Ireland*, Irish Texts Society, vol. 41 (London, 1941), 240–83.

37 'Tuirill Bicrenn und seine Kinder,' ed. R. Thurneysen, *Zeitschrift für celtische*

Philologie 12 (1918), 239–50 at 246. An interesting example of whether to give credence to a fabulous tale occurs in that section of the *Lebor Gabhála Érenn* on the sons of Míl dealing with their encounters with the primordial women of Ireland, Éiriu, Banba, and Fodla. The Book of Druim Snechta is quoted with reference to Banba: *Atbert Lebur Dromma Snechta cor iarfaig Amairgen dia cenél. Do chlaind Ádham dam, ar sí; Cid cenél do maccaib Náe duit? Ol sé. Am sini-sea anás Náe, ol sí; for rind sléibe ro basa isin dílind; cosa tel-sa anois, ol sí dechaid tonda dílend. Is de sin do garar Tel Tuindi. Acht chena is ingantach in slecht sin anúas. Canait íarum diceltta forri 7 attarbanath úadaib* [The Book of Druim Snechta says that Amorgen enquired after her race. 'Of the progeny of Adam am I,' said she. 'Which branch of the sons of Noah are you from?' said he. 'I am older than Noah,' said she; 'on a peak of a mountain was I in the flood; to this present mound the waves of the Flood attained.' Therefore it is called Tel Tuinne (Teltown). Nevertheless the foregoing is a wonderful passage. Thereafter they sing spells against her, and drive her away from them] (*Lebor Gabhála Érenn*, vol. 5, 52–5, no. 390). The passage immediately before, which is unique to Ms. F, concerns the Fomorians who fought in the shape of giants on the side of the Tuatha Dé against the sons of Míl. It is not clear if this – also part of (ante)-diluvian apocryphal lore – is also intended to be seen as a matter of wonder.

38 Perhaps the most interesting usages – other than Augustine's comment in *The City of God* – that Ó Néill cites occur in Servius's Commentary on Virgil, which was known to Irish scholars in some form. There the meanings are descriptive and not pejorative. See the Old Irish glosses on Servius printed in *Thesarus Paleohibernicus* II, 235 and xxv.

39 'The Uses of Tradition in *Serglige Con Culainn*,' *Ulidia*, 77–84. The text was edited by Myles Dillon, *Compert Con Culainn and Other Tales* (Dublin, 1953).

40 I have repunctuated Dillon's text here. I have also taken *cathaigtis* in the sense 'used to tempt' from the extended use of the verb to signify the act of temptation: cf. *DIL sub cathugud*.

41 This has also been noted by Ó Néill. The female seduction aspect of the *praestrigia demonum* term becomes even clearer when the colophon in LL is compared with the language of the Hiberno-Latin *De ordine creaturum*, in the passage cited by Carey, 'The Uses of Tradition in *Serglige Con Culaind*,' 79: But those lying and impure spirits, fleeting and insubstantial, are capable of sensation and, clothed in bodies of air, never grow old and swell with pride as they wage war with men. Liars, and skilled in deceit, they move the senses of men, filling mortals with fear, troubling their lives with disturbances in their dreams and with movements and twisting of their limbs, concocting apparitions and oracles (*praestrigia atque oracula fingentes*), and governing the casting of lots. They fill human hearts with yearning for

unlawful love and desire: telling lies which seem like truth, and they put on the appearance and radiance of good angels (Manuel Díaz y Díaz, *Liber de ordine creaturarum: un anónimo irlandés del siglo VII* [Santiago de Compostela, 1972], 142–4.

42 Whitley Stokes, ed. 'The Irish Ordeals, Cormac's Adventure in the Land of Promise, and the Decision as to Cormac's Sword,' *Irische Texte* 3 (1901), 183–229, at 202.

43 The entry *prull* concerns the shape-shifting churl who transforms into a beautiful youth and is interpreted as *Spiritus Poematis*; cf. *Sanas Chormaic,* ed. Kuno Meyer, *Anecdota from Irish Manuscripts*, vol. 5 (Dublin, 1913), 90–5.

44 See my comments on this tale in 'Early Irish Literature and Contemporary Disciplines,' in R. Wall ed., *Medieval and Modern Ireland* (Totowa, NJ, 1988), 60–74, at 68–71. More recently, Máirín Ní Dhonnchadha has amplified my argument in providing a text and translation of the entry, 'The *Prull* Narrative in *Sanas Cormaic*,' in *Cín Chille Cúile: Texts, Saints and Places. Essays in Honour of Pádraig Ó Riain*, ed. John Carey, M. Herbert, and Kevin Murray (Aberystwyth, 2004), 163–78.

45 For the uses made of some other-world women in the *Acallam*, see Dooley, 'The Date and Purpose of *Acallam na Senórach*,' *Éigse* 34 (2004), 97–126.

46 Note the skillful use of alliteration here.

47 Cf. *A ríoghan deas mhilis, más cinniúin domh tú féin mar stór,/ tabhair léigse is gealladh domh sul fá n-aistre mé leat siar sa ród:/ má éagaim fán tSeannainn, i gcrích Mhanainn, nó san Éiphte mhór,/ gurb ag Gaeil chumhra an Creagáin a leagfar mé i gcré faoi fhód* [O sweet lovely queen, if I am fated to love you, give me bond and promise before I go my way with you: should I die by the Shannon, in Man or in Egypt great, that I be put in the grove with the lovely Gael of Cill Creggan]; Art Mac Cumhaigh, '*Úr-chill an Chreagain*,' *An Duanaire: Poems of the Dispossessed*, ed. and trans. Seán Ó Tuama and Thomas Kinsella (Portlaoise, 1981), 176–81 at 181 (my translation).

48 I use this term in the Kristevan sense; cf. Julia Kristeva, *Powers of Horror: An Essay on Abjection* (New York, 1982), 86–9, 207–10. See my reference to Kristeva and abjection in chapter 6, note 5.

49 W.B. Yeats, *Collected Poems* (London, 1950), 395–6.

Epilogue: Their Bodies, Ourselves

1 For heroic attitudes to personal glory, see Patrick Ford, 'The Idea of Everlasting Fame in the *Táin*,' *Ulidia*, 255–62. For the persistence of Celtic warlike traditions, see Christophe Veille, 'The Oldest Narrative Attestations of a Celtic Mythical and Traditional Heroic Cycle,' *Ulidia*, 217–27.

2 Philip O'Leary, 'Honour-bound: The Social Context of Early Irish Heroic *Geis,' Celtica* 20 (1988), 85–107; P. O'Leary, 'Magnanimous Conduct in Irish Heroic Literature,' *Éigse* 25 (1991), 28–44; W. Sayers, 'Games, Sport, and Para-Military Exercise in Early Ireland,' *Aethlon* 10 (1992), 105–23.

3 The most influential general work here is Ward Parks, *Verbal Dueling in Heroic Narrative: Homeric and Old English Traditions* (Princeton, 1990). For an application to the *Táin* see Will Sayers, 'Contracting for Combat: Flyting and Fighting in *Táin Bó Cúailnge,' Emania* 16 (1997), 49–62.

4 Beyond the horror lies also the question of how a society creates responsive memorials to such an event of common trauma. Such a question on sites of memory, particularly as they pertain to the First World War and after, has received a number of important recent studies but it lies outside the scope of this work.

5 I discuss the larger scene of heroic investiture of which this is a part in chapter 5.

6 Perhaps the most 'authoritative' touch in the sequence is the use of the chariot's wheel rims to create the basic design. The image gains its greatest currency value from its use in royal inauguration scenes. See *Audacht Morainn: The Testimony of Morann,* ed. Fergus Kelly (Dublin, 1976), 8–9.

7 Susan Sontag has compared image with narrative as media for horror. She sees narrative as better able to convey compassion because, for our times, the image has become counter-reflective and banal. But narrative also mutes compassion in its formal need for closure and for moving on. See her *Regarding the Pain of Others* (New York, 2003).

8 Kenneth Hurlstone Jackson, *The Oldest Irish Tradition: A Window on the Iron Age* (Cambridge, 1964); J.P. Mallory, 'The World of Cú Chulainn: The Archaeology of the Táin Bó Cúailnge,' in *Aspects of the Táin,* 103–59.

9 For a description of these, see 'Le sanctuaire de Ribemont-sur-Ancre: vainqueurs et vaincus séparés dans la mort,' *Historia Thematique. Comment vivaient vraiment nos 'ancetres' les Gaulois* 77 (May–June 2002), 34–5.

10 In the words of Hartog concerning Herodotus' description of Scythian custom, this piling up of heads, this '*mutilation guerrière est, avant tout, une arithmétique de l'áristeia*'; cited by Jean-Louis Brunaux, *Guerre et religion en Gaule: essai d'anthropologie celtique* (Paris, 2004), 112, from François Hartog, *Le miroir d'Herodote* (Paris, 1980), 179.

11 'Huit cavaliers gaulois et leurs chevaux on été découverts dans une seule tombe de terre arverne,' Pierre Barthélmy, *Le Monde,* 31 May 2002.

12 See in this respect Jean-Louis Brunaux's earlier *Les religions gauloises: rituels celtiques de la Gaule indépendante* (Paris, 1996), 141–66.

Bibliography

Alexiou, Margaret. *Ritual Lament in Greek Tradition*. Cambridge, 1974.

Anderson, Alan Orr, and Marjorie Anderson. *Adomnán's Life of Columba*. Edinburgh, 1961.

Anderson, Benedict. *Imagined Communities: Reflections on the Origin and Spread of Nationalism*. Rev. ed. London, 1991.

Barthes, Roland. *Mythologies*. Paris, 1957.

– *The Pleasure of the Text*, trans. R. Miller. New York, [1973] 1975.

– *S/Z: An Essay*, trans. Richard Miller. New York, [1970] 1974.

– 'Textual Analysis: Poe's "Valdemar."' In *Modern Criticism and Theory*, ed. David Lodge. London, 1988.

Baumgarten, Rolf. 'Etymological Aaetiology and Irish Tradition.' *Ériu* 61 (1990), 115–23.

– 'Varia III. A Note on *Táin Bó Regamna*.' *Ériu* 34 (1983), 189–92.

Benveniste, Emile. *Problèmes de linguistique générale*. 2 vols. Paris, 1966–74.

Bergin, Osborn. 'Syntax of the Verb in Old Irish.' *Ériu* 13 (1925), 198–203.

Bergin, Osborn, ed. *Anecdota from Irish manuscripts*. 5 vols. Berlin, 1907–13.

– *Irish Bardic Poetry*, trans. David Greene. Dublin, 1970.

Best, Richard I. 'Notes on the Script of Lebor na hUidre.' *Ériu* 6 (1912), 161ff.

Best, R.I., ed. 'The Graves of the Kings at Clonmacnois.' *Ériu* 2 (1905), 163–71.

Best, R.I., and O Bergin, eds. *Lebor na hUidre: Book of the Dun Cow*. Dublin, 1929.

Best, R.I., et al., eds. *The Book of Leinster*. 6 vols. Dublin 1954–83.

Bernard, J.H., and R. Atkinson, eds. *The Irish Liber Hymnorum*. 2 vols. Henry Bradshaw Society. London, 1898.

Biddick, Kathleen. 'Genders, Bodies, Boundaries: Technologies of the Visible.' *Speculum* 68 (1993), 389–418.

Bieler, Ludwig, ed. *Four Latin Lives of Saint Patrick*. Dublin, 1971.

– *Libri Epistolarum Sancti Patricii Episcopii*. Dublin, 1952.

– *The Patrician Texts in the Book of Armagh*. Dublin, 1979.

Binchy, Daniel. 'Distraint in Irish Law.' *Celtica* 10 (1973), 22–71.

– 'Mellbretha.' *Celtica* 8 (1968), 144–54.

– 'Varia Hibernica.' In *Indo-Celtica: Gedächtnisschrift für Alf Sommerfelt*, ed. H. Pilch and J. Thurow, 29–38. Munich, 1972.

Binchy, Daniel, ed. *Críth Gablach*. Dublin, 1979.

– *Corpus Iuris Hibernici*. Dublin, 1978.

Bitel, Lisa M. '"Conceived in Sins, Born in Delights": Stories of Procreation from Early Ireland.' *Journal of the History of Sexuality* 3 (1992), 181–202.

Bloch, R. Howard. *Medieval Misogyny and the Invention of Western Love*. Chicago, 1991.

Bloomfield, Morton. *The Seven Deadly Sins: An Introduction to the History of a Religious Concept with Special Reference to Medieval English Literature*. East Lansing, MI, 1967.

Bourke, Angela, et al., eds. *The Field Day Anthology of Irish Writing*, part 4. Dublin, 2002.

Bourke, Cormac. 'A Note on the *Delg Aidechta*.' In *Studies in the Cult of St Columba*, ed. C. Bourke, 185–93. Dublin, 1997.

Bowen, Charles. 'Great Bladdered Medb: Mythology and Inventionn in the *Táin Bó Cúailnge*.' *Éire-Ireland* 10 (1987), 14–34.

Breatnach, Caoimhín, ed. *Patronage, Politics and Prose*. Maynooth, 1996.

Breatnach, Liam. 'The Ecclesiastical Element in the Old Irish Legal Tract *Cáin Fuithirbe*.' *Peritia* 5 (1986), 36–52.

Breatnach, P.A. 'The Chief's Poet.' *Proceedings of the Royal Irish Academy* C 83 (1983).

Breatnach, Risteard A. 'The Lady and the King: A Theme in Irish Literature.' *Studies: An Irish Quarterly Review* 42 (1953), 321–6.

Brunaux, Jean-Louis. *Guerre et religion en Gaule: essai d'anthropologie celtique*. Paris, 2004.

– *Les religions gauloises: riuels celtiques de la Gaule indépendante*. Paris, 1996.

Burkert, Walter. *Structure and History in Greek Mythology and Ritual*. Berkeley, 1979.

Butler, Judith. *Gender Trouble: Feminism and the Subversion of Identity*. New York and London, 1990.

Bynum, Caroline Walker. *Holy Feast and Holy Fast: The Religious Significance of Food to Medieval Women*. Berkeley, and Los Angeles, 1987.

Byrne, F.J. 'The Trembling Sod: Ireland in 1169.' In *A New History of Ireland*. Vol. 2. *Medieval Ireland, 1169–1534*, ed. Art Cosgrove, 1–66. Oxford, 1987.

Cairns, David and Shaun Richards. *Writing Ireland: Colonialism, Nationalism and Culture*. Manchester, 1988.

Calame, Claude. 'Herodotus: Historical Discourse or Literary Narrative.' In *The Craft of Poetic Speech in Ancient Greece*, trans. Janice Orion, 75–96. Ithaca, NY, 1995.

– *Poétique des mythes dans la Grèce antique*. Paris, 1999.

Calder, George, ed. *Auraicept na n-Éces: The Scholars' Primer; Being the texts of the Ogham tract from the Book of Ballymote and the Yellow book of Lecan, and the text of the Trefhocul from the Book of Leinster*. Edinburgh, 1917.

Campanile, Enrico. 'Old Irish *Bóand*.' *Journal of Indo-European Studies* 13 (1985), 477–9.

Carey, John. 'Eithne in Gubai.' *Éigse* 28 (1994–5), 160–4.

– *King of the Mysteries: Early Irish Religious Writing*. Dublin, 1988.

– 'The Uses of Tradition in *Serglige Con Culaind*.' In *Ulidia: Proceedings of the First International Conference on the Ulster Cycle of Tales, Belfast 1994*, ed. James P. Mallory and Gerard Stockman, 77–84. Belfast, 1994.

– 'Varia II: The Address to Fergus's Stone.' *Ériu* 51 (2000), 183–7.

Carmichael, Alexander, ed. and trans. *Carmina Gadelica: Ortha nan Gaedel*. 6 vols. Edinburgh, 1928–54.

Carney, James, 'The Dating of Early Irish Verse.' *Éigse* 19 (1983), 177–216.

– 'The History of Early Irish Literature: The State of Research.' In *Proceedings of the Sixth International Congress of Celtic Studies*, ed. G. Mac Éoin, 113–30. Dublin, 1990.

– *Studies in Early Irish Literature and History*. Dublin, 1955.

Carney, James, ed. *Medieveal Irish Lyrics*. Port Laoise, 1967.

– *The Poems of Blathmac Son of Cú Brettain and the Gospel of Thomas*. Irish Texts Society, vol. 47. London, 1964.

Cavafy, Constantine. *Collected Poems*, trans. Edmund Keeley and Philip Sherrard, ed. George Savadis. London, 1984.

Cavallo, Guglielmo. 'Le rossignol et l'hirondelle: Lire et écrire à Byzance et en Occident.' *Annales* 56 (2000), 4–5, 349–61.

Chadwick, Nora. 'Imbas forosnae.' *Scottish Gaelic Studies* 4 (1954), 39–64.

Charles-Edwards, Thomas M. 'The Context and Uses of Literacy in Early Christian Ireland.' In *Literacy in Medieval Celtic Societies*, ed. Huw Pryce. Cambridge Studies in Medieval History 33, 62–82. Cambridge, 1998.

– 'Geis, Prophecy, Omen, and Oath.' *Celtica* 23 (1999), 38–99.

Chartier, Roger. 'Texts, Printing, Readings.' In *The New Cultural History*, ed. Lynn Hunt. Berkeley, 1989.

Collingwood, R.G., and P.P. Wright. *The Roman Inscriptions of Britain*. Oxford, 1965.

Corthals, Johan. 'Zur Frage des mündlichen oder schriftlichen Ursprungs der Sagen *roscada*.' In *Early Irish Literature: Media and Communication / Mündlich-*

keit und Schriftlichkeit in der frühen irischen Literatur, ed. Stephen N. Tranter and H.L.C. Tristram, 201–20. Tubingen, 1989.

Culler, Jonathan. 'In Defence of Overinterpretation.' In Umberto Eco, Richard Rorty, and Christine Brook-Rose, *Interpretation and Overinterpretation*, with ed. Stefan Collini. Cambridge, 1991.

Davies, Sioned. 'Written Text as Performance: The Implications for Middle Welsh Prose Narratives.' In *Literacy in Medieval Celtic Societies*, ed. Huw Pryce, 133–48. Cambridge Studies in Medieval History 33. Cambridge, 1998.

Davies, Wendy. 'The Latin Charter Tradition in Western Britain, Brittany and Ireland in the Early Medieval Period.' In *Ireland and Medieval Europe*, ed. Dorothy Whitelock, R. McKitterick, and D. Dumville, 553–7. London, 1982.

Detienne, Marcel. *L'invention de la mythologie*. Paris, 1981.

Derrida, Jacques. 'Structure, Sign, and Play in the Discourse of the Human Sciences.' In *Writing and Difference*, trans. Alan Bass, 278–94. Chicago, 1978.

Diaz y Diaz, Manuel, ed. *Liber de ordine creaturarum: un anónimo irlandés del siglo VII*. Santiago de Compostela, 1972.

Dillon, Myles. *Compert Con Culaind and Other Tales*. Dublin, 1953.

Dooley, Ann. *The Celtic Consciousness*, ed. Robert O'Driscoll, 155–61. Portlaoise, 1981.

– 'The Date and Purpose of Acallam na Senórach.' *Éigse* 34 (2004), 97–126.

– 'Early Irish Literature and Contemporary Disciplines.' In *Medieval and Modern Ireland*, ed. Richard Wall, 60–74. Totowa, NJ, 1988.

– 'The Gospel of Nicodemus in Ireland.' In *The Medieval Gospel of Nicodemus: Texts, Intertexts, and Contexts in Western Europe*, ed. Zbigniew Izydorczyk, 361–402. Tempe, AZ, 1997.

– 'The Heroic Word: On the Reading of Early Irish Sagas.' In *The Celtic Consciousness*, ed. Robert O'Driscoll, 155–61. Portlaoise, 1982.

Douglas, Mary. *Purity and Danger: An Analysis of the Concepts of Pollution and Taboo*. Hammondsworth, 1970.

Dragonetti, Roger. *Mirage des sources: l'art du faux dans le roman médiéval*. Paris, 1987.

Dronke, Peter. 'Towards the Interpretation of the Leiden Love-spell.' *Cambridge Medieval Celtic Studies* 16 (1988) 61–74.

Dumézil, Georges. *The Destiny of the Warrior*, trans. Alf Hiltenbeitel. Chicago, 1970.

– *Mythe et épopée*. 2 vols. Paris, 1971.

Dumville, David N. '*Scéla Laí Brátha* and the Collation of Leabhar na hUidhre.' *Éigse* 16 (1975), 24–8.

– 'Ulster Heroes in the Early Irish Annals: A Caveat.' *Éigse* 17 (1977), 47–54.

Dunn, Francis M. 'Ends and Means in Euripedes' *Heracles*.' In *Classical Closure:*

Reading the End in Greek and Latin Literature, ed. Deborah Roberts, Francis M. Dunn, and Don Fowler, 83–111. Princeton, 1997.

Dupont, Florence. *The Invention of Literature: From Greek Intoxication to the Latin Book*, trans. Janet Lloyd. Baltimore and London, 1999.

Durkheim, Emile. *The Elementary Forms of Religious Life*. London, 1957.

Easterling, P.E. 'Men's *kleos* and Women's *goos*: Female Voices in the *Iliad*.' *Journal of Modern Greek Studies* 9 (1991), 145–51.

Eco, Umberto. *The Limits of Interpretation*. Bloomington, IN, 1990.

– *The Role of the Reader: Explorations in the Semiotics of Texts*. Bloomington, IN, 1979.

Enright, Michael. *The Lady with the Mead Cup: Ritual, Prophecy and Lordship in the European Warband from La Tène to the Viking Age*. Dublin, 1996.

Ferguson, Samuel. 'A Dialogue between the Head and the Heart of an Irish Protestant.' *Dublin University Magazine* 2, 9 (November 1883), 586–93.

Findon, Joanne. *A Woman's Words: Emer and Female Speech in the Ulster Cycle*. Toronto, 1998.

Foley, John Miles. *Homer's Traditional Art*. Philadelphia, 1999.

– *The Singer of Tales in Performance*. Bloomington, IN, 1995.

Ford, Patrick. 'The Idea of Everlasting fame in the *Táin*.' In *Ulidia*, ed. J.P. Mallory, 255–62.

Forsyth, Kathryn. 'Literacy in Pictland.' In *Literacy in Medieval Celtic Societies*, ed. Huw Pryce. Cambridge Studies in Medieval Literature 33, 39–61. Cambridge, 1999.

Fowler, Don. 'Second Thoughts on Closure.' In *Classical Closure*, ed. D. Roberts, 3–22.

Freud, Sigmund. 'Medusa's Head.' In *Sexuality and the Psychology of Love*, ed. Philip Rieff, 212–13. New York, 1963.

Geertz, Clifford. *The Interpretation of Cultures*. New York, 1973.

Genette, Gérard. *Figures III* (Paris, 1972). In Scott Simpkins, *Literary Semiotics: A Critical Approach*, 57–86. Lanham, MD, and Oxford, 2001.

Gilbert (Gilla Easpuig) of Limerick. *De Statu Ecclesiastico*. In James Ussher, *Whole Works*. Vol. 4. Dublin, 1847.

Gray, Elizabeth A. 'Cath Maige Tuired: Myth and Structure.' *Éigse* 18 (1981), 183–209; 19 (1983), 230–62.

Gray Elizabeth A., ed. *Cath Maige Tuired*. Irish Texts Society vol. 52. London, 1983.

Great Britain, Public Record Office. *Ancient Laws of Ireland*. H.M.S.O. 6 vols. London, 1865–1901.

Greene, David, ed. *Fingal Rónáin and Other Stories*. Dublin, 1975.

Greimas, Algirdas Julien. 'La description de la signification et la mythologie comparée.' *L'Homme* (Sept.–Dec. 1963), 51–66; English translation: 'Comparative Mythology.' In *On Meaning: Selective Writings on Semiotic Theory*, trans. Paul J. Perron and Frank. H. Collins, Theory and History of Literature 38, 3–18. Minneapolis, 1987.

– *Structural Semantics: An Attempt at a Method*, trans. Danielle McDowell et al. Lincoln, NE, 1983.

Greenwood, Eamon. 'Some Aspects of the Evolution of Táin Bó Cúailnge from TBC I to LL TBC.' In *Ulidia*, ed. J.P. Mallory, 47–54.

Gwynn, Aubrey. 'Six Irish Papal Legates, 1101–1198.' *Irish Ecclesiastical Record* 63 (1944), 361–7.

Gwynn, Edmund, ed. *The Metrical Dindshenchas*. Royal Irish Academy Todd Lecture Series, vols. 8–11. Dublin, 1903–24.

Haley, G. 'The Topography of the Táin Bó Cúailnge.' PhD diss., Harvard University, 1970.

Halperin, David, J.J. Winkler, and F. Zeitlin. *Before Sexuality: The Construction of Erotic Experience in the Ancient Greek World*. Princeton, 1990.

Hänsel, Bernhard, ed. *Die Indo-Germanen und das Pferd: Akten des Internationalen interdisziplinären Kolloquiums*. Berlin, 1994.

Harbison, Peter. 'Church Reform and Irish Monastic Culture in the Twelfth Century.' *Journal of the Galway Archaeological and Historical Society* 52 (2000), 1–11.

– *The High Crosses of Ireland: An Iconographical and Photographic Survey*. Romisch-Germanisches Zentralmuseum, Forschunginstitut für Vor- und Frühegeschichte, Band 17, 1–3. Bonn, 1992.

Hartog, François. *Le miroir d'Herodote*. Paris, 1980.

Harvey, Anthony. 'Early Literacy in Ireland: The Evidence from Ogam. *Cambridge Medieval Celtic Studies* 14 (1987), 1–15.

Hauck, Karl. *Goldenbrakteaten aus Sievern: spätantike Amulett-Bilder der Saxonica und die sachsen-'Origo' bei Widikund von Corvey*. Munich, 1970.

Heaney, Seamus. 'Station Island.' In *Station Island*. London, 1984.

Hennessy, William M., ed. *The Annals of Loch Cé*. London, 1871.

Henry, P.L. 'Interpreting the Gaulish Inscription of Chamalières.' *Études celtiques* 21 (1984), 144–50.

– 'Táin Roscada: Discussion and Edition.' *Zeitschrift für celtische Philologie* 47 (1995), 32–75.

Herbert, Máire. 'Celtic Heroine? The Archaeology of the Deirdre Story.' In *Gender in Irish Writing*, ed. Toni O'Brien Johnson and David Cairns, 13–22. Philadelphia, 1991.

– 'Goddes and King: The Sacred Marriage in Early Ireland.' In *Women and Sovereignty*, ed. Louise Fradenberg, 264–75. Cosmos 7. Edinburgh, 1992.

- 'The Preface to the *Amra Choluim Cille*: A Re-appraisal.' In *Sages, Saints and Storytellers: Celtic Studies in Honour of Professor James Carney*, ed. Donnchadh Ó Corráin, Liam Breatnach, and Kim McCone. Maynooth Monographs 2, 67–75. Maynooth, 1989.
- 'The Seven Journeys of the Soul.' *Éigse* 17 (1977), 1–12.
Herren, Michael. *The Hisperica Famina: Related Poems*. Toronto, 1992.
Hogan, Edmund. *Onomasticon Goedelicum*. Dublin and London, 1910.
Hollo, Kaarina. 'A Context for *Fled Bricrenn ocus Loinges Mac nDúil Dermait*.' In *Ulidia*, ed. J.P. Mallory, 91–8.
- 'Cú Chulainn and Síd Truim.' *Ériu* 49 (1998), 13–22.
- 'The Feast of Bricriu and the Exile of the Sons of Dúil Dermait.' *Emania* 10 (1992), 18–24.
Hughes, Ian, ed. *Stair Nicoméid: The Irish Gospel of Nicodemus*. Irish Texts Society, vol. 55. Dublin, 1991.
Hull, Vernam, ed. *Loinges Mac nUislenn: The Exile of the Sons of Uisliu*. London, 1949.
Ireland, Colin, ed. *Old Irish Wisdom Attributed to Aldfrith of Northumbria: An Edition of Bríathra Flainn Fhína maic Ossu*. Medieval and Renaissance Texts and Studies 205. Tempe, AZ, 1999.
Ireland, Sean. *Roman Britain: A Sourcebook*. London and New York, 1996.
Irigaray, Luce. *Speculum of the Other Woman*, trans. Gillian C. Gill. Ithaca, NY, 1985.
- *This Sex Which Is Not One*, trans. Catherine Porter with Carolyn Burke. Ithaca, NY, 1985.
Jackson, Kenneth H. 'The Historical Grammar of Irish: Some Actualities and Some Desiderata.' In *Proceedings of the Sixth International Congress of Celtic Studies, Galway 1979*, 1–18. Galway, 1983.
- *The Oldest Irish Tradition: A Window on the Iron Age*. Cambridge, 1964.
Jacquard, Danielle, and Claude Thomasset, eds. *Sexuality and Medicine in the Middle Ages*. Princeton and Cambridge, 1988.
Jaski, Bart. 'Cú Chulainn, *gormac* and *dalta* of the Ulstermen.' *Cambrian Medieval Celtic Studies* 37 (Summer 1999), 9–11.
- *Early Irish Kingship and Succession*. Dublin, 2001.
Joynt, Maud, ed. *Tromdám Guaire*. Dublin, 1931.
Kelleher, John. 'The *Táin* and the Annals.' *Ériu* 22 (1971), 107–27.
Kelly, Fergus. *A Guide to Early Irish Law*. Dublin, 1988.
- ed. *Audacht Morainn: The Testimony of Morann*. Dublin, 1976.
Kelly, Patricia. 'The *Táin* as Literature.' In *Aspects of the Táin*, ed. K.P. Mallory, 69–102. Belfast, 1992.
Kermode, Frank. *The Sense of an Ending*. Oxford, 1967.

Kiberd, Declan. *Inventing Ireland: The Literature of the Modern Nation*. Cambridge, MA, 1995.

Knipp, David. *Christus 'Medicus' in der frühchristlichen Sarkophagskulptur: Ikonigraphische Studien der Sepulkralkunst des späten vierten Jahrhunderts*. Leiden, 1998.

Knott, Eleanor, ed. *Togail Bruidne da Derga*. Medieval and Modern Irish Series 8. Dublin, 1975.

Kristeva, Julia. *Powers of Horror: An Essay on Abjection*, trans. Louis S. Roudiez. New York, 1982.

Krueger, Roberta. *Women Readers and the Ideology of Gender in Old French Verse Romance*. Cambridge, 1993.

Kundera, Milan. *Immortality*. In *Homo Sentimentalis*, part four. New York, 1991.

LaCapra, Dominic. *History and Criticism*. Ithaca, NY, 1985.

Lacy, Brian, trans. *Manus O'Donnell, The Life of Colum Cille*. Dublin, 1998.

Lambert, Pierre-Yves. '"Style de traduction": les traditions celtiques de textes historiques.' *Revue d'histoire des textes* 24 (1994), 375–91.

Landes, Christian, ed. *Dieux guerrisseurs en Gaule romaine*. Paris, 1992.

Laqueur, Thomas W. *Making Sex: Body and Gender from the Greeks to Freud*. Cambridge, MA, 1990.

Lawlor, H.J., ed. 'The Cathach of St Columba.' *Proceedings of the Royal Irish Academy* C 33 (1916), 408–12.

Lejeune, Michel, et al., eds. 'Le plomb magique du larzac et les sorcières gauloises.' *Études celtiques* 22 (1985), 88–177.

Lerer, Seth. *Literacy and Power in Anglo-Saxon England*. Lincoln, NE, 1991.

Lévi-Strauss, Claude. *Histoire du lynx*. Paris, 1991.

– 'The Story of Asdiwal.' In *The Structural Study of Myth and Totemism*, ed. Edmund Leach, 1–48. London, 1968.

– *Structural Anthropology*. Trans. Claire Jacobson and Brooke Grundfest Schoepf. 2 vols. New York, 1963, 1976.

Lincoln, Bruce. *Myth, Cosmos and Society: Indo-European Themes of Creation and Destruction*. Cambridge, MA, and London, 1986.

– *Priests, Warriors and Cattle: A Study in the Ecology of Religions*. Berkeley, 1981.

– *Theorizing Myth: Narrative, Ideology, and Scholarship*. Chicago and London, 1999.

Little, Lester K. *Benedictine Maledictions: Liturgical Cursing in Romanesque France*. Ithaca, NY, 1993.

Loraux, Nicole. *Born of the Earth: Myth and Politics in Athens*, trans. Selina Stewart. Ithaca, NY, 2000.

Lord, Albert B. 'Perspectives on Recent Work on the Oral Traditional Formula.' *Oral Tradition* 1 (1996), 467–503.

Mac Cana, Proinsias. 'Aspects of the Theme of King and Goddess in Early Irish Literature.' *Études celtiques* 7 (1955–6), 356–413; 8 (1958–9), 58–65.

– *Celtic Mythology*. London, 1975.

– *The Learned Tales of Medieval Ireland*. Dublin, 1980.

– 'The Motif of Trivial Cause.' In *Seanchas: Studies in Early and Medieval Irish Archaeology, History and Literature in Honour of Francis J. Byrne*, ed. Alfred P. Smyth, 205–11. Dublin 2000.

– 'Mythology in Early Irish Literature.' In *The Celtic Consciousness*, ed. Robert O'Driscoll, 143–54. Portlaoise, 1981.

– '*Regnum* and *Sacerdotium*: Notes on Irish Tradition,' *Proceedings of the British Academy* 65 (1979), 443–75.

– 'The Three Languages and the Three Laws.' *Studia Celtica* 5 (1970), 62–78.

Mac Gearailt, Uaiter. '*Cath Ruis na Ríg* and Twelfth-century Literary and Oral Tradition.' *Zeitschrift für celtische Philologie* 44 (1991), 128–45.

McNamara, Martin. *The Apocrypha in the Irish Church*. Dublin, 1975.

McManus, Damian. *A Guide to Ogam*. Maynooth, 1991.

Malinoski, Bernard. *The Sexual Life of Savages*. 3rd ed. London, 1932.

Mallory, James P., ed. *Aspects of the Táin*. Belfast, 1992.

Mallory, James P., and Gerard Stockman., eds. *Ulidia: Proceedings of the First International Conference on the Ulster Cycle of Tales*. Belfast, 1994.

Marstrander, Carl, ed. 'The Deaths of Lugaid and Derbforgaill.' *Ériu* 5 (1911), 201–18.

Mauss, Marcel. *The Gift: Form and Function of Exchange in Archaic Societies*. Trans. Ian Cunnison. New York, 1954. English translation of *Essais sur le don*.

McAlister, H.M.V., ed. *Lebor Gabhála Érenn: The Book of Invasions of Ireland*. Irish Texts Society, vols. 34, 35, 39, 41, 44. London, 1938–56.

McCone, Kim. *Pagan Past and Christian Present*. Maynooth, 1990.

– 'A Tale of Two Ditties: Poet and Satirist in *Cath Maige Tuired*.' In *Sages, Saints and Storytellers: Celtic Studies in Honour of Professor James Carney*, ed. Donnchadh Ó Corráin, Liam Breatnach, and Kim McCone, 122–43. Maynooth Monographs 2. Maynooth, 1989.

– 'Werewolves, *Cyclopes*, *Díberga* and *Fíanna*: Juvenile Delinquincy in Early Ireland.' *Cambridge Medieval Celtic Studies* 12 (1986) 1–22.

McCone, Kim, and Katharine Simms, eds. *Progress in Medieval Irish Studies*. Maynooth, 1996.

Meid, Wolfgang. *Gaulish Inscriptions*. Budapest, 1992.

Meid, Wolfgang, ed. *Die Romanze von Froech und Findabair: Táin Bó Fróich*. Innsbruck, 1970.

Meroney, Howard. 'A mo comdhiu néll! Cid do-dhén fri Firu Arddae?' *Journal of Celtic Studies* 2 (1958), 96–101.

Meyer, Kuno, ed. 'Echtra Nerai: The Adventures of Nera.' *Revue celtique* 10 (1889), 212–28.

– *Fianaighecht.* Royal Irish Academy Todd Lecture Series 16. London, 1910.
– 'Finn and the Man in the Tree' *Revue celtique* 25 (1904), 344–9.
– *Hibernica Minora.* Oxford, 1894.
– *King and Hermit.* London, 1901.
– 'The Laud Genealogies and Tribal Histories,' *Zeitschrift für celtische Philologie* 8 [1911], 317–20.
– *Sanas Chormaic: Cormac's Glossary.* In *Anecdota from Irish Manuscripts* vol. 5. Dublin, 1913.
– 'Siaburcharpat Conculaind.' In *Anecdota from Irish Manuscripts*, vol. 3, 49–56. Dublin, 1910.

Miller, A.W.K., ed. 'O'Clery's Irish Glossary.' *Revue celtique* 4 (1880), 349–428.

Moi, Toril. *French Feminist Thought: A Reader.* Oxford, 1987.

Motz, L. 'Thorr's River Crossing.' *Saga Book* 23 (1993), 469–87.

Muhr, Kay. 'The Location of the Ulster Cycle: Part I: *Tóchustal Ulad*.' In *Ulidia: Proceedings of the First International Conference on the Ulster Cycle of Tales*, ed. James P. Mallory and Gerard Stockman, 149–58. Belfast, 1994.

Mulchrone, Kathleen, ed. *Vita tripartita.* Dublin, 1939.

Muldoon, Paul. *Paul Muldoon: Poems. 1968–1998.* New York, 2001.

Murnahan, Sheila. 'The Poetics of Loss in Greek Epic.' In *Epic traditions in the Contemporary World: The Poetics of Community*, ed. Margaret Bessinger, Jane Tytlus, and Suzanne Wofford. 203–20. Berkeley and Los Angeles, 1999.

Murphy, Gerard. *Early Irish Lyrics.* Oxford, 1956.

Murray, Kevin. 'The Finding of the *Táin*.' *Cambridge Medieval Celtic Studies* 41 (Summer 2001), 17–24.

Mynors, R.A.B., completed by R.M. Thomson and M. Winterbottom. *William of Malmesbury's Gesta Regum Anglorum: The History of the English Kings.* Oxford, 1998.

Nagy, Gregory. 'Epic as Genre.' In *Epic Traditions in the Contemporary World: The Poetics of Community*, ed. Margaret Beissinger, Jane Tylus, and Susanne Wofford. Berkeley, 1999.
– *Homeric Questions.* Ithaca, NY, 1996.

Nagy, Joseph F. 'Close Encounters of a Traditional Kind.' In *Celtic Folklore and Christianity: Studies in Memory of William Heist*, ed. Patrick Ford, 129–49. Los Angeles, 1983.
– *Conversing with Angels and Ancients: Literary Myths of Medieval Ireland.* Ithaca, NY, and London 1987.
– 'Liminality and Knowledge in Irish Tradition.' *Studia Celtica* 16–17 (1981–2), 135–43.

– Review of *Ulidia*. *Éigse* 28 (1994–5), 183–8.
– *The Wisdom of the Outlaw: The Boyhood Deeds of Finn in Gaelic Narrative Tradition*. Berkeley, 1985.

Nettlau, Max. 'The Fragment of the *Táin Bó Cuailnge* in MS Egerton 93.' *Revue celtique* 14 (1893), 254–6; 15 (1894), 62–78, 198–208.

Ní Dhonnchadha, Máirin. '"Caillech" and Other Terms for Veiled Women in Medieval Irish Texts.' *Éigse* 28 (1994–5), 71–96.
– 'The Prull Narrative in Sanas Cormaic.' In *Cín Chille Cúile: Texts, Saints and Places. Essays in Honour of Pádraig Ó Riain*, ed. John Carey, Máire Herbert and Kevin Murray, 163–78. Aberystwyth, 2004.

Ní Dhonnchadha, Máirin, ed. 'An Address to a Student of Law.' In *Sages, Saints and Storytellers: Celtic Studies in Honour of Professor James Carney*, ed. Donnchadh Ó Corráin, Liam Breatnach, and Kim McCone. 159–77, Maynooth Monographs 2. Maynooth, 1989.
– *Cáin Adamnáin*. Forthcoming.

O'Brien, Michael, ed. *Corpus Genealogiarum Hiberniae*. Vol 1. Dublin, 1962.
– 'Miscellanea Hibernica.' *Études celtiques* 3 (1946), 372–3.

Ó Cathasaigh, Tomás. '*Cath Maige Tuired* as Exemplary Myth.' In *Folia Gadelica: Essays Presented to R.A. Breatnach*, ed. Pádraig de Brún et al., 1–19. Cork, 1983.
– 'The Eponym of Cnogba,' *Éigse* 23 (1989), 27–38.
– *The Heroic Biography of Cormac mac Airt*. Dublin, 1977.
– 'Mythology in *Táin Bó Cúailnge*.' In *Studien zur Táin Bó Cúailnge*, ed. Hildegard L.C. Tristram, 114–32. Scriptoralia 52. Tübingen, 1993.
– 'Pagan Survivals: The Evidence of Early Irish Narrative.' In *Ireland und Europa: die Kirche im frühen Mittlealter / Ireland and Europe: The Early Church*, ed. Michael Richter and Proinseas Ní Chatháin, 291–307. Stuttgart, 1984.
– 'The Rhetoric of *Scéla Cano Meic Gartnáin*.' In *Sages, Saints and Storytellers: Celtic Studies in Honour of Professor James Carney*, ed. Donnchadh Ó Corráin, Liam Breatnach, and Kim McCone, 239–45. Maynooth Monographs 2. Maynooth, 1989.
– 'The Sister's Son in Early Irish Literature.' *Peritia* 5 (1986), 128–60.

Ó Coileáin, Seán. 'The Making of *Tromdám Guaire*.' *Ériu* 28 (1977), 32–70.
– 'The Structure of a Literary Cycle,' *Ériu* 25 (1974), 88–125.

Ó Concheannain, Tomás. '*Aided Nath Í* and Uí Fhiachrach Genealogies.' *Éigse* 25 (1991), 1–27.
– 'LL and the Date of the Reviser of LU.' *Éigse* 20 (1984), 212–25.
– 'The Manuscript Tradition of *Mesca Ulad*.' *Celtica* 31 (1989), 13–30.
– 'The Reviser of Leabhar na hUidhre.' *Éigse* 15 (1973–4), 277–88.

O'Conor, Kieran. 'The Morphology of Gaelic Lordly Sites in North Connacht.' In *Gaelic Ireland c.1250–c.1650: Land, Lordship and Settlement*, ed. Patrick J. Duffy, David Edwards, and Elizabeth Fitzpatrick, 329–45. Dublin, 2001.

Ó Corráin, Donnchadh. 'The Education of Diarmait mac Murchada.' *Ériu* 37 (1986), 78–81.

– 'Historical Need and Literary Narrative.' In *Proceedings of the 7th International Congress of Celtic Studies, Oxford 1983*, ed. D. Ellis Evans, John G. Griffith, and E.M. Jope, 141–58. Oxford, 1986.

– 'Marriage in Early Ireland.' In *Marriage in Ireland*, ed. Art Cosgrove, 5–24. Dublin, 1985.

Ó Corráin, Donnchadh, Aidan Breen, and Liam Breatnach. 'The Laws of the Irish.' *Peritia* 3 (1984), 382–438.

– 'Muirchertach Mac Lochlainn and the *Circuit of Ireland*,' In *Seanchas*, ed. Alfred P. Smyth, 238–50. Dublin 1999.

Ó Cróinín, Dáibhí. *Early Medieval Ireland 400–1200*. London, 1995.

Ó Cuív, Brian. 'A Poem of Prophecy on Ua Conchobair kings of Connacht.' *Celtica* 21 (1989), 31–54.

– 'Tradition and Innovation in Irish Literature.' In *Proceedings of the British Academy* 49 (1963), 233–62.

O'Donovan, John, ed. 'The Circuit of Muircheartach mac Neill.' In *Tracts Relating to Ireland*, 24–58. Dublin, 1841.

– 'Fearghal Og Mac an Bhaird's Poem on the Battle of Down.' In *Miscellany of the Celtic Society*, 404–15. Dublin, 1849.

Ó hAodha, Donncha, ed. *Bethu Brigte*. Dublin, 1978.

Ó hUiginn, Ruairi. 'The Background and Development of *Táin Bó Cuailnge*.' In *Aspects of the Táin*, ed. J.P. Mallory, 29–68. Belfast, 1992.

– 'Tongu do dia toinges mo thúath and Related Expressions.' In *Sages, Saints and Storytellers: Celtic Studies in Honour of Professor James Carney*, ed. Donnchadh Ó Corráin, Liam Breatnach, and Kim McCone, 332–41. Maynooth Monographs 2. Maynooth, 1989.

O'Keeffe, J.G., ed. *Buile Suibhne*. Irish Texts Society 11. London 1910.

– 'Cuchulinn and Conlaech' *Ériu* 1 (1904), 123–7.

O'Kelleher, A., and G. Schoepperle, eds. *Betha Colaim Chille: Life of Columcille*. Urbana, IL. 1918.

O'Leary, Philip. 'Honour-bound: The Social Context of Early Irish Heroic *Geis*.' *Celtica* 20 (1988), 85–107.

– 'The Honour of Women in Early Irish Literature.' *Ériu* 38 (1987), 27–44.

– 'Magnanimous Conduct in Irish Heroic Literature.' *Éigse* 25 (1991), 28–44.

– 'Verbal Deceit in the Ulster Cycle. *Éigse* 21 (1986), 16–26.

Olsen, Karin. 'The Cuckold's Revenge: Reconstructing Six Irish *Roscada* in *Táin Bó Cúailnge*.' *Cambrian Medieval Celtic Studies* 28 (1994), 51–69.

Olson, Glending. *Literature as Recreation in the Later Middle Ages*. Ithaca, NY, 1982.

Ó Maille, Tomás. 'Medb Cruachna.' *Zeitschrift für celtische Philologie* (1927), 129–46.

O'Neill, Timothy. *The Irish Hand*. Portlaoise, 1984.

Ó Néill, Pádraig. 'An Irishman at Chartres in the Twelfth Century: The Evidence of Oxford, Bodleian Library MS Auct. F. 15.' *Ériu* 48 (1997), 1–35.

– 'The Latin Colophon to the *Táin Bó Cúailnge* in the Book of Leinster: A Critical View of Old Irish Literature.' *Celtica* 23 (1999), 269–75.

O'Rahilly, Cecile. 'Ferdai écin.' *Éigse* 16 (1976), 326.

– *Táin Bó Cúalnge from the Book of Leinster*. Dublin, 1967.

– *Táin Bó Cúailnge: Recension I*. Dublin, 1976.

O'Rahilly, T.F. *Early Irish History and Mythology*. Dublin, 1946.

Ó Riain, Pádraig. 'Boundary Association in Early Irish Society.' *Studia Celtica* 7 (1972), 12–29.

– 'A Study of the Irish Legend of the Wild Man.' *Éigse* 14 (1972), 179–206.

– 'The Táin: A Clue to Its Origins.' In *Ulidia: Proceedings of the First International Conference on the Ulster Cycle of Tales*, ed. James P. Mallory and Gerard Stockman, 31–38. Belfast, 1994.

Oskamp, Hans, ed. 'Mael Muire: Compiler or Reviser?' *Éigse* 15 (1973–4), 177–82.

– *The Voyage of Máel Dúin*. Groningen, 1970.

O'Sullivan, Aidan. 'Crannogs in Late Medieval Ireland.' In *Gaelic Ireland, c.1250–c.1650: Land, Lordship and Settlement*, ed. Patrick J. Duffy, David Edwards, and Elizabeth Fitzpatrick, 397–417. Dublin, 2001.

O'Sullivan, Anne, ed. *The Book of Leinster*, vol. 6. Dublin 1983.

Ó Tuama, Sean, ed. *An Duanaire, 1600–1900: Poems of the Dispossessed*, trans. Thomas Kinsella. Portlaoise, 1981.

Parkes, Malcolm. 'The Contribution of Insular Scribes of the Seventh and Eighth Centuries to the 'Grammar of Intelligibility.' In *Grafia e interpunzione del latine nel medioevo*, ed. A. Maierù, 1–18. Rome, 1987.

Parkes, Ward. *Verbal Dueling in Heroic Narrative: Homeric and Old English Traditions*. Princeton, 1990.

Partner, Nancy. 'No Sex, No Gender.' *Speculum* 68 (1993), 419–44.

Paulin, Tom. *The Invasion Handbook*. London, 2002.

Pearson, A.J. 'A Medieval Glossary.' *Ériu* 13 (1940), 61–87.

Picard, Jean-Michel. 'Structural Patterns in Early Hiberno-Latin Hagiography.' *Peritia* 4 (1985), 67–82.

Picard, Jean-Michel, and Y. de Pontfarcy, eds. *The Vision of Tnugdal*. Dublin, 1989.

Plummer, Charles. *Vitae Sanctorum Hiberniae*. 2 vols. Oxford, 1910.

Poppe, Erich. 'Grammatica, grammatic, Augustine, and the *Táin*.' In *Ildánach*

Ildírech: A Festschrift for Proinsias Mac Cana, ed. John Carey, John Koch, and Pierre-Yves Lambert, 203–10. Aberystwyth, 1999.

Power, Annie. 'The Common Authorship of Some Book of Leinster Texts.' *Ériu* 9 (1923), 126–8.

Propp, Vladimir. *Morphology of the Folktale*, trans. Laurence Scott. Austin, 1968. First published in Russian, 1927.

Puhvel, Jaan. 'Mythological Reflections of Indo-European Medicine.' In *Indo-European and Indo-Europeans*, ed. George Cardona et al., 369–82. Philadelphia, 1970.

Radcliffe-Brown, A.R. *Structure and Function in Primitive Society*. New York, 1952.

Radner, Joan. '"Fury Destroys the World": Historical Strategy in Ireland's Ulster Epic.' *Mankind Quarterly* 23 (1982), 41–60.

Rastier, François. *Meaning and Textuality*, trans. Frank Collins and Paul Perron. Toronto, 1997; first pub. 1989.

Rees, Alwyn, and Brinley Rees. *Celtic Heritage: Ancient Tradition in Ireland and Wales*. London, 1961.

Ricoeur, Paul. *Temps et recit II. la configuration dans le récit de fiction*. Paris, 1984.

Riffaterre, Michael. 'The Interpretant in Literary Semiotics.' In *Reading Eco: An Anthology*, ed. Rocco Capozzi, 173–84. Bloomington, IN, 1977.

Ross, Margaret Clunies. 'An Interpretation of the Myth of Thorr's Encounter with Geirrothr and His Daughters.' In *Speculum Norroenum: Norse Studies in Honour of Gabriel Turville-Petre*, ed. Ursula Dronke et al., 370–91. Odense, 1981.

Rousselle, Aline. *Croire et guérir: la foi en Gaule dans l'antiquité tardive*. Paris, 1990.

Royal Irish Academy. *Dictionary of the Irish Language*. Dublin, 1983.

Said, Edward. 'Thoughts on Late Style.' *London Review of Books* 26, no. 15 (August 2004), 3–7.

Sayers, Will. 'Contracting for Combat: Flyting and Fighting in *Táin Bó Cúailnge*.' *Emania* 16 (1997), 49–62.

– 'Cú Chulainn, The Heroic Imposition of Meaning on Signs, and the Revenge of the Sign.' *Incognita: International Journal for Cognitive Studies in the Humanities* 2 (1991), 79–105.

– 'Fergus and the Cosmogonic Sword.' *History of Religions* 25 (1985), 30–56.

– 'Games, Sport and Para-military Exercise in Early Ireland.' *Aethlon: The Journal of Sport Literature* 10 (1992), 105–23.

Schatzer, Danuta. '"Iuvenes vestri visiones videbunt"': Visions and the Literary Sources of Patrick's *Confessio*.' *Journal of Medieval Latin* 3 (1993), 169–201.

Schwartz, Dorothy Dilts. 'Balance in the Book of Leinster *Táin Bó Cúailnge* and in Neo-classical Rhetoric.' *Proceedings of the Harvard Celtic Colloquium* 6 (1986), 29–46.

– 'The Beautiful Women and the Warriors in the LL *TBC* and in Twelfth-century Neo-classical Rhetoric.' *Proceedings of the Harvard Celtic Colloquium* 5 (1985), 128–46.

– 'The Problem of Classical Influence in the Book of Leinster *Táin Bó Cuailnge*: Significant Parallels with Twelfth-century Neo-classical Rhetoric.' *Proceedings of the Harvard Celtic Colloquium* 6 (1986) 96–125.

– 'Repetition in the Book of Leinster *Táin Bó Cúailnge* and in Neo-classical Rhetoric.' *Proceedings of the Harvard Celtic Colloquium* 4 (1984), 45–81.

Selden, Raman, Peter Widdowson, and Peter Brooker. *A Reader's Guide to Contemporary Literary Theory.* 4th ed. London and New York, 1997.

Sharpe, Richard. *Adomnán's Life of Saint Columba.* Oxford, 1998.

Simms, Katharine. *From Kings to Warlords: The Changing Political Structures of Gaelic Ireland in the Later Middle Ages.* London 1987.

Simpkins, Scott. *Literary Semiotics: A Critical Approach.* Oxford, 2001.

Sims-Williams, Patrick. 'Person-switching in Celtic Panegyric: Figure or Fault?' In *Heroic Poets and Poetic Heroes: A Festschrift for Patrick Ford.* CSANA Yearbook 3–4, ed. J.F. Nagy and L.E. Jones, 315–26. Dublin, 2005.

Sjoesdedt-Lanval, Marie. *Dieux et héros des Celtes.* Paris, 1940.

Sklute, L.H. '*Freothuwebbe* in Old English Poetry.' *Neophilologische Mitteilungen* 71 (1970), 534–41.

Slotkin, Edgar W. 'Medieval Irish Scribes and Fixed Texts.' *Éigse,* 17 (1978–9), 437–50.

– 'Noínden: Its Semantic Range.' In *Celtic Language, Celtic Culture: A Festschrift for Eric P. Hamp,* ed. A.T.E. Matonis and D.F. Melia, 137–50. Van Nuys, CA, 1995.

Smith, Peter. 'Aimirgein Glúngel Tuir Tend: A Middle-Irish Poem on the Authors and Laws of Ireland.' *Peritia* 8 (1994), 129–36.

Sontag, Susan. *Regarding the Pain of Others.* New York, 2003.

Spiegel, Gabrielle. *The Past as Text: The Theory and Practice of Medieval Historiography.* Baltimore and London, 1997.

Stahl, William H., ed. *Commentary on the Dream of Scipio.* New York, 1952.

Stevenson, Jane. 'The Beginnings of Literacy in Ireland.' *Proceedings of the Royal Irish Academy* 89 C (1989), 127–65.

Stock, Brian. *The Implications of Literacy.* Princeton, 1983.

Stokes, Whitley, ed. *Acallam na Senórach. Irische Texte,* vol. 4, pt 1. Leipzig, 1900.

– 'Cóir Anman.' *Irische Texte,* vol. 3. Leipzig, 1897.

– *Félire Óengusso Céli Dé: The Martyrology of Oengus the Culdee*. London, 1905.
– 'The Irish Ordeals, Cormac's Adventures in the Land of Promise, and the Decision as to Cormac's Sword.' *Irische Texte* 3, pt 1, 183–229. Leipzig, 1897.
– 'O'Mulconry's Glossary.' In *Archiv für celtische Lexicographie*. Vol. 1, ed. Whitley Stokes and Kuno Meyer. Halle, 1900.
– *Scél na Fír Flatha. Irische Texte* 3, 183–229. Berlin, 1891.
– *Three Irish Glossaries*. Edinburgh, 1862.
Taylor, Andrew. *Textual Situations: Three Medieval Manuscripts and Their Readers*. Philadelphia, 2002.
– 'Was There a Song of Roland?' *Speculum* 76, 1 (January 2001), 28–65.
Tertullian. *De Anima*, 57, 10 (*Patrologia Latina* 2, 794).
Thurneysen, Rudolf. *Die irische Helden-und Königsage bis zum siebzehnten Jahrhundert*. Halle, 1913; Berlin 1921.
– 'Die Überlieferung der *Táin Bó Cúailnge*.' *Zeitschrift für celtische Philologie* 9 (1913), 418–43.
Thurneysen, Rudolf, ed. *Scéla Mucce Meic Dathó*. Dublin, 1935.
– '*Táin Bó Cuailnge* nach H. 2. 17.' *Zeitschrift für celtische Philologie* 8 (1912), 525–54.
– 'Tuirill Bicrenn und seine Kinder.' *Zeitschrift für celtische Philologie* 12 (1918), 239–50.
Todd, James Henthorn, ed. *Cogadh Gaedhel re Gallaib: The Wars of the Gaedhil with the Gaill*. London, 1871.
Toner, Gregory. 'The Ulster Cycle: Historiography or Fiction?' *Cambrian Medieval Celtic Studies* 40 (2000), 1–20.
Trindade, Ann. 'Irish Gormlaith as a Sovereignty Figure.' *Études celtiques* 23 (1986), 143–6.
Tristram, Hildegard. 'The Cattle Raid of Cuailnge in Tension and Transition between the Oral and the Written, Classical Subtexts and Narrative Heritage.' In *Cultural Identity and Cultural Integration*, ed. Doris Edel, 61–81. Dublin, 1996.
– 'Latin and Latin Learning in the Táin Bó Cuailnge.' *Zeitschrift für celtische Philologie* 49–50 (1997), 847–77.
– 'Mimesis and Diegesis in the Cattle Raid of Cuailgne.' In *Ildánach Ildírech: A Festschrift for Proinsias Mac Cana*, ed. John Carey, John Koch, and Pierre-Yves Lambert, 263–76. Aberystwyth, 1999.
– 'What Is the Purpose of Táin Bó Cúailnge?' In *Ulidia*, ed. J.P. Mallory, 11–23.
Turner, Victor. *The Ritual Process: Structure and Anti-structure*. London, 1969.
Van Gennep, Arnold. *The Rites of Passage*. London, 1960.
Van Hamel, A.G., ed. 'Conle's Abenteurliche Fahrt.' *Zeitschrift für celtische Philologie* 17 (1928).
– *Immrama*. Dublin, 1941.

Vance, Eugene. *Mervelous Signals: Poetics and Sign Theory in the Middle Ages.* Lincoln, NE, 1986.

Veille, Christophe. 'The Oldest Narrative Attestations of a Celtic Mythical and Traditional Heroic Cycle.' In *Ulidia: Proceedings of the First International Conference on the Ulster Cycle of Tales*, ed. James P. Mallory and Gerard Stockman, 217–27. Belfast, 1994.

Vendryes, Jean, and P.-Y. Lambert, eds. *Lexique étymologique de l'Irlandais ancien.* Paris, 1960–1996.

Vernant, Jean-Pierre. *Mythe et société en Grèce ancienne.* Paris, 1974; translated as *Myth and Society in Ancient Greece*, by Janet Lloyd. New York, 1984.

Vidal-Naquet, Pierre. 'The Black Hunter and the Origin of the Athenian *Ephebia*.' Revised version in *The Black Hunter: Forms of Thought and Forms of Society in the Greek World*, trans. Andrew Szegedy-Maszak, 106–28. Baltimore and London, 1986.

Walsh, Paul, *Irish Leaders and Learning through the Ages*, ed. Nollaig Ó Muraíle. Dublin, 2003.

Walsh, Paul, ed. *Beatha Aodha Ruaidh uí Dhomhnaill / The Life of Aodh Ruadh O Domhnaill*, part 1. Irish Texts Society, 42. London, 1948.

Walsh, Paul, and Colm O Lochlainn, eds. *Beatha Aodha Ruaidh uí Dhomhnaill / The Life of Aodh Ruadh O Domhnaill*, part 2. Irish Texts Society, 45. London, 1957.

Watkins, Calvert. 'Some Celtic Phrasal Echoes.' In *Celtic Language, Celtic Culture: A Festschrift for Eric P. Hamp*, ed. A.T.E. Matonis and Daniel F. Melia, 47–56. Van Nuys, CA, 1990.

– *How to Kill a Dragon.* Ithaca, NY, 1999.

Wiley, Dan. 'The Maledictory Psalms.' *Peritia* 15 (2001), 261–79.

Windish, Ernst, ed. 'Das Fest des Bricriu und die Verbannung der Mac Dúil Dermait.' *Irische Texte* 2 (1884), 164–217.

– '*Táin Bó Cuailnge* nach der hs. Egerton 1782.' *Zeitschrift für celtische Philologie* 9 (1913), 121–58.'

– *Táin Bó Regamna. Irische Texte* 2, 239–56. Leipzig, 1889.

Wright, R.P. 'Roman Britain in 1968: II, Inscriptions.' *Journal of Roman Studies* 59 (1969), 235–46.

Yeats, W.B. *Collected Poems.* London, 1950.

Zumthor, Paul. *Essai de poetique medievale.* Paris, 1972.

Index